TRENCH DOGS

IAN DENSFORD

DEAD RECKONING

ANNAPOLIS, MARYLAND

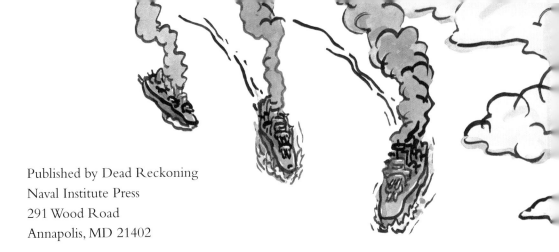

Published by Dead Reckoning
Naval Institute Press
291 Wood Road
Annapolis, MD 21402

ISBN: 978-1-68247-233-0 (paperback)
ISBN: 978-1-68247-234-7 (eBook)

Library of Congress Control Number: 2018941320

∞ Print editions meet the requirements of ANSI/NISO z39.48-1992 (Permanence of Paper).
Printed in the United States of America.

26 25 24 23 22 21 20 19 18   9 8 7 6 5 4 3 2 1
First printing

ROLL CALL

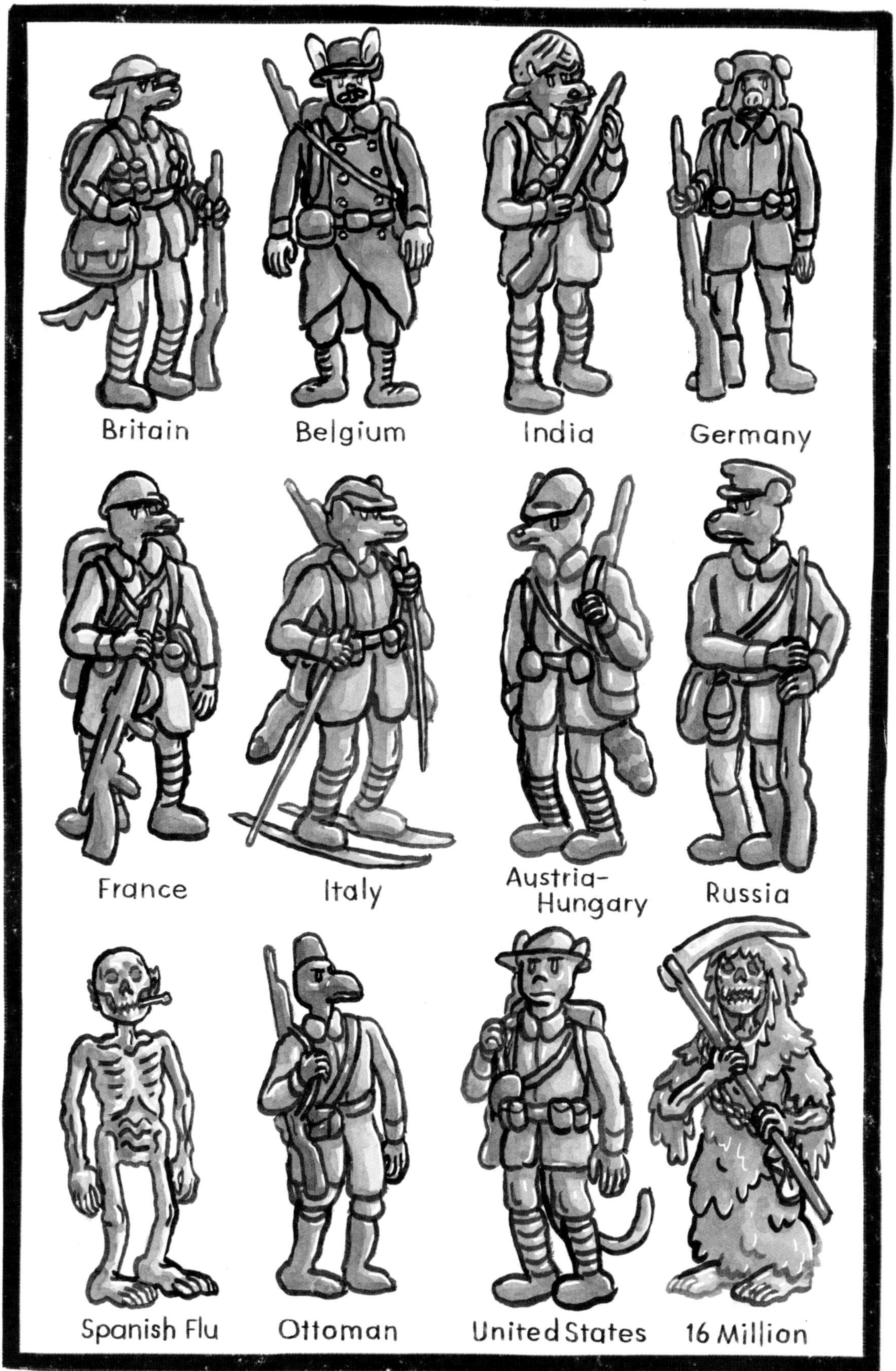

Britain
Belgium
India
Germany
France
Italy
Austria-Hungary
Russia
Spanish Flu
Ottoman
United States
16 Million

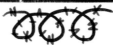

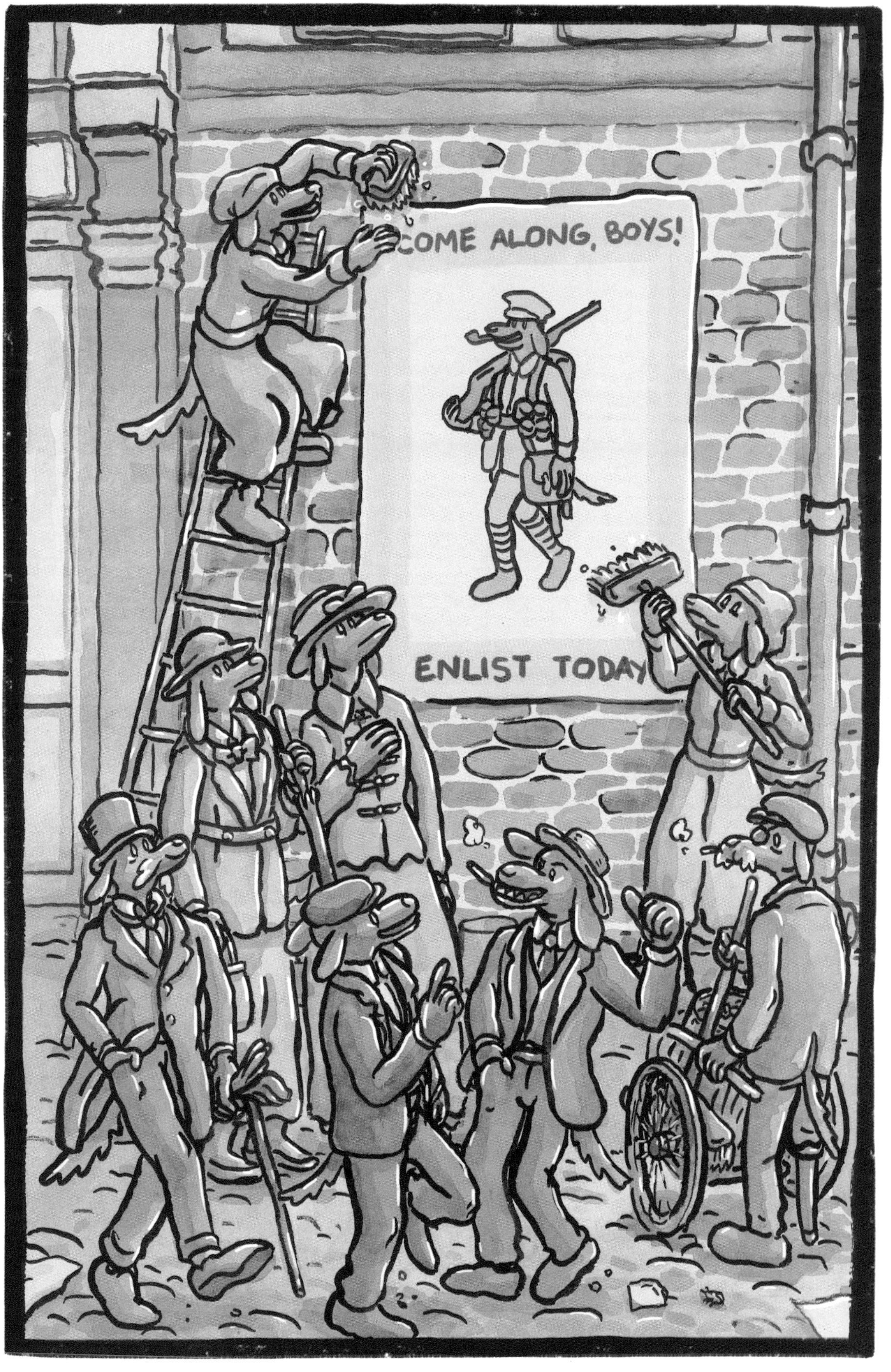
COME ALONG, BOYS!
ENLIST TODAY

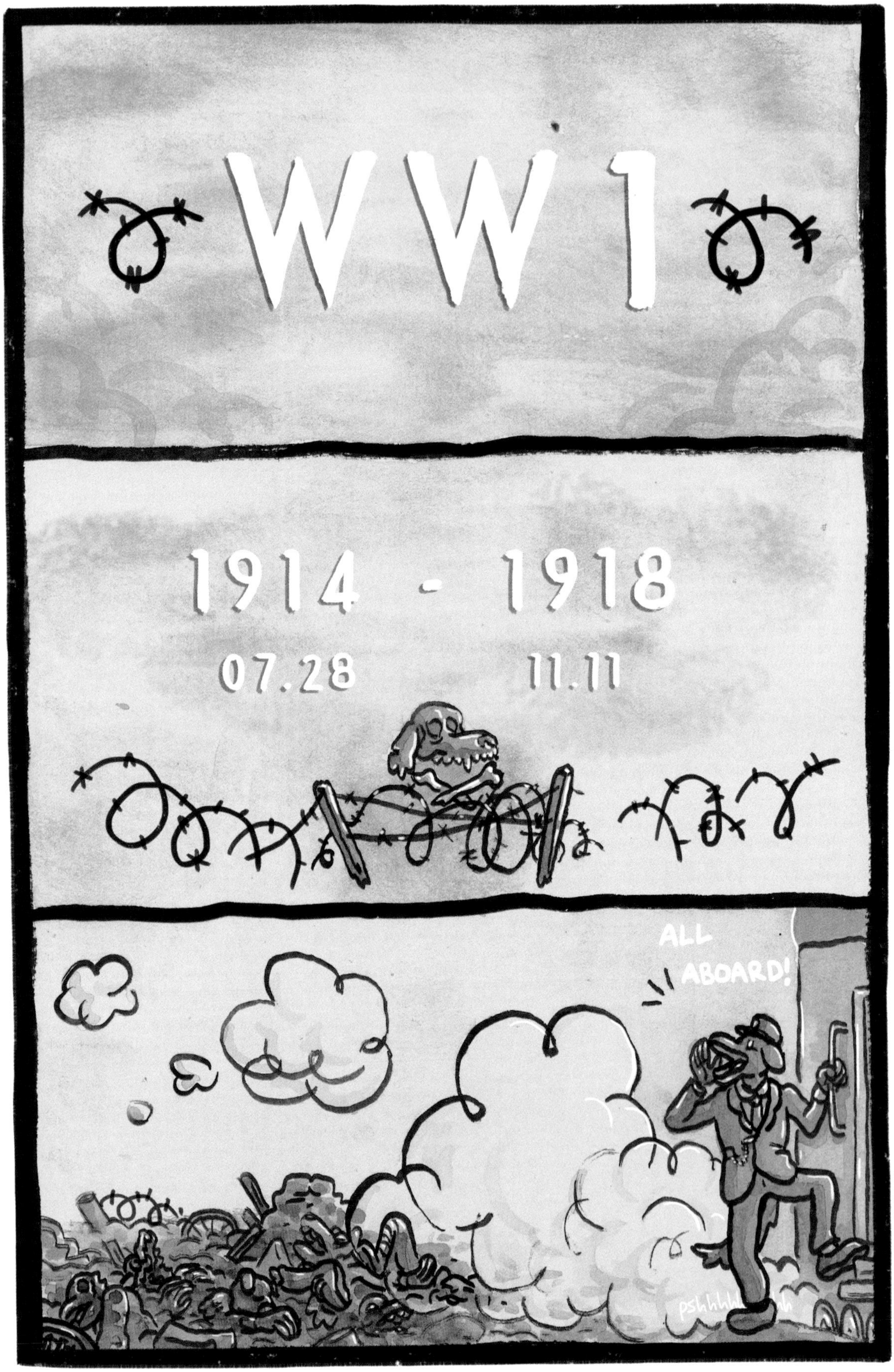
WW1
1914 - 1918
07.28
11.11
ALL ABOARD!

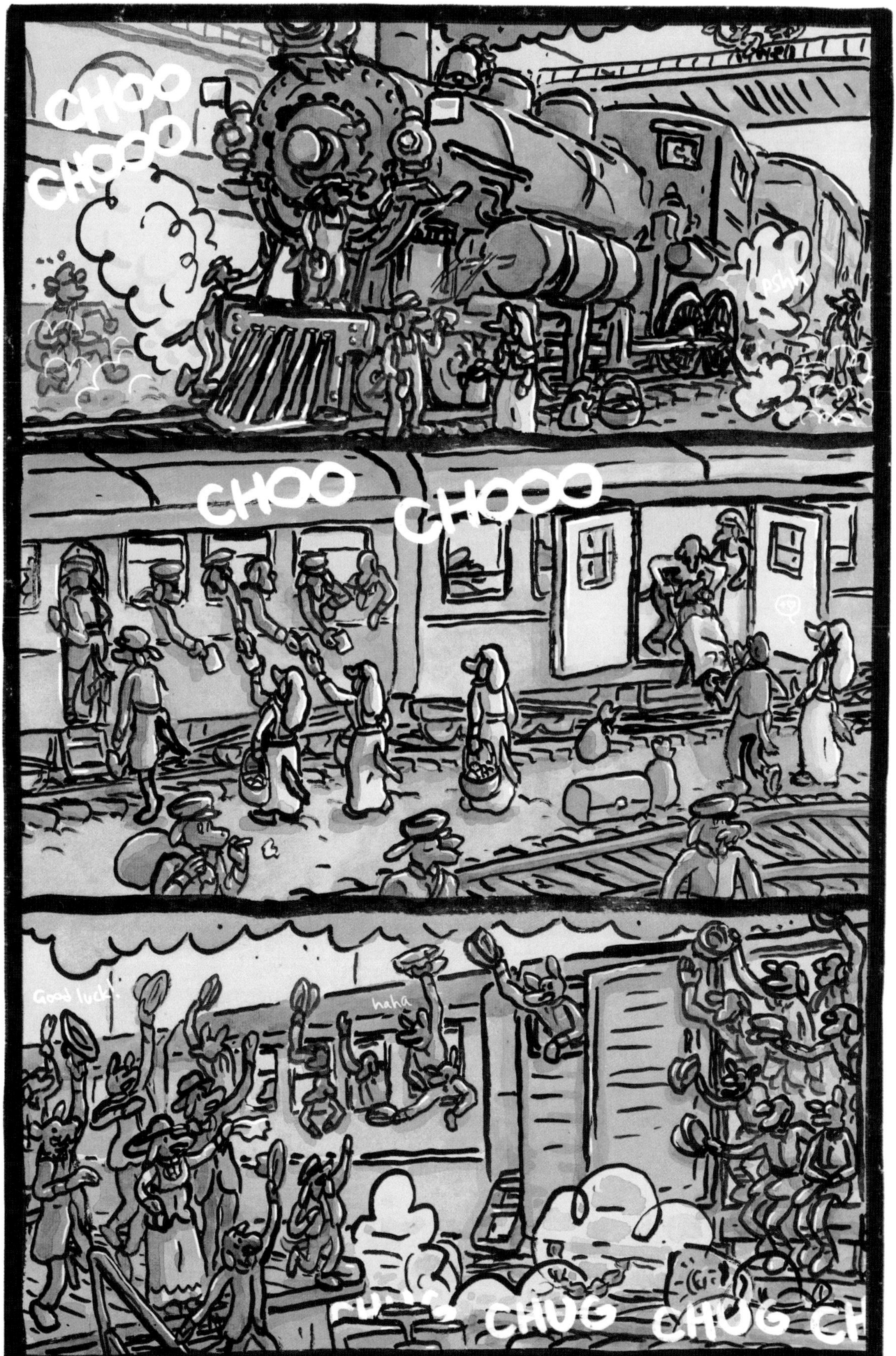
CHOO
CHOOO
pshh
CHOO
CHOOO
Good luck!
haha
CHUG
CHUG

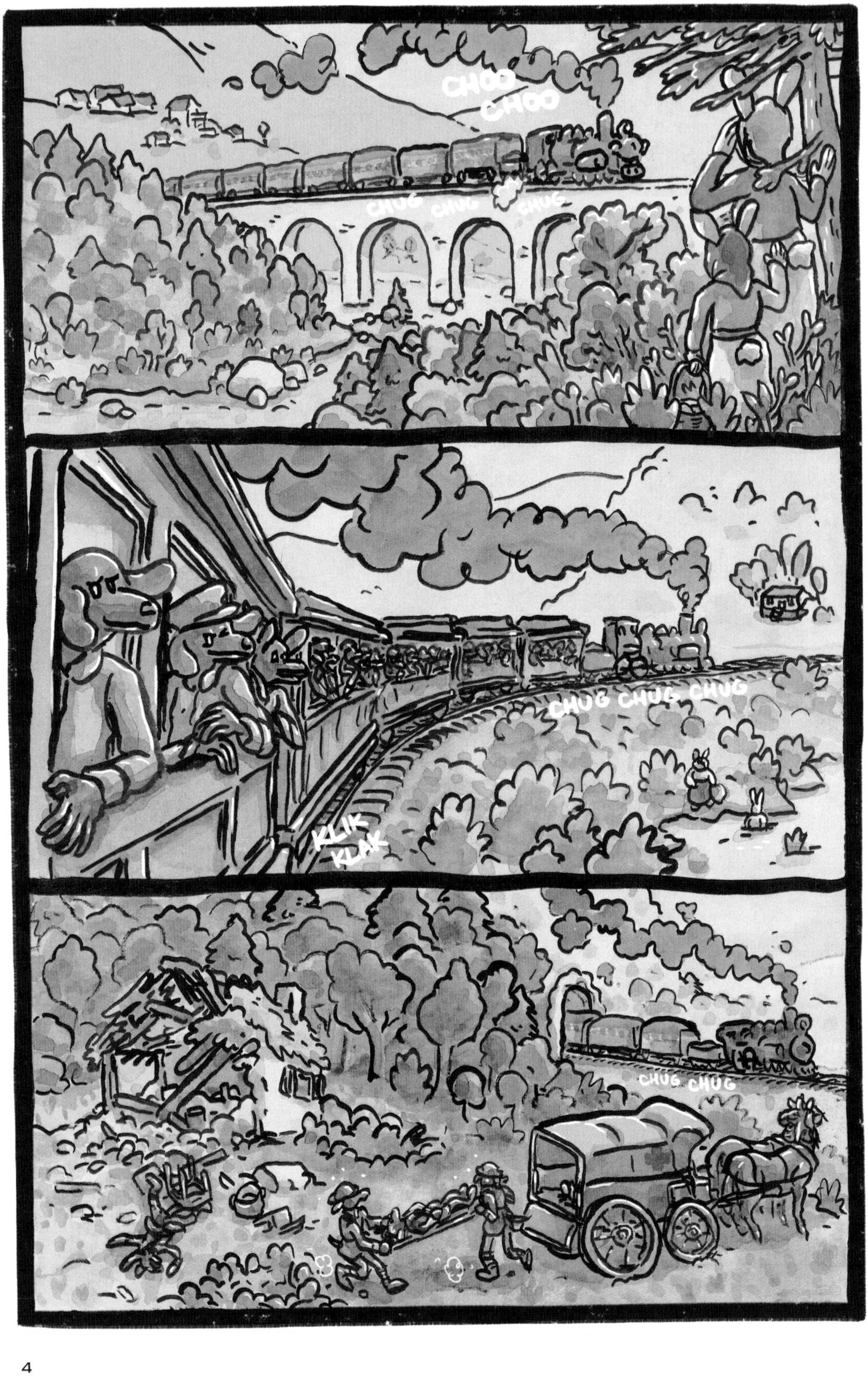
CHOO CHOO
CHUG CHUG CHUG
CHUG CHUG CHUG
KLIK KLAK
CHUG CHUG

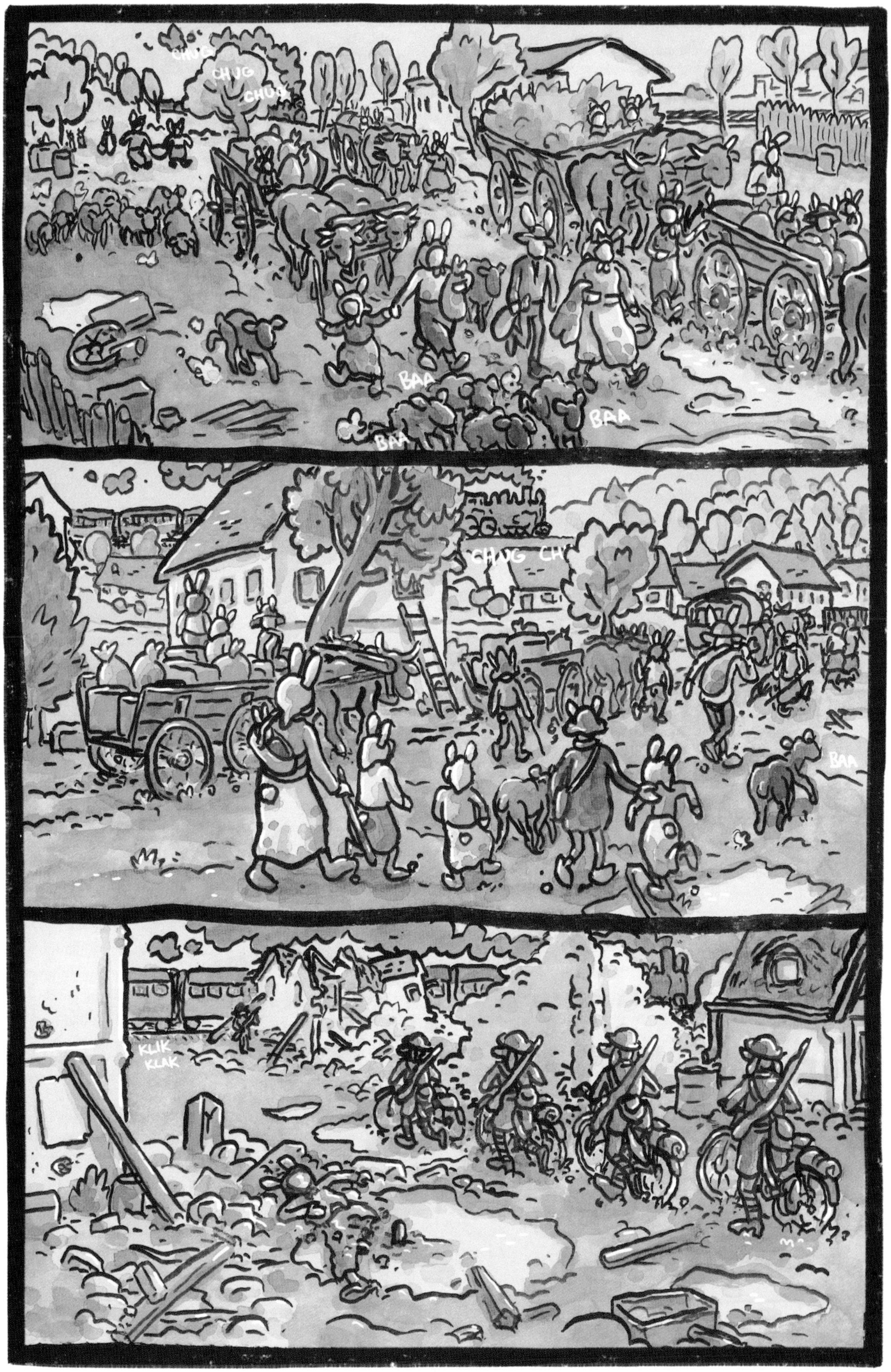
CHUG
CHUG
CHUG
BAA
BAA
BAA
CHUG CH
BAA
KLIK
KLAK

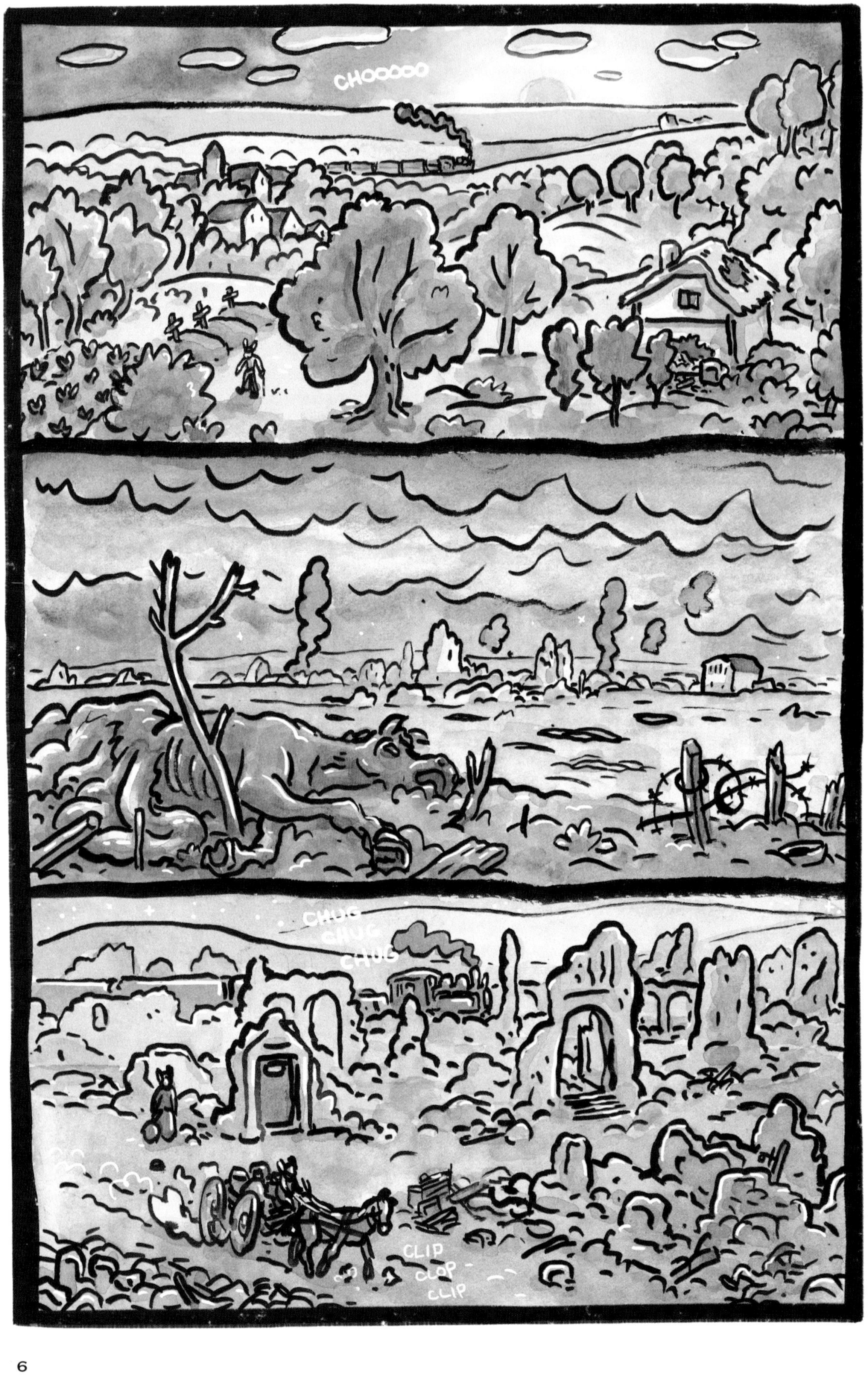
CHOOOOO
CHUG
CHUG
CHUG
CLIP
CLOP
CLIP

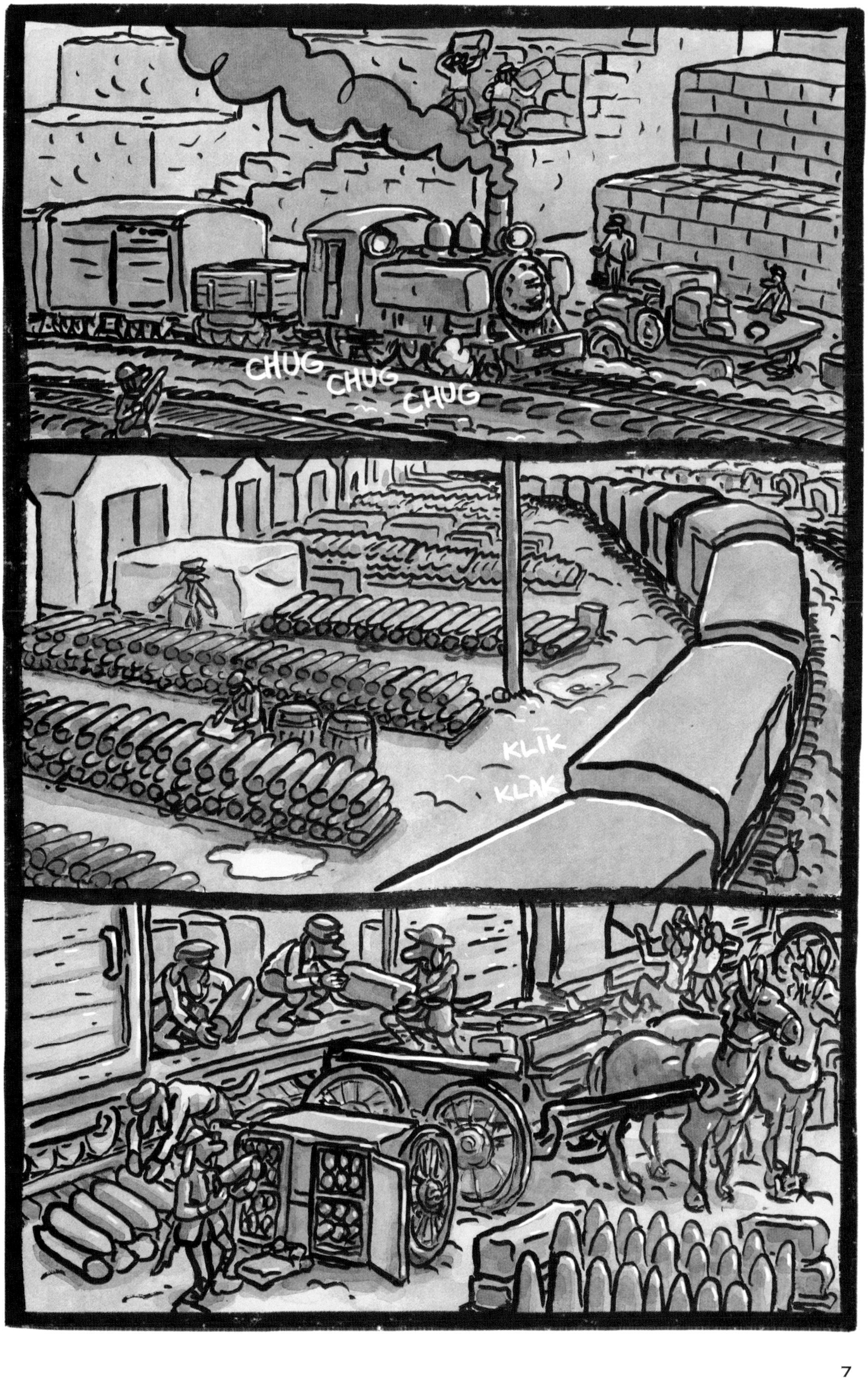
CHUG
CHUG
CHUG
KLIK
KLAK

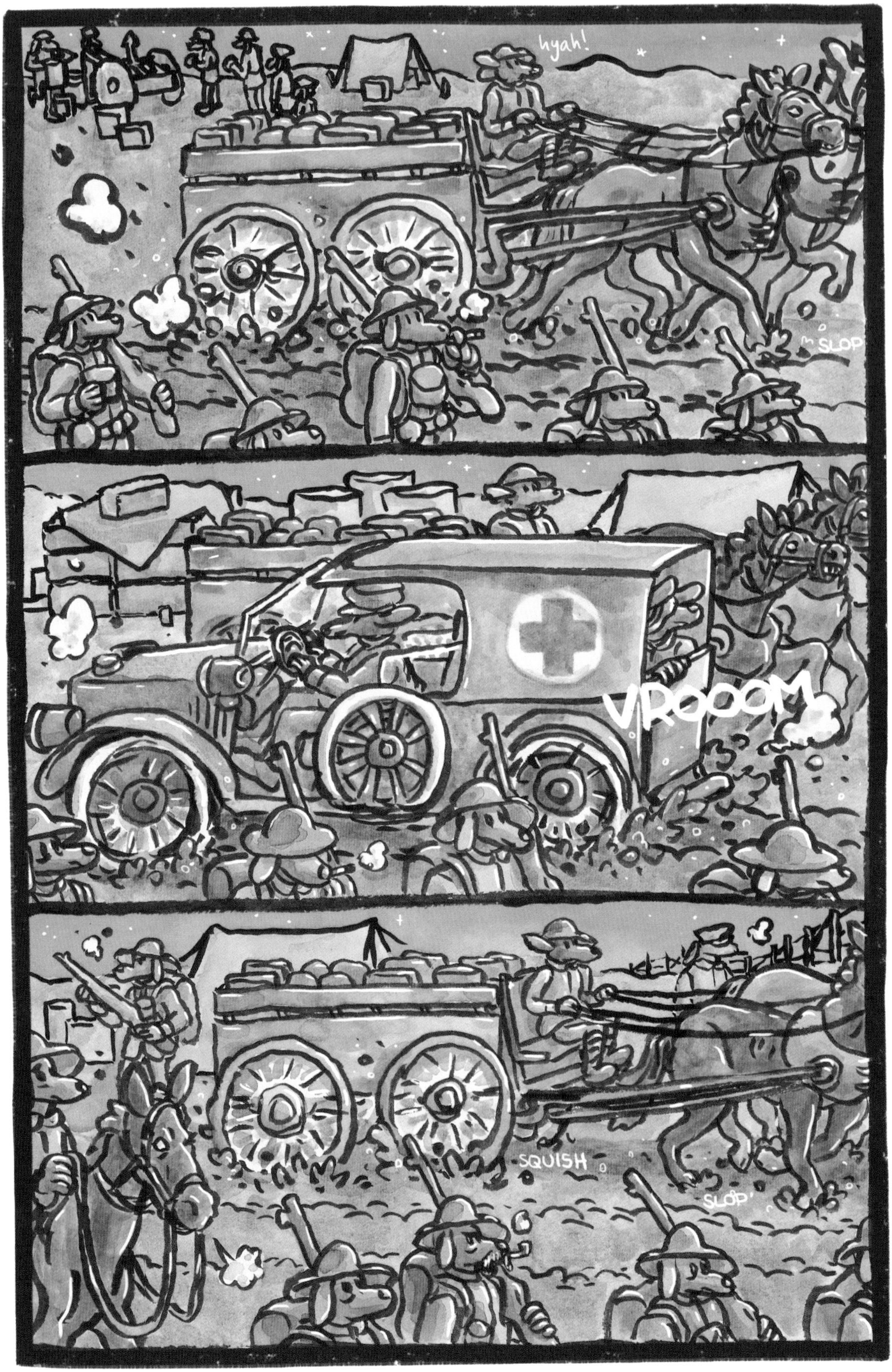
hyah!
SLOP
VROOOM
SQUISH
SLOP

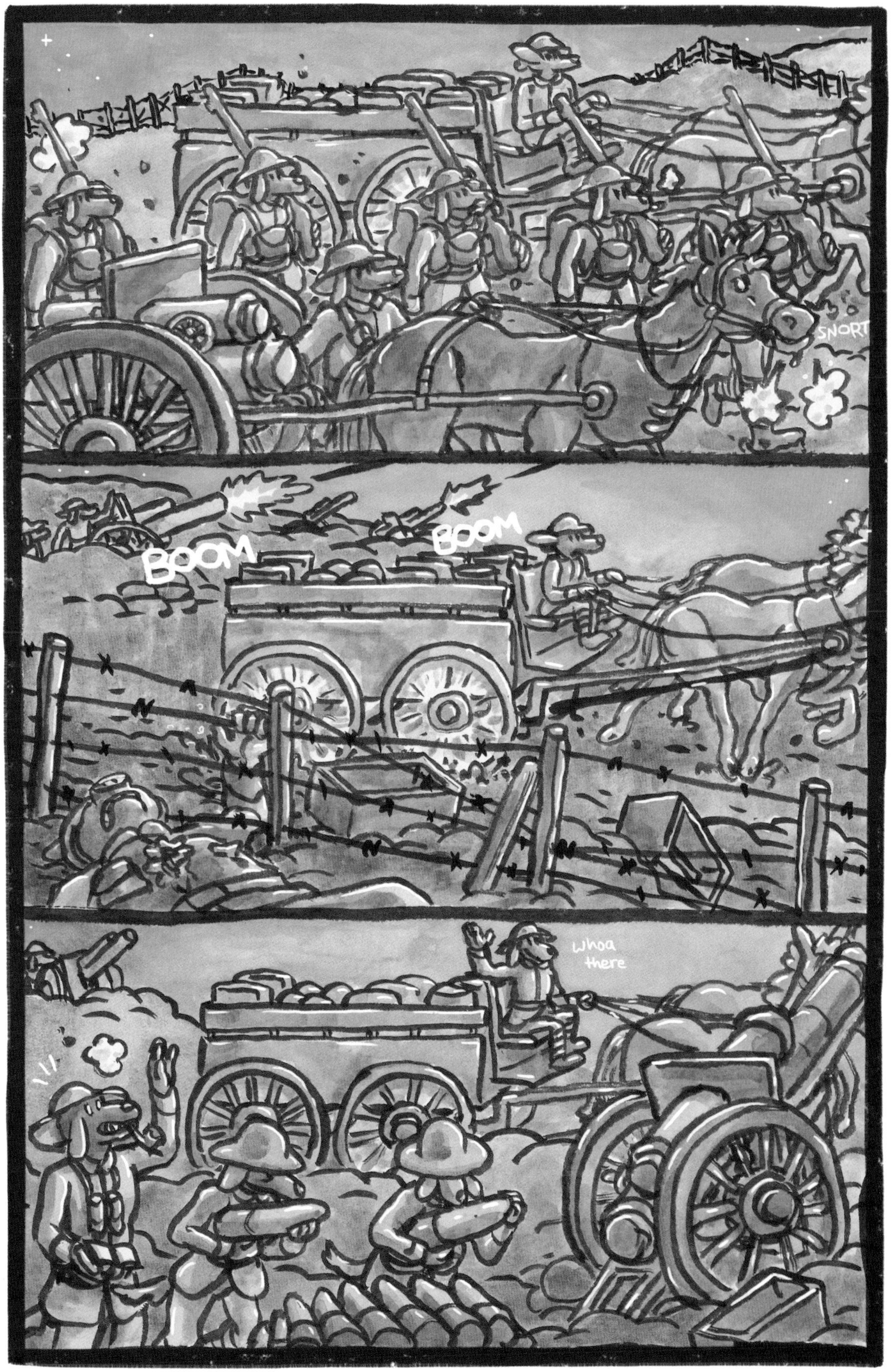
SNORT
BOOM
BOOM
Whoa
there

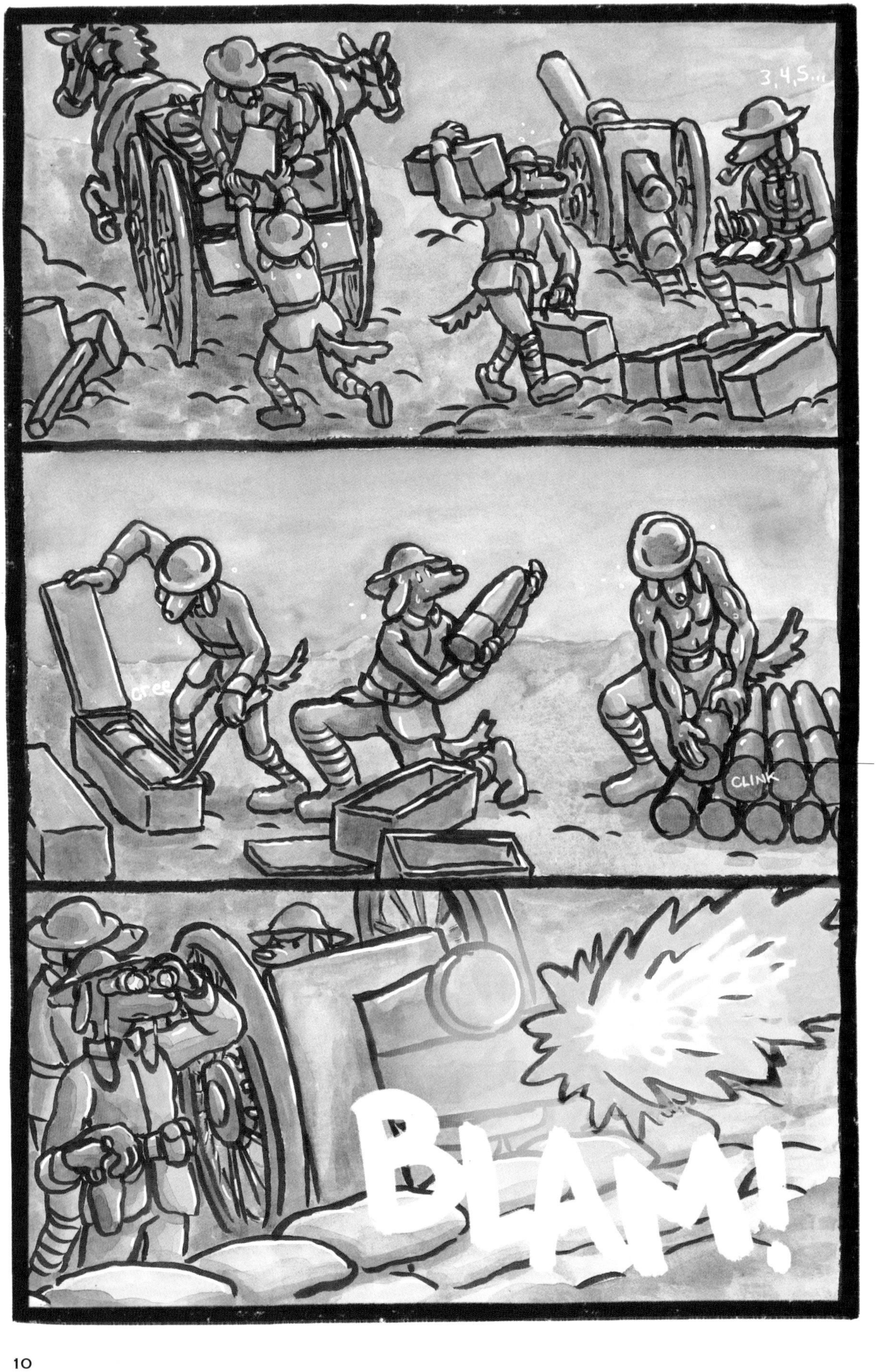
3,4,5...
cree
CLINK
BLAM!

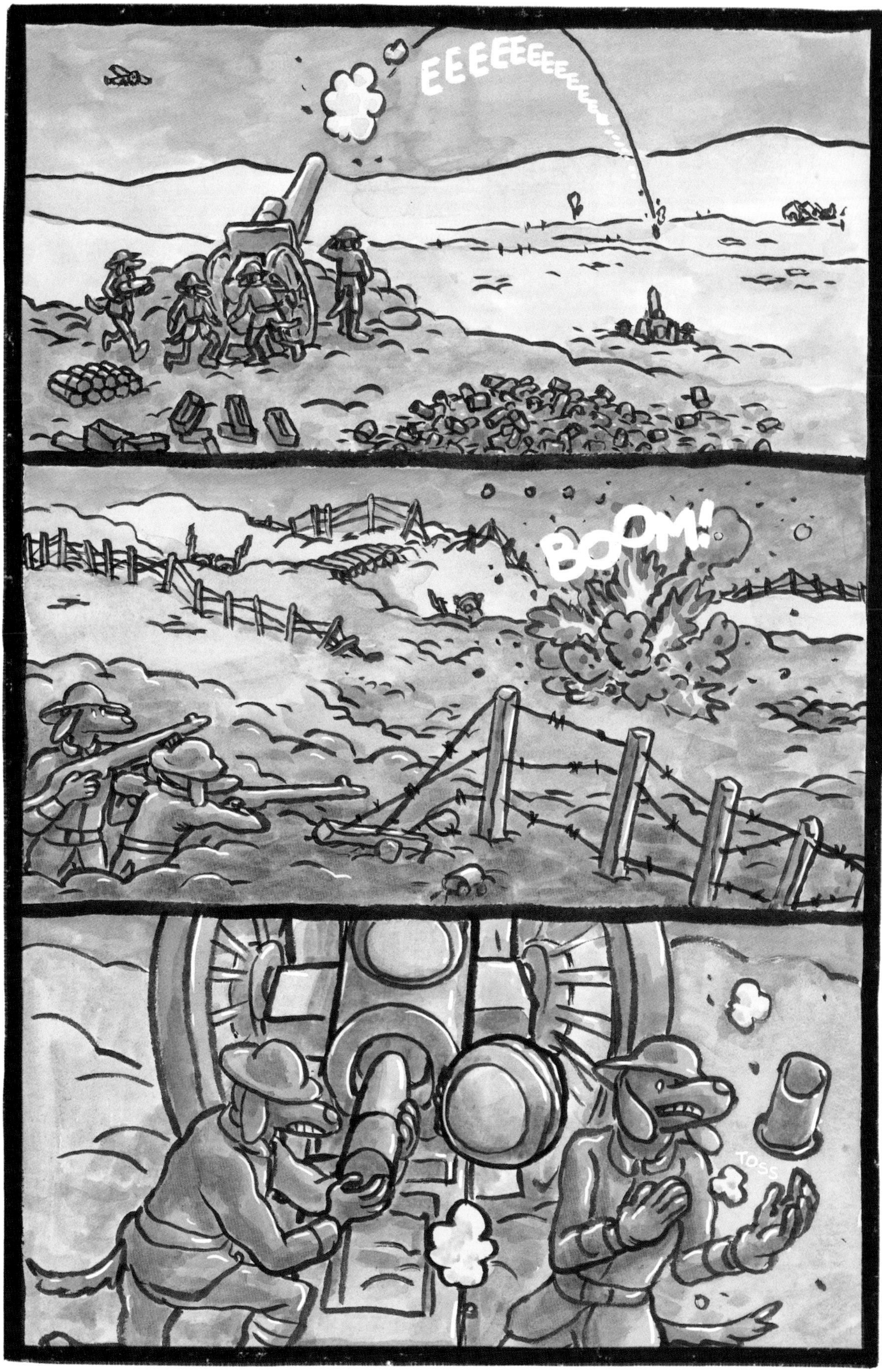
EEEEEEEEEEEEEEEEE
BOOM!
TOSS

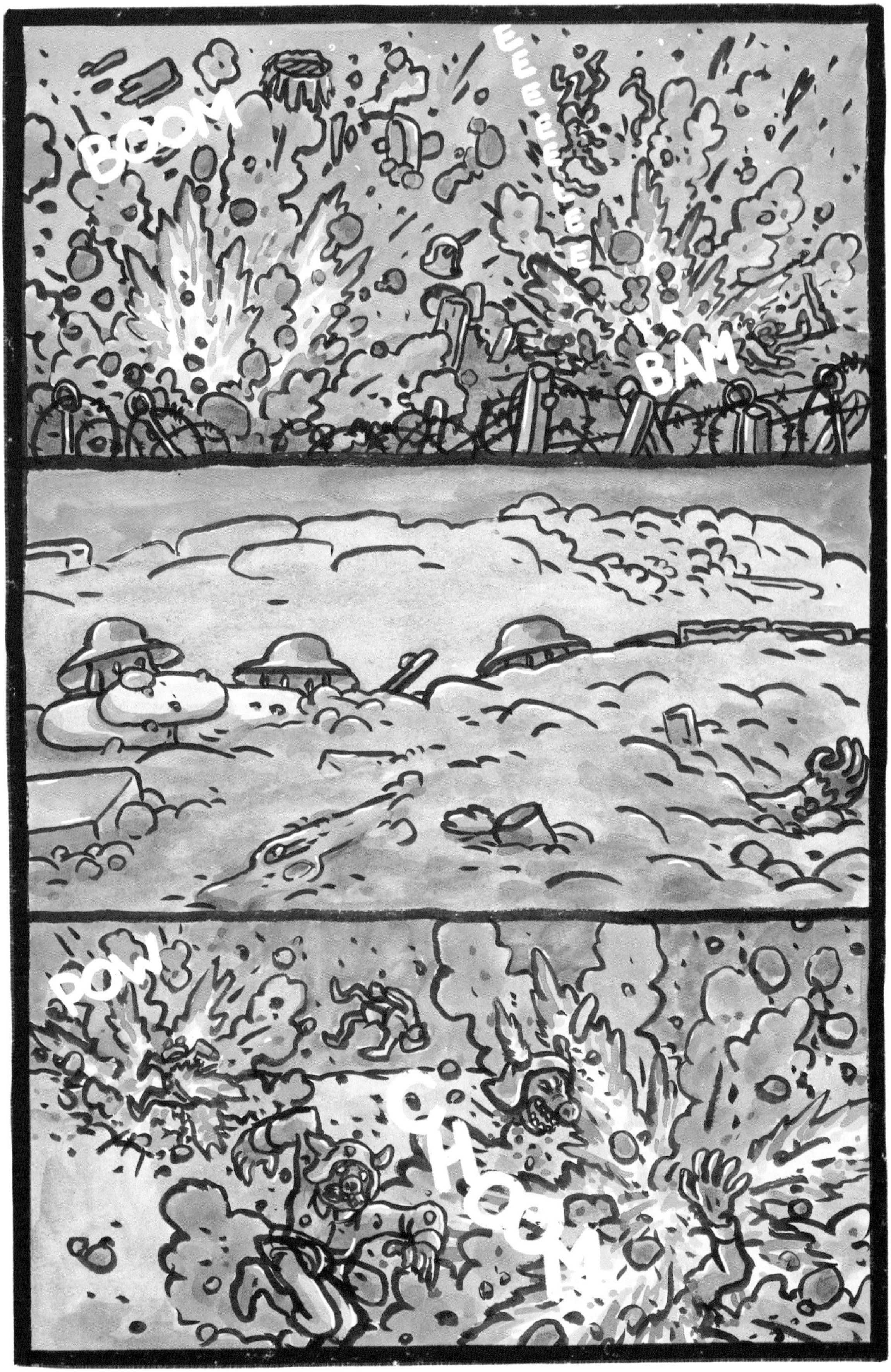
BOOM
EEEEEEEE
BAM
POW
CHOOM

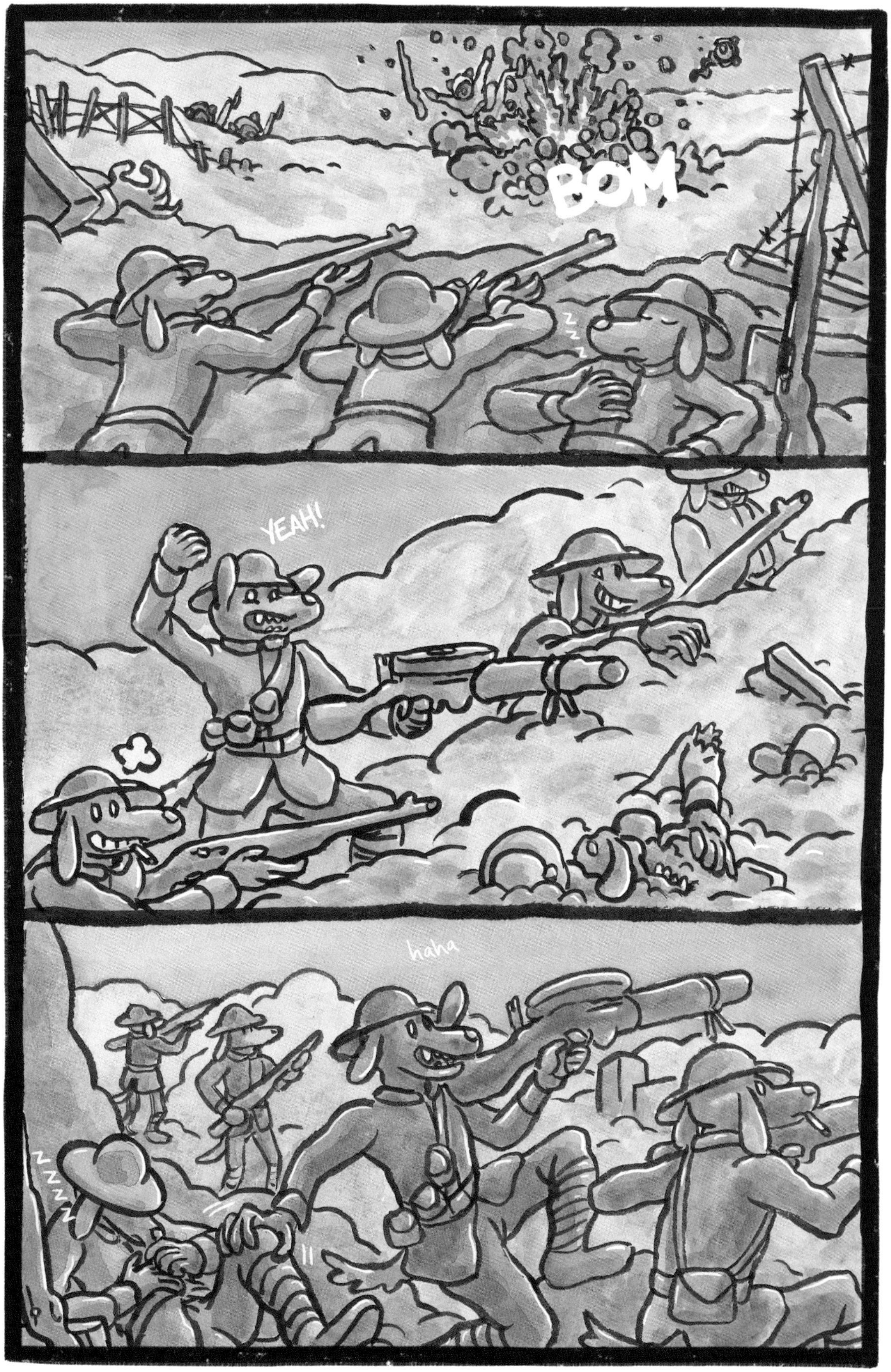
BOM
YEAH!
haha

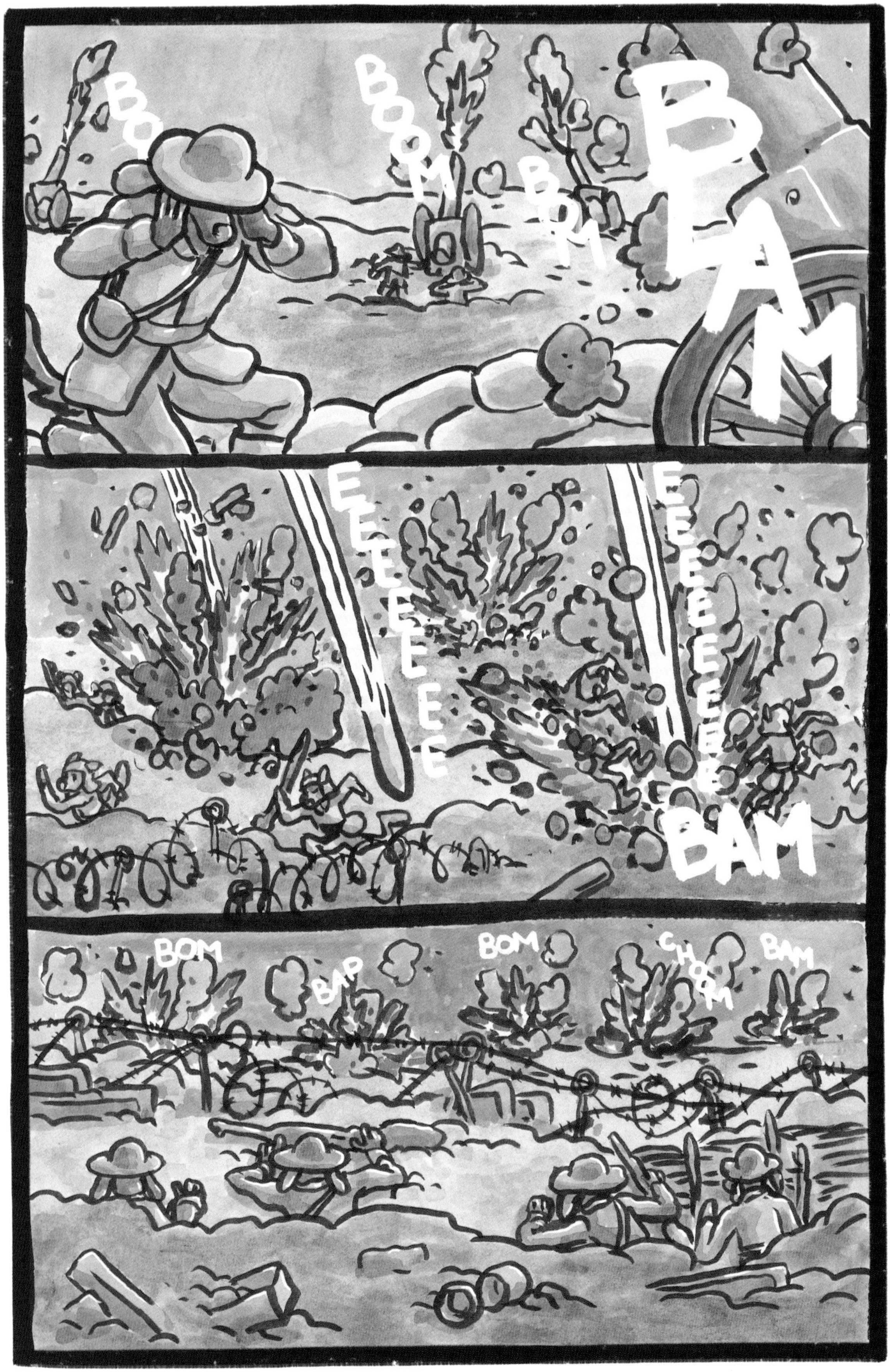

BO
BOOOM
BOM
BLAM
EEEEEEEE
EEEEEEEEEEEE
BAM
BOM
BAP
BOM
CHOOM
BAM

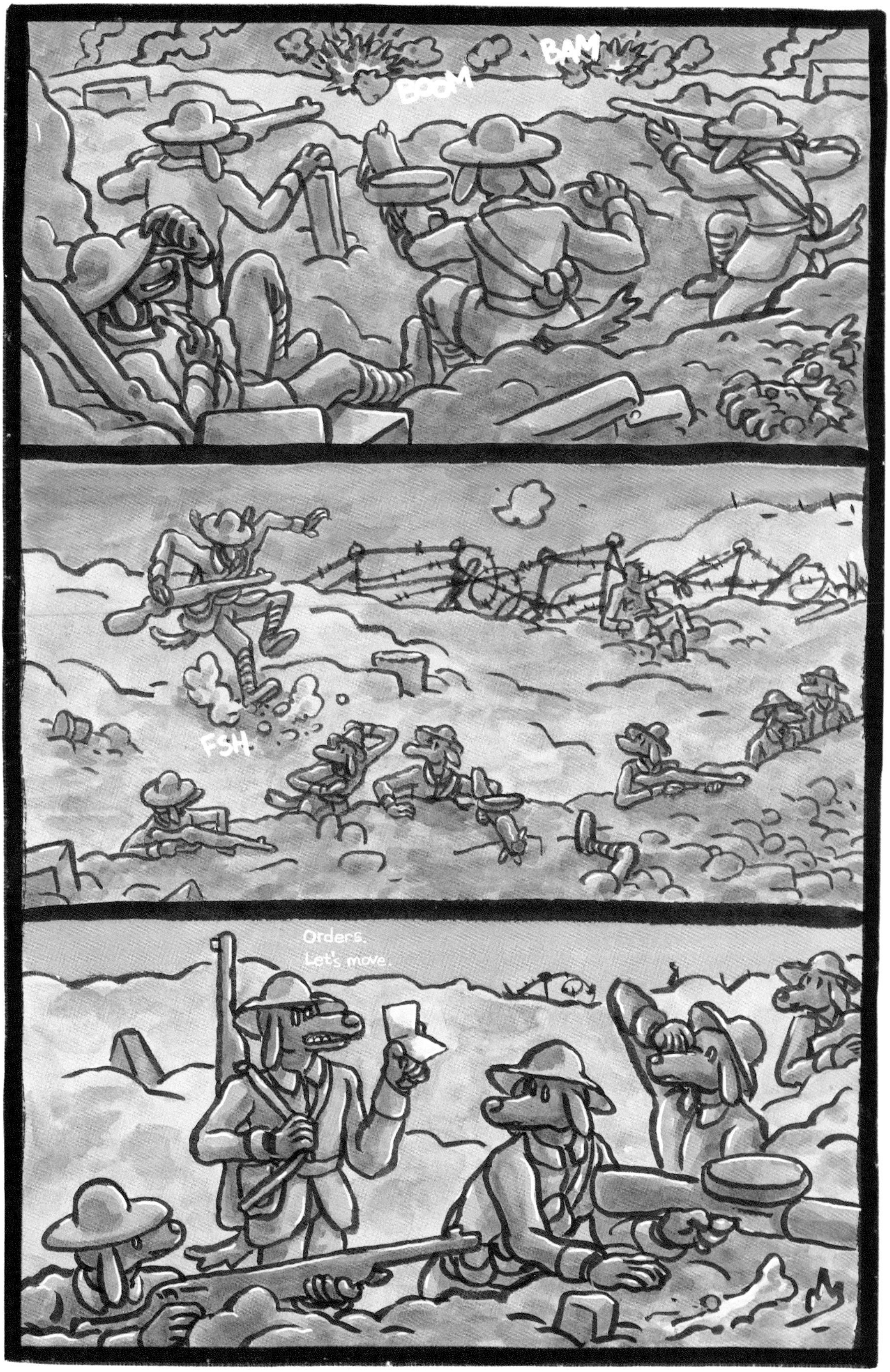
BOOM
BAM
FSH
Orders.
Let's move.

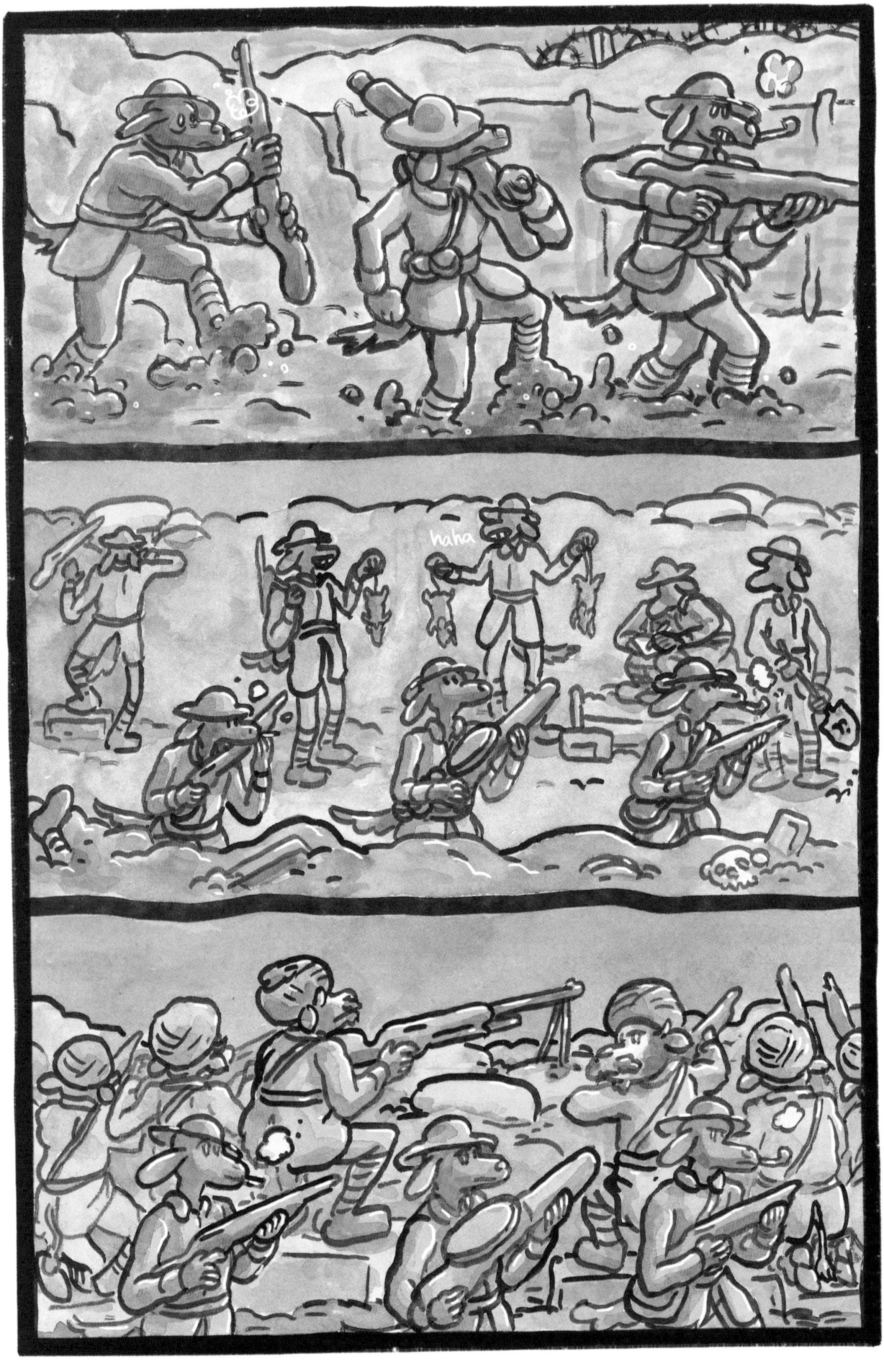
haha

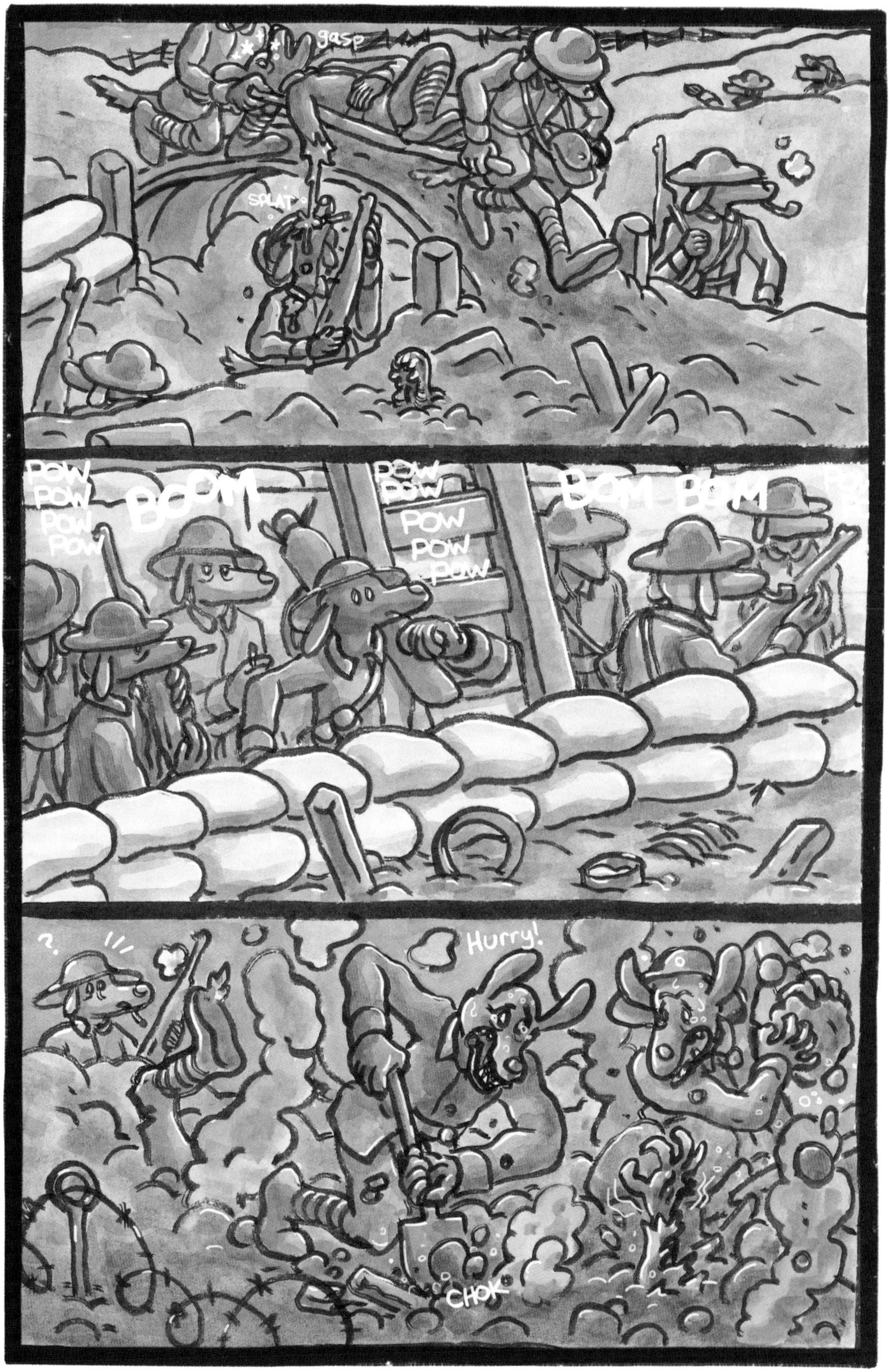
gasp
SPLAT
POW
POW
POW
POW
BOOM
POW
POW
POW
POW
POW
BOM BOM
?
Hurry!
CHOK

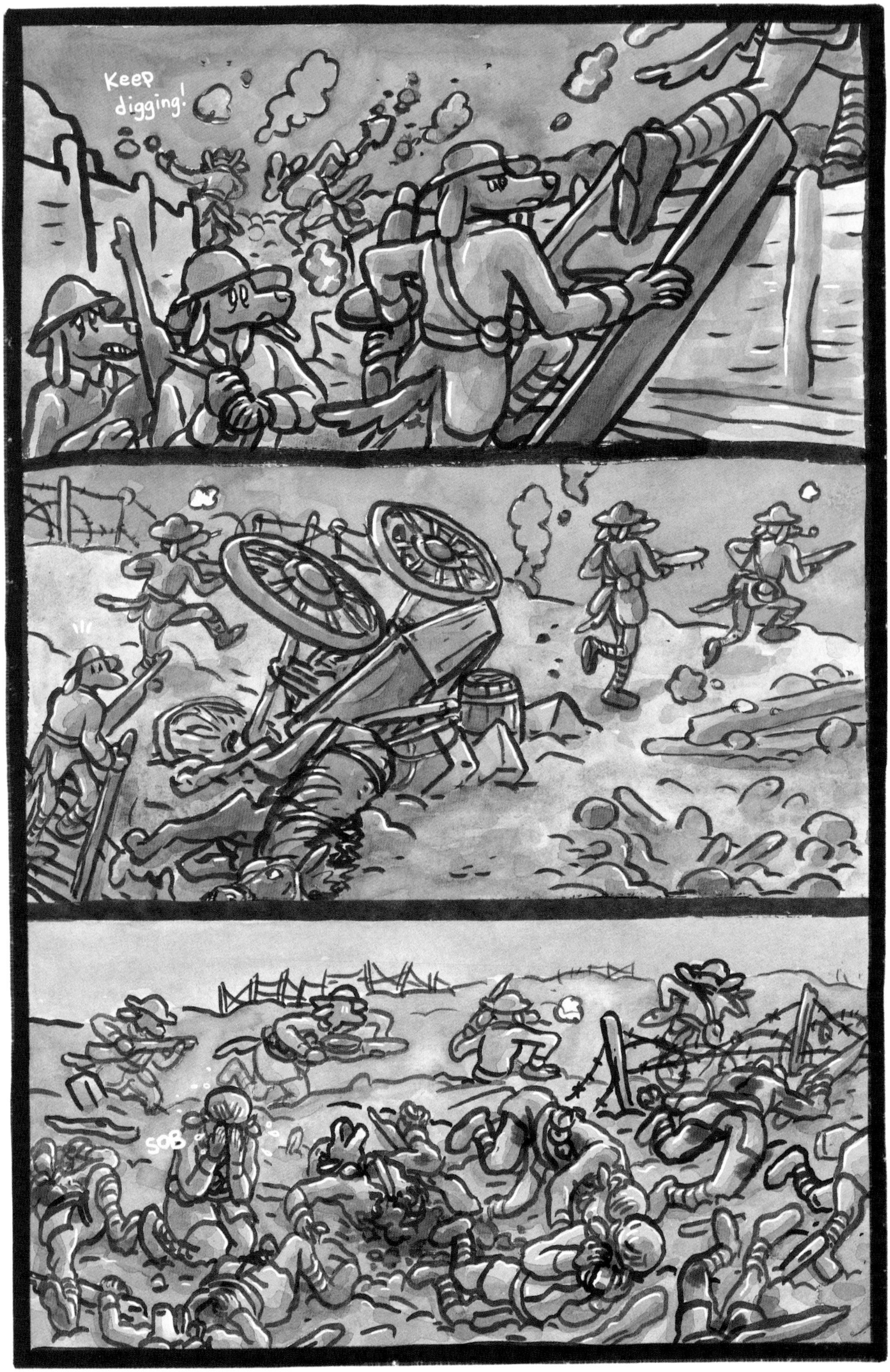
Keep digging!
SOB

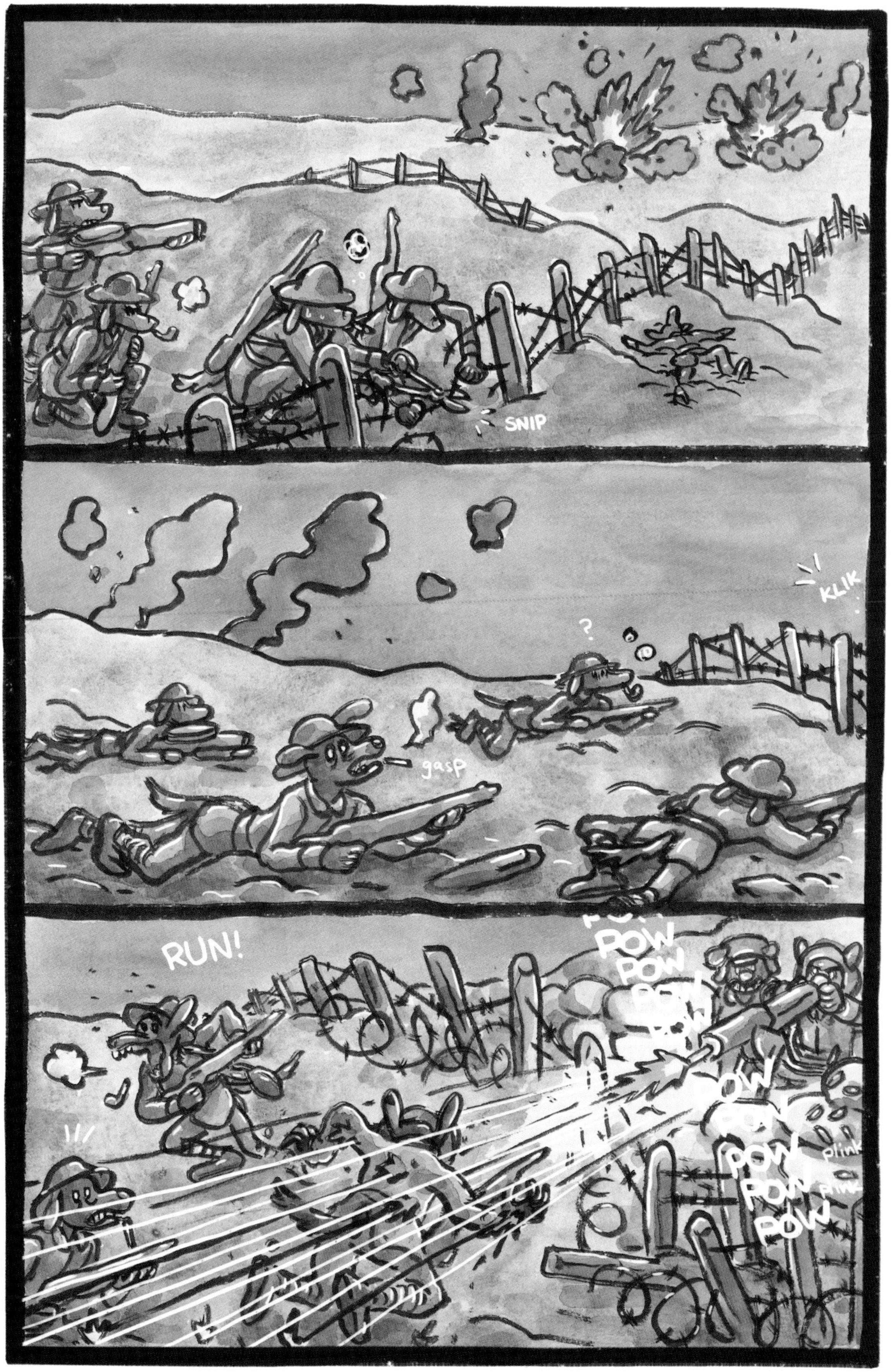
SNIP
KLIK
?
gasp
RUN!
POW
POW
POW
POW
POW
POW
POW
plink
plink

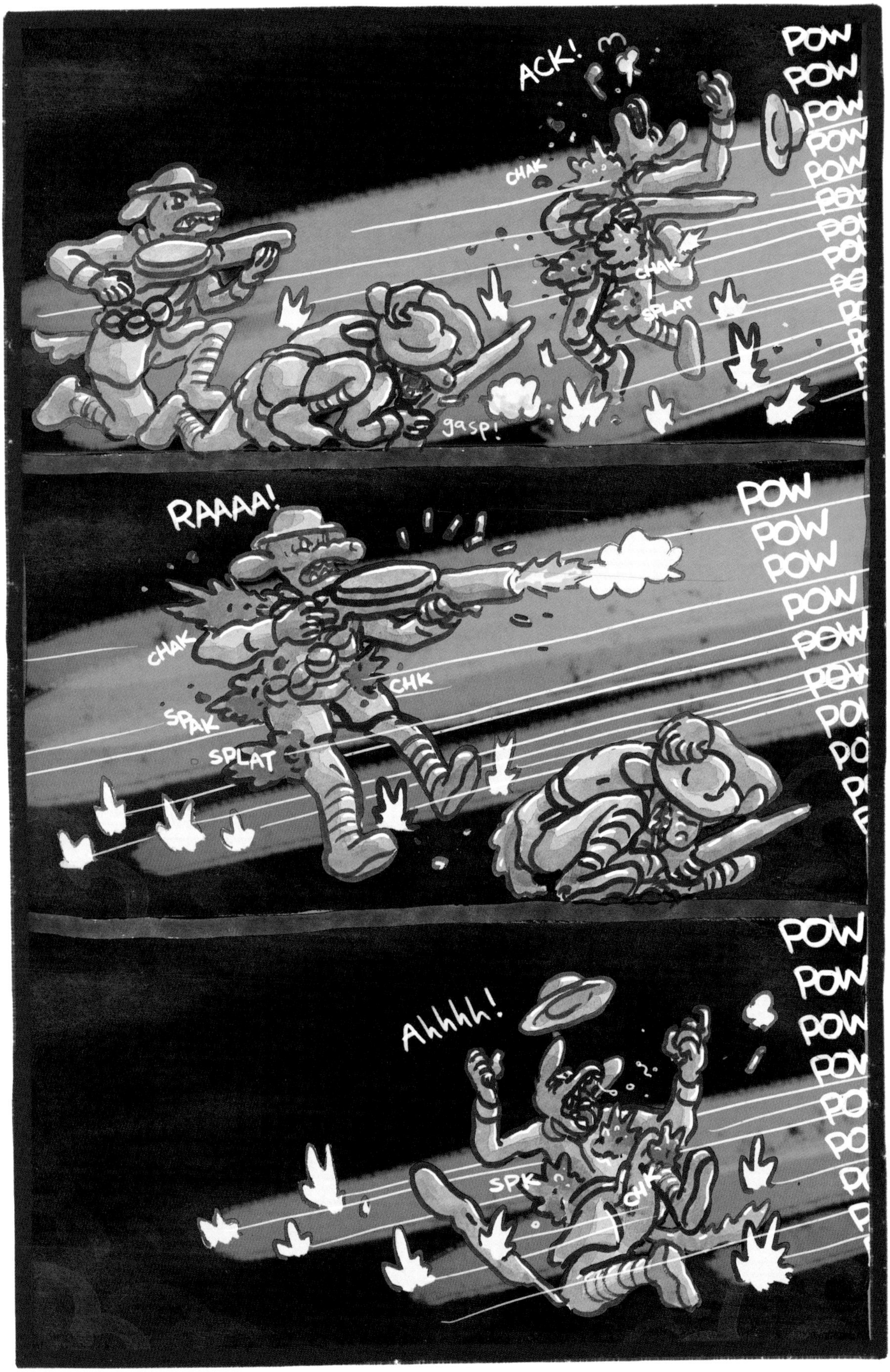
ACK!
POW
POW
POW
POW
POW
CHAK
CHAK
SPLAT
gasp!
RAAAA!
POW
POW
POW
POW
POW
CHAK
CHK
SPAK
SPLAT
Ahhhh!
POW
POW
POW
POW
SPK
CHK

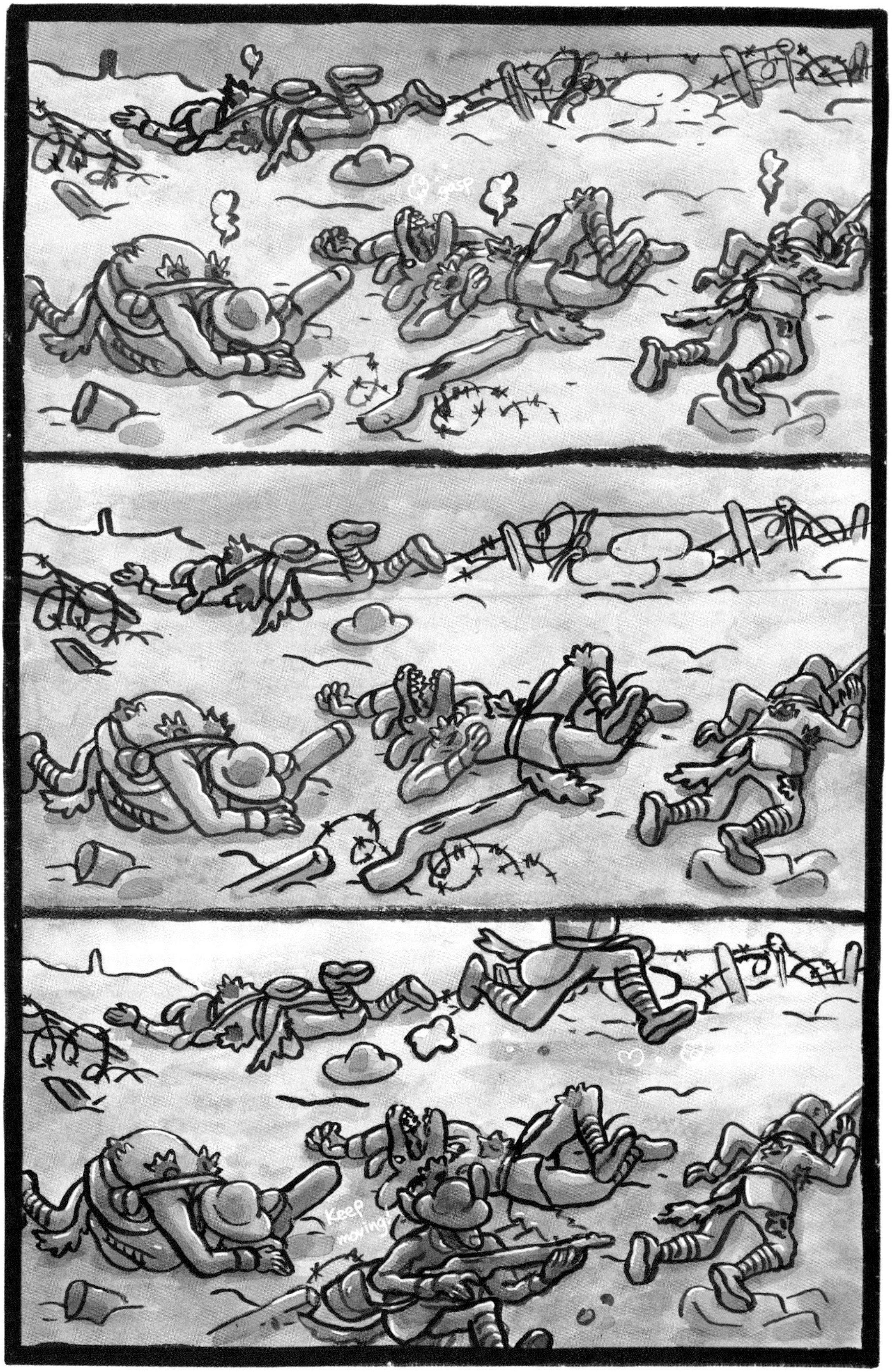
gasp
Keep moving!

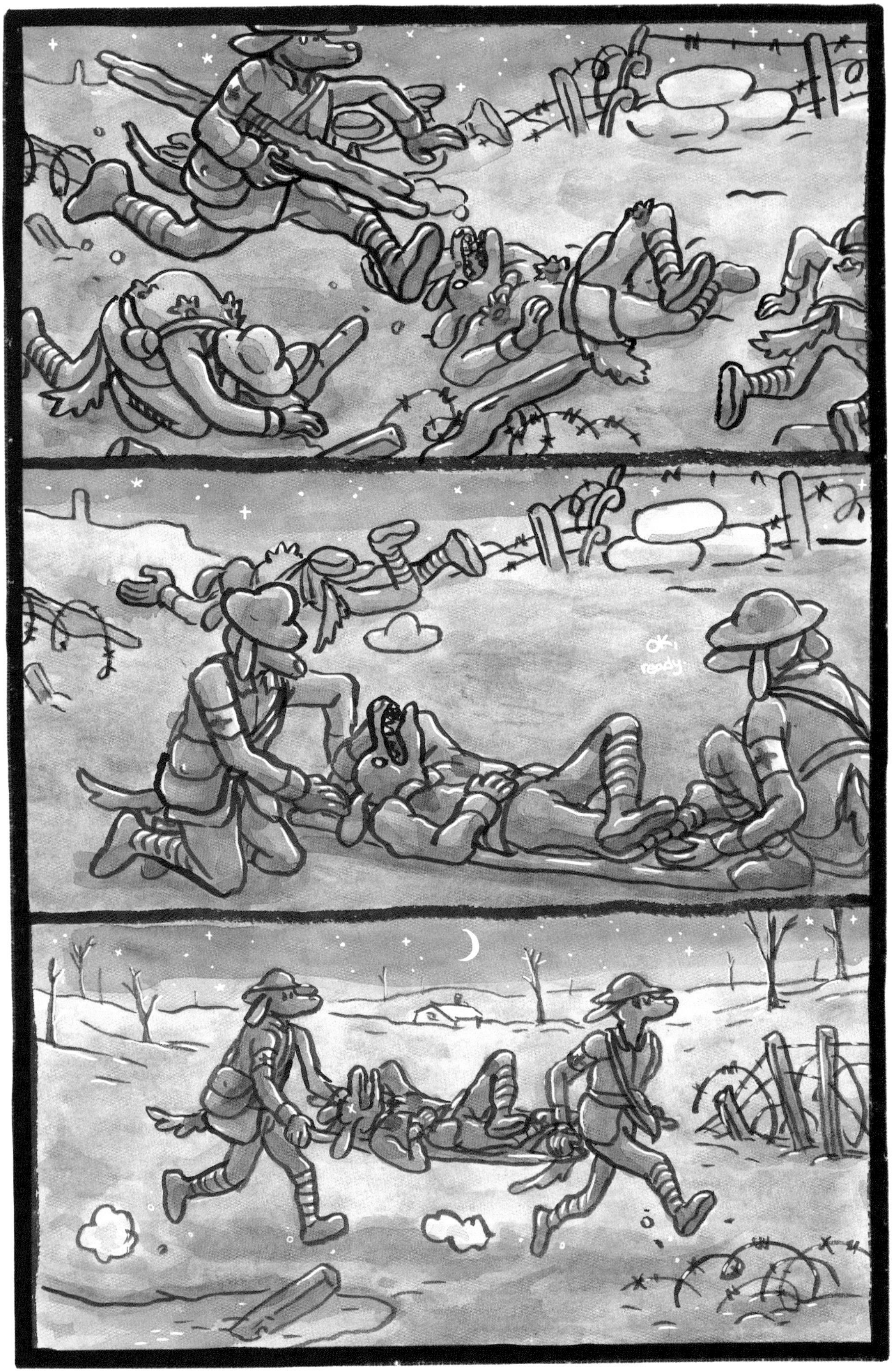
ok,
ready.

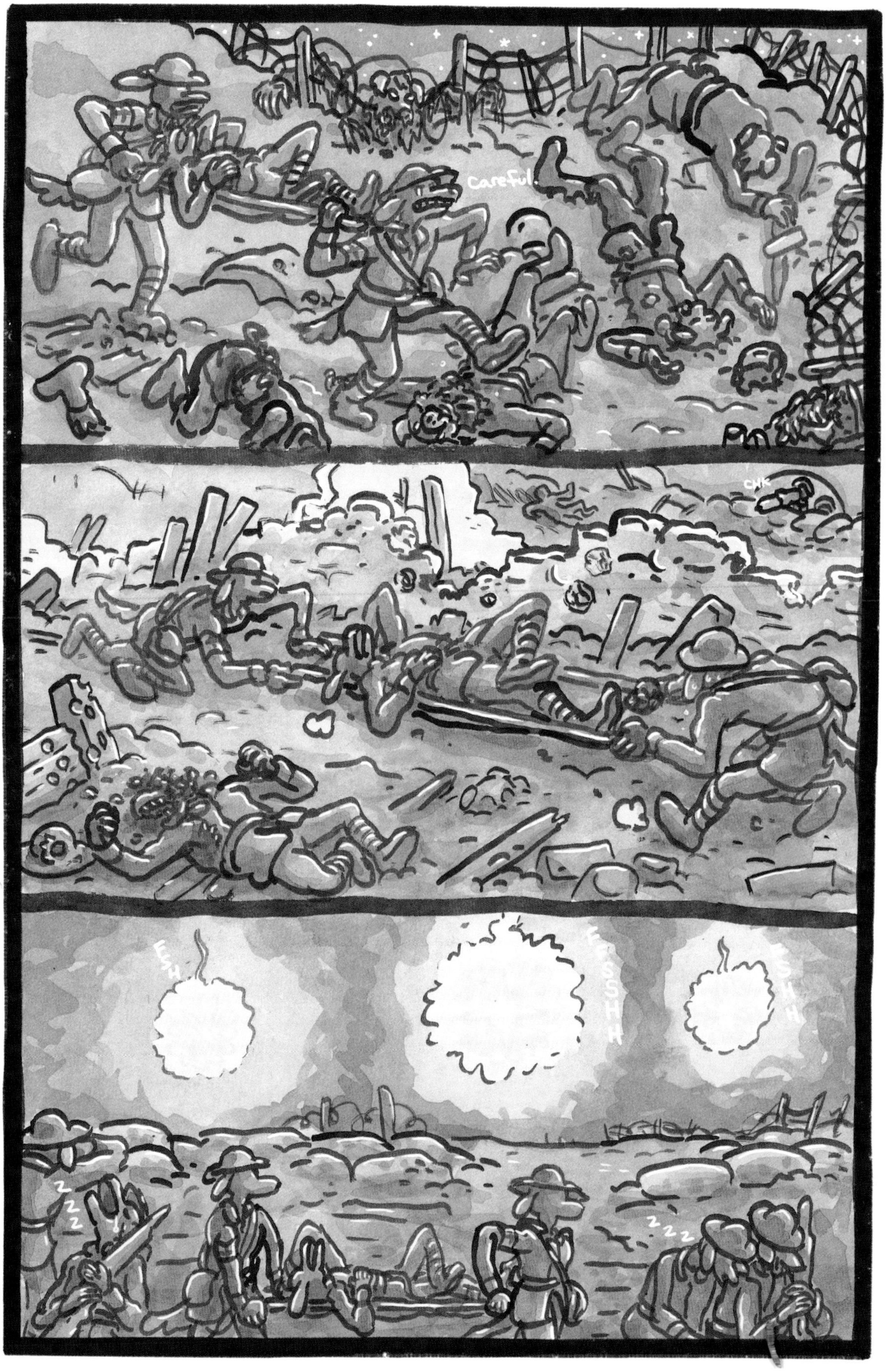
careful.
CHK
FSH
FFSSHH
FSHH
zzz
zzz

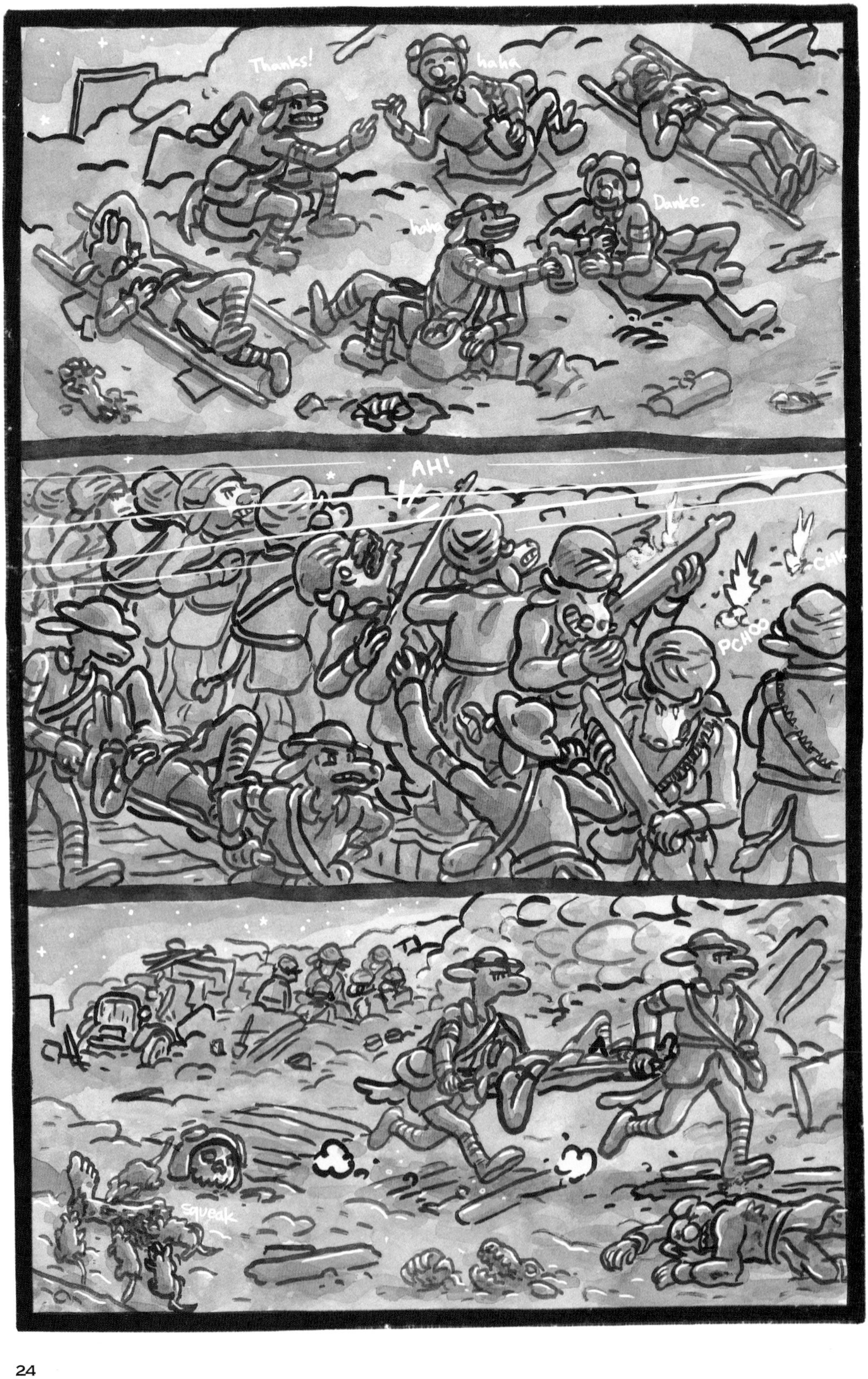
Thanks!
haha
haha
Danke.
AH!
CHK
PCHOO
squeak

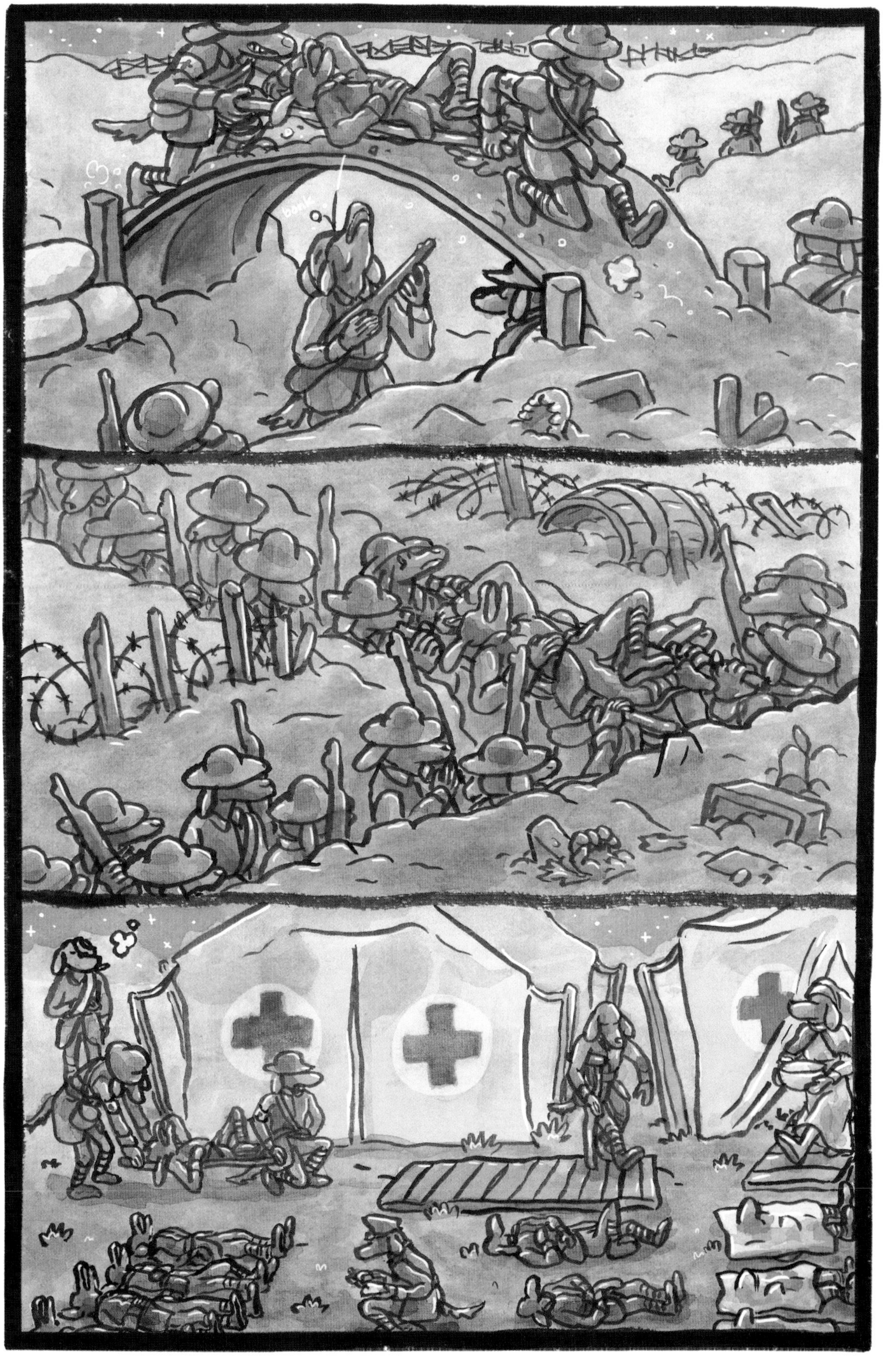
bonk

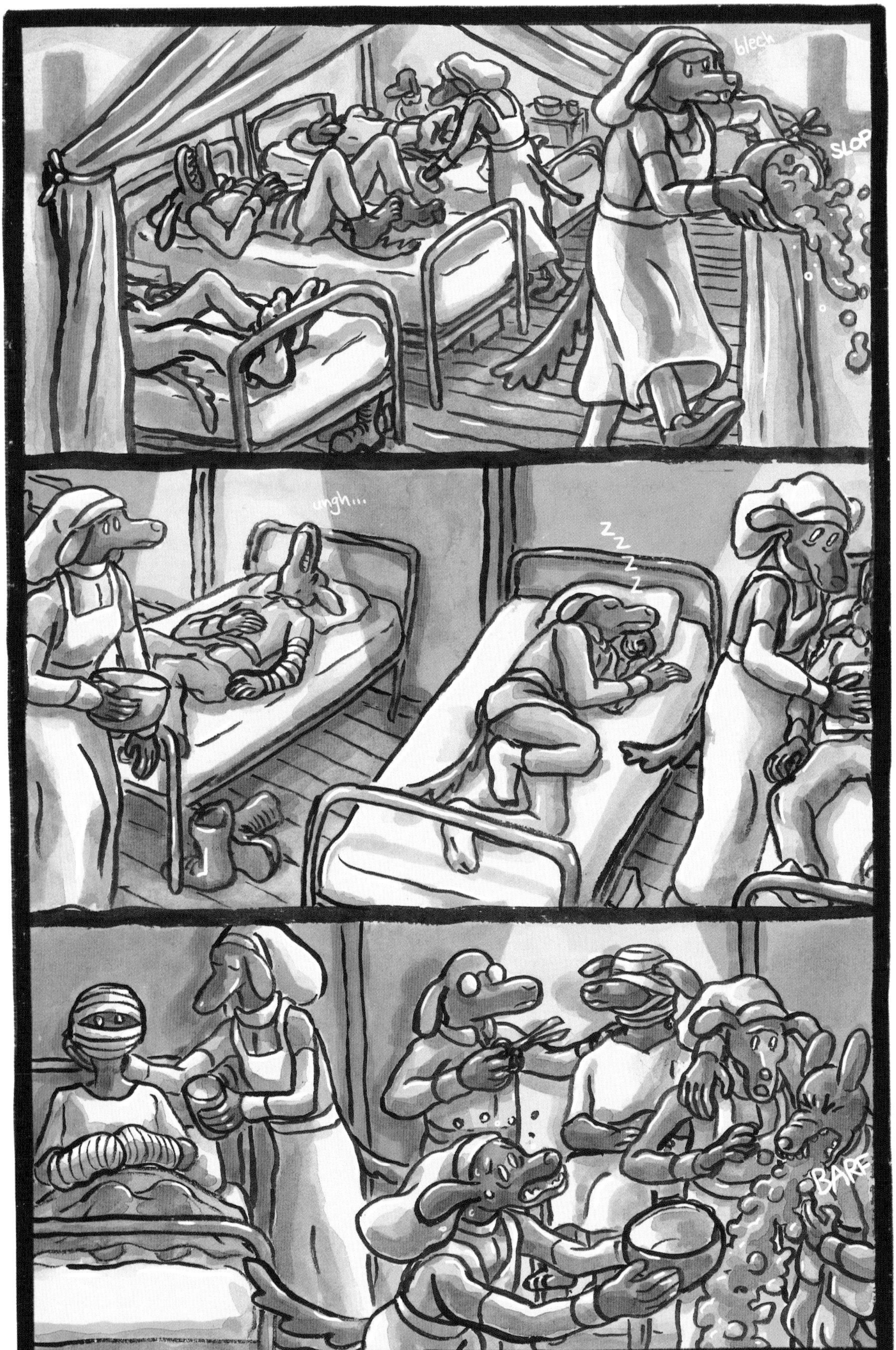
blech
SLOP
ungh...
ZZZZ
BARF

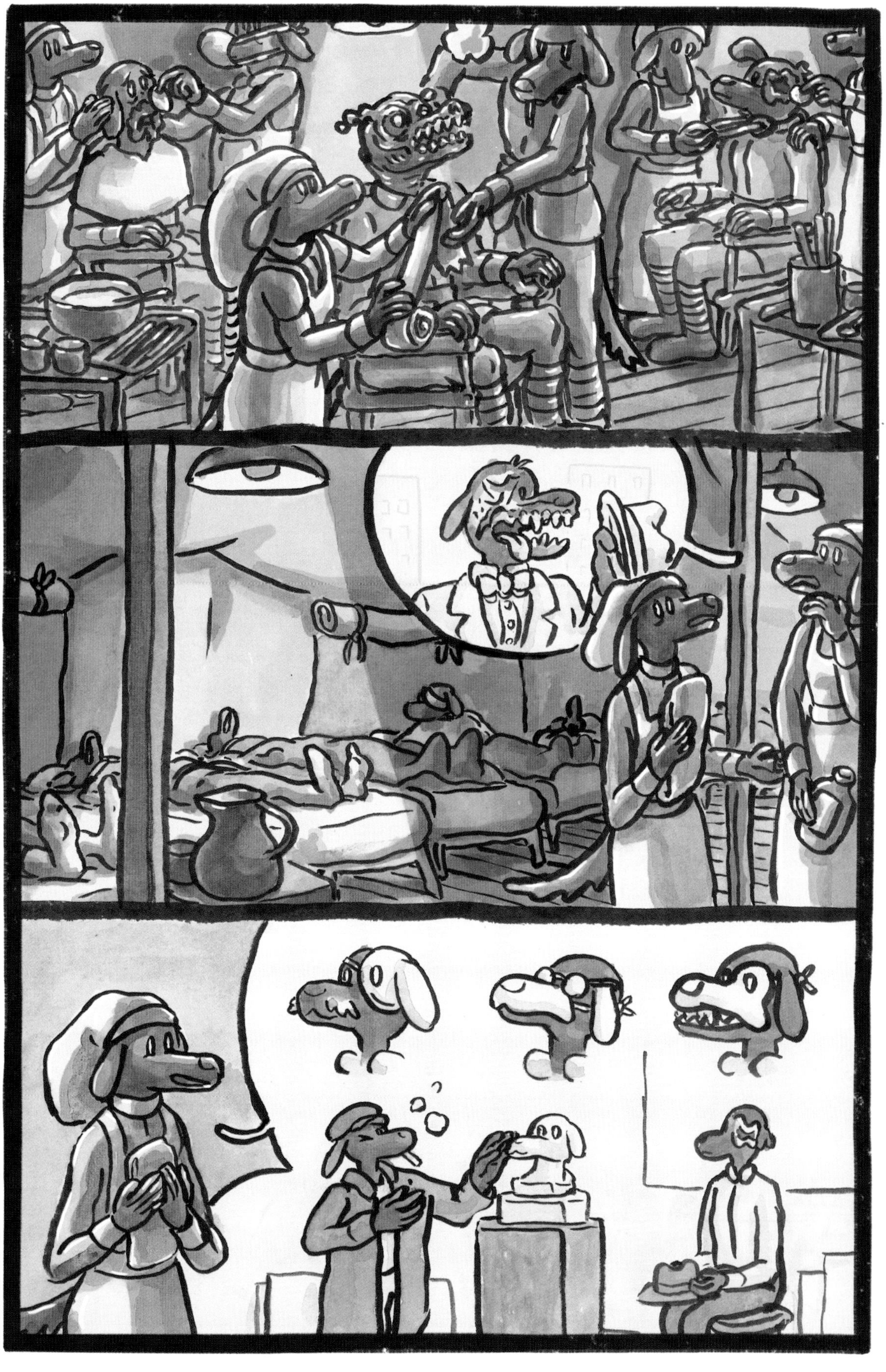

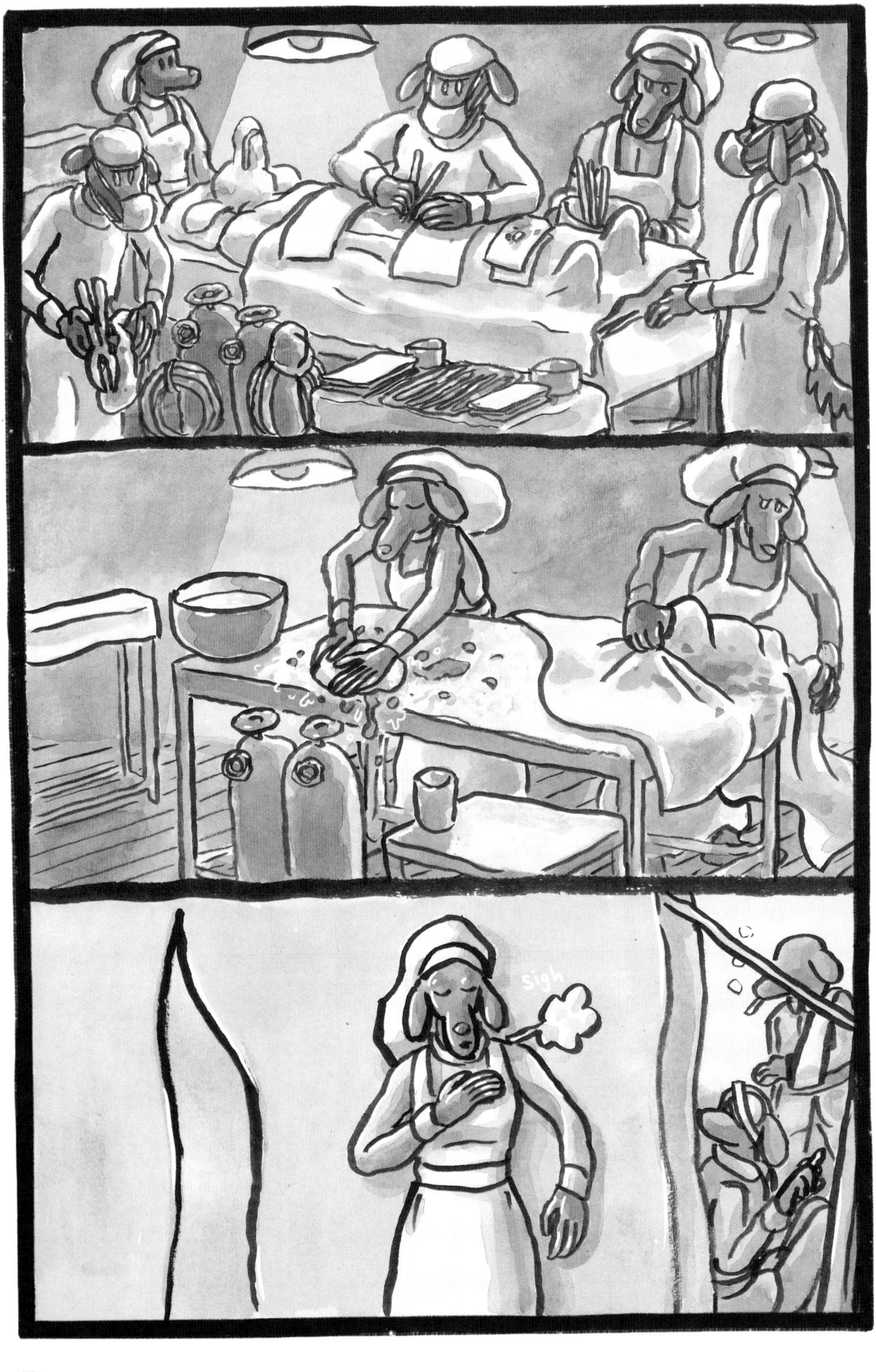
sigh

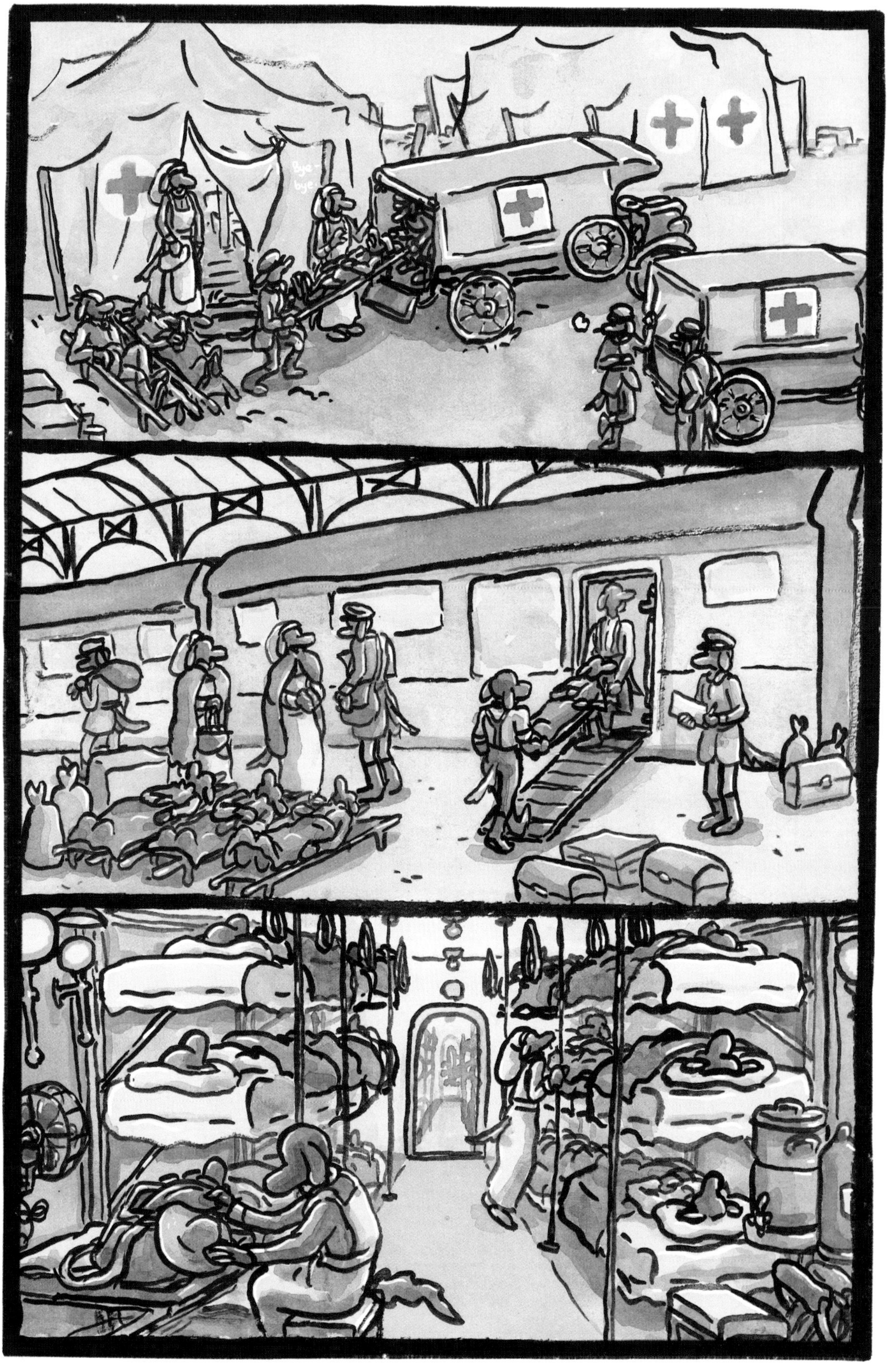
Bye bye

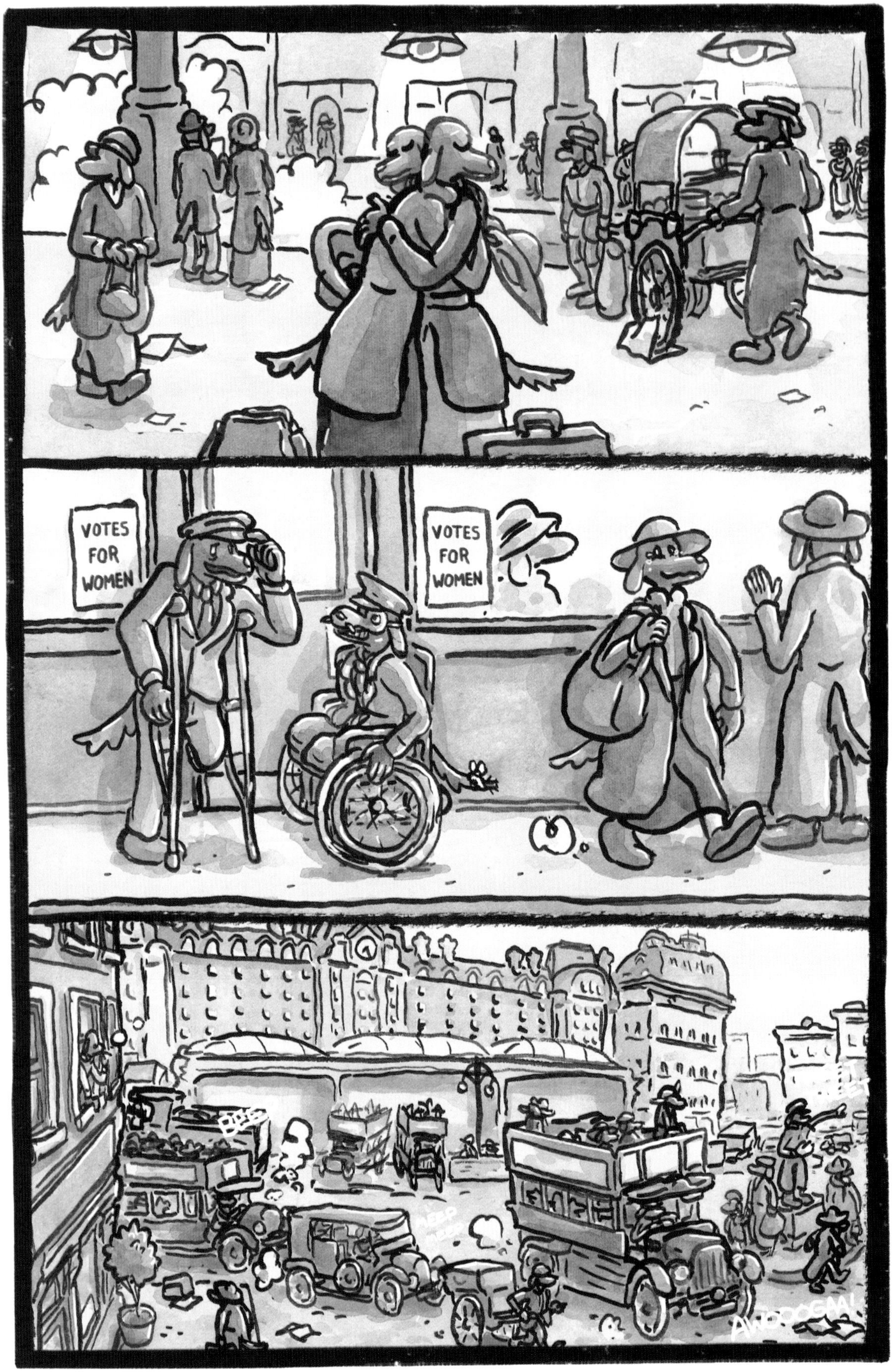
VOTES FOR WOMEN
VOTES FOR WOMEN
AWOOOGAA!

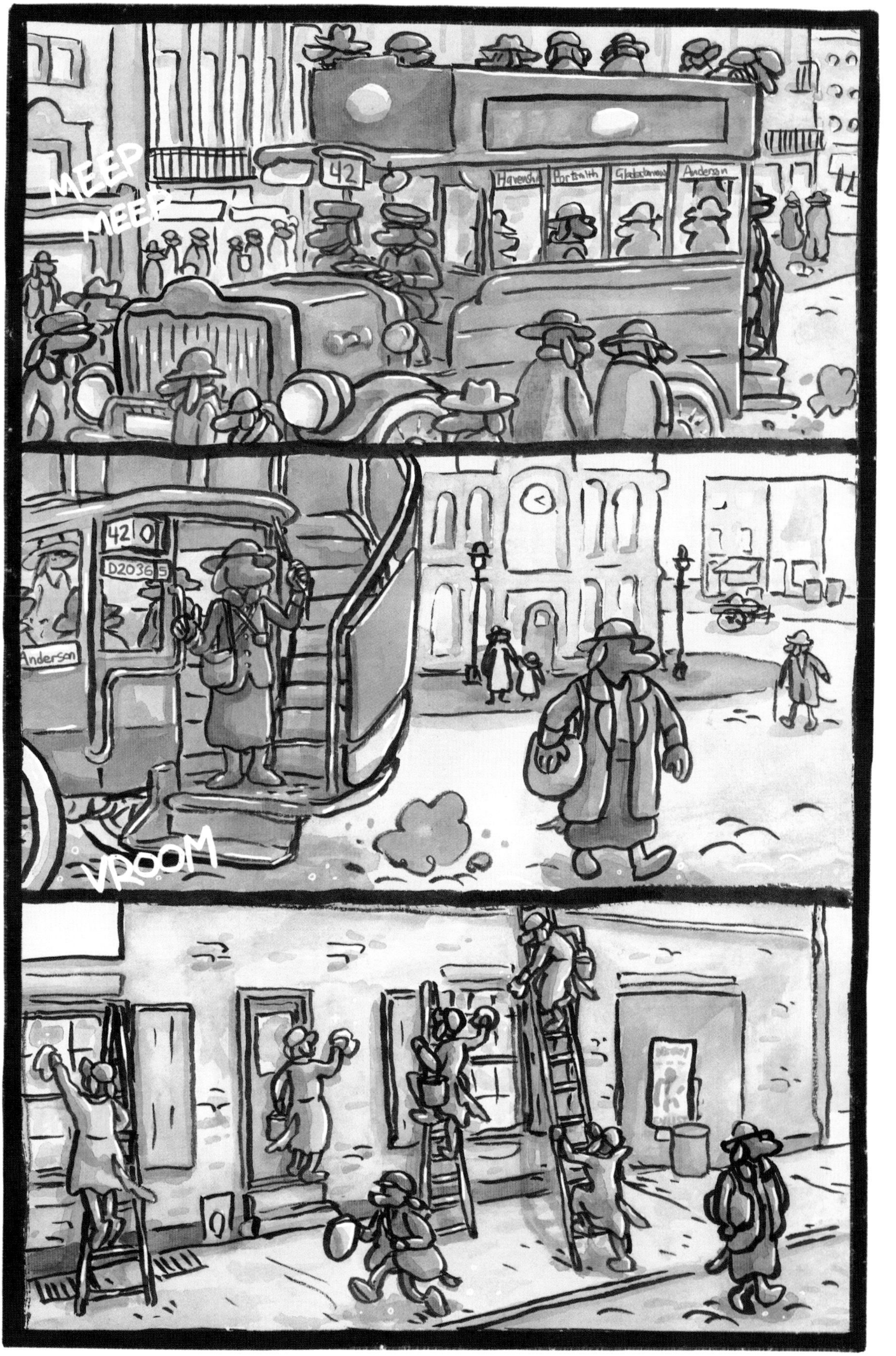
MEEP MEEP
42
Anderson
42 0
D2036 5
Anderson
VROOM

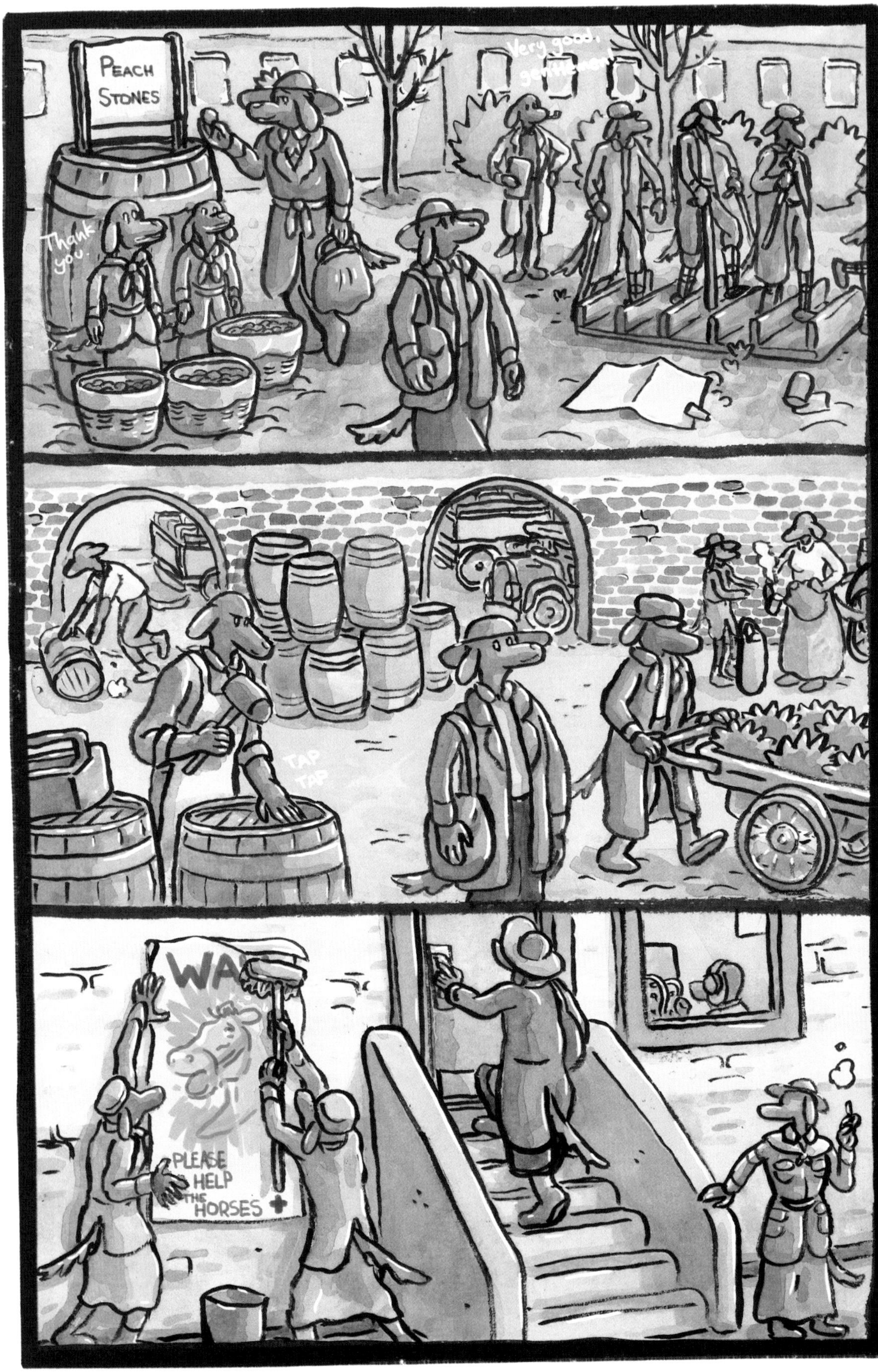
PEACH STONES
Thank you.
Very good, gentlemen!
TAP TAP
PLEASE HELP THE HORSES

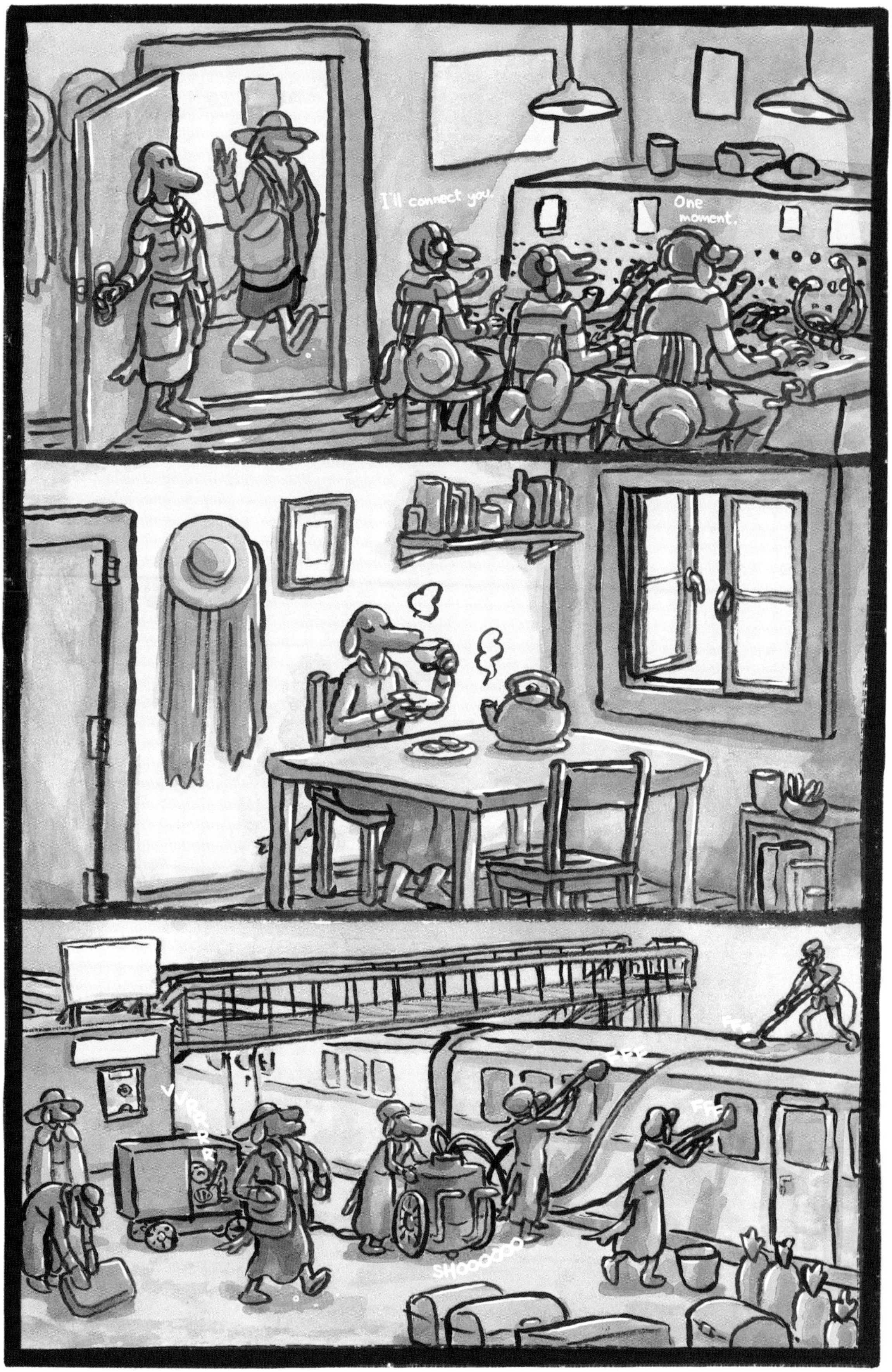

I'll connect you.
One moment.
VVRRRRR
FFF
FFF
FFF
SHOOOOOO

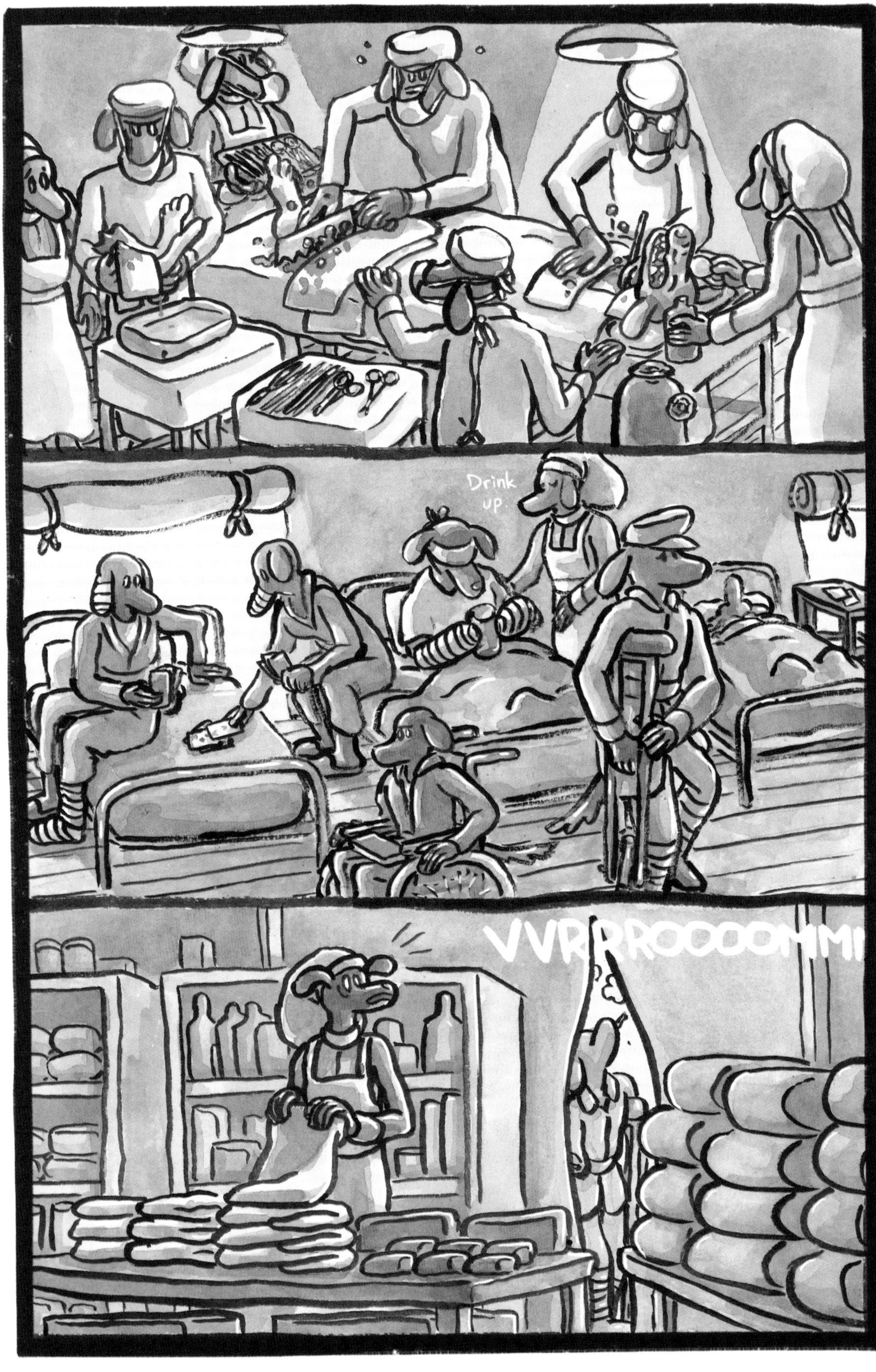
Drink up.
VVRRROOOOOMM!

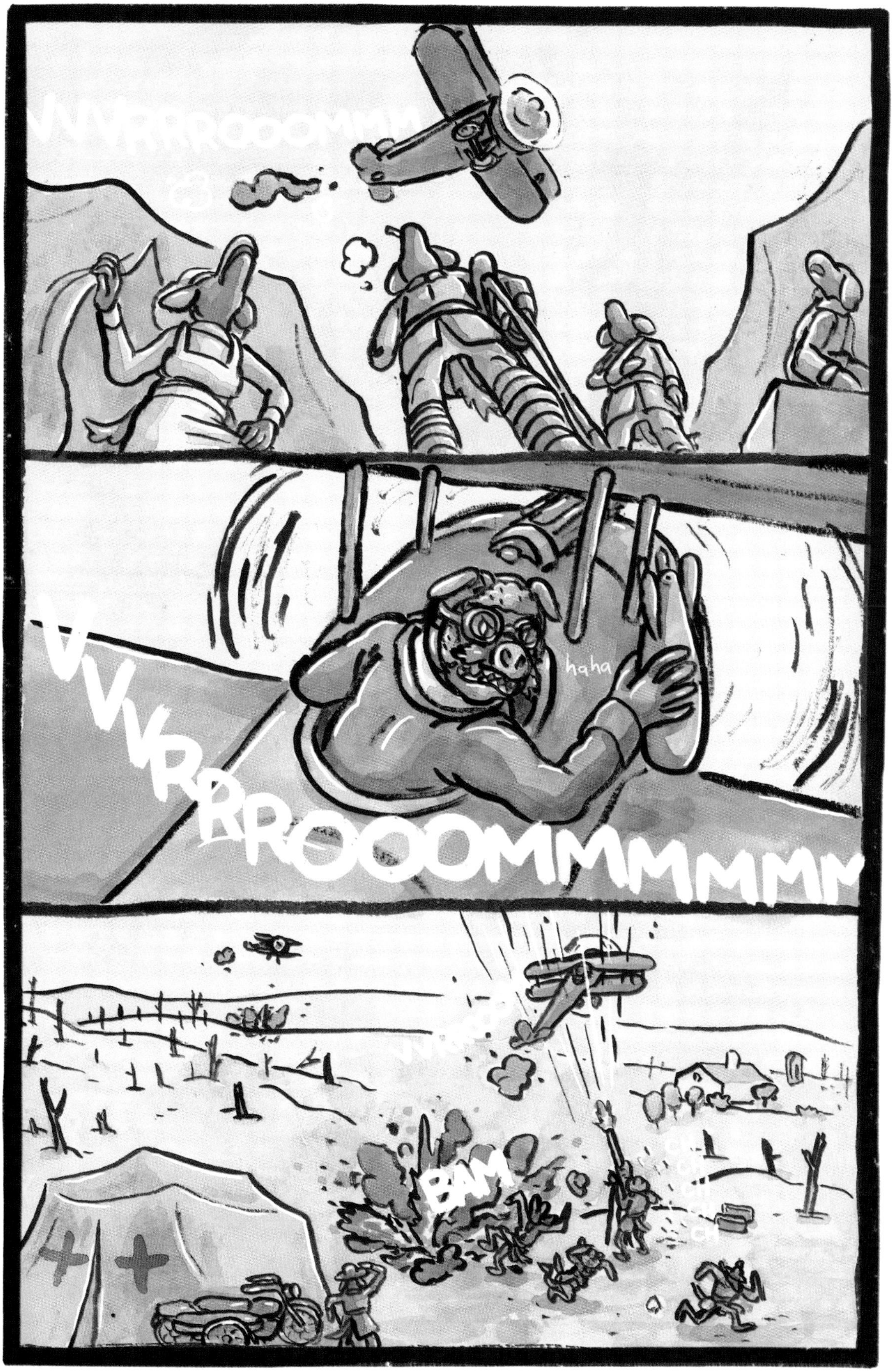
VVVRRROOOMMM
haha
VVVRRROOOMMMMMM
BAM
CH CH CH CH CH

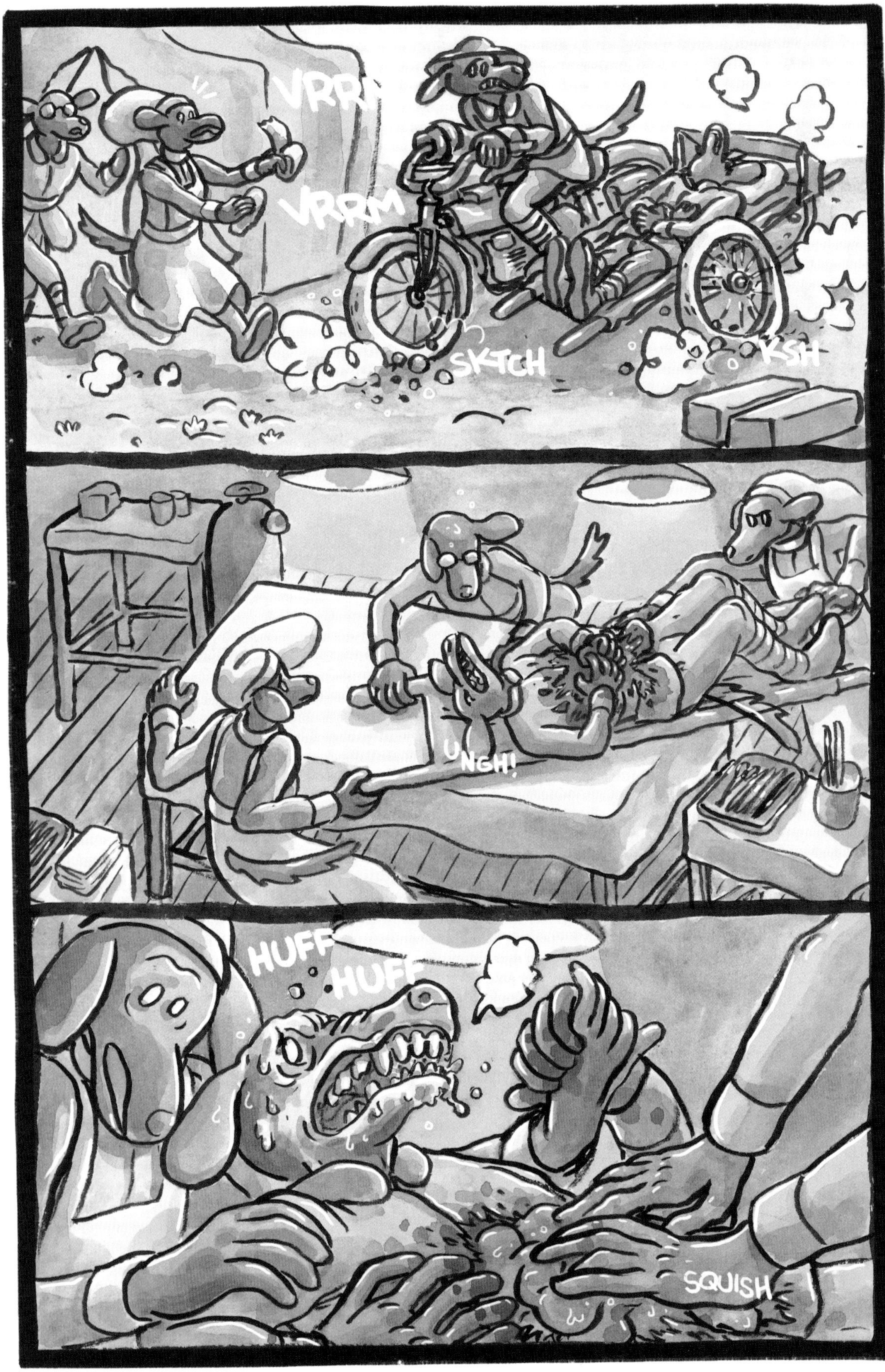
VRRM
VRRM
SKTCH
KSH
UNGH!
HUFF
HUFF
SQUISH

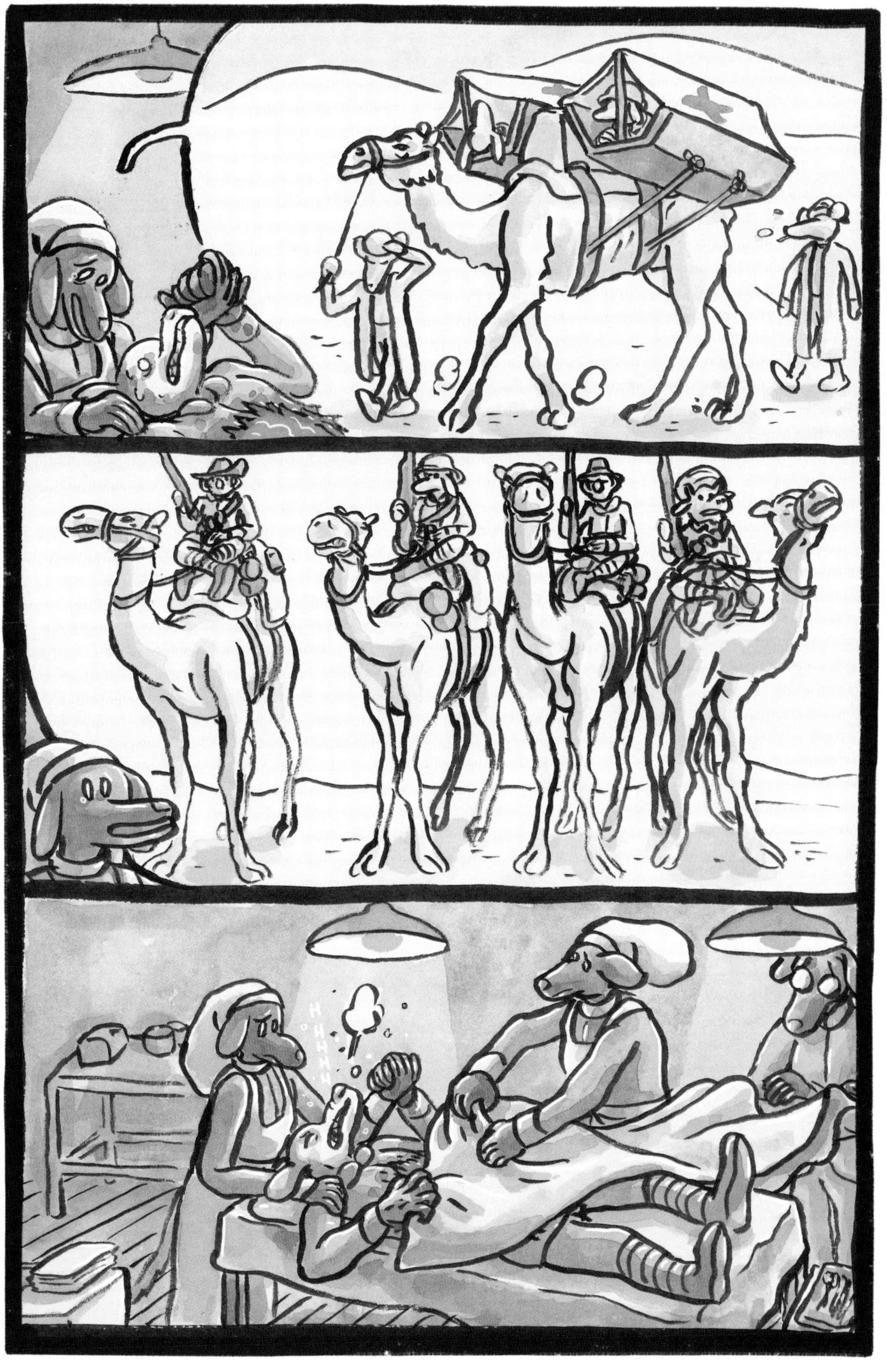

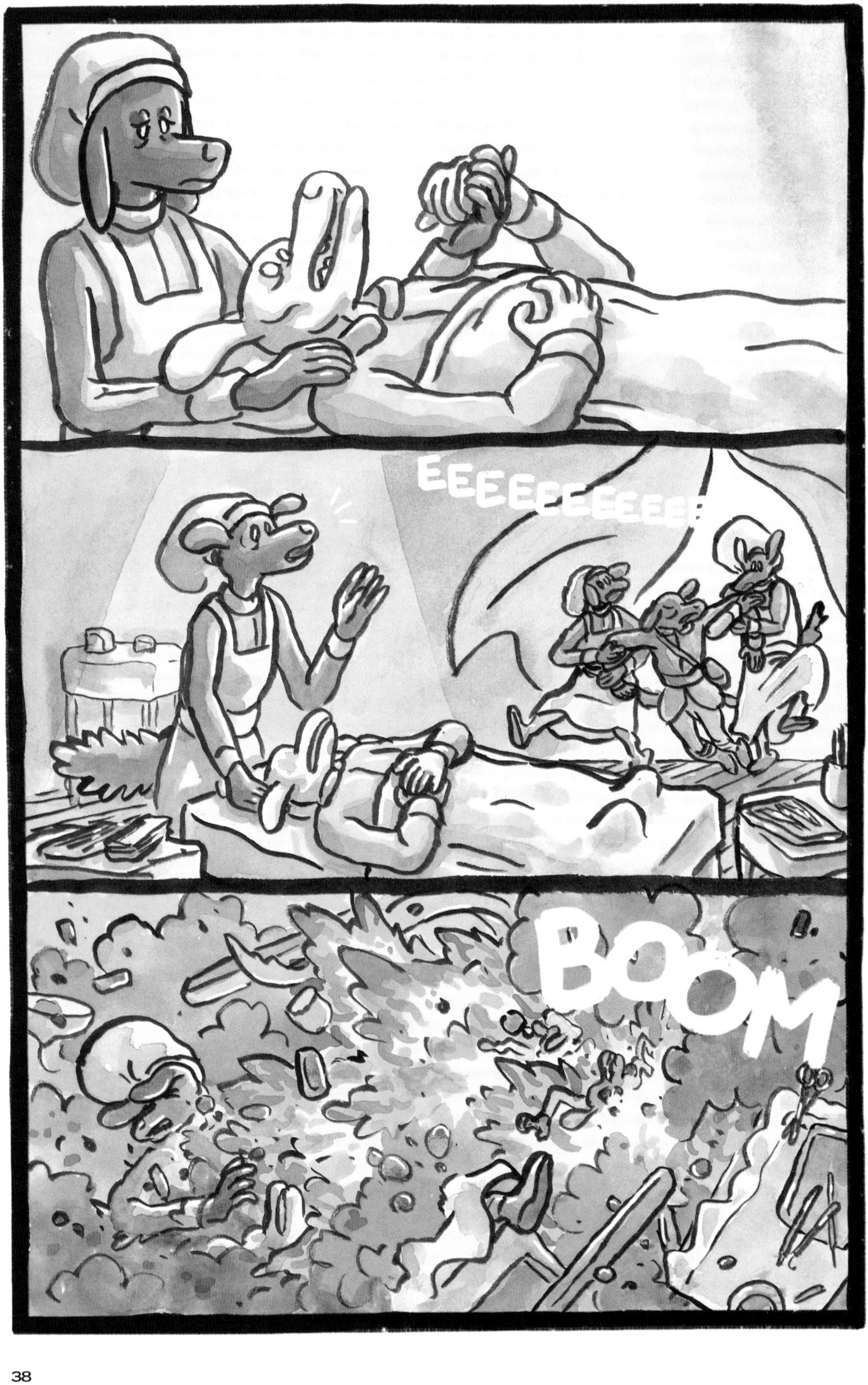
EEEEEEEEEEEE
BOOM

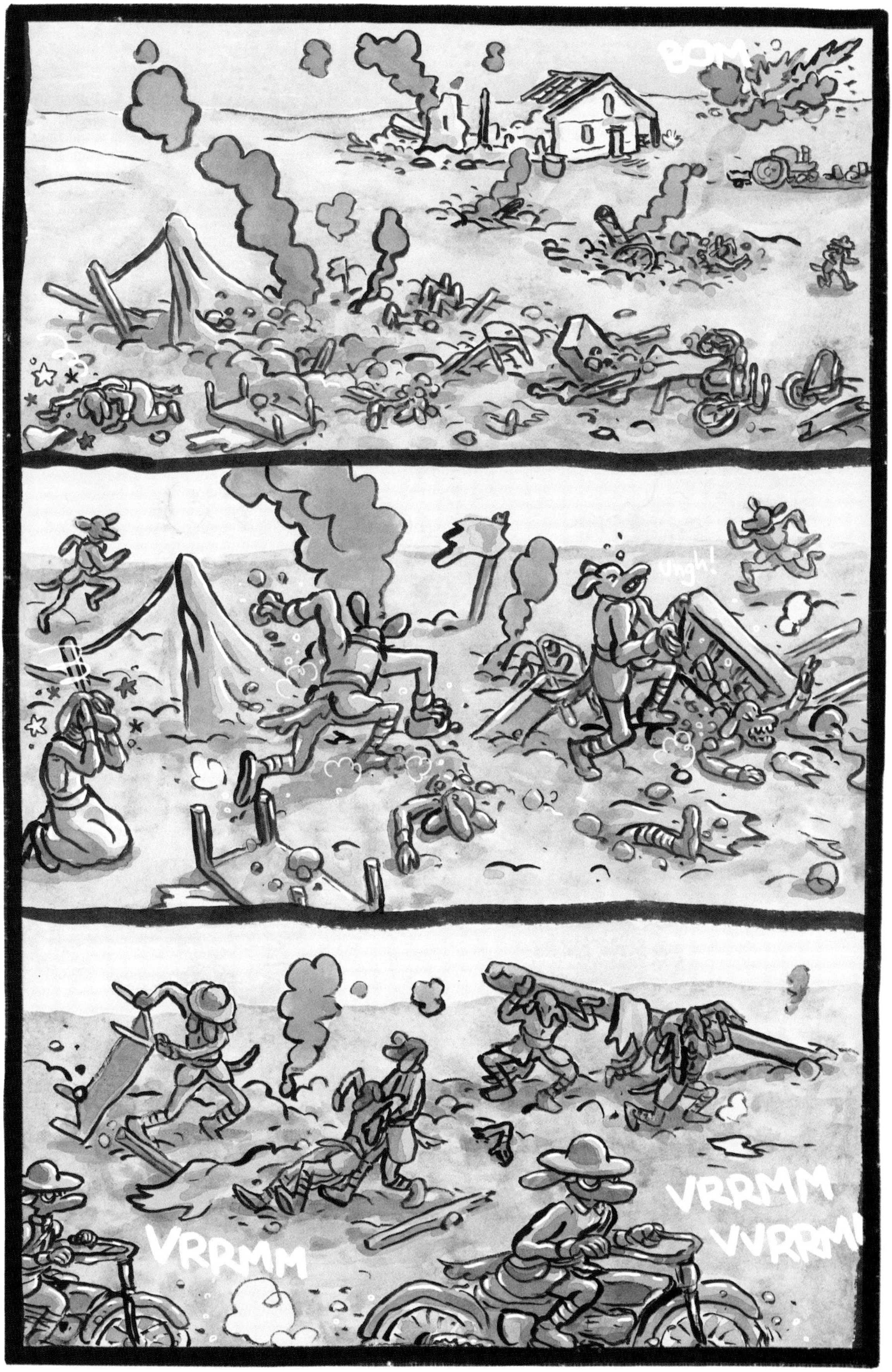
BOM
Ungh!
VRRMM
VRRMM
VVRRM

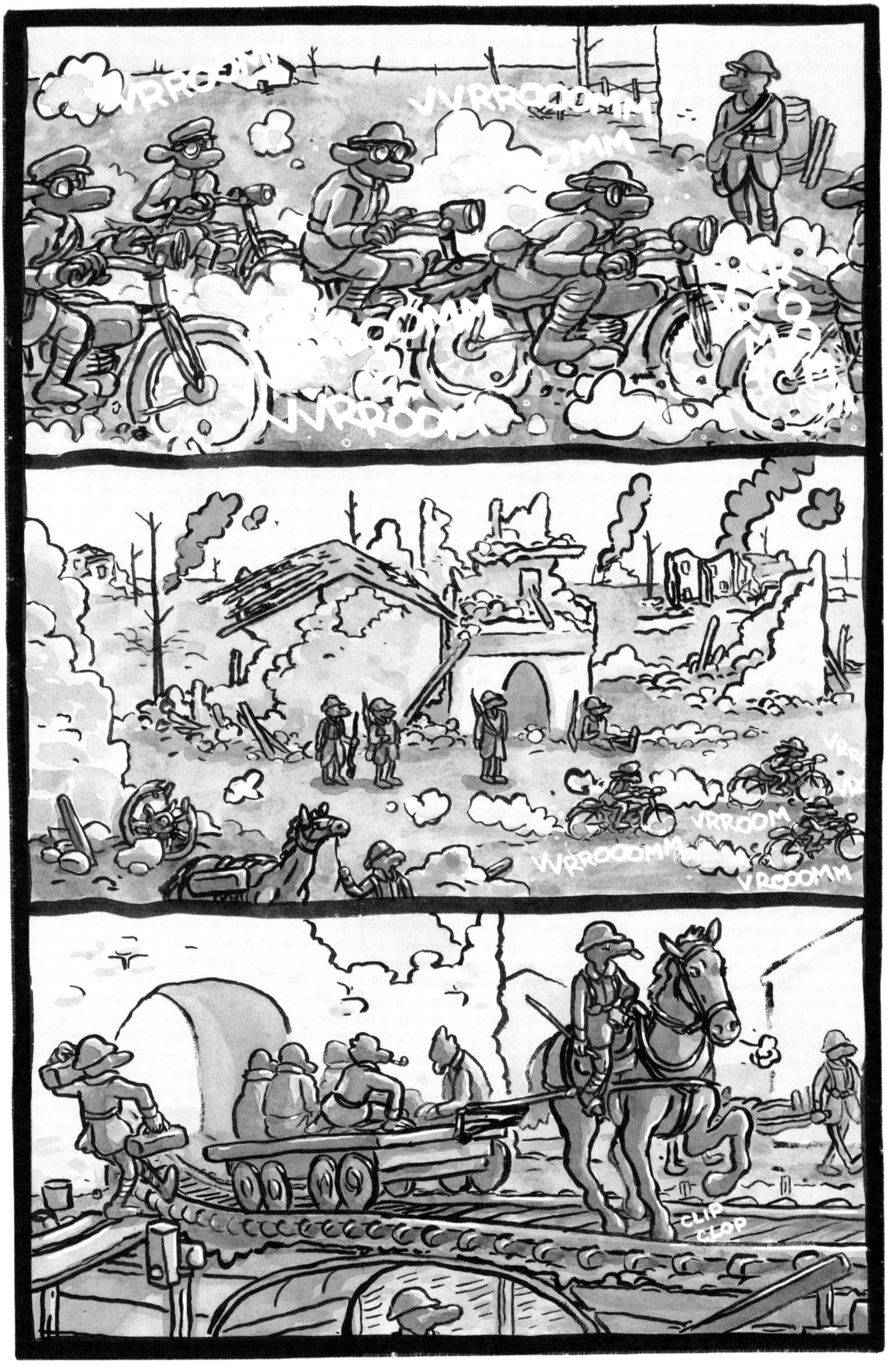
VRROOMM
VVRROOOMM
VVRROOM
VRROOM
VVRROOOMM
VROOOMM
CLIP
CLOP

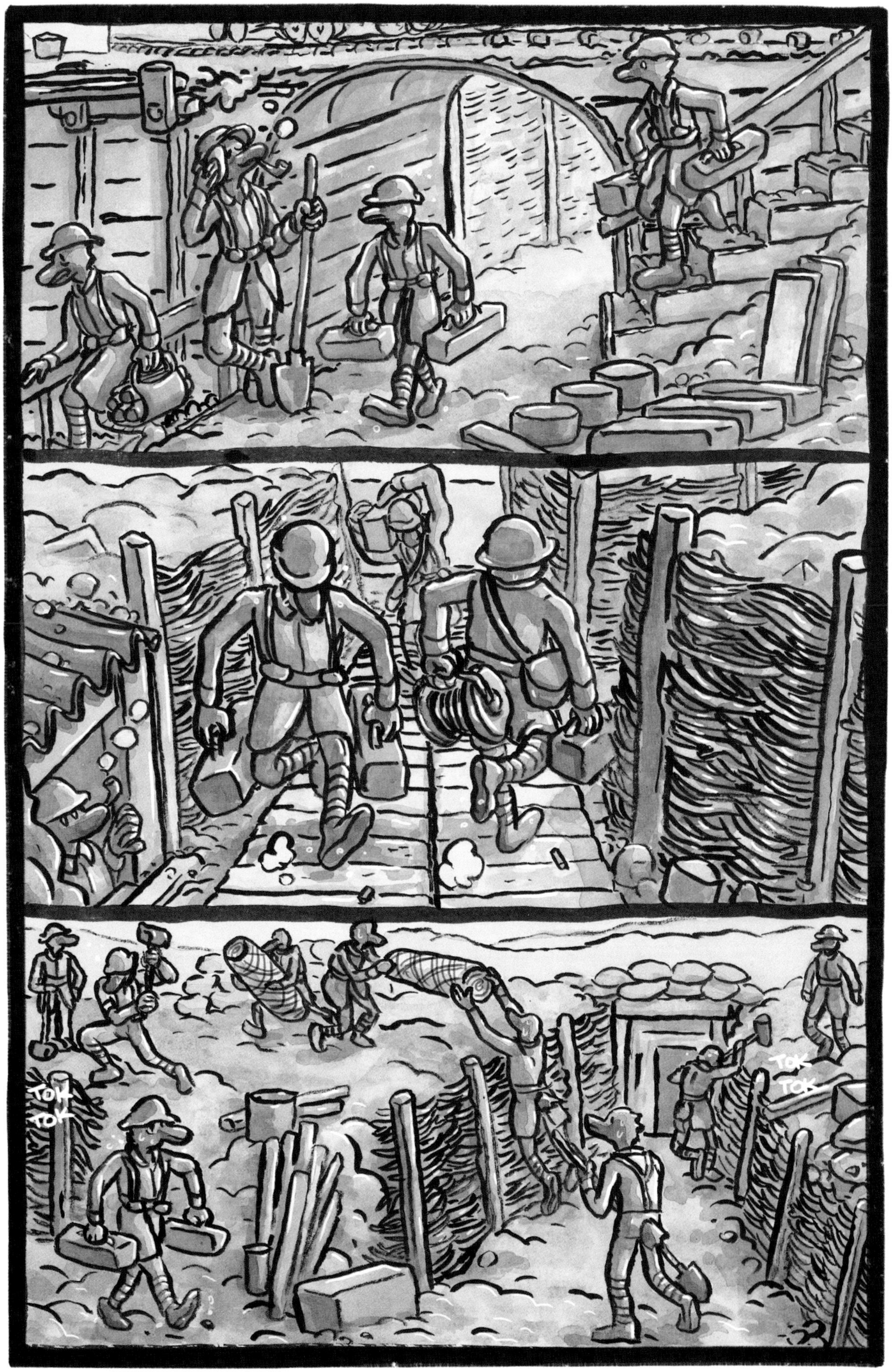
TOK
TOK
TOK
TOK

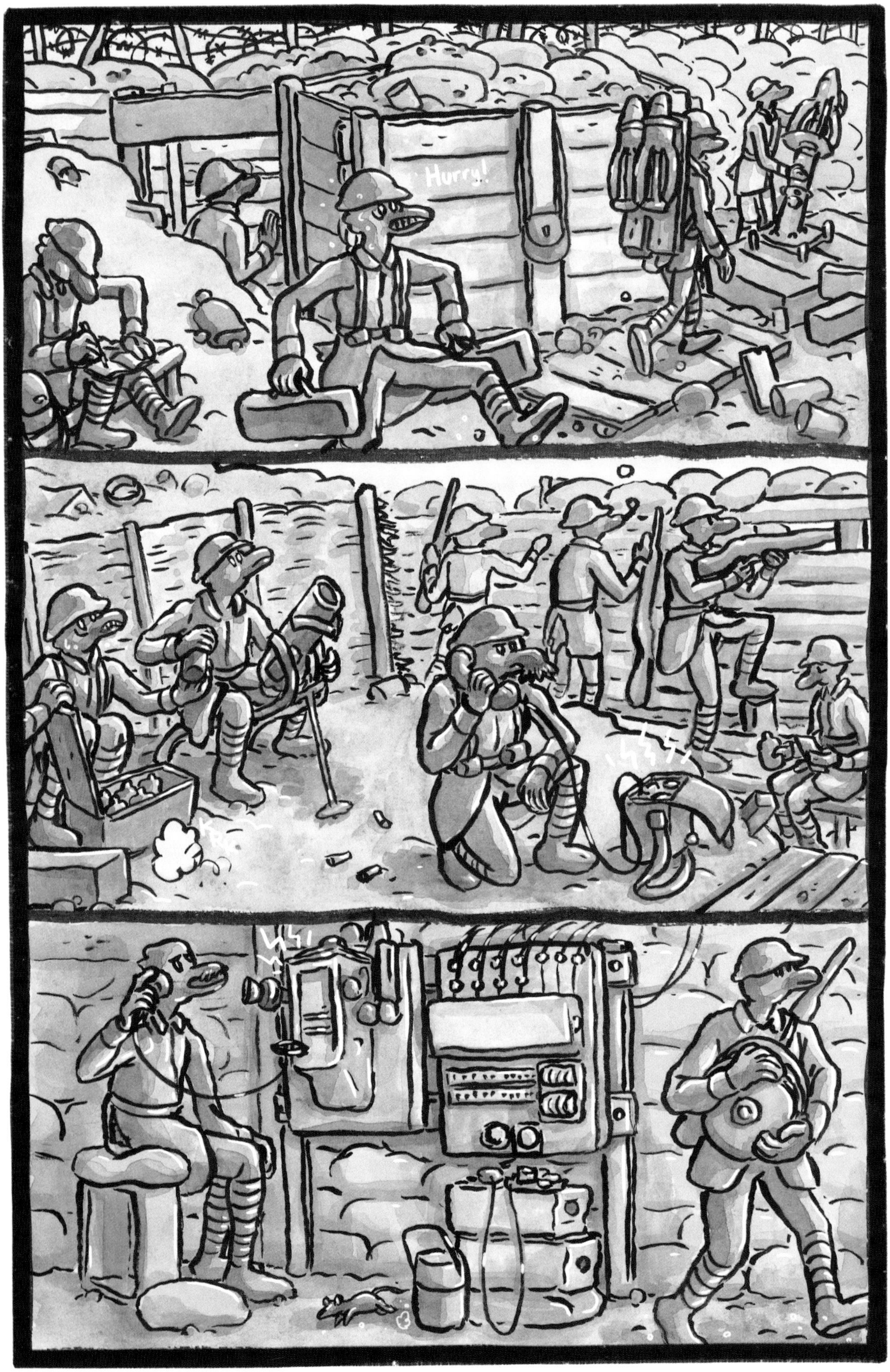
Hurry!

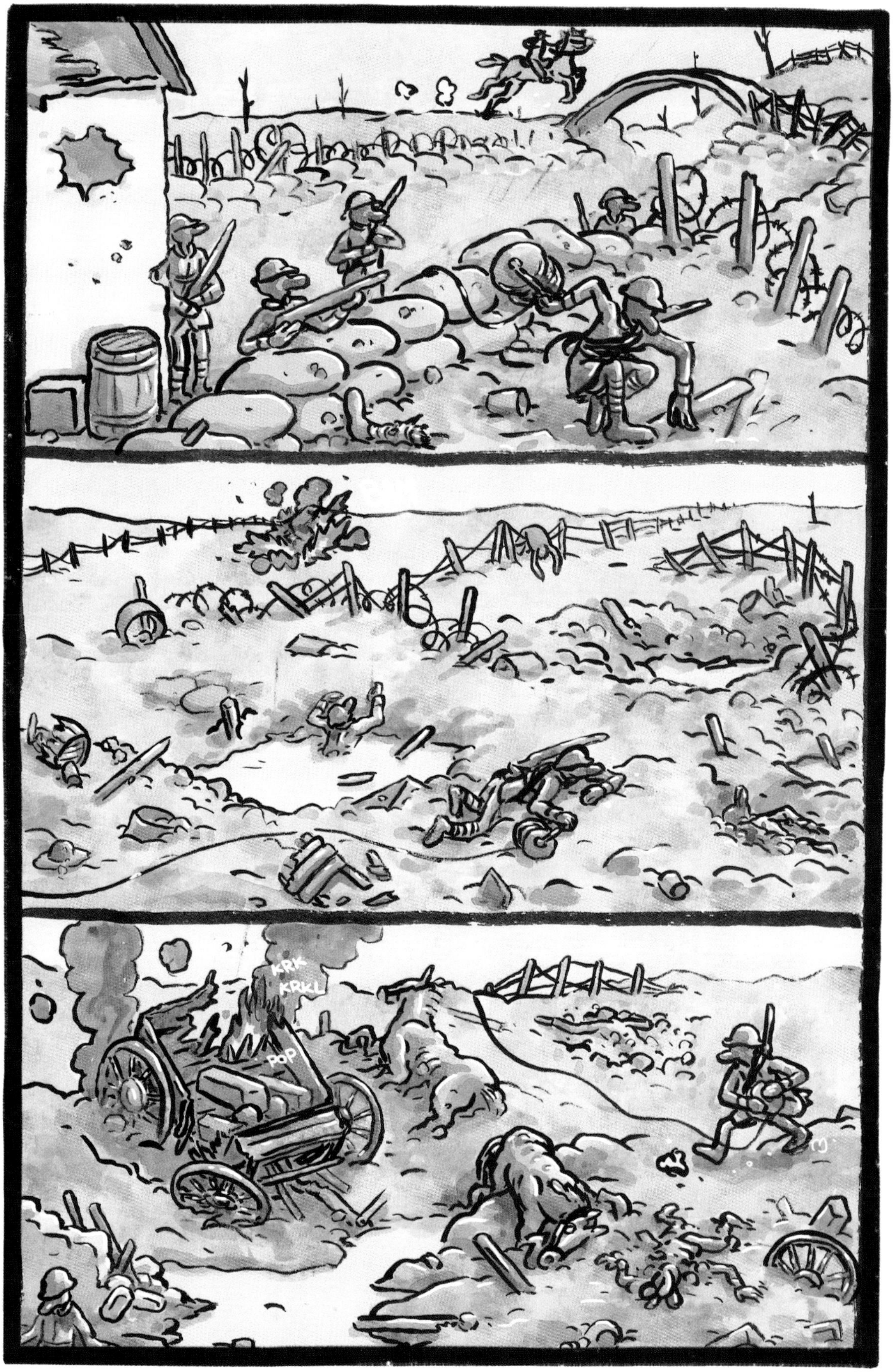
KRK
KRKL
POP

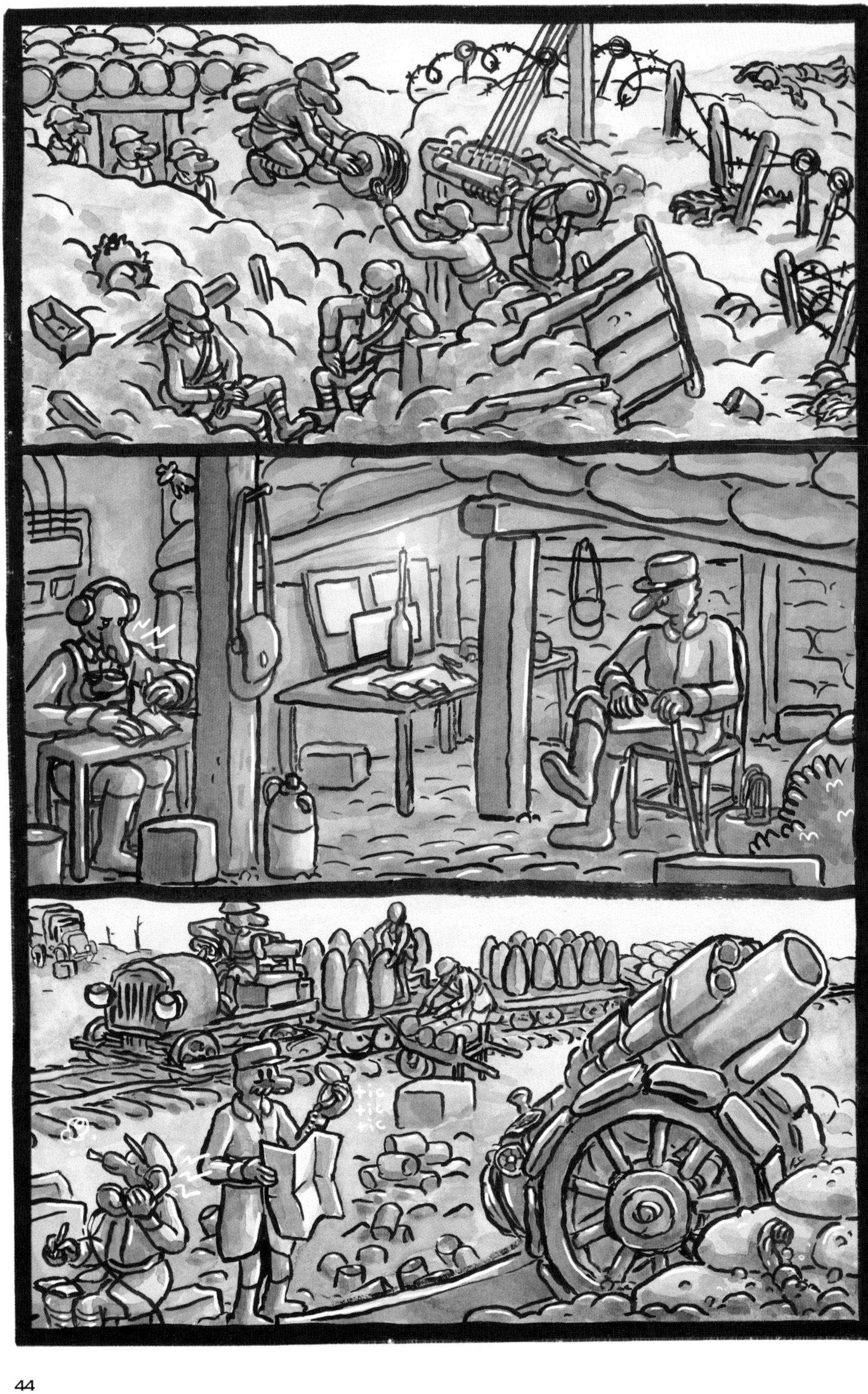
tic
tic
tic

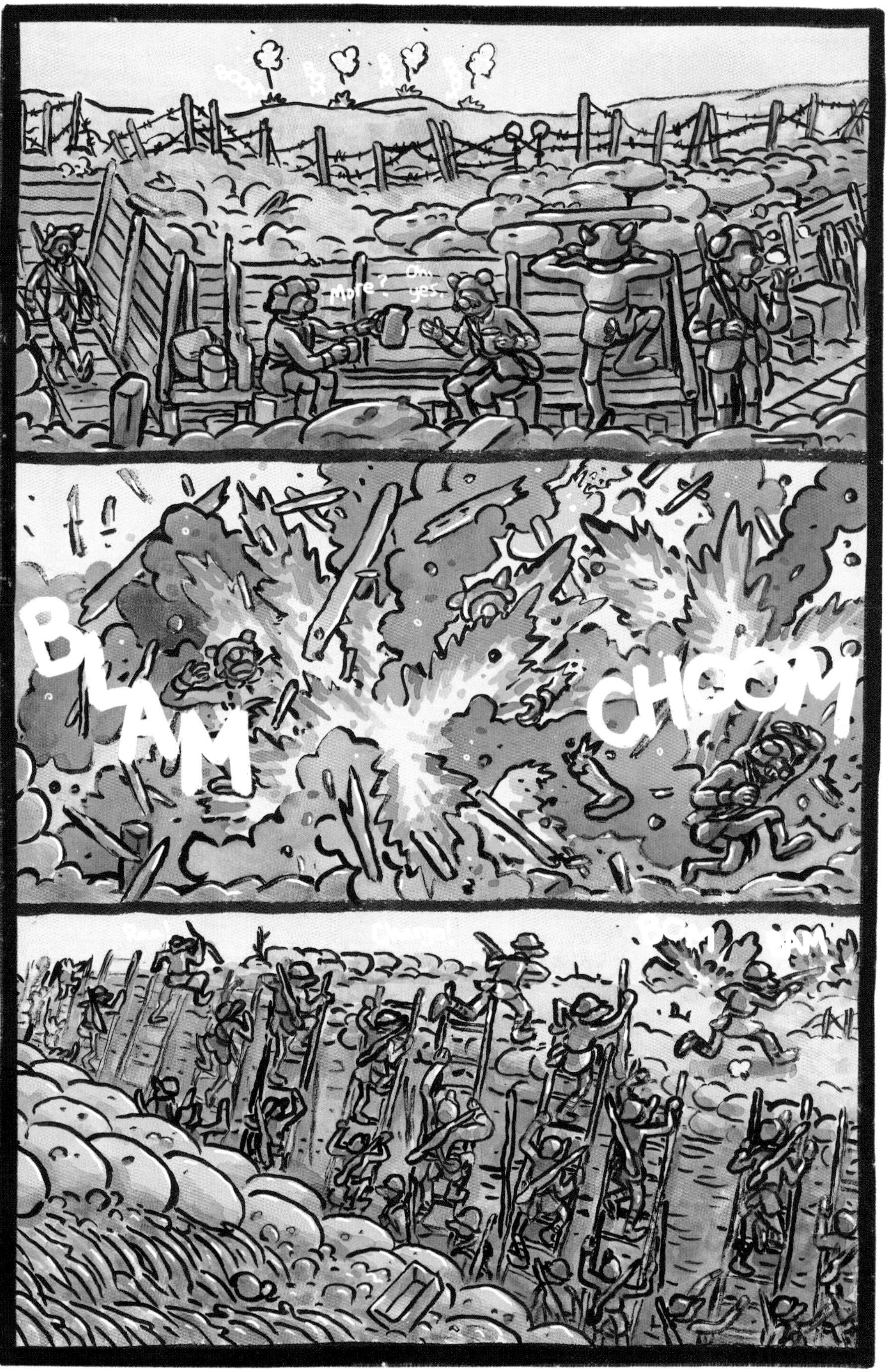
BOOM
More?
Om yes.
BLAM
CHOOM
Raa!
Charge!

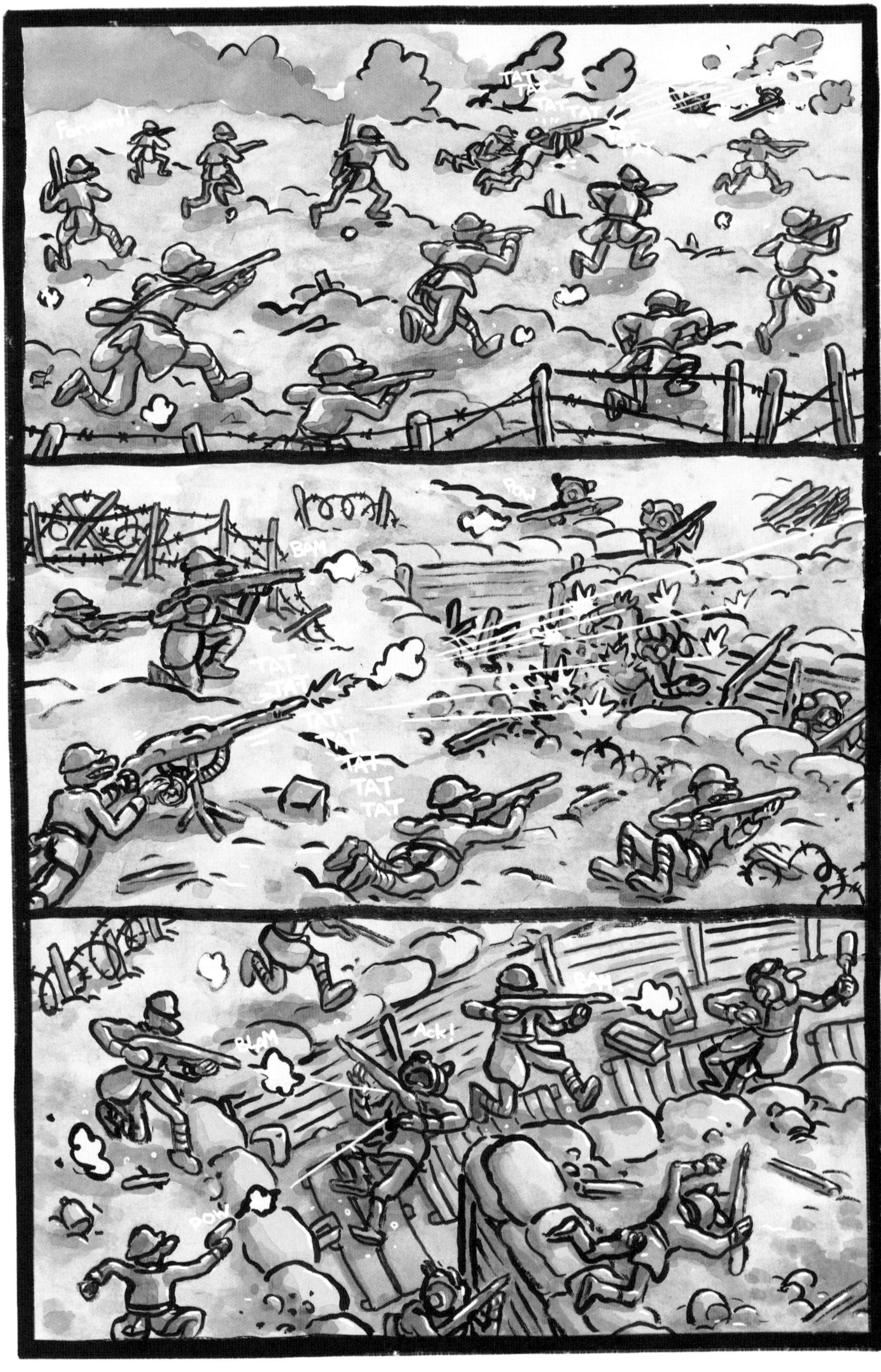
Forward!
TAT TAT TAT TAT
POW
BAM
TAT TAT TAT TAT TAT TAT TAT
BAM
BLAM
Ack!
POW

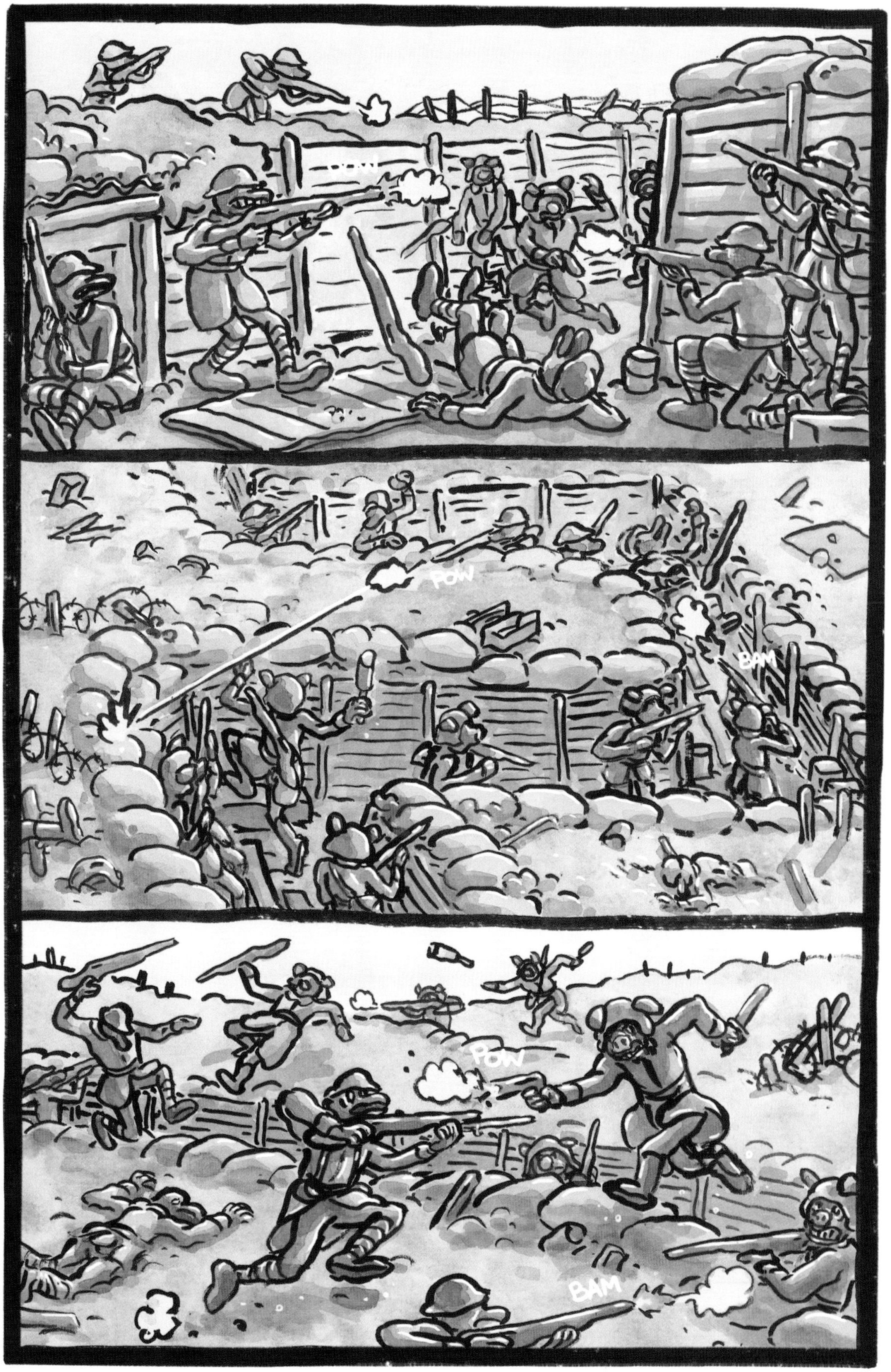
POW
POW
BAM
POW
BAM

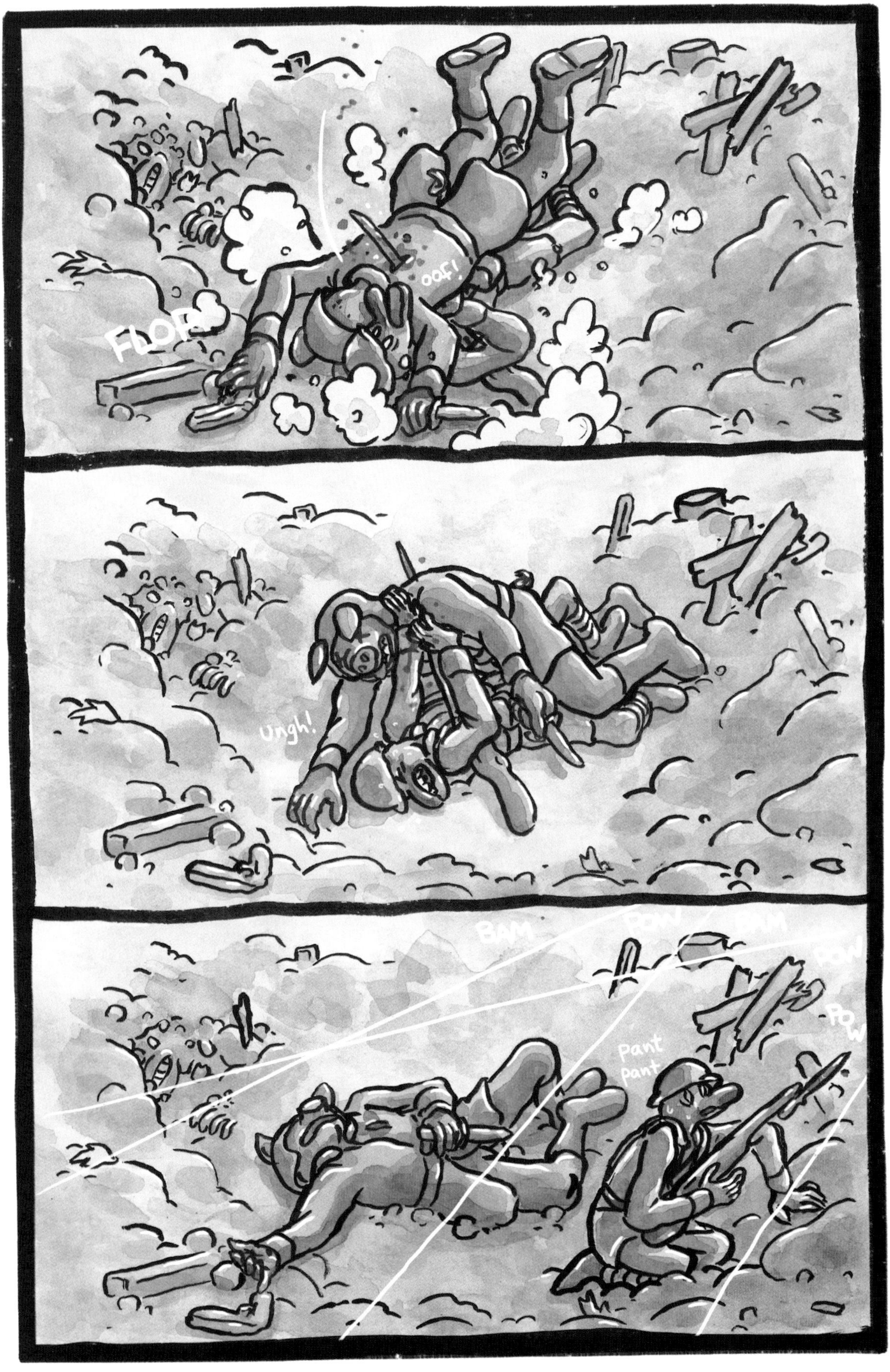
FLOP
oof!
Ungh!
BAM
POW
BAM
POW
POW
Pant pant

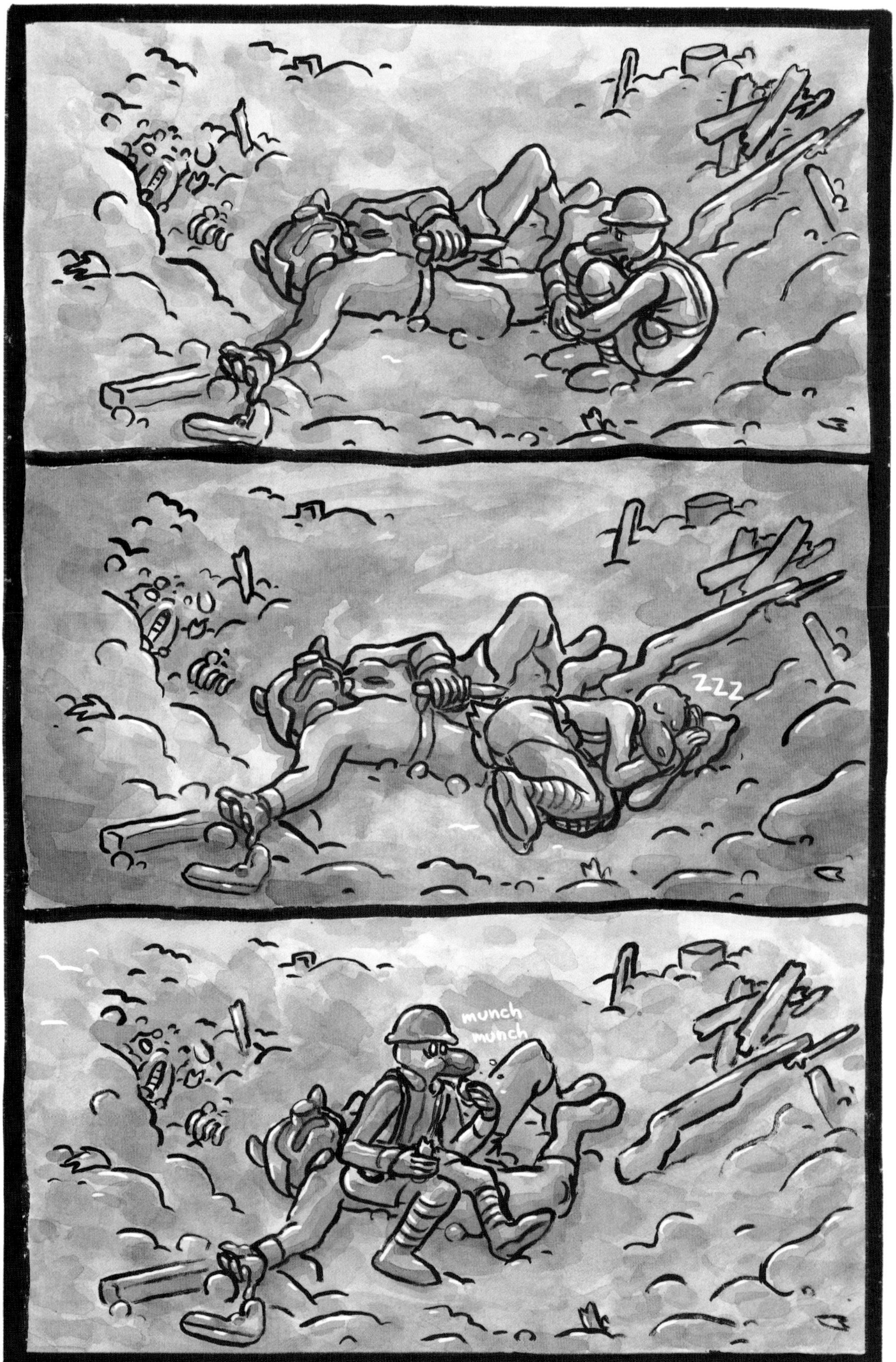
ZZZ
munch
munch

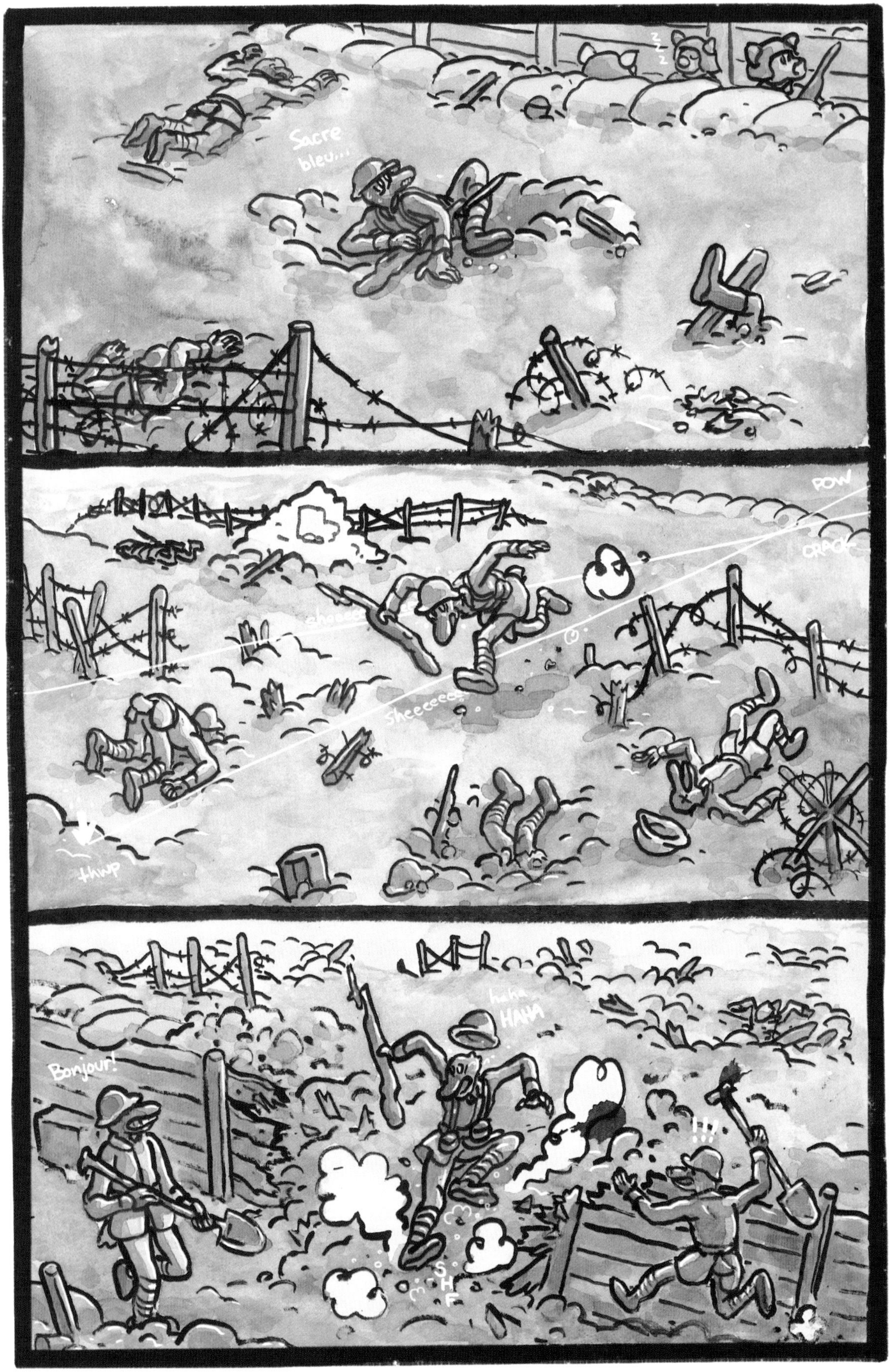
Sacre bleu...
POW
CRACK
sheeeeeee
sheeeeeeee
thwp
haha HAHA
Bonjour!
!!!
SHF

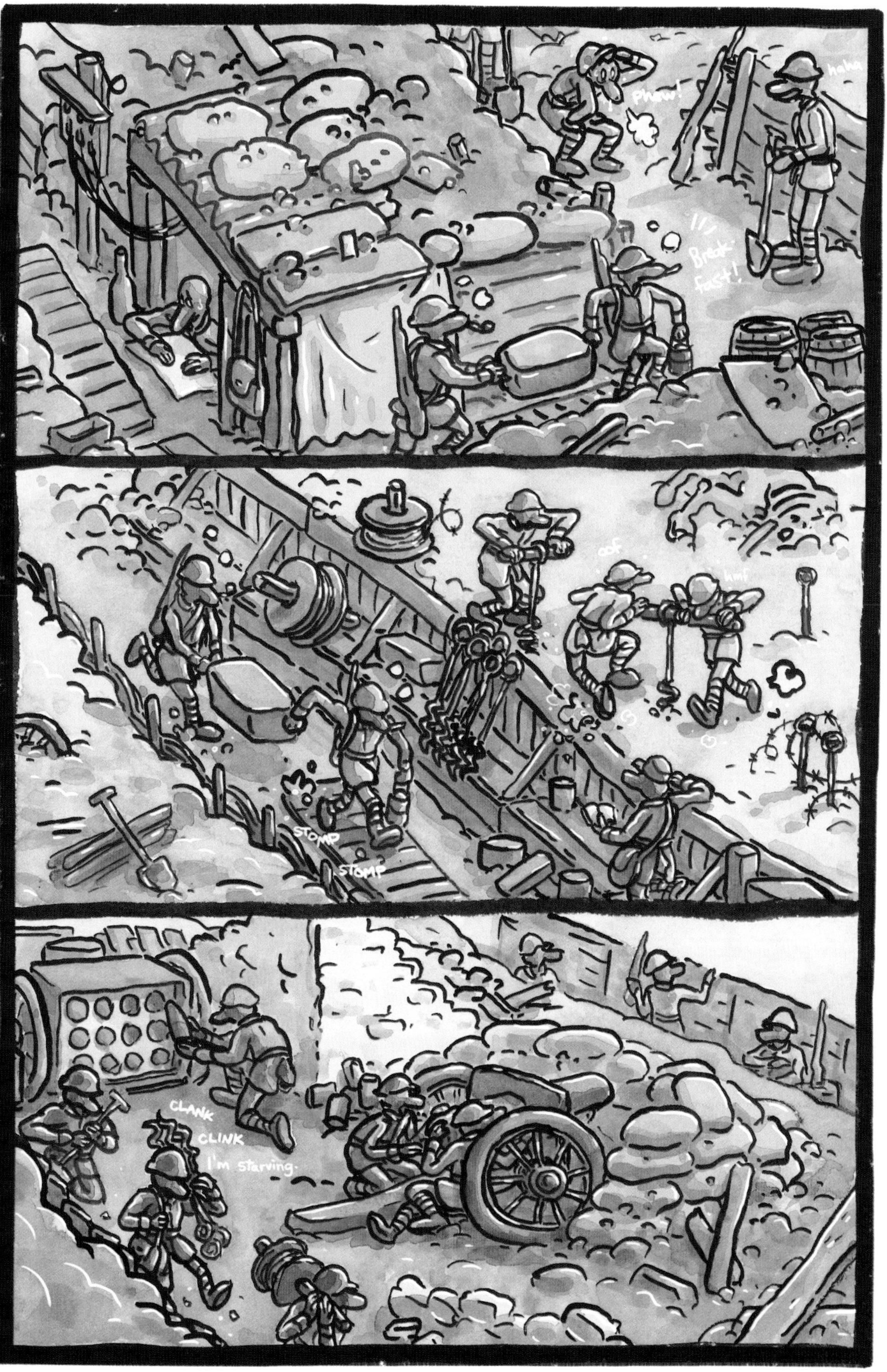
Phew!
haha
Break-fast!
oof
hmf
STOMP
STOMP
CLANK
CLINK
I'm starving.

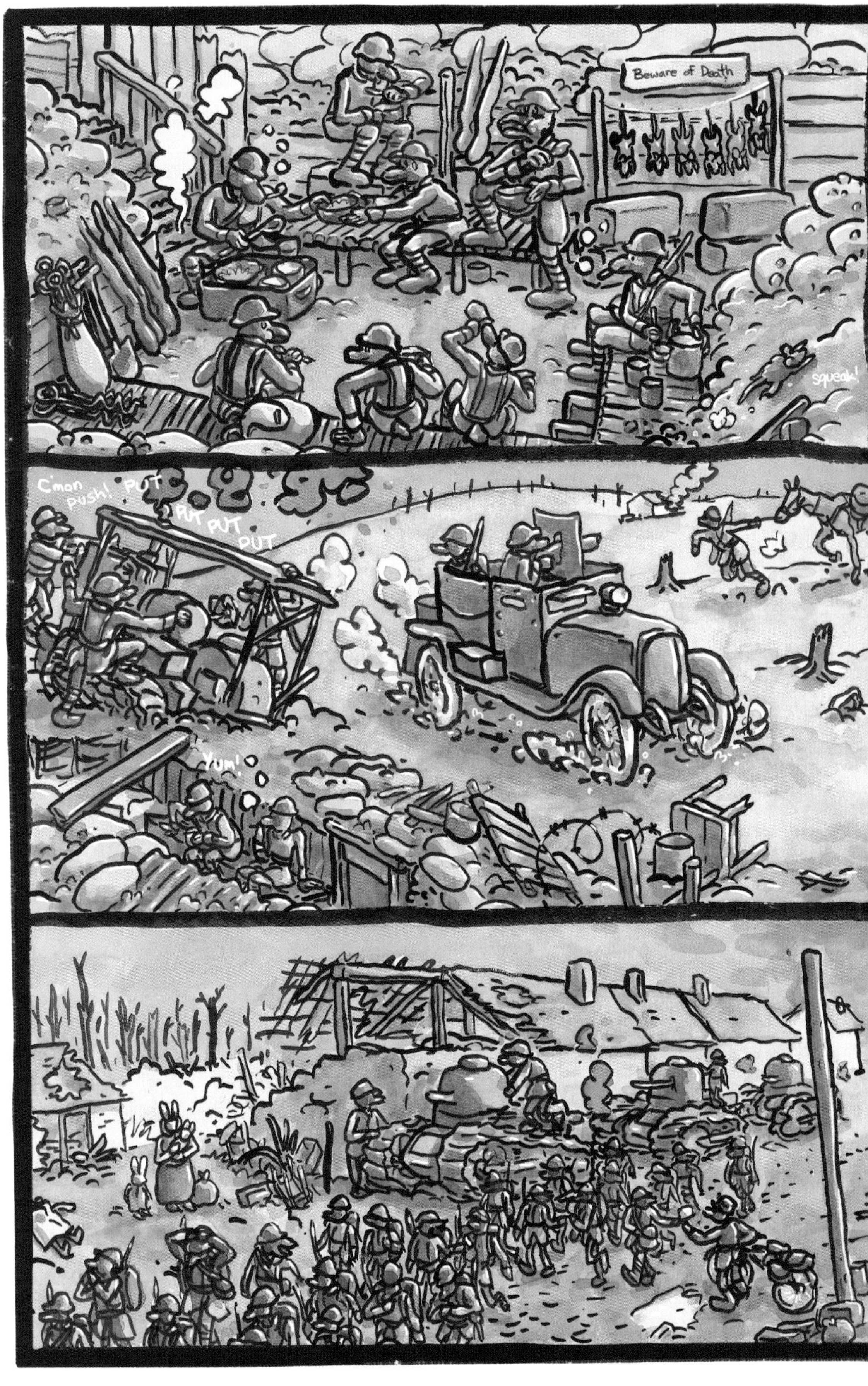
Beware of Death
squeak!
C'mon push!
PUT PUT PUT PUT
YUM!

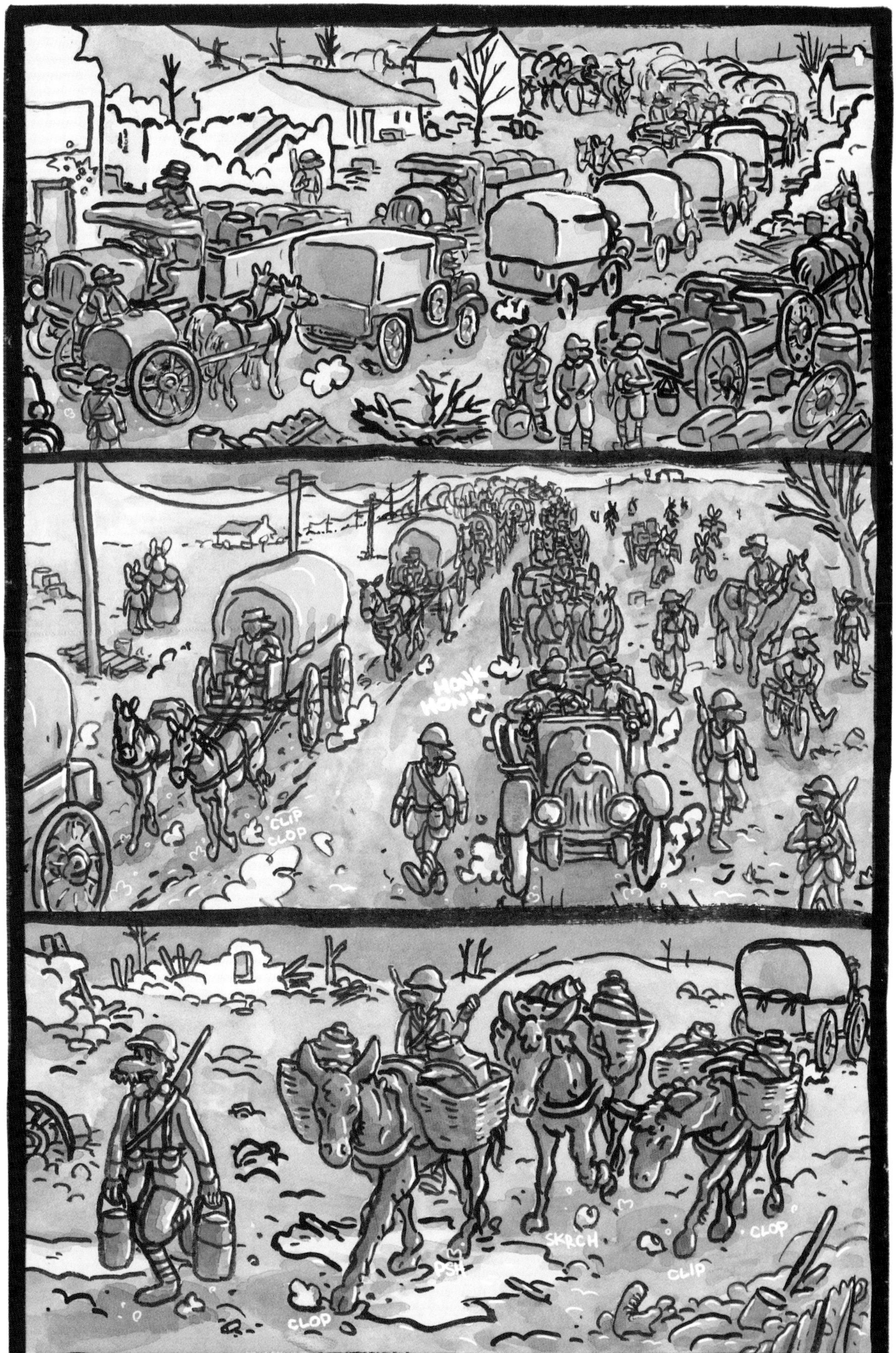
HONK
HONK
CLIP
CLOP
CLOP
PSH
SKRCH
CLIP
CLOP

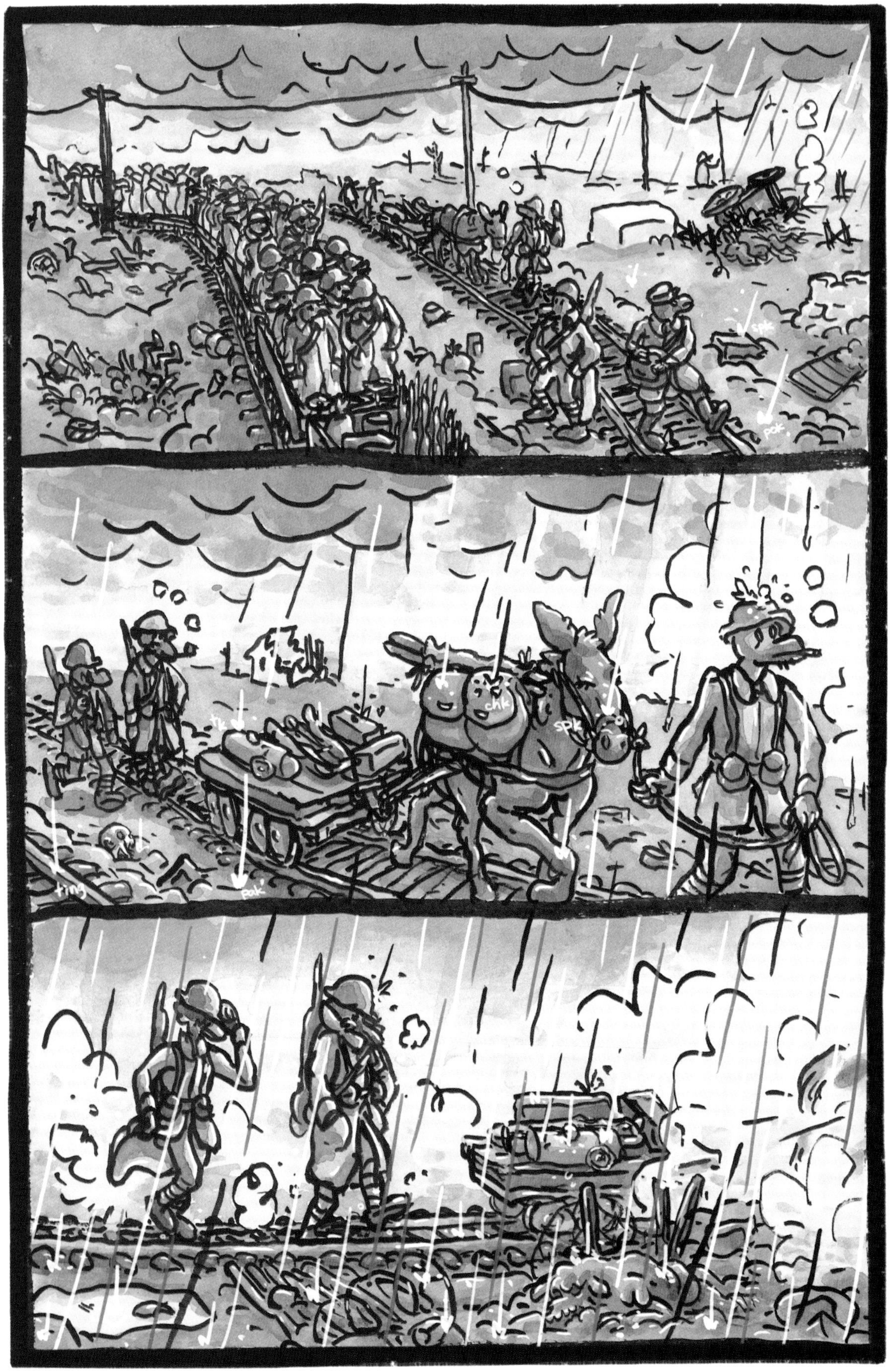
spk
pok
tk
chk
spk
ting
pok

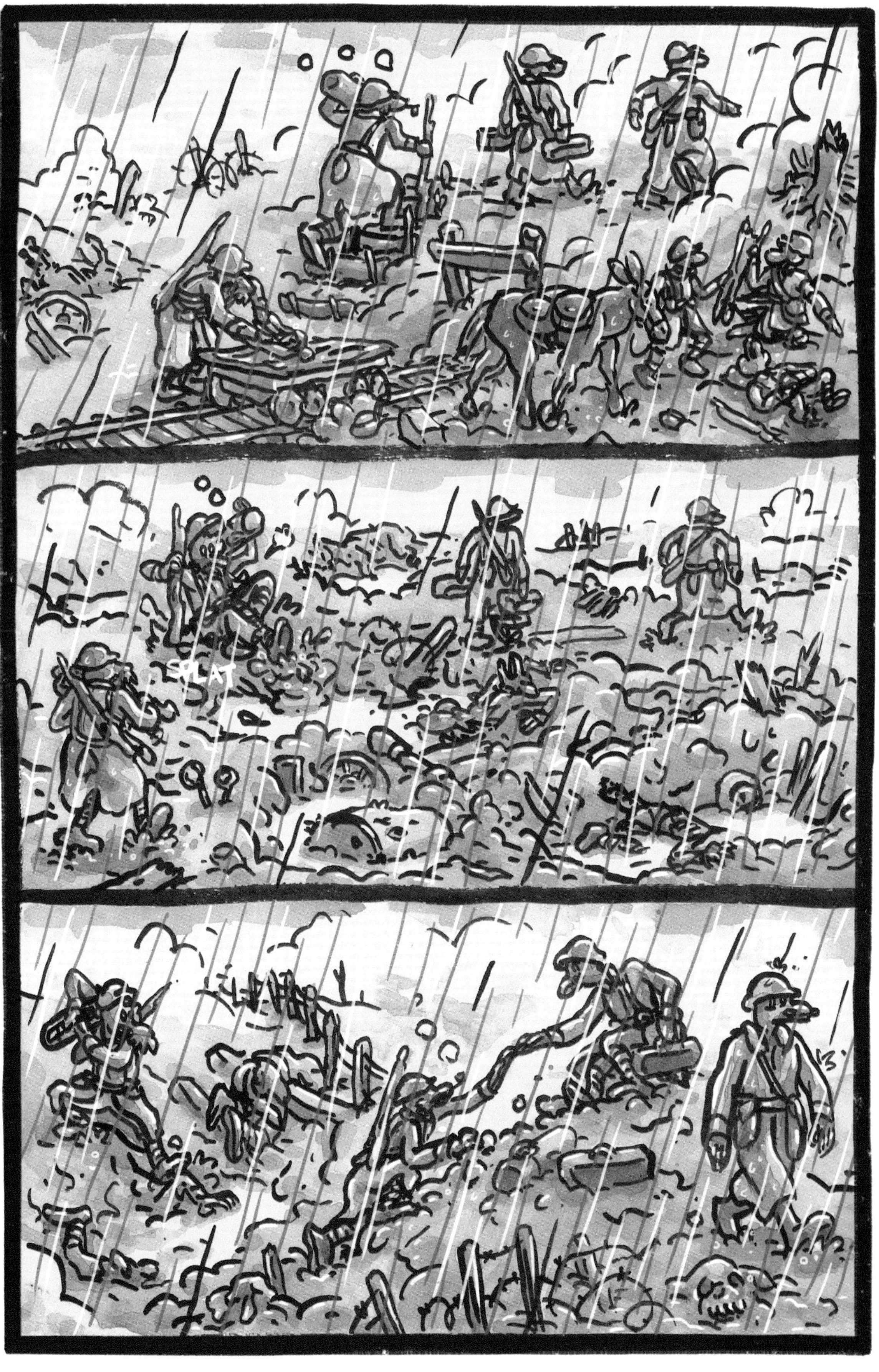
SPLAT

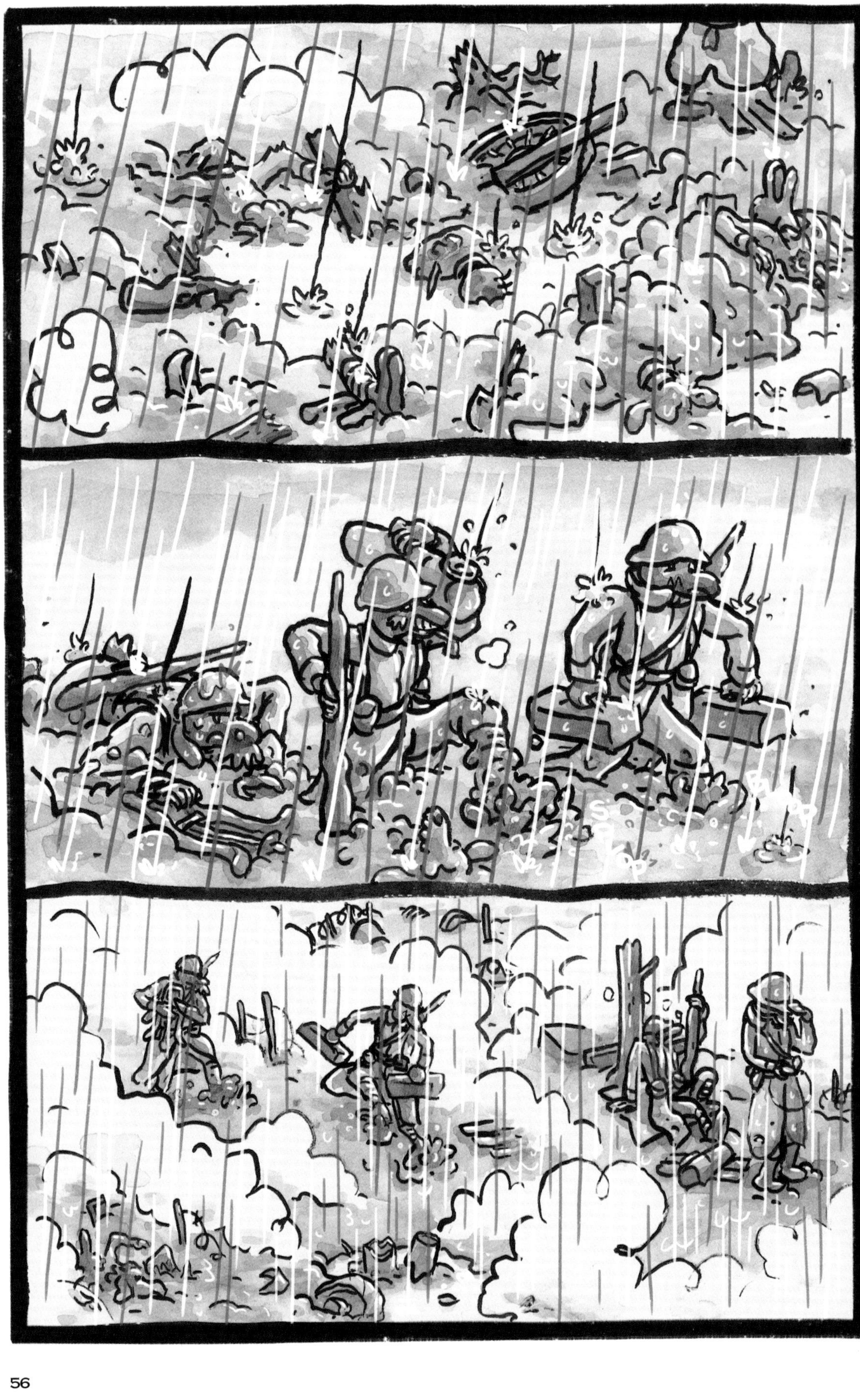

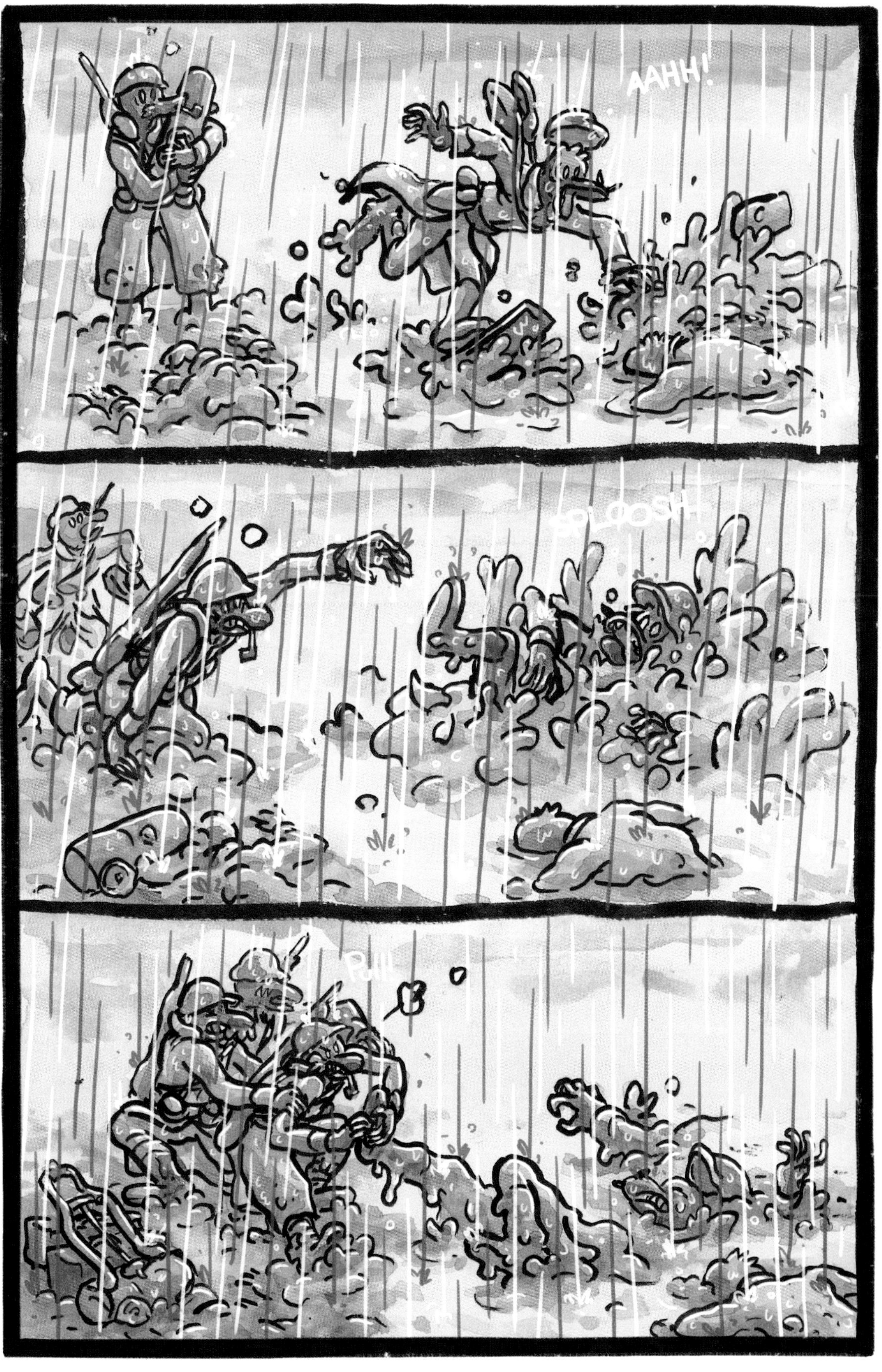
AAHH!
SPLOOSH
PULL

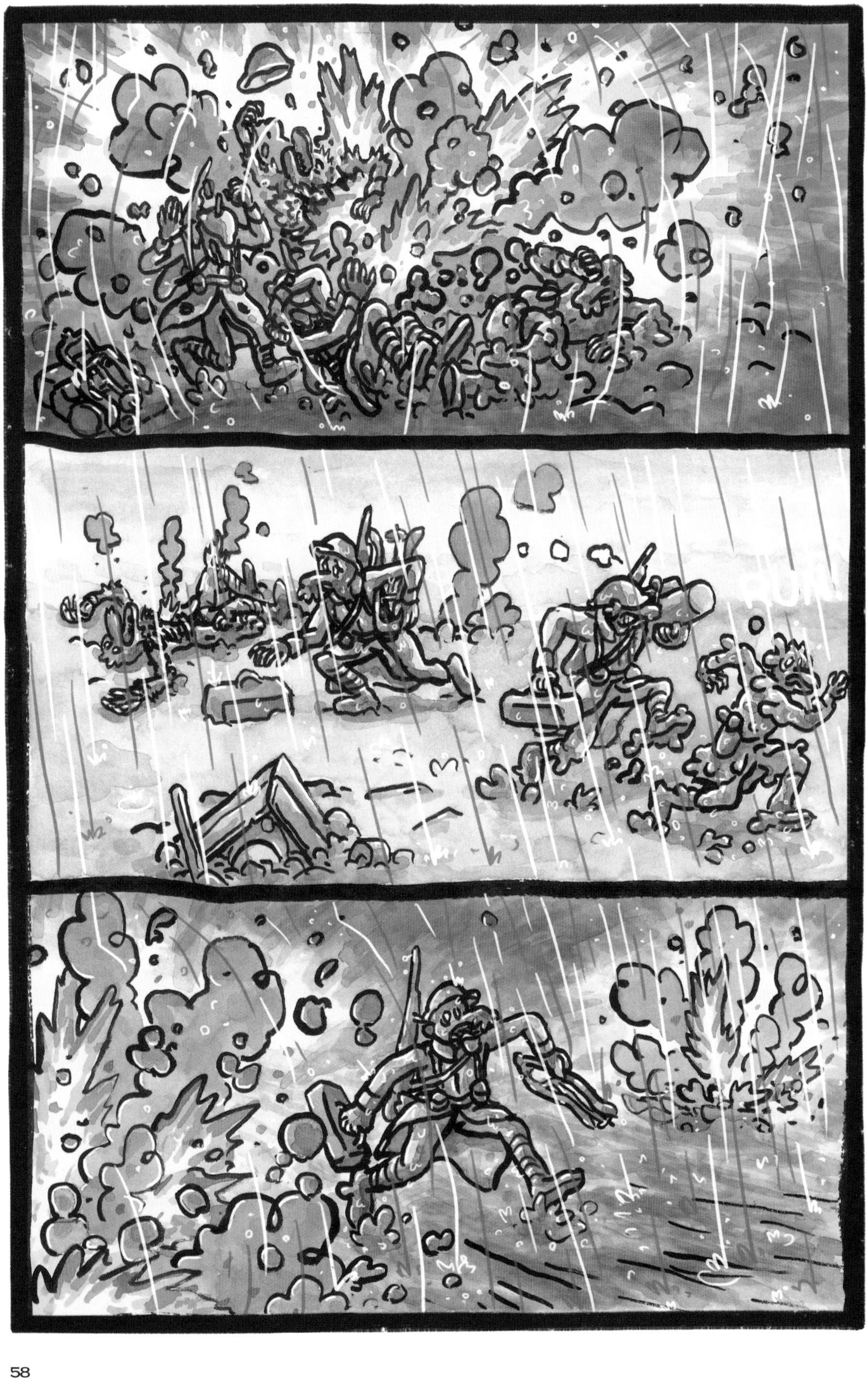

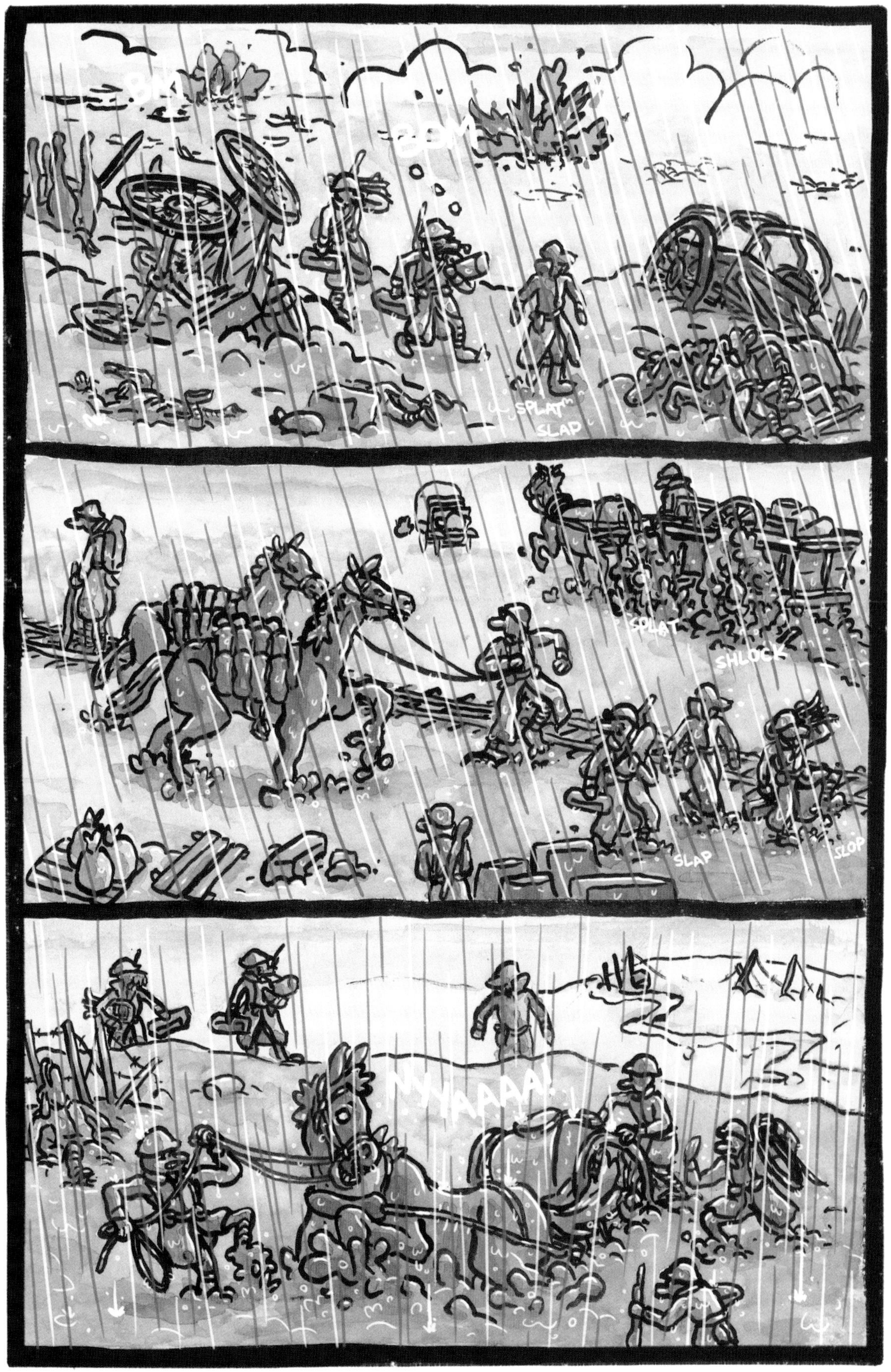
BM
BOOM
SPLAT
SLAP
SPLAT
SHLOCK
SLAP
SLOP
NYAAAA!

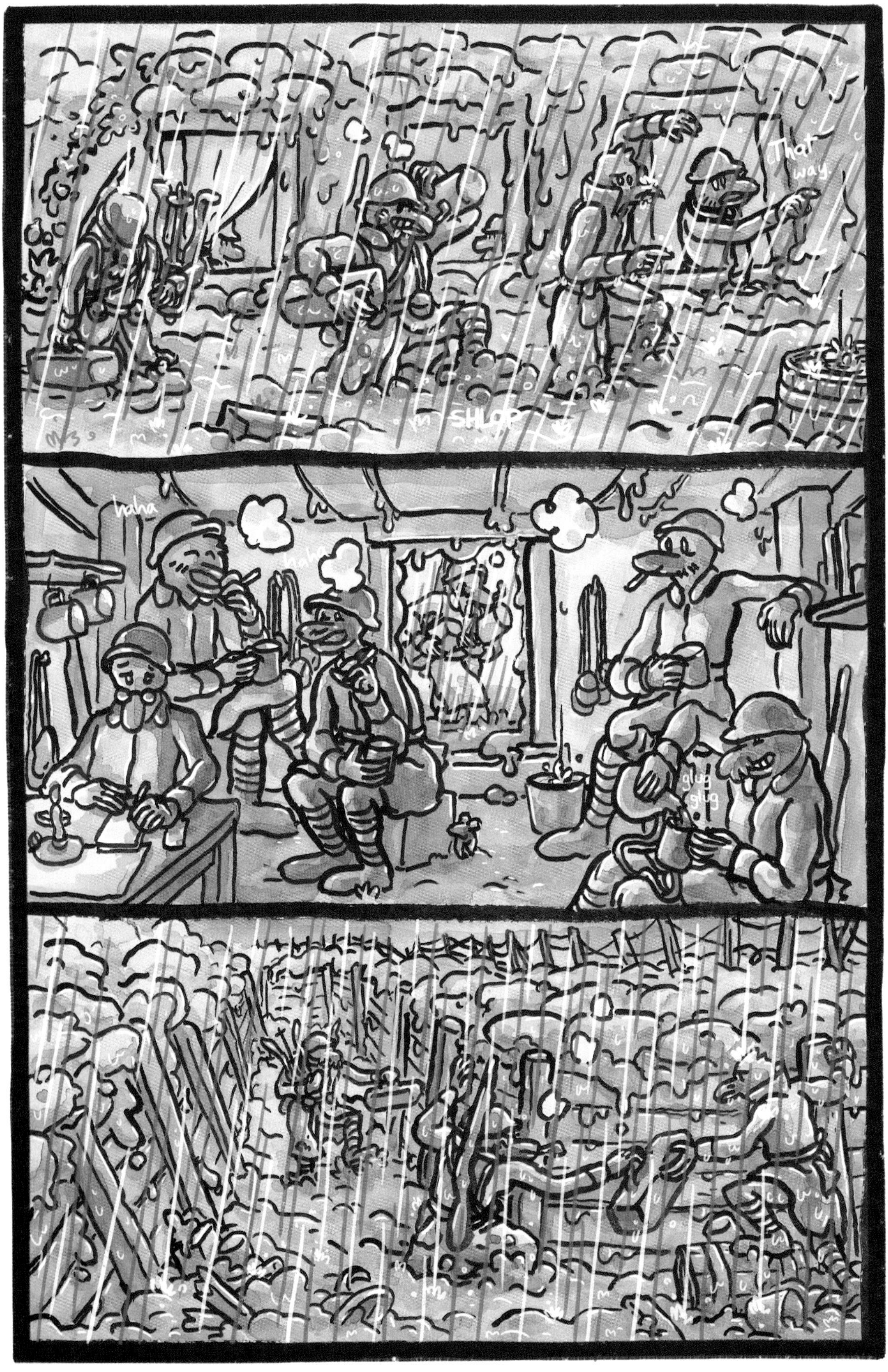
That way.
SHLOP
haha
haha
glug glug

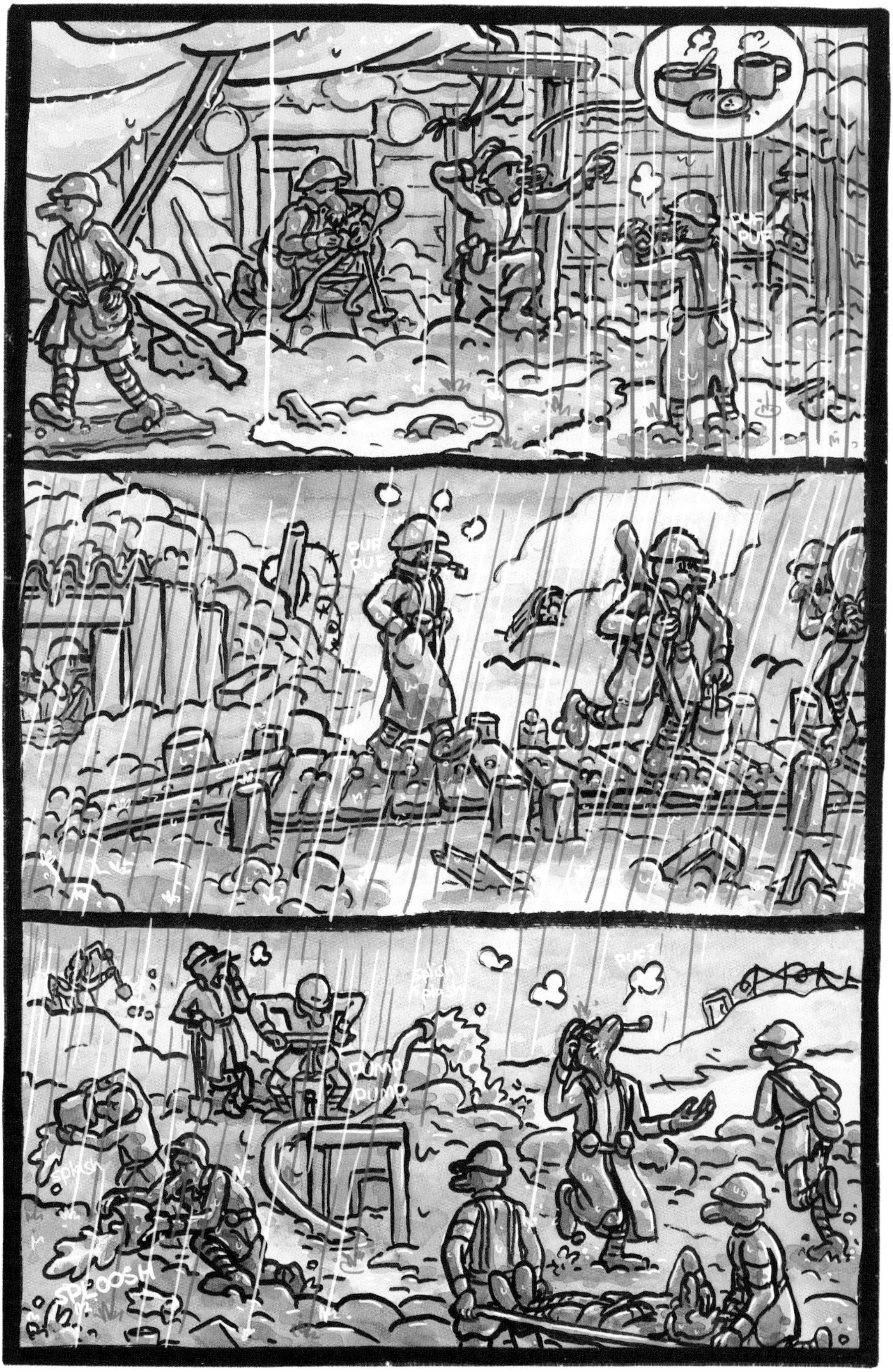
PUF
PUF
PUF
PUF
Splash
Splash
PUF?
PUMP
PUMP
Splash
SPLOOSH

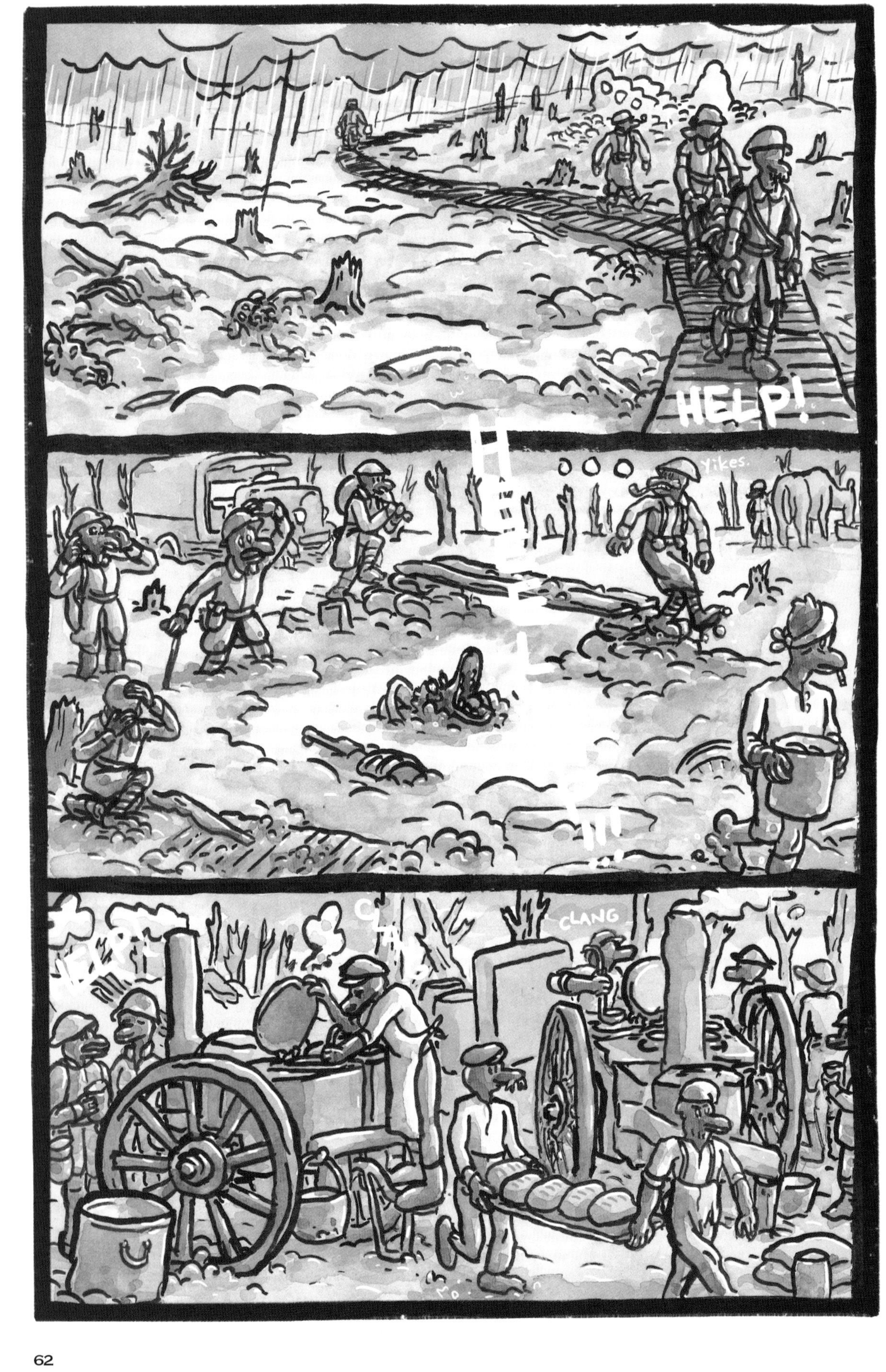
HELP!
Yikes.
CLANG

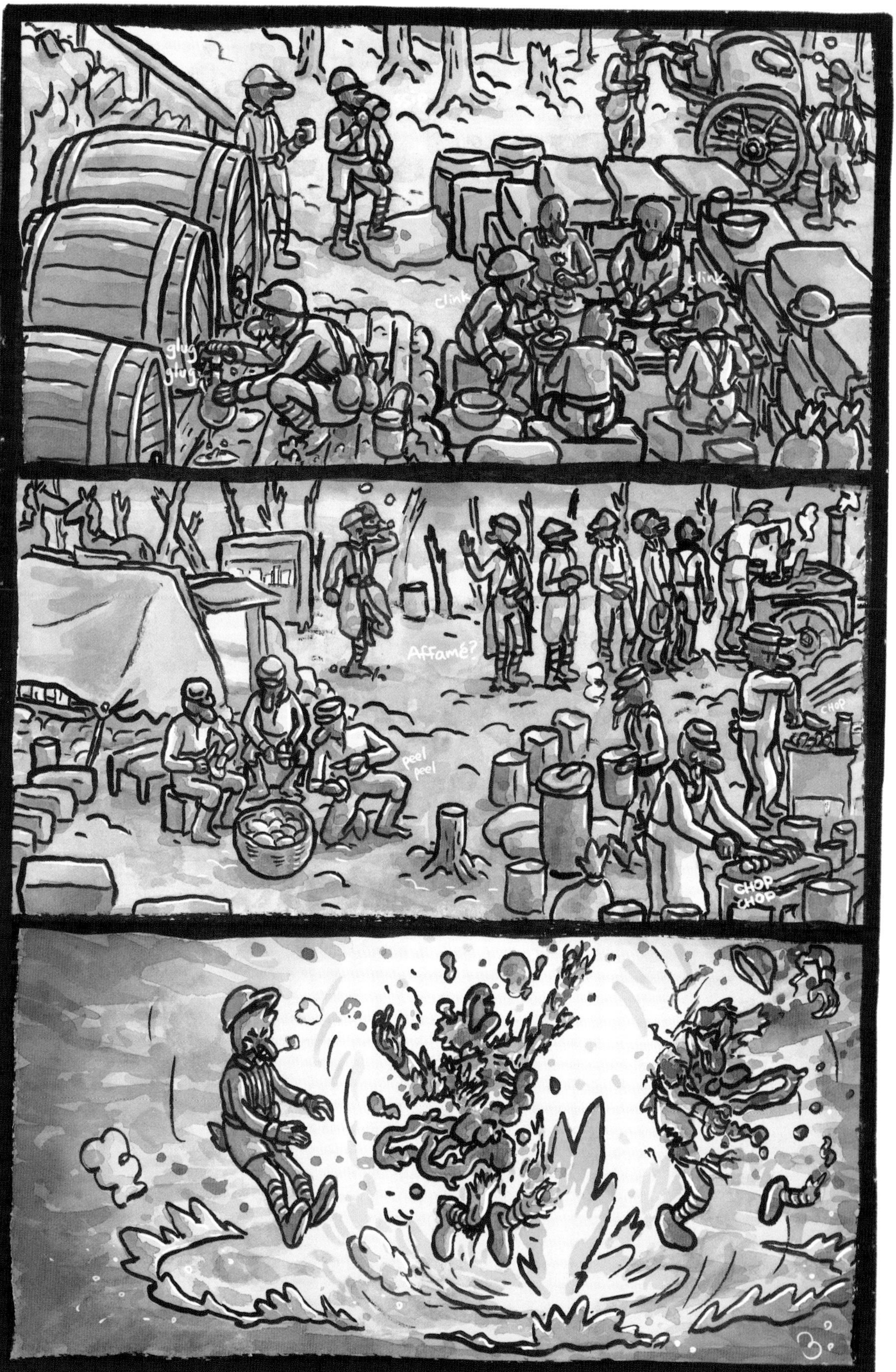
glug
glug
clink
clink
Affamé?
peel
peel
CHOP
CHOP
CHOP

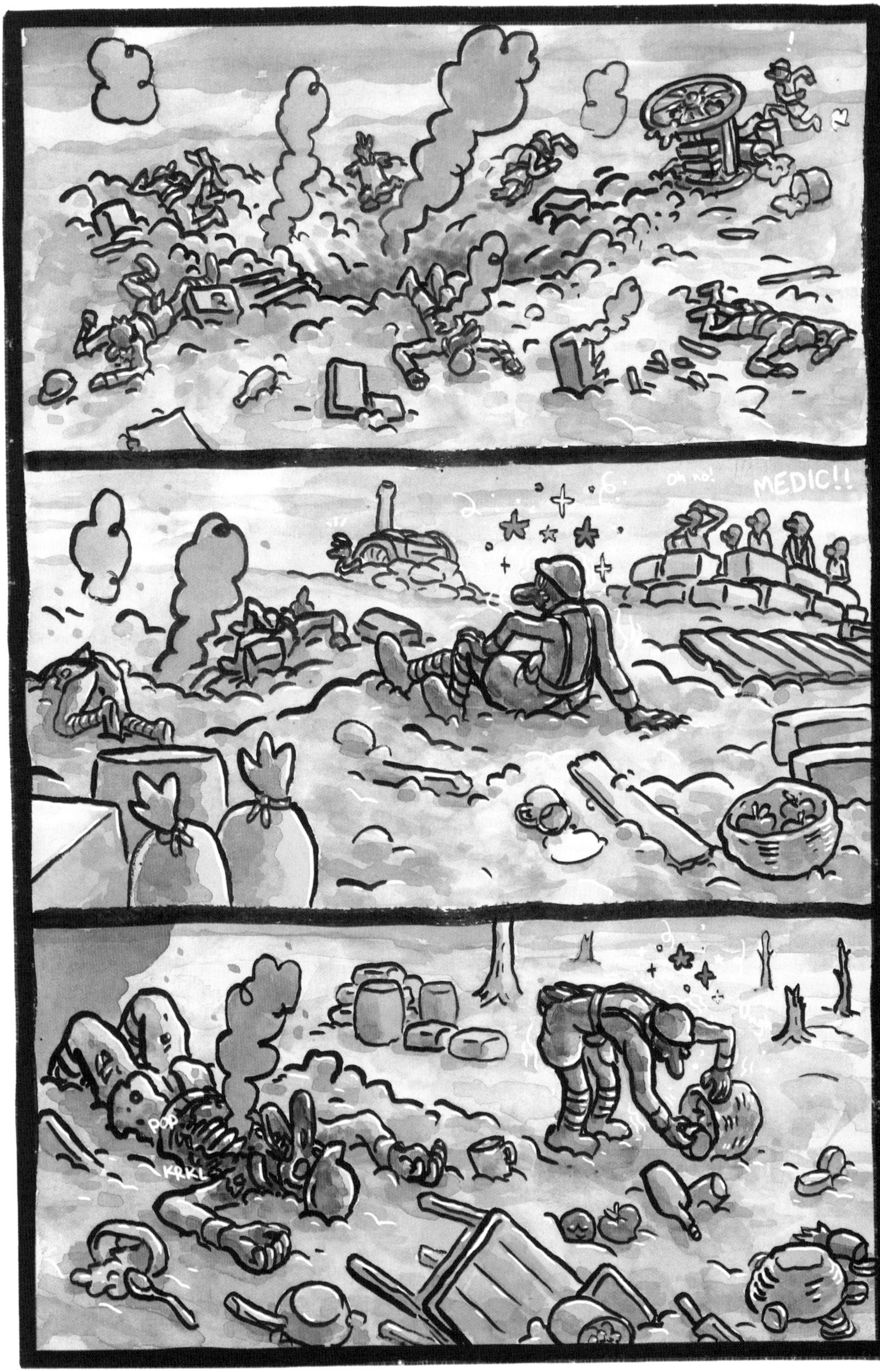
Oh no!
MEDIC!!
POP
KRKL

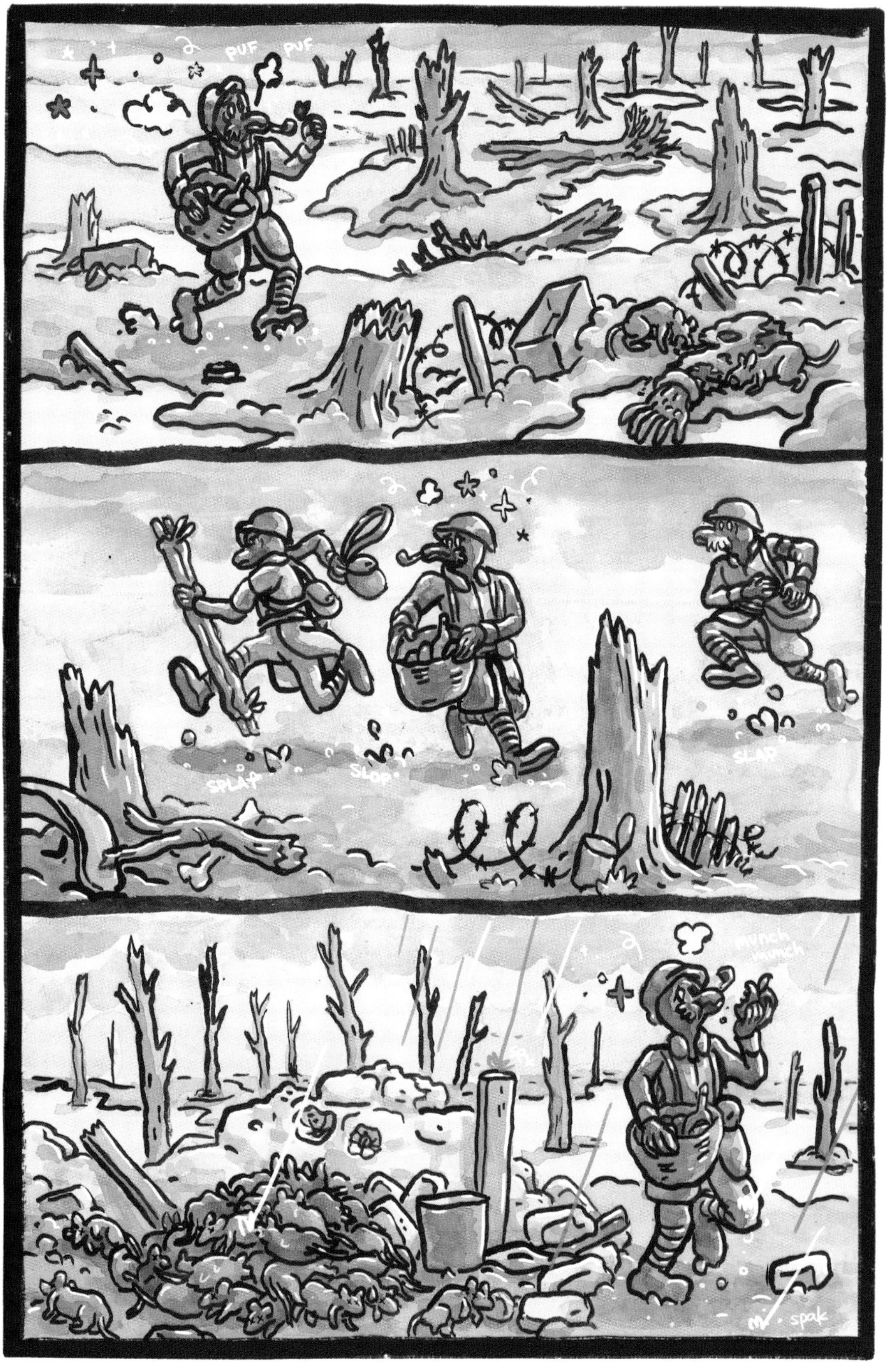
PUF PUF
SPLAT
SLOP
SLAP
munch
munch
spak

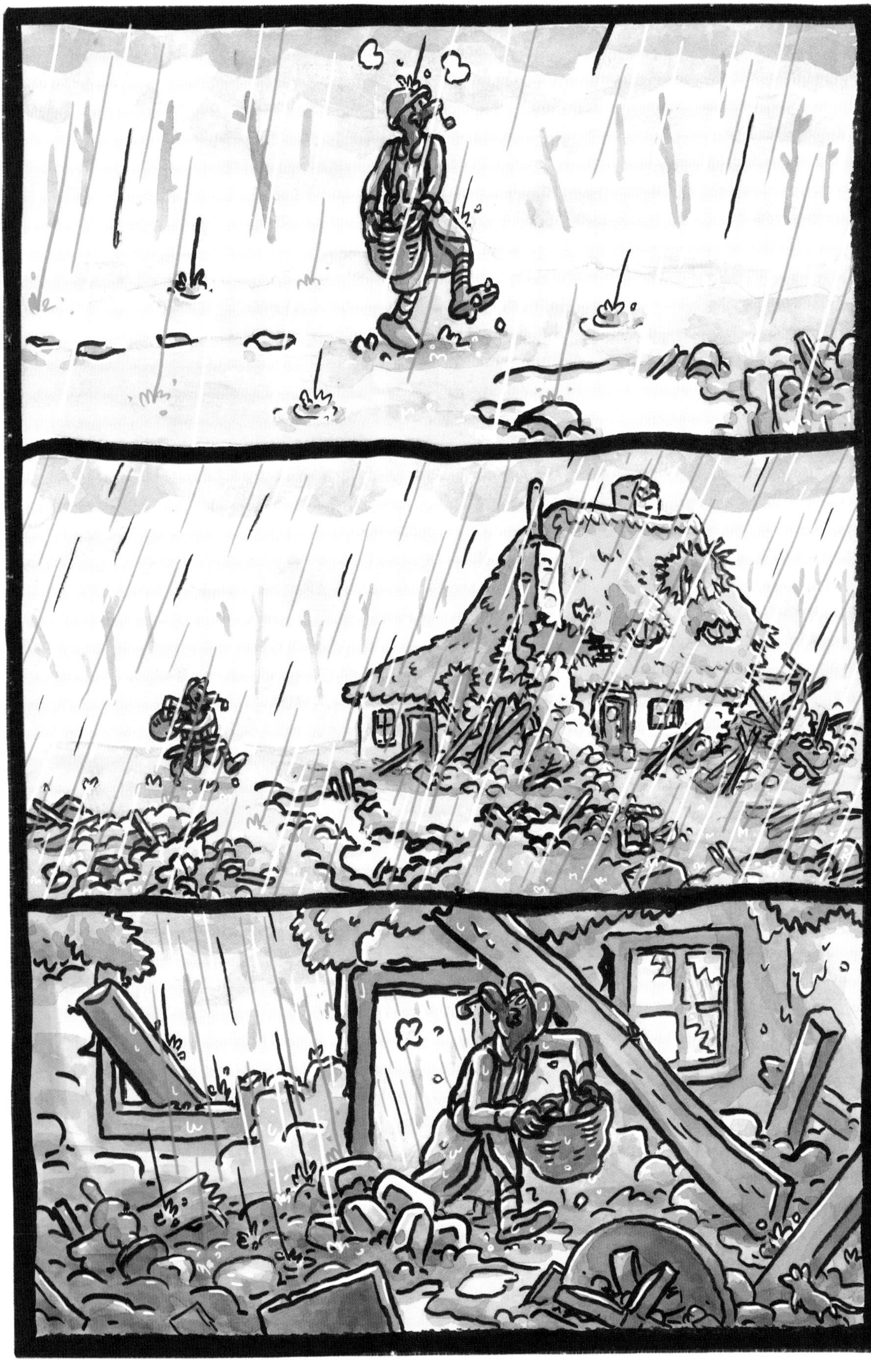

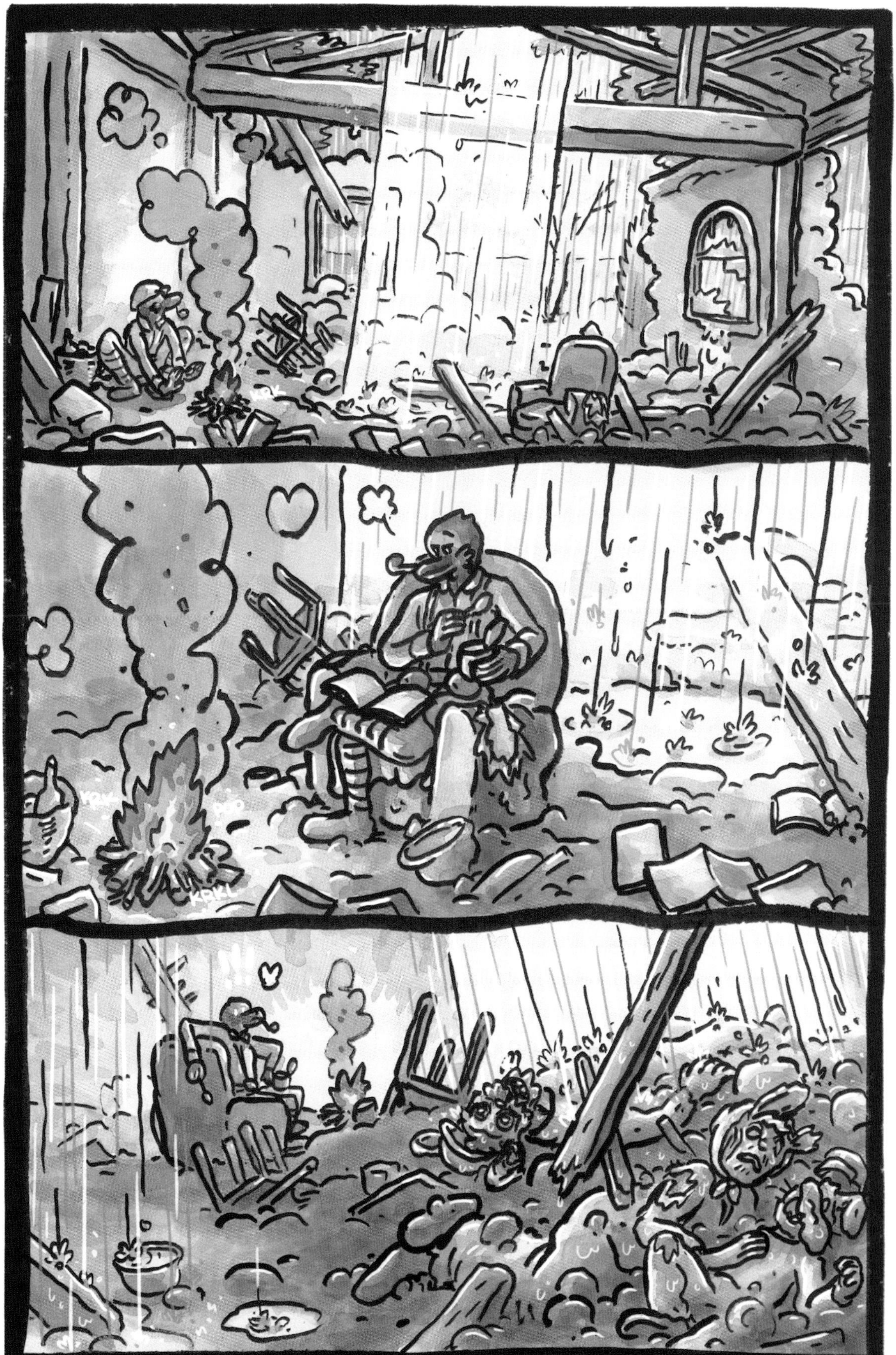
KRK
KRK
POP
KRKL

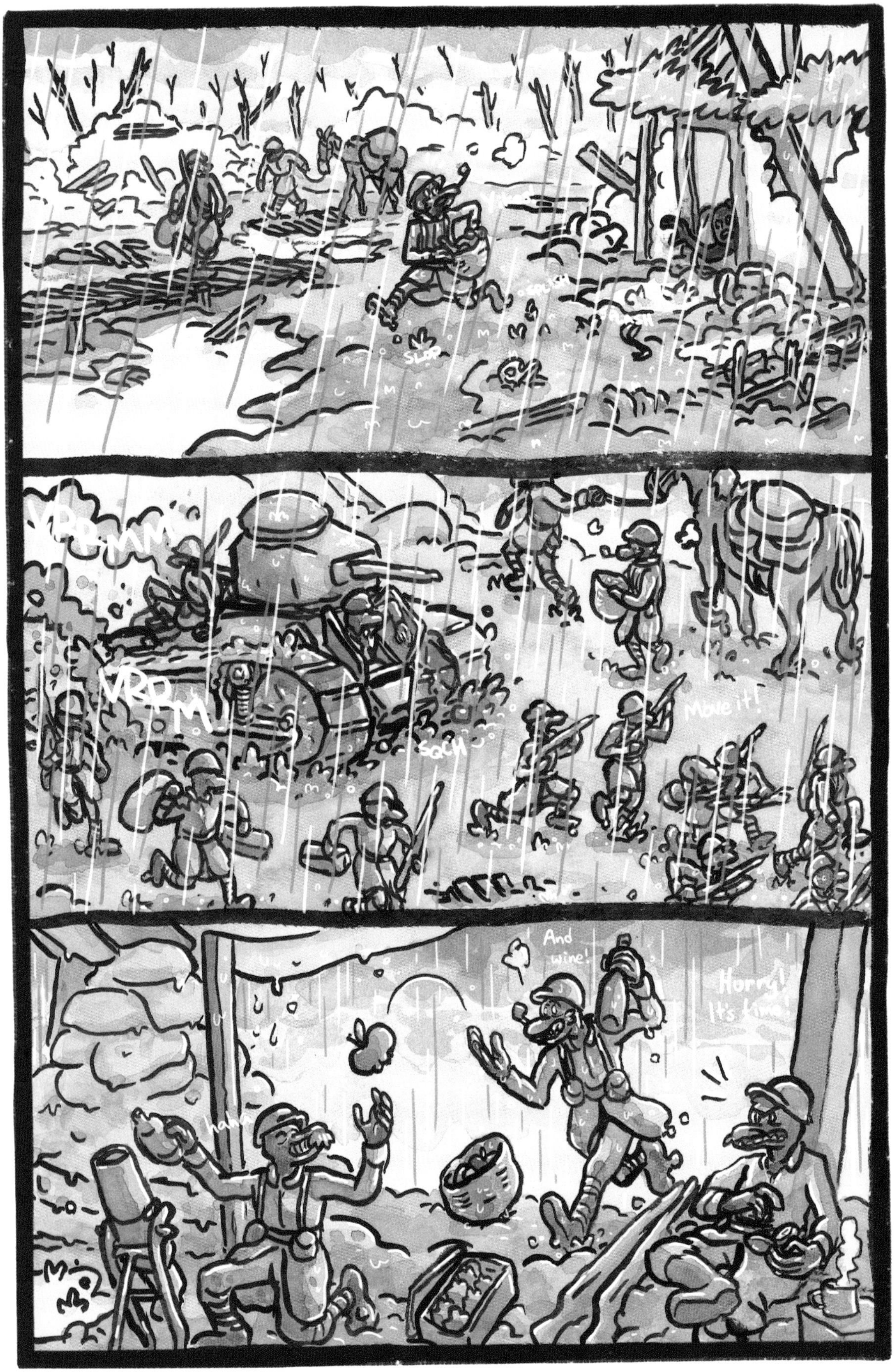
Yikes!
SPLISH
SPLASH
SLOP
VRRMM
VRRM
SQCH
Move it!
haha
And wine!
Hurry! It's time!

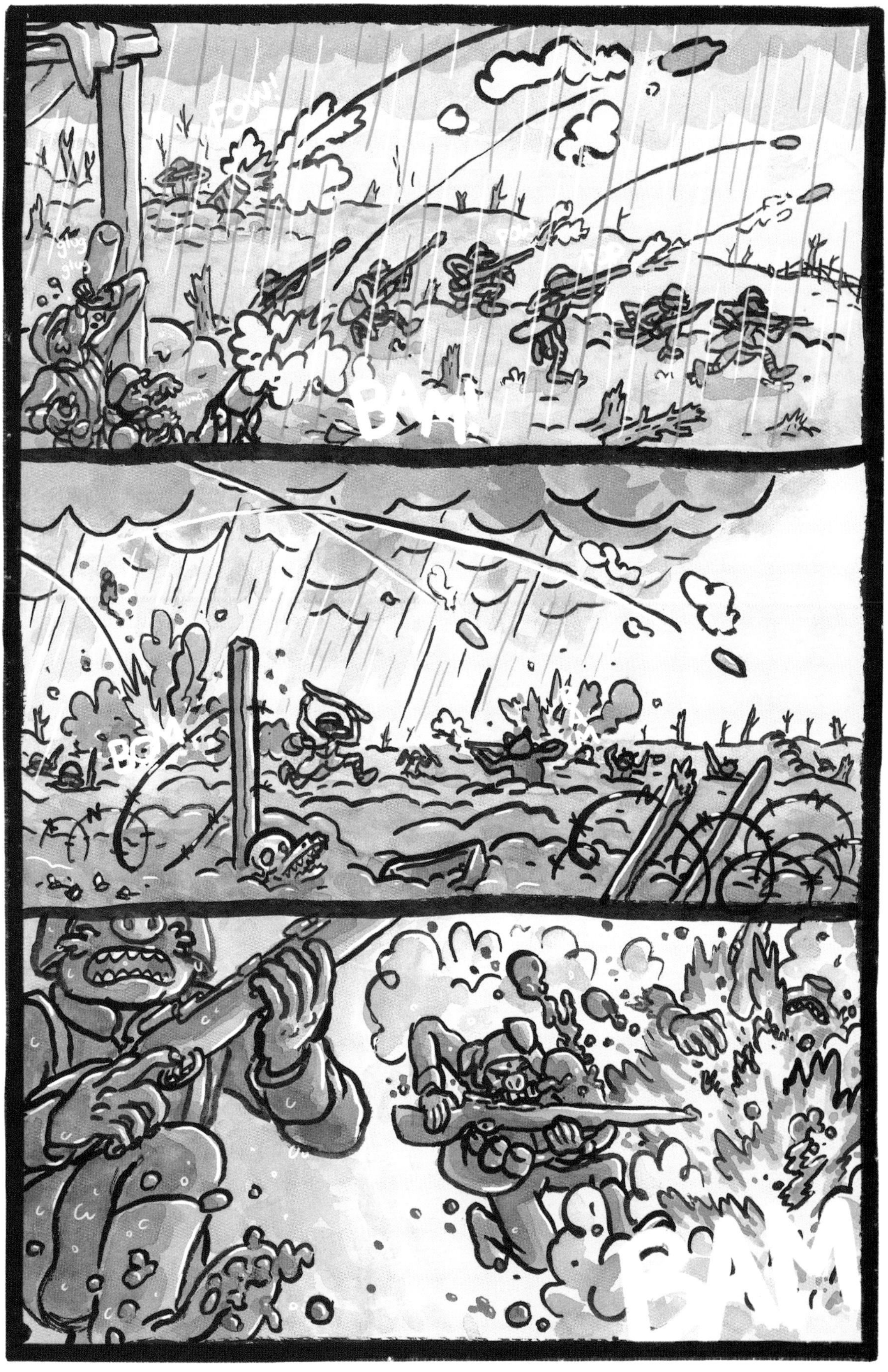
POW!
glug
glug
munch
POW
POP
BAM!
BAM

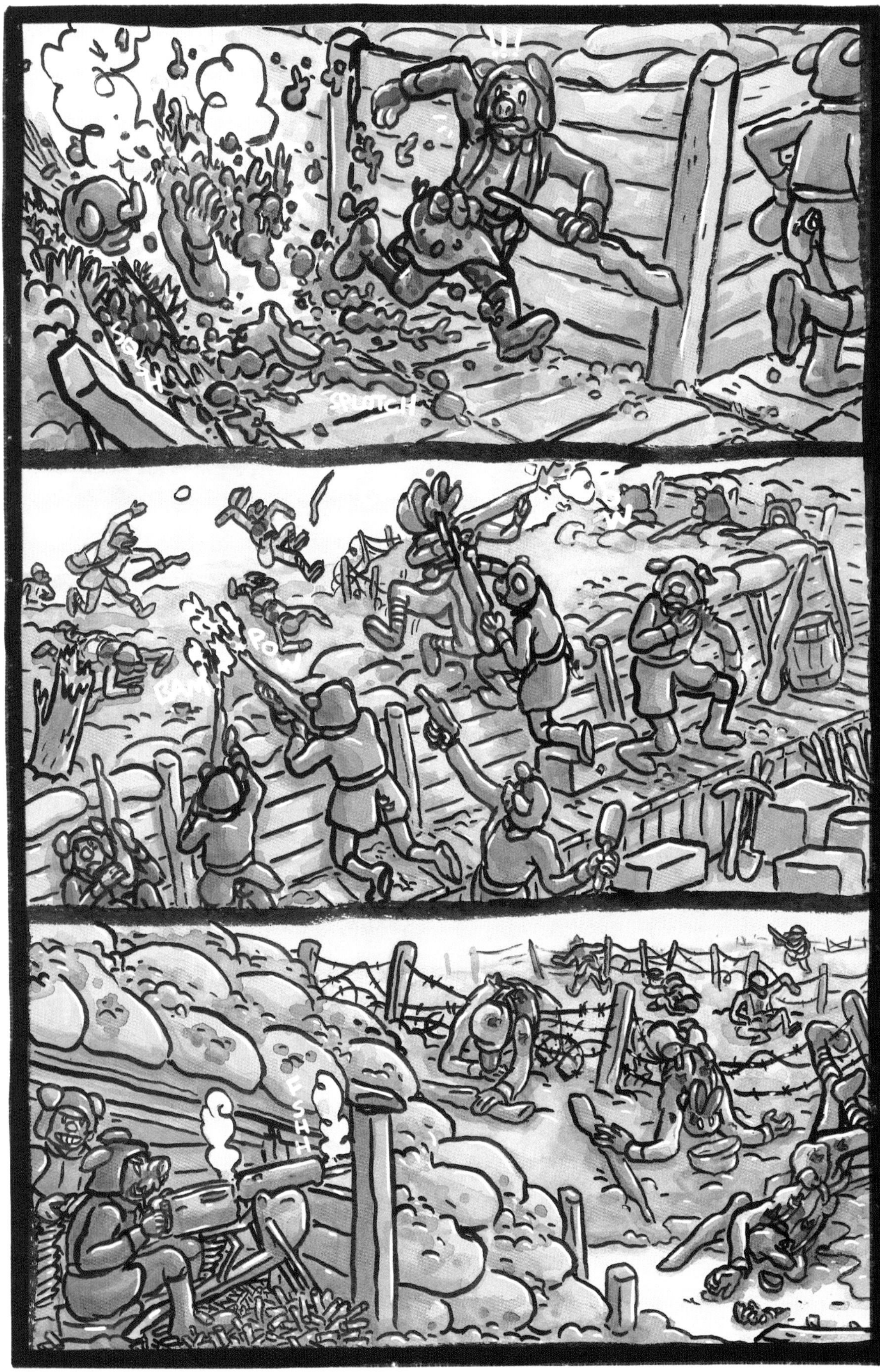
!!!
SPLOTCH
POW
BAM
FSHH

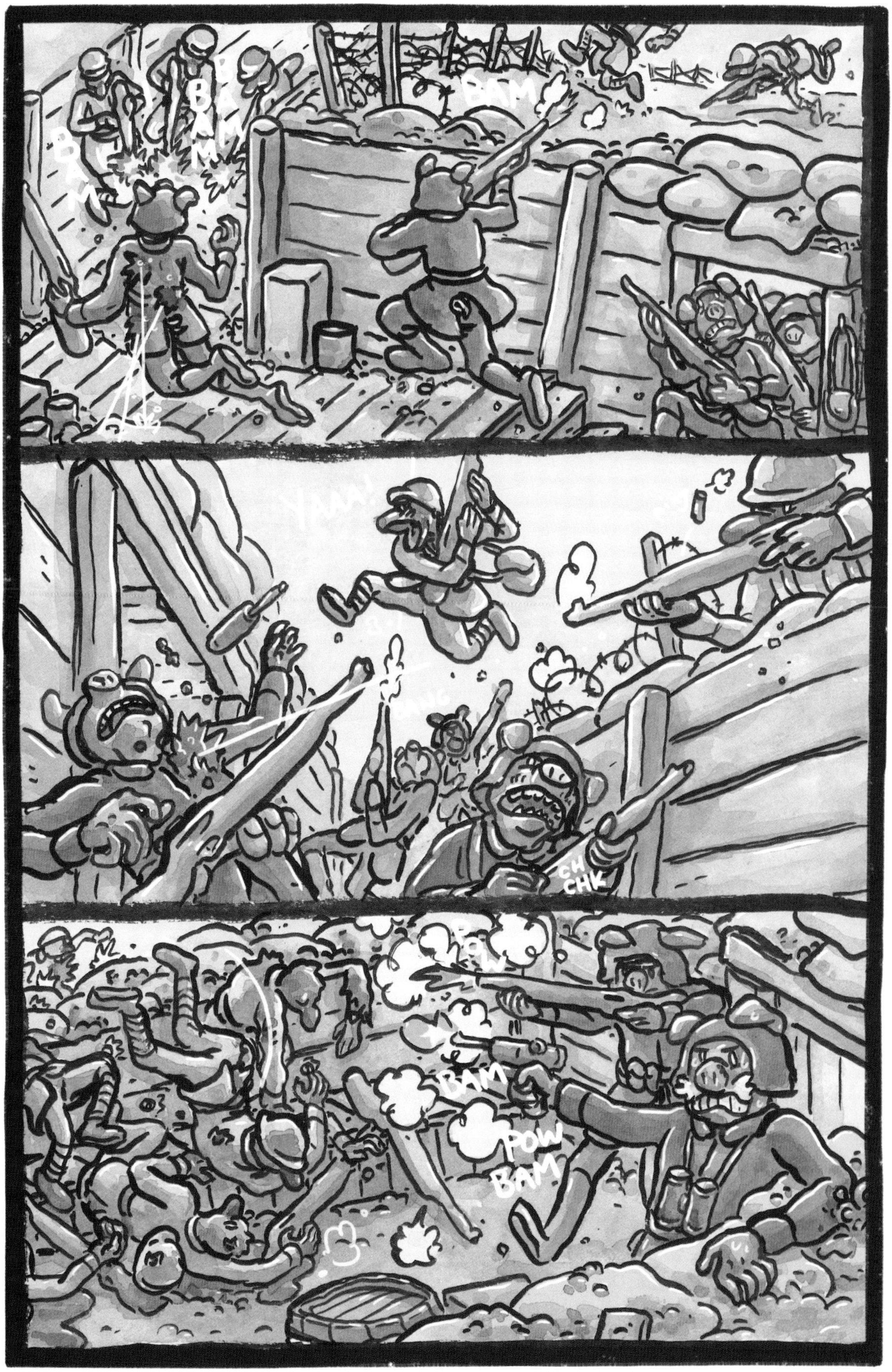
BAM
BBAM
BAMM
BAM
YAAA!
BANG
CH
CHK
POW
BAM
POW
BAM

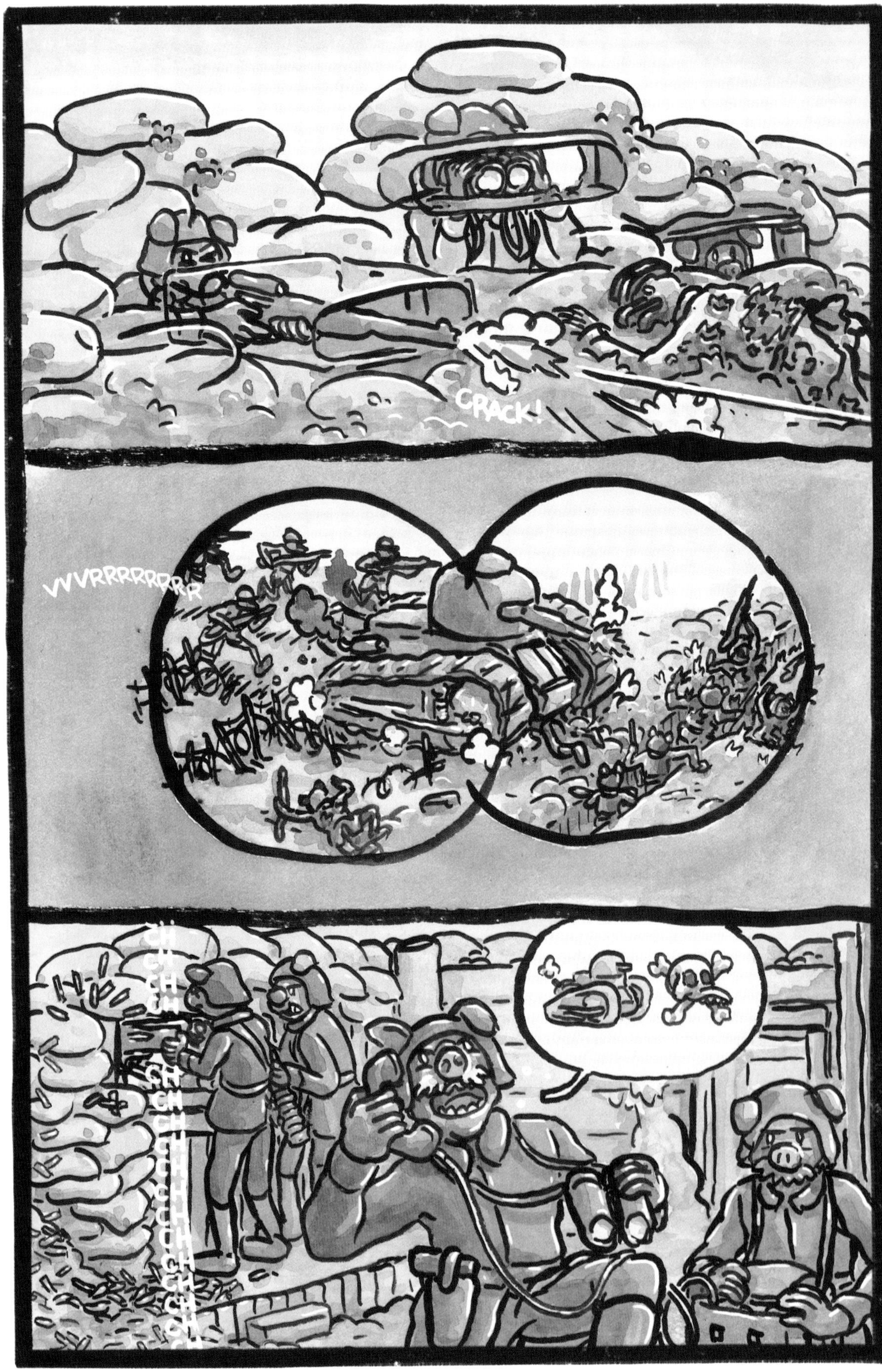
CRACK!
VVVRRRRRRRR
CHCHCHCH
CHCHCHCHCHCHCHCHCHCH

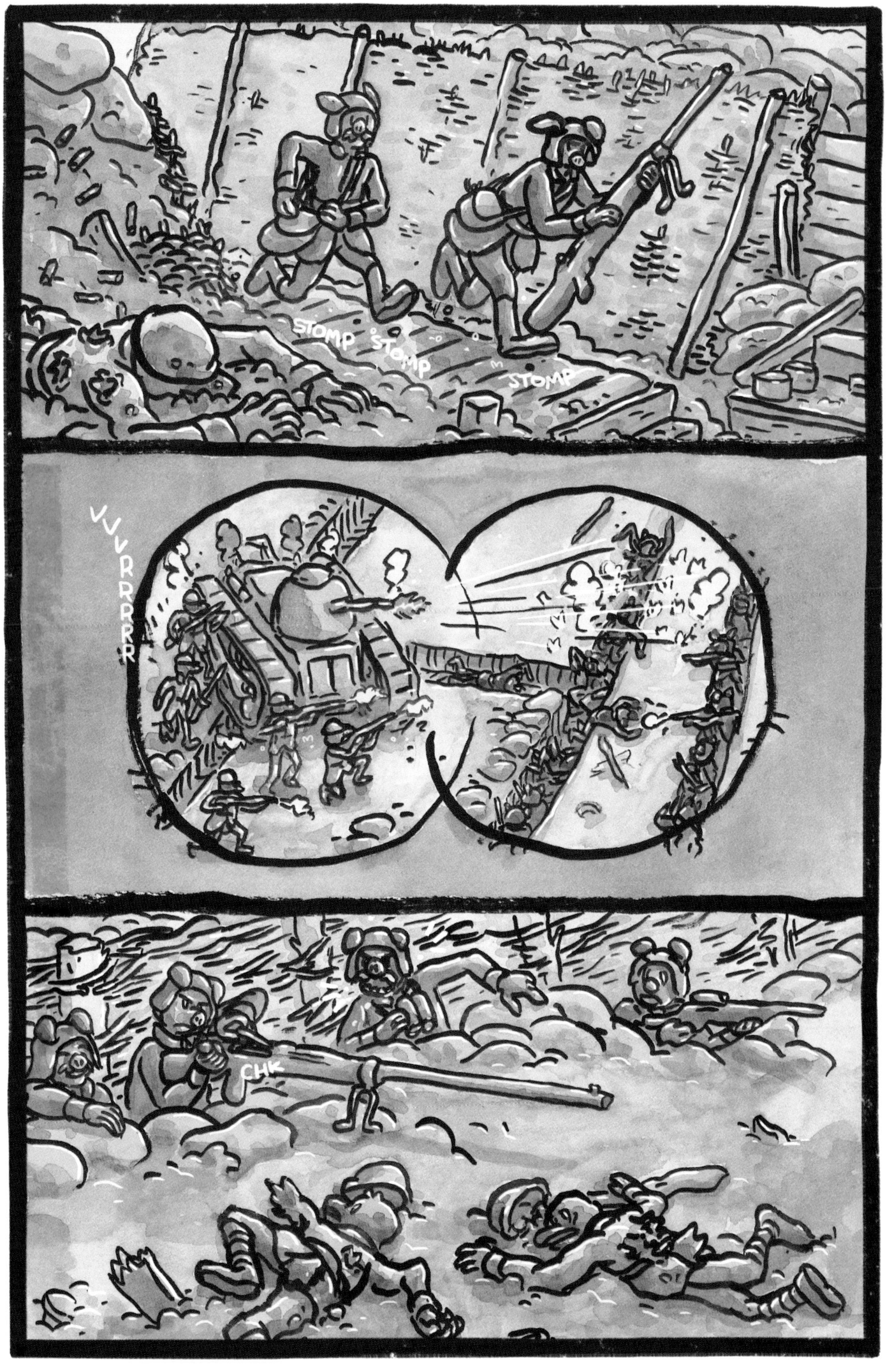
STOMP
STOMP
STOMP
VVVRRRRR
CHK

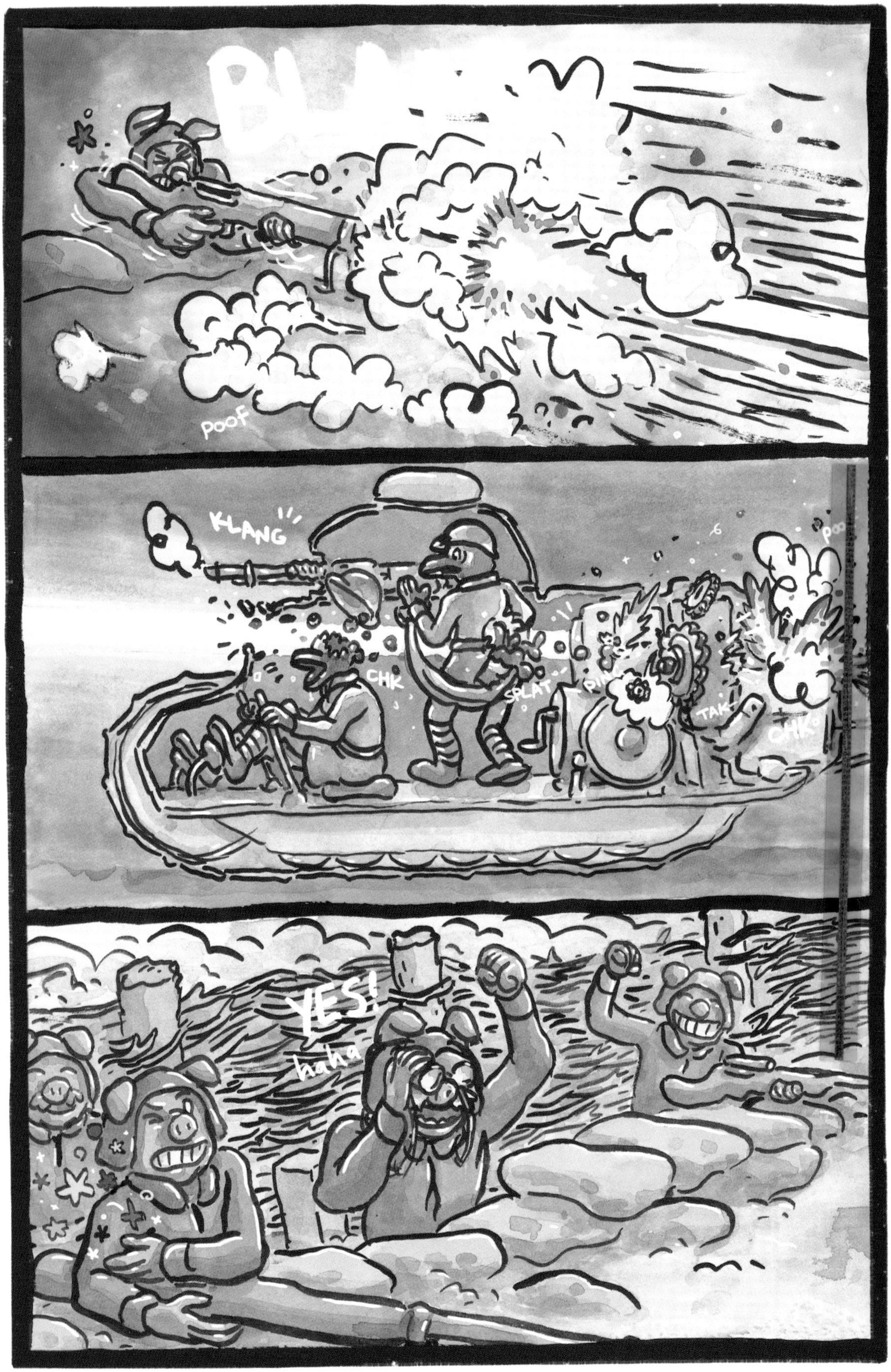
POOF
KLANG
CHK
SPLAT
PING
TAK
CHK
YES!
haha

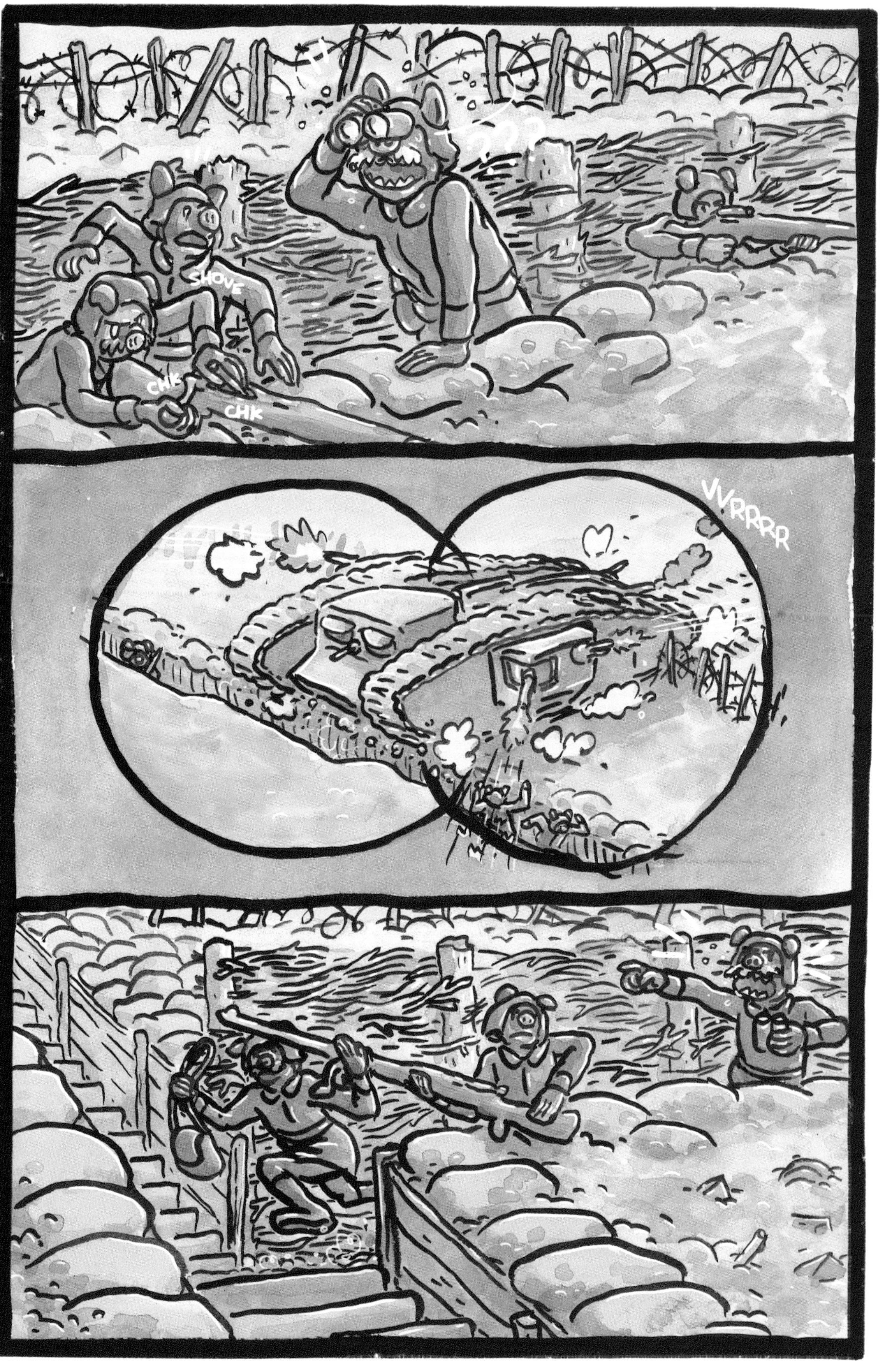
???
SHOVE
CHK
CHK
VVRRRRR

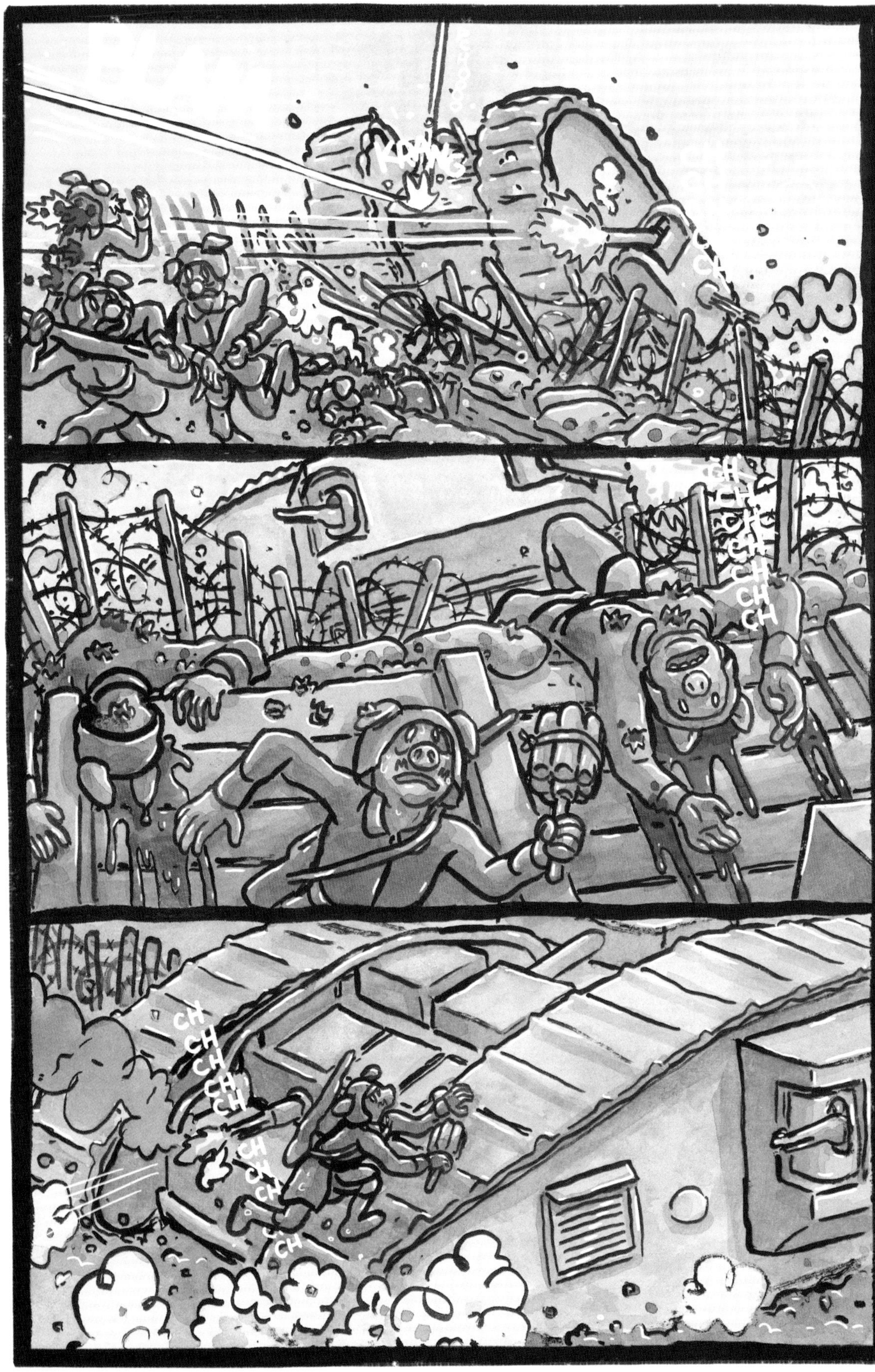

CH CH CH CH CH CH CH CH
CH CH CH CH CH
CH CH CH CH

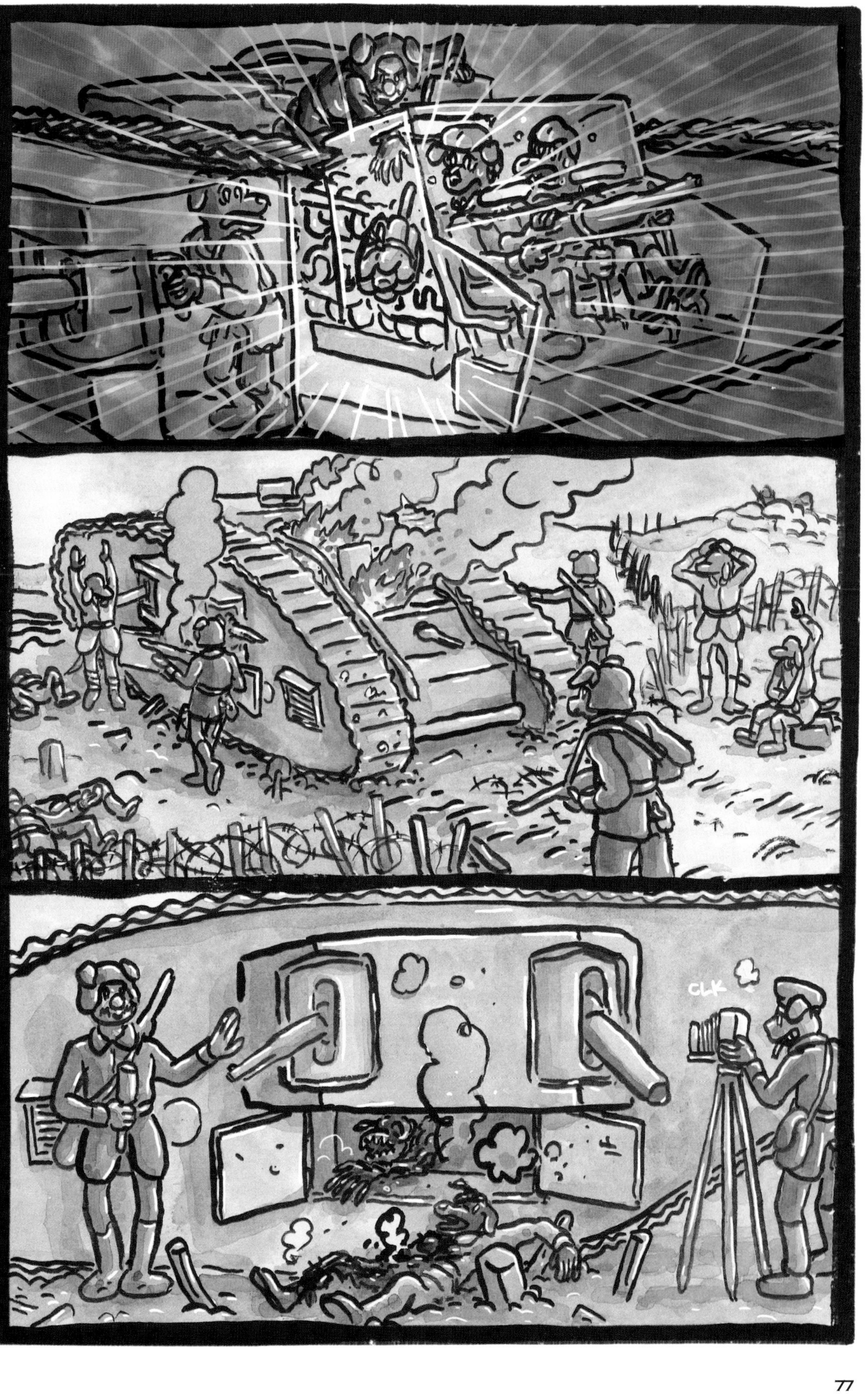
CLK

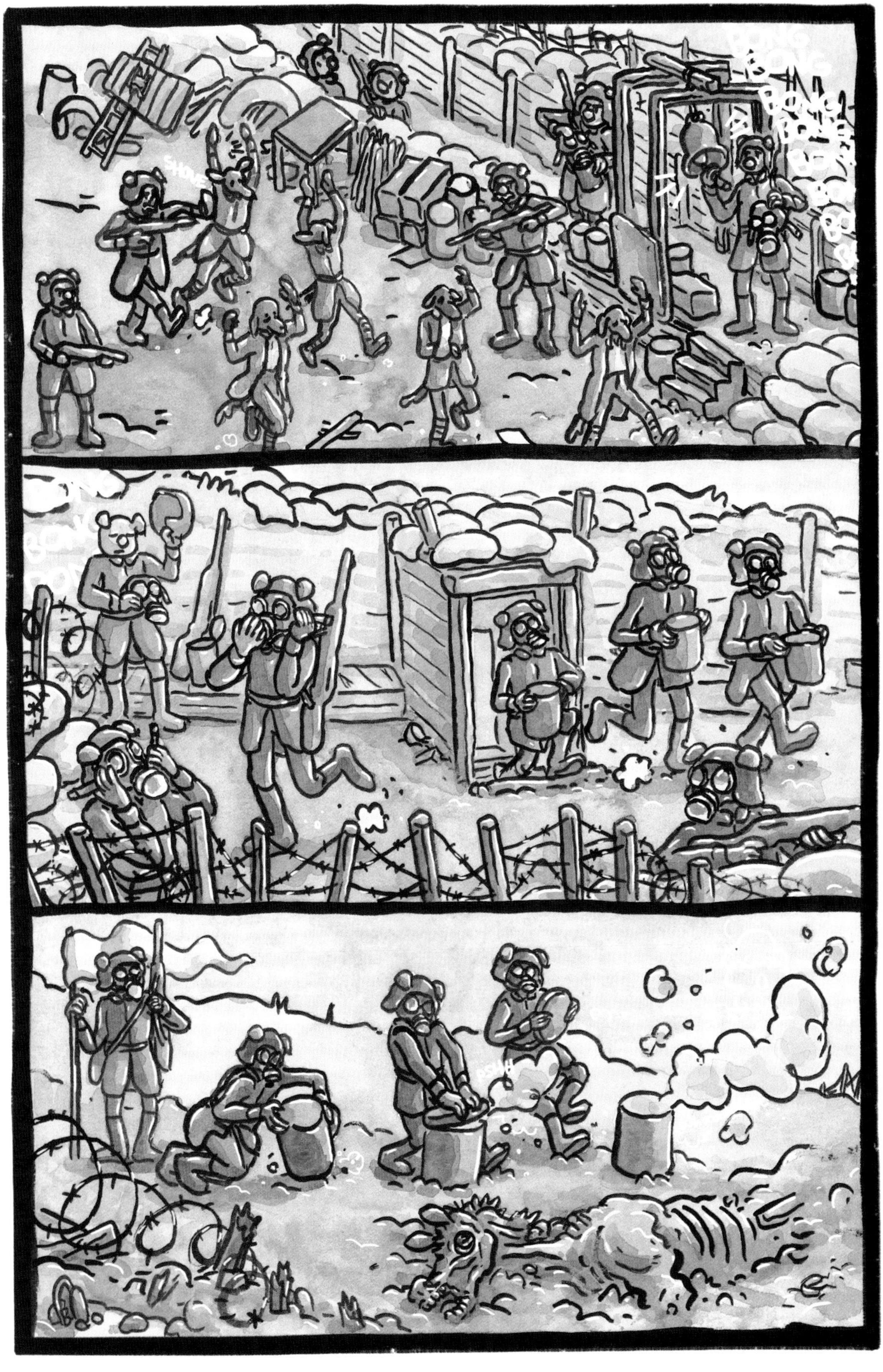
BONG BONG
SHOVE
BONG BONG
PSHH

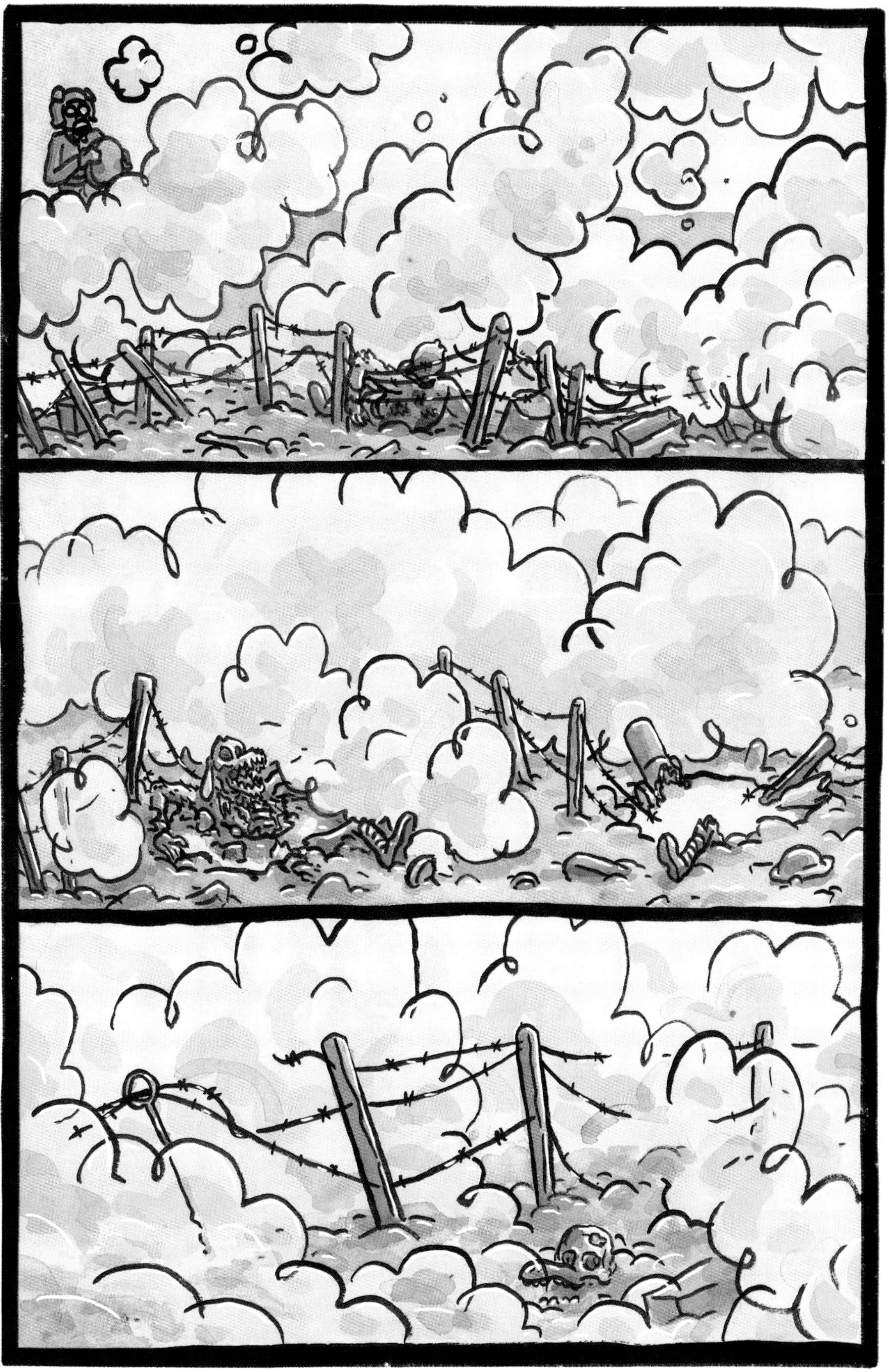

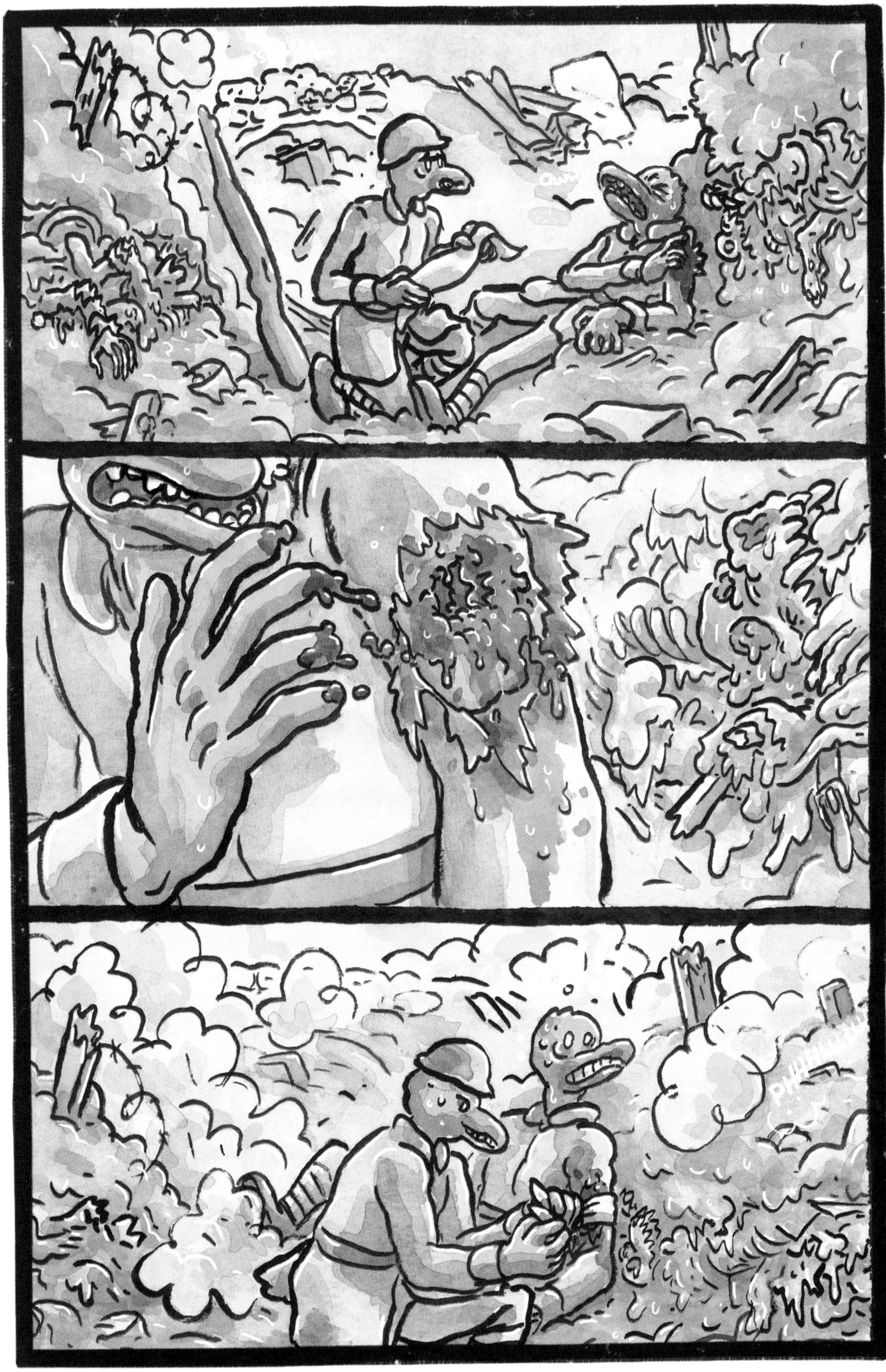

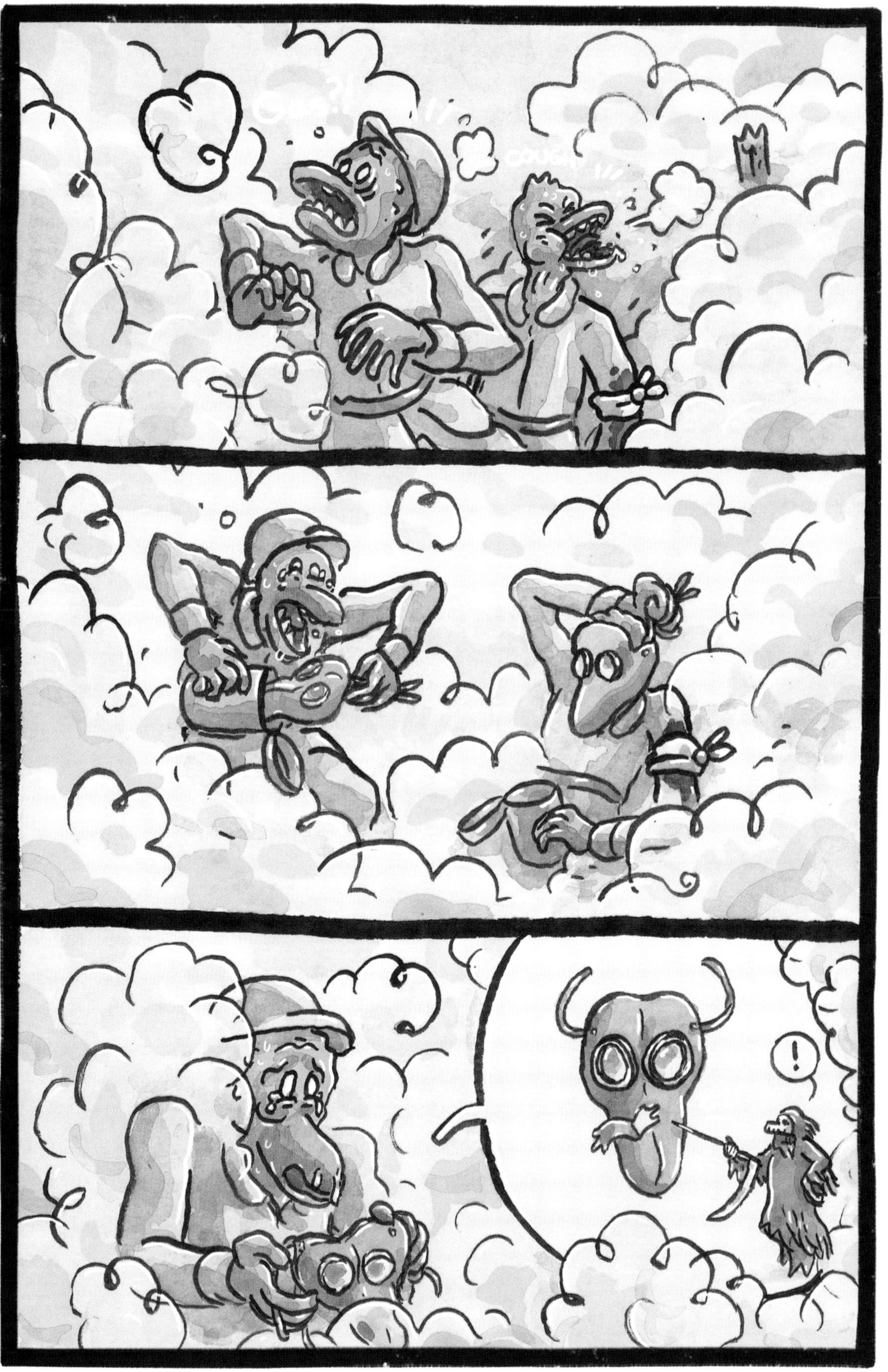
COUGH
!

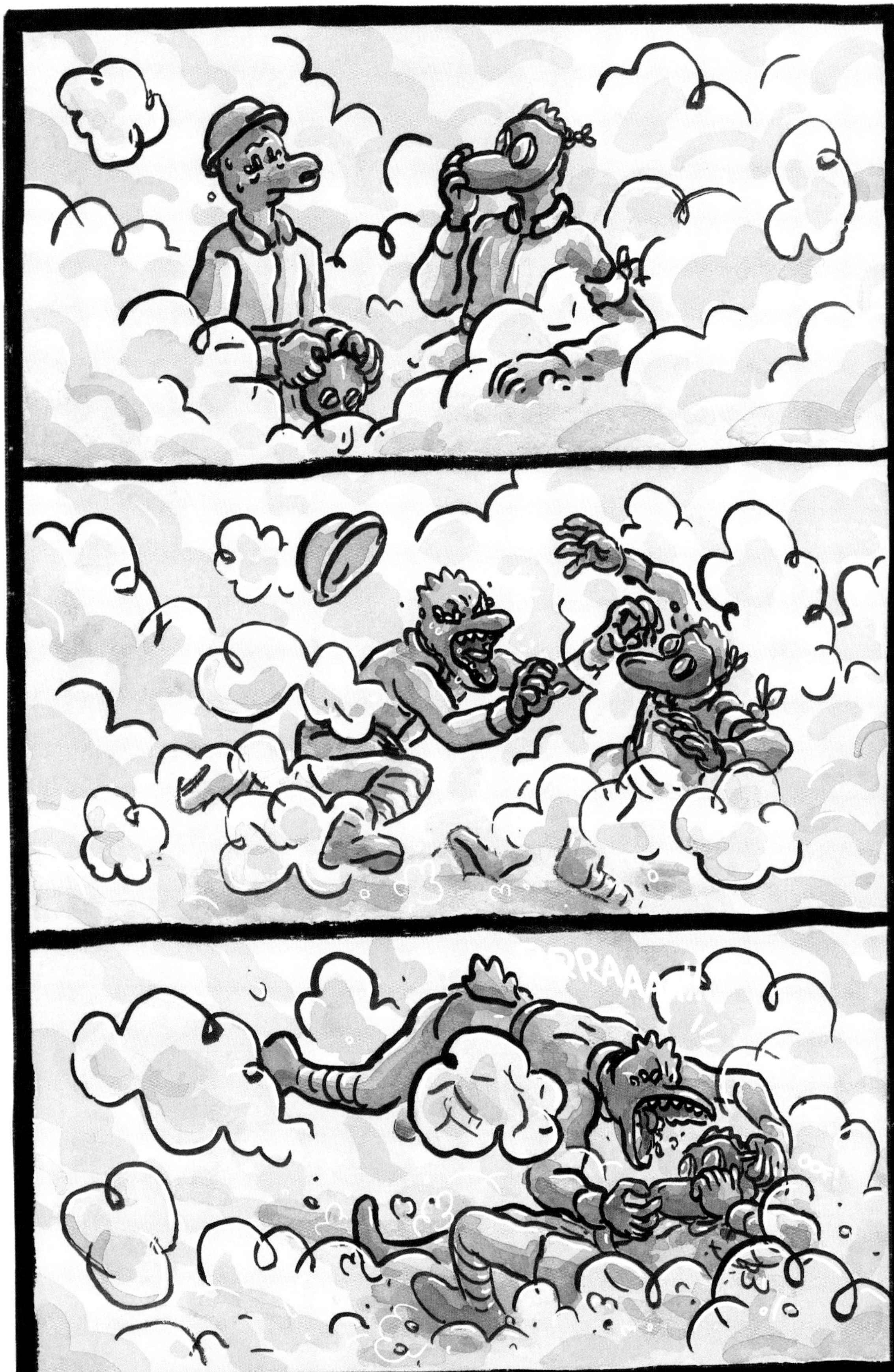
RRAAA
OOF!

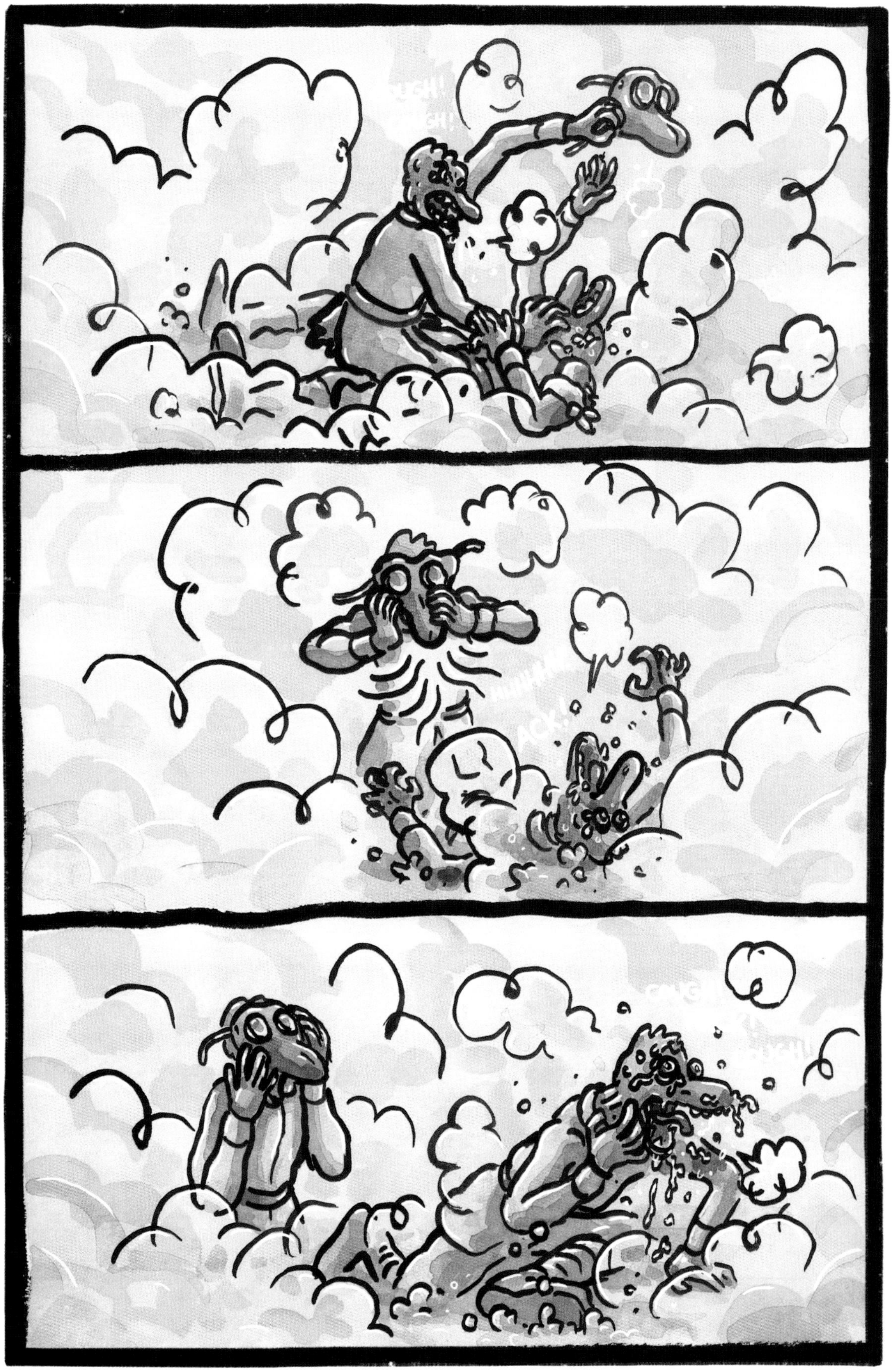
ACK!

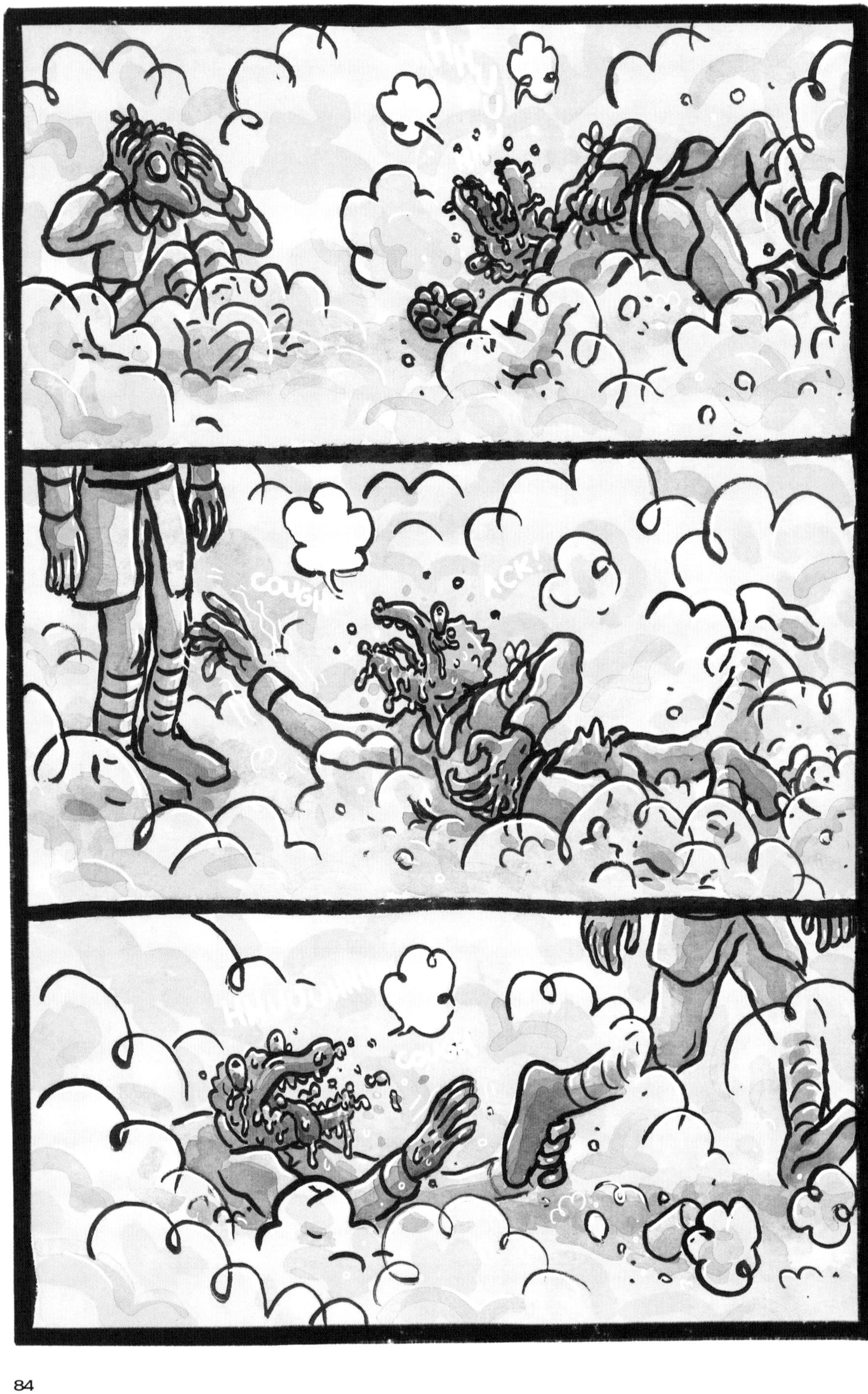
COUGH
ACK!

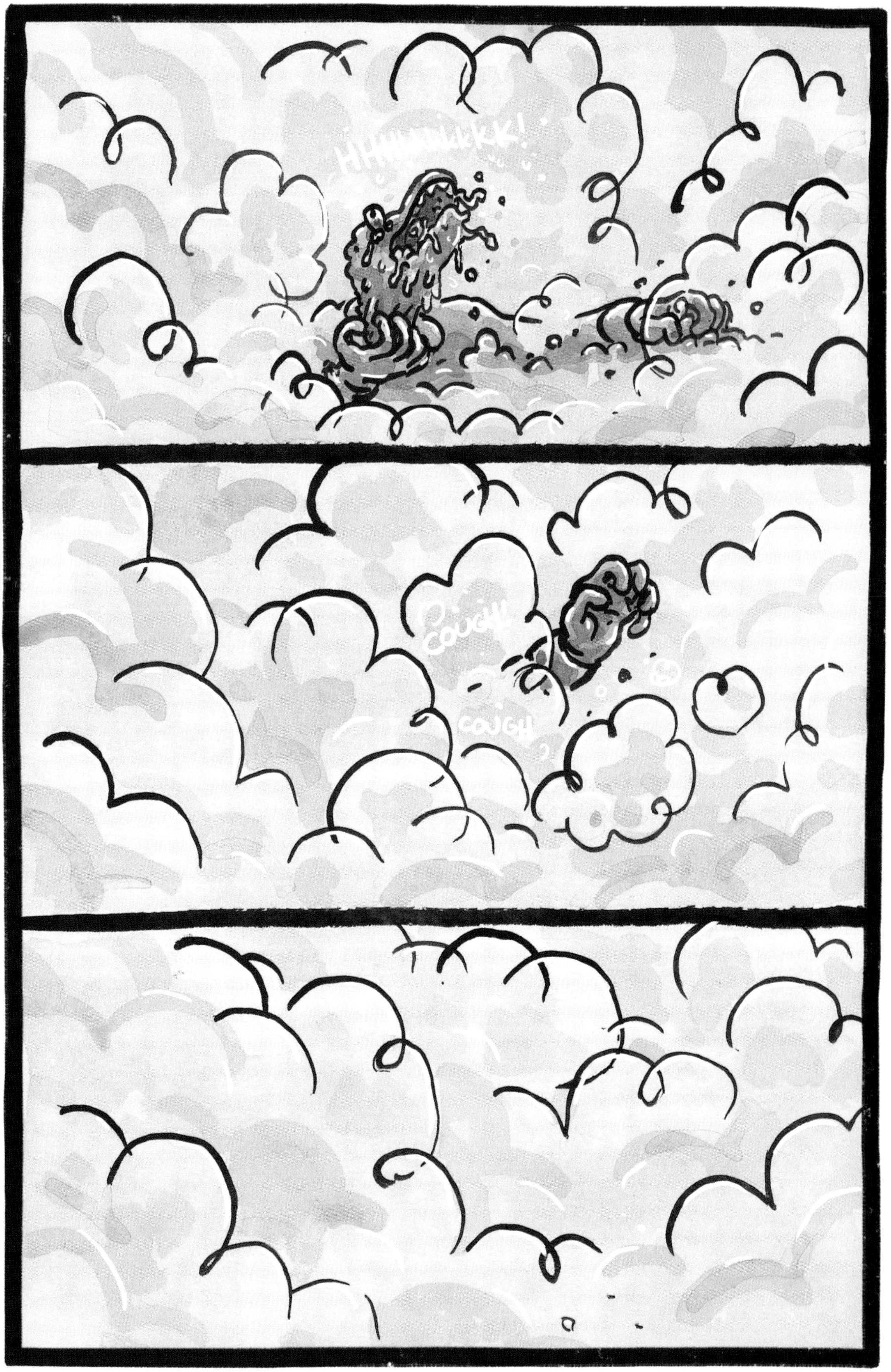
COUGH!
COUGH

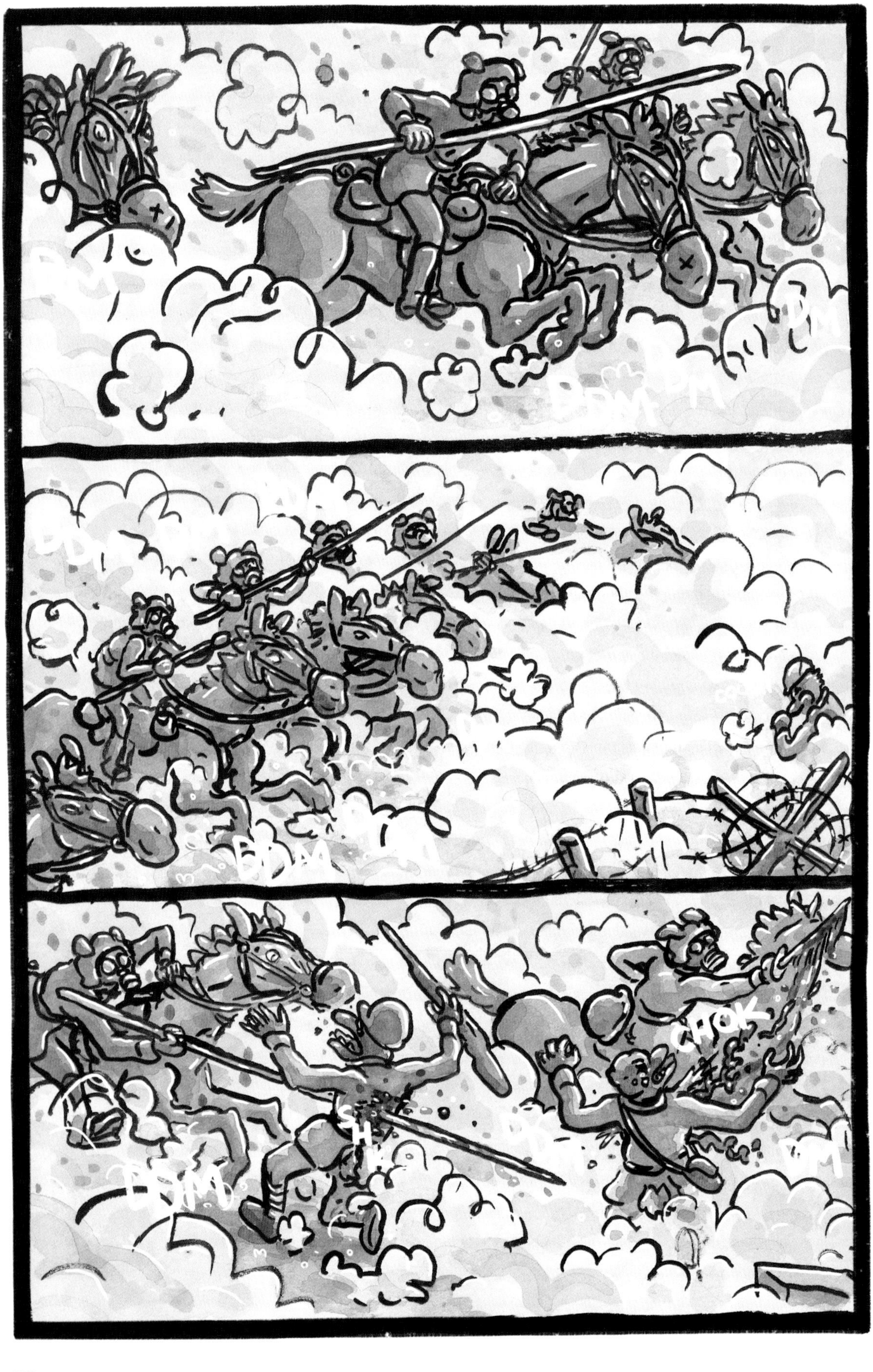
BDM
BDM
BDM
CHOK

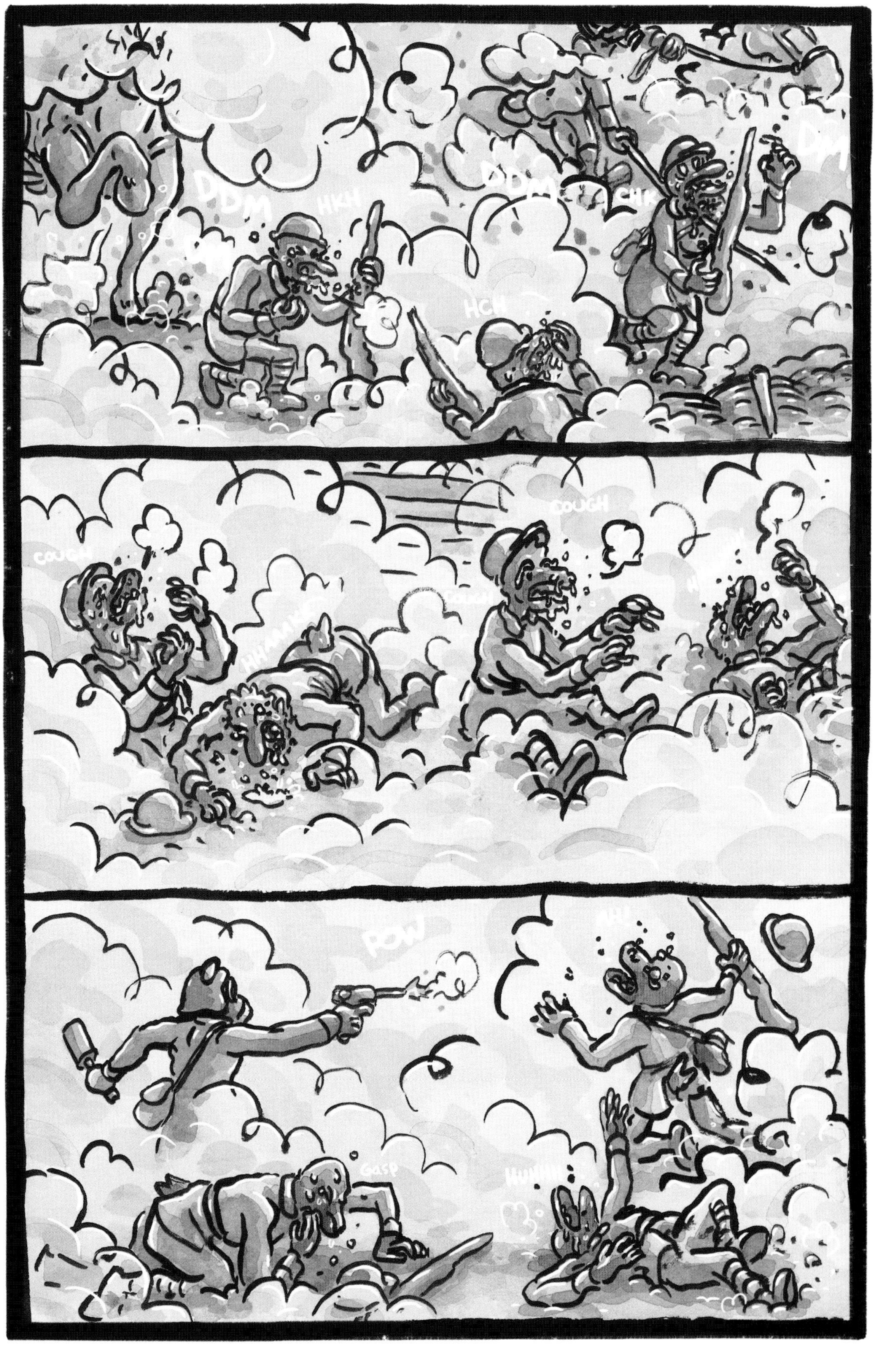
DDM
HKH
DDM
CHK
HCH
COUGH
COUGH
COUGH
POW
AH
Gasp

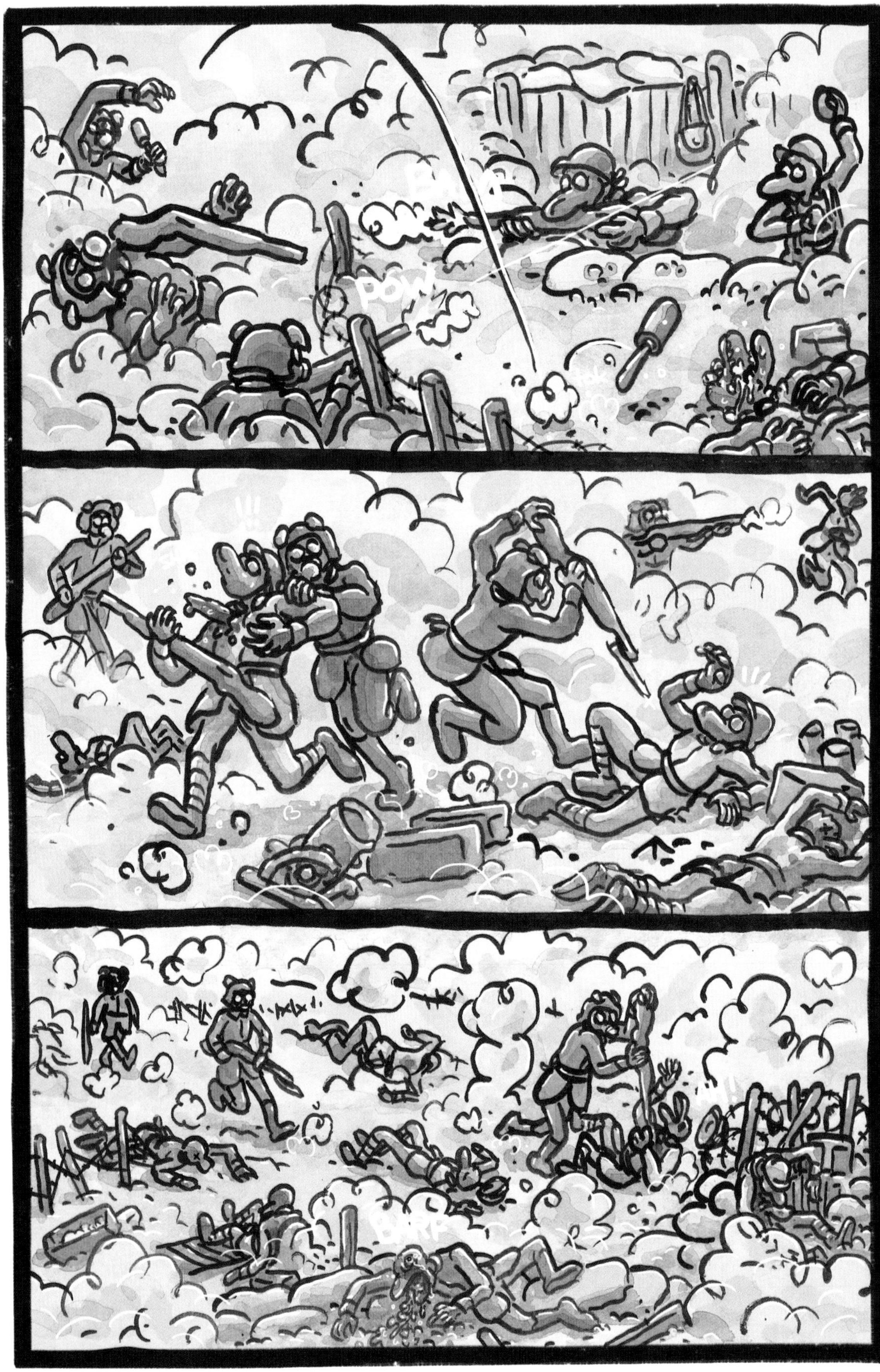
POW

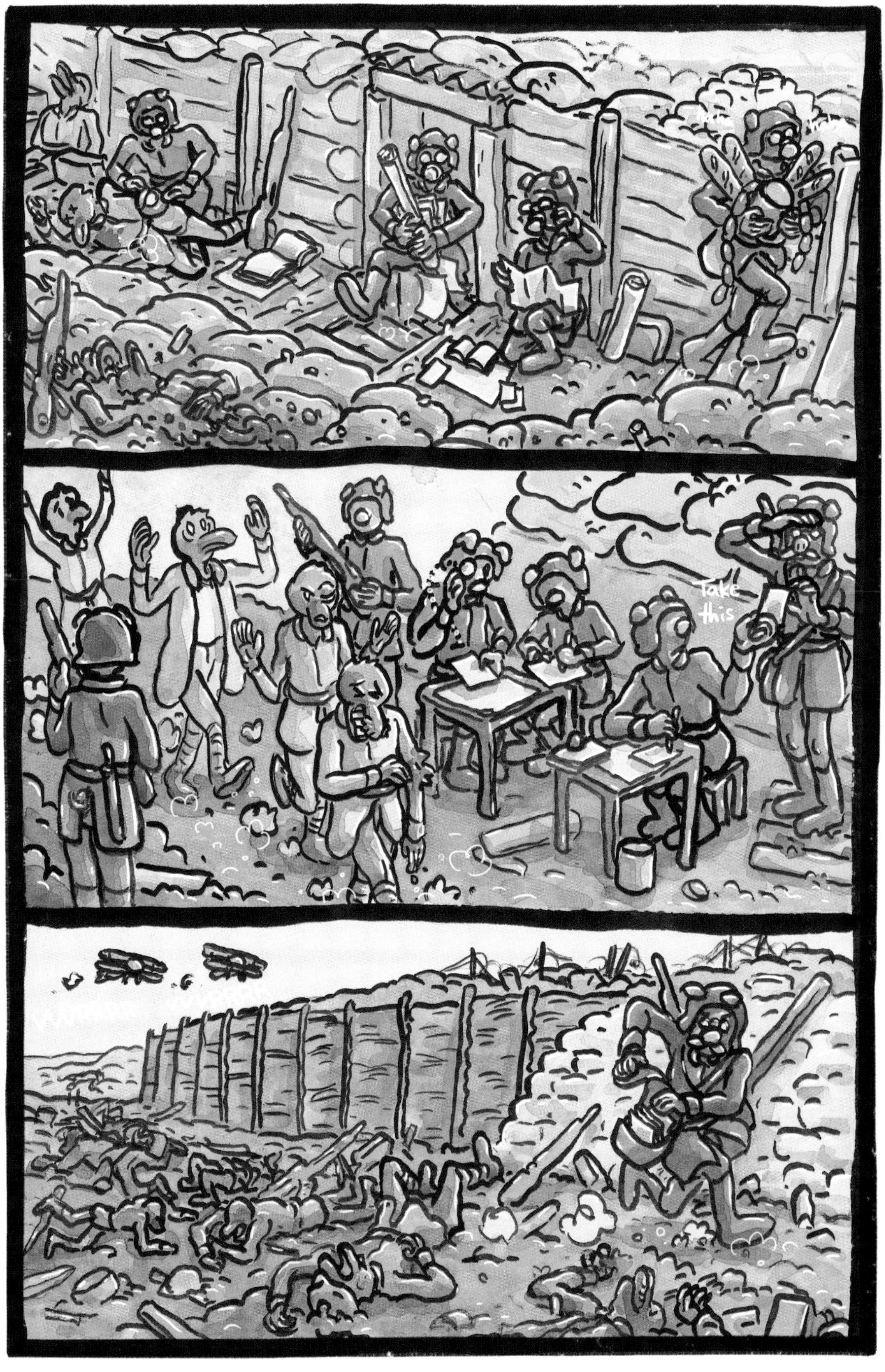
Take this

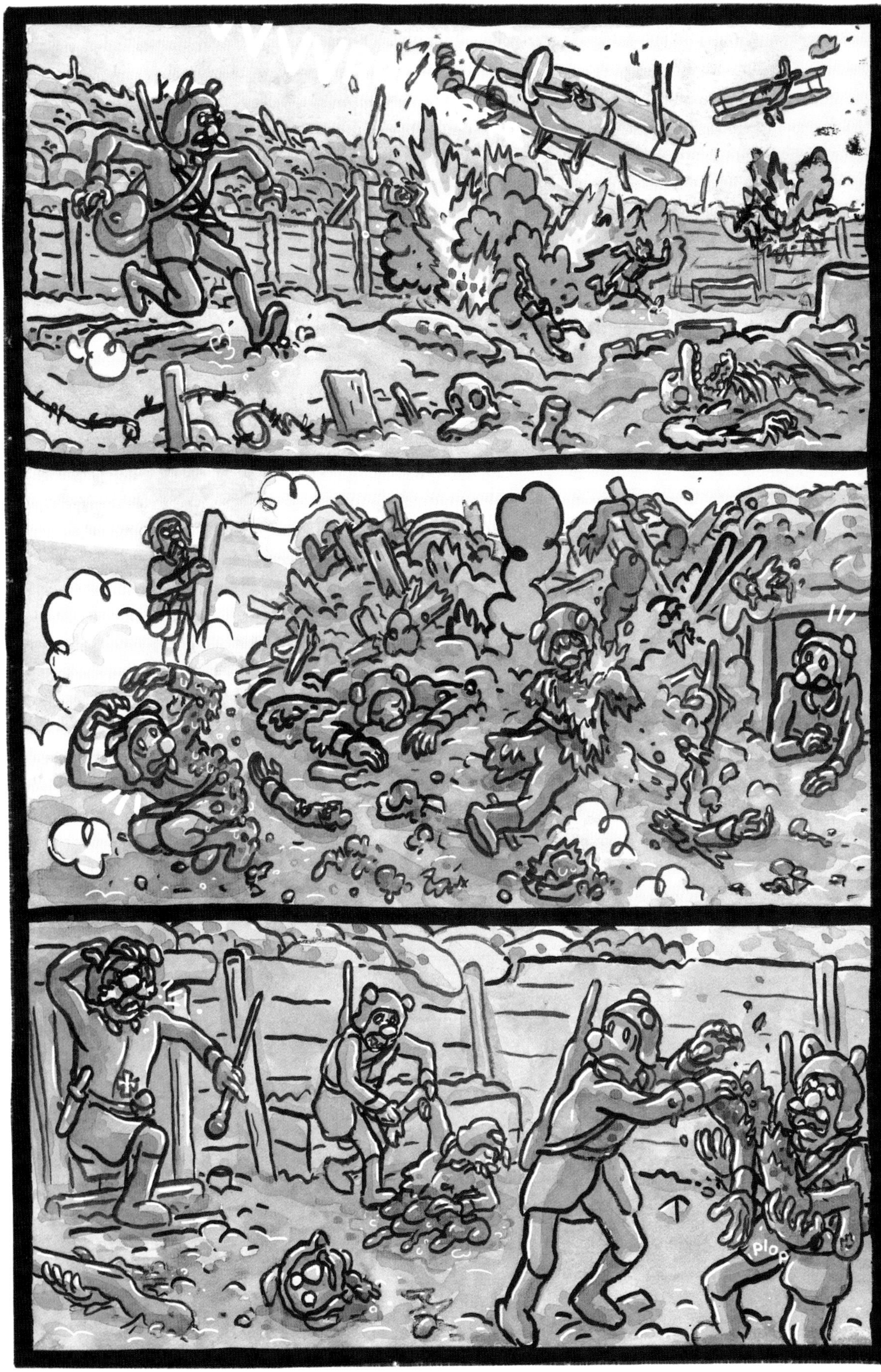
PLOP

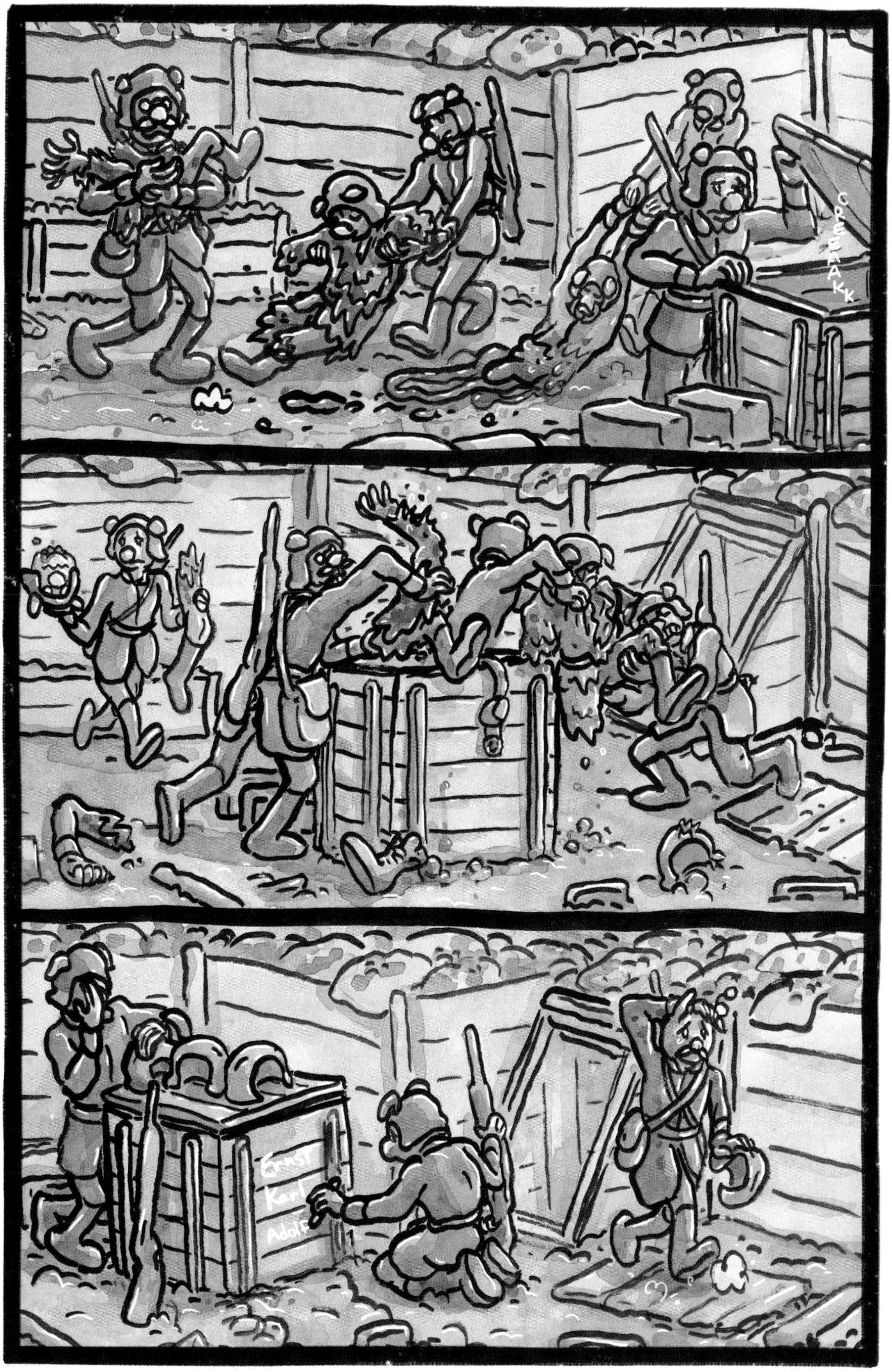
CREEAKK
Ernst
Karl
Adolf

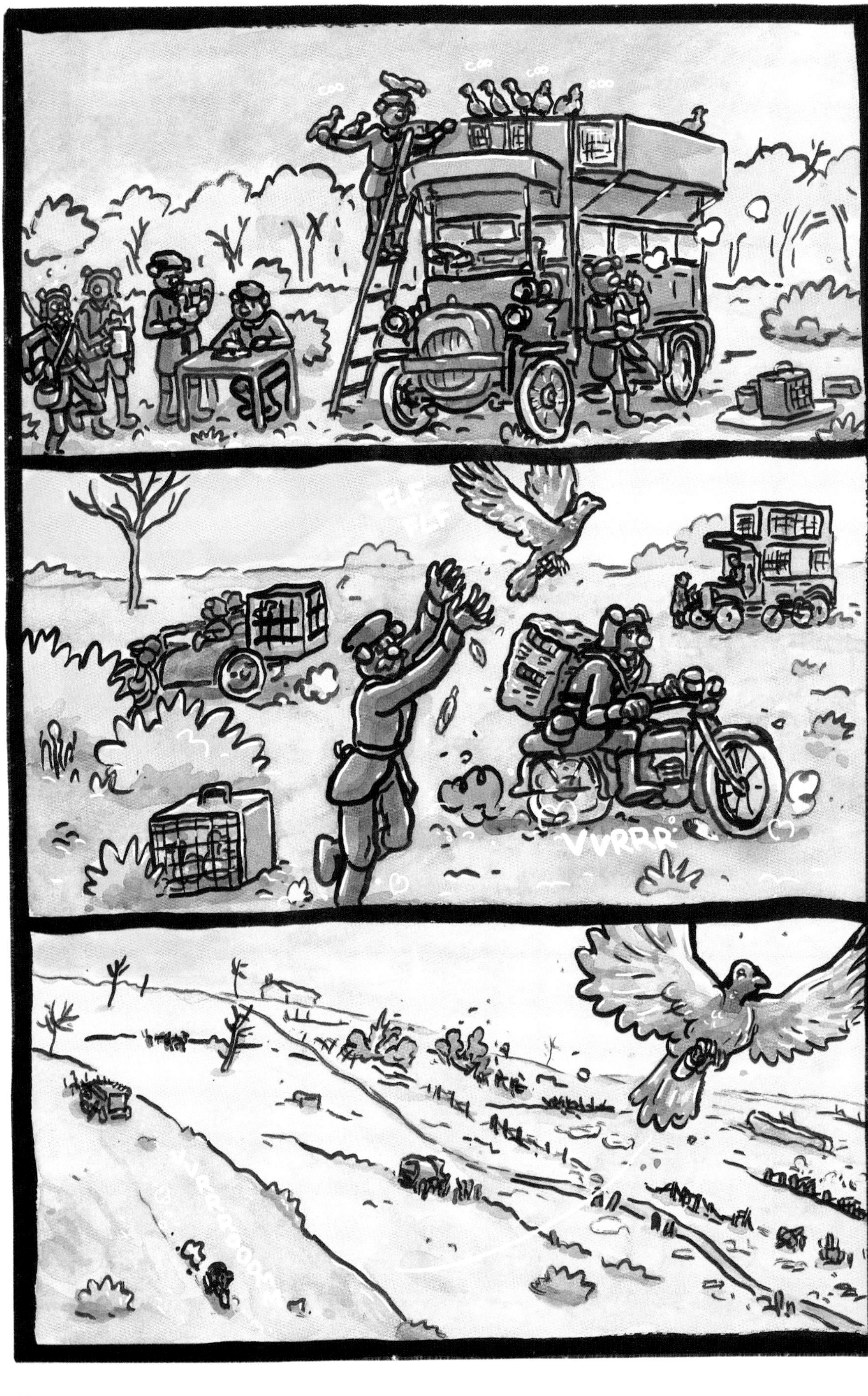
COO
COO
COO
COO
FLF
FLF
VVRRR
VRRROOOM

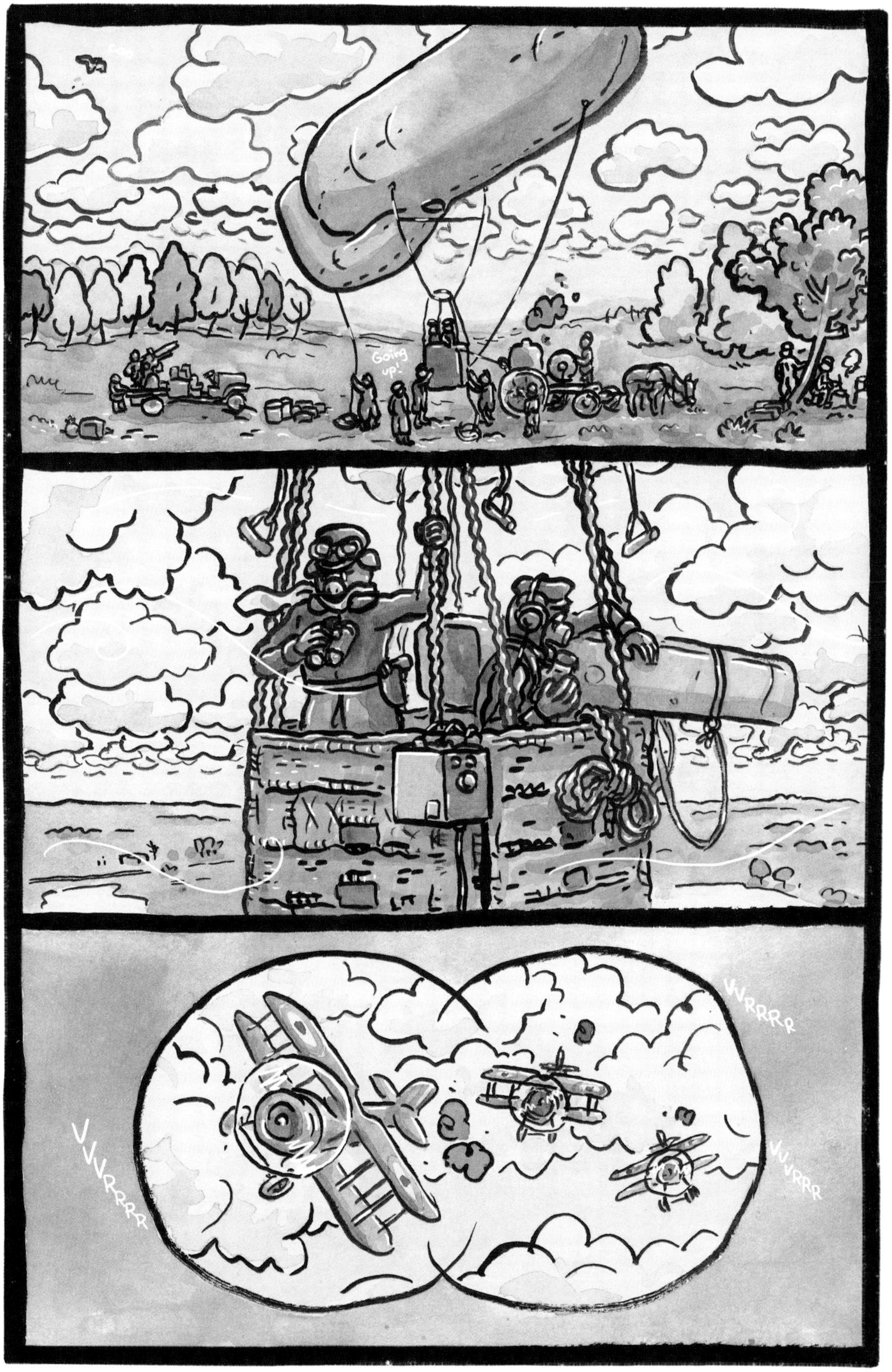
Going up!
VVRRRRR
VVVRRRRR
VVVRRRR

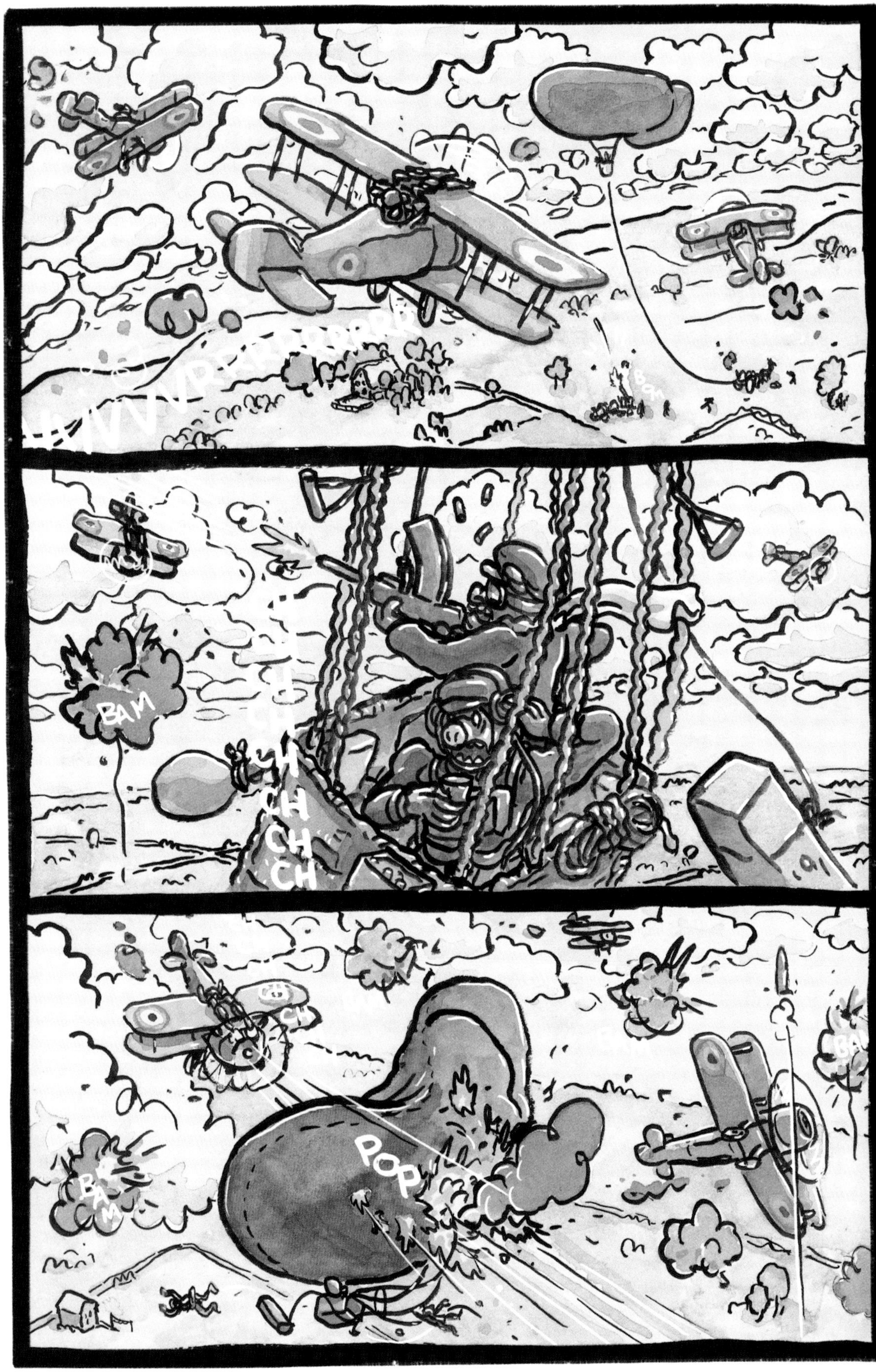
BAM
BAM
POP
BAM

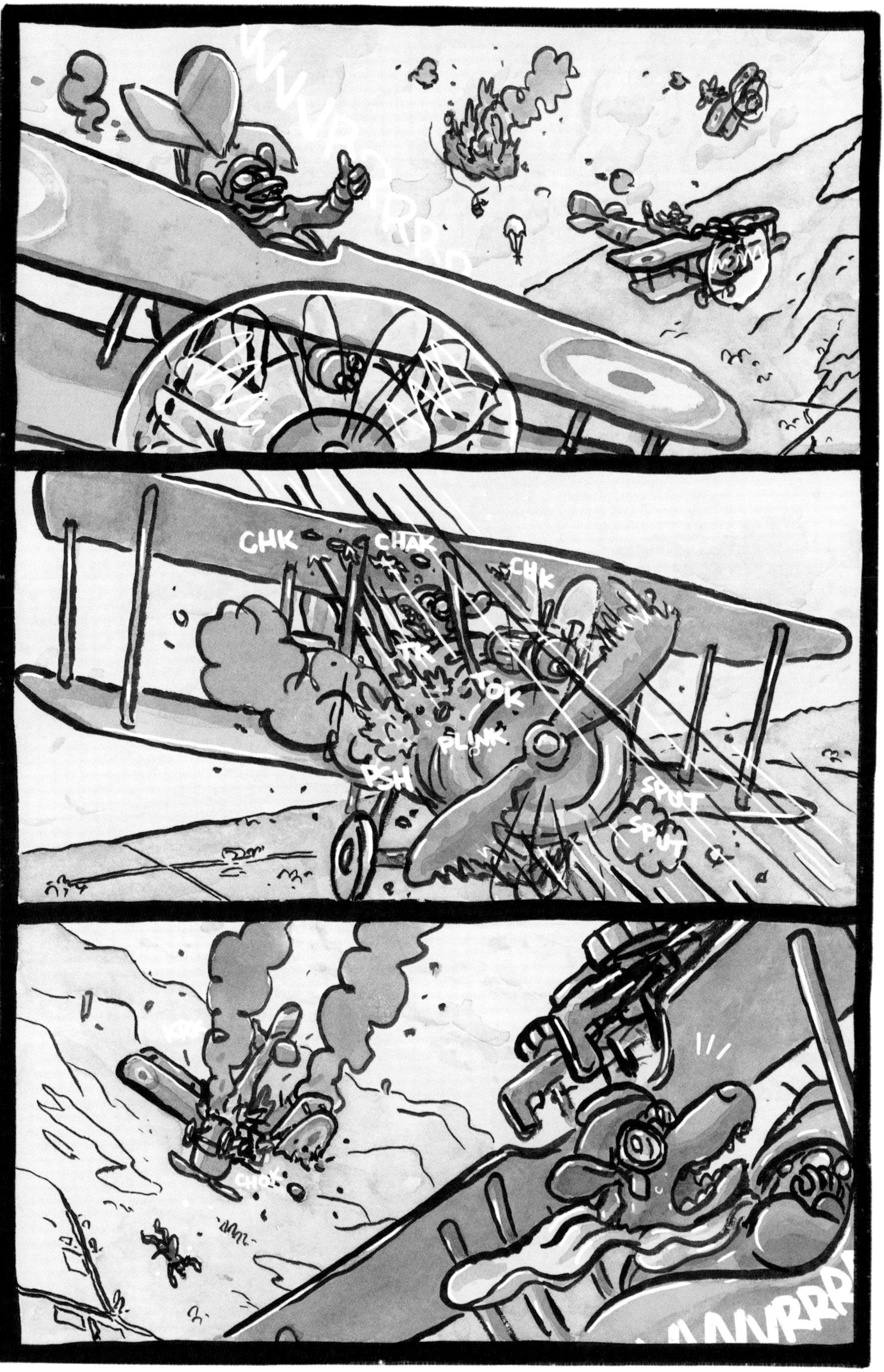
CHK
CHAK
CHK
TK
TOK
PLINK
PSH
SPUT
SPUT
CHOK

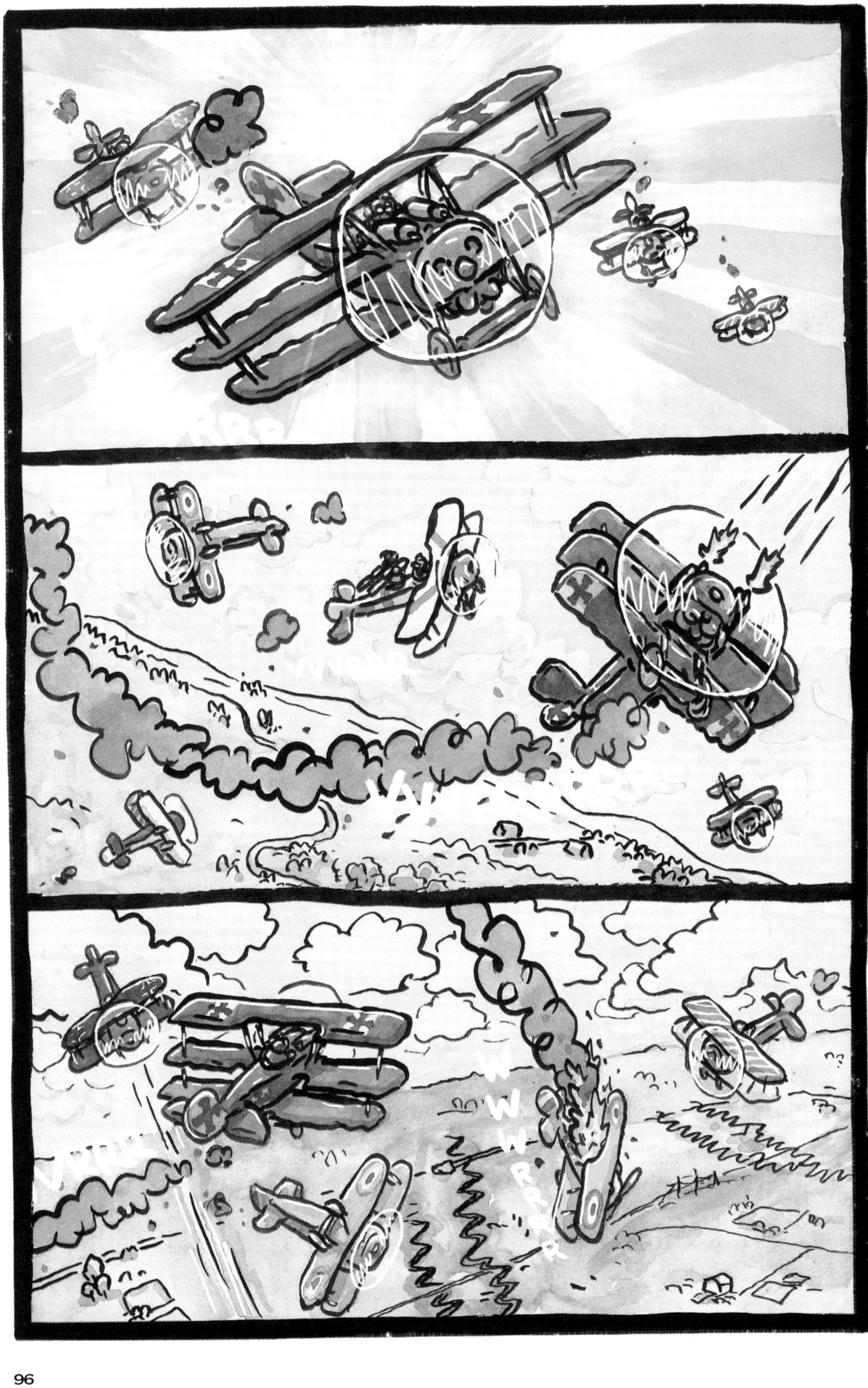
WWWRRRR

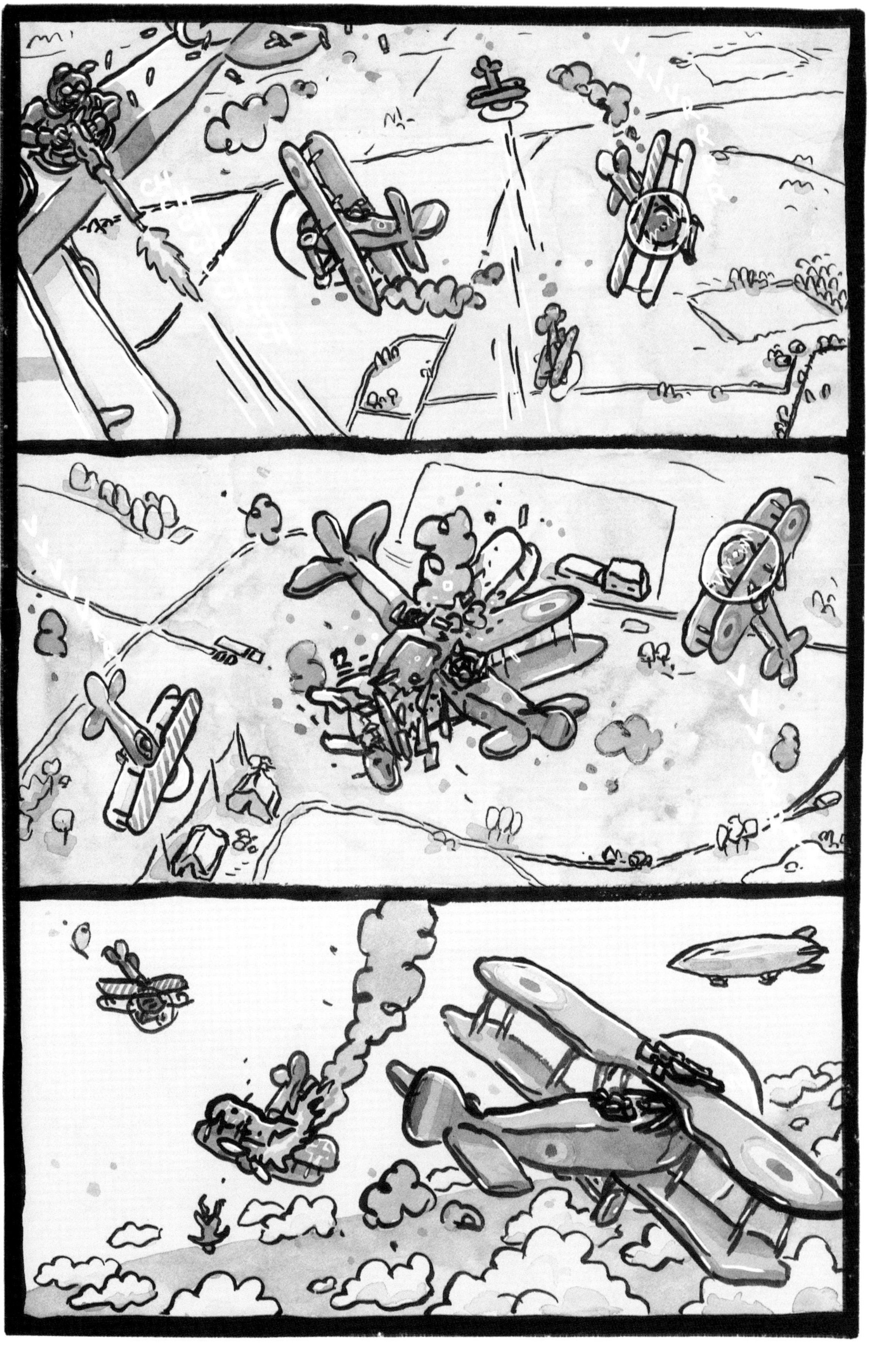

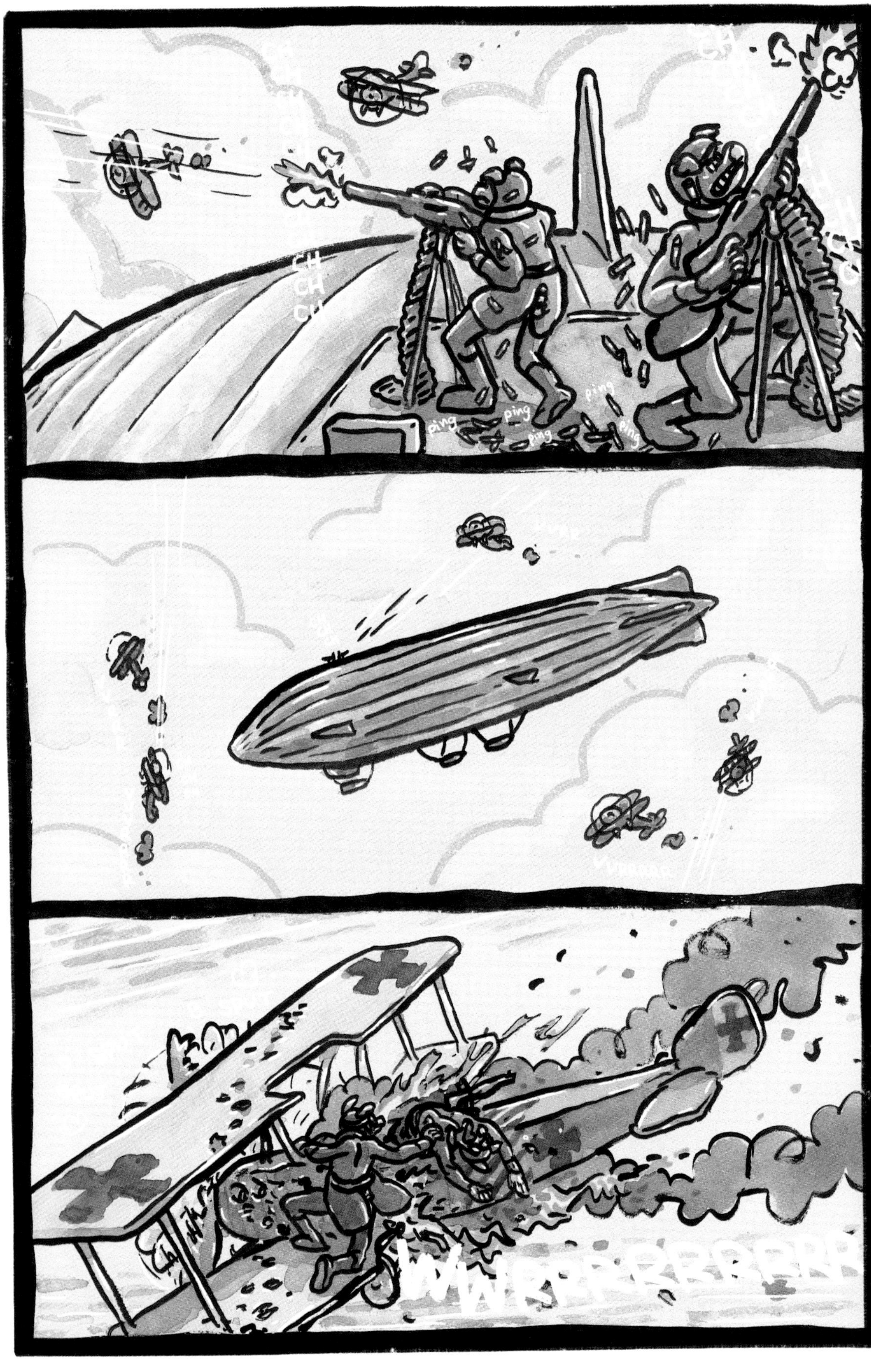
CH
CH
CH
CH
CH
ping
ping
ping
ping
ping
WWRRRRRRRR

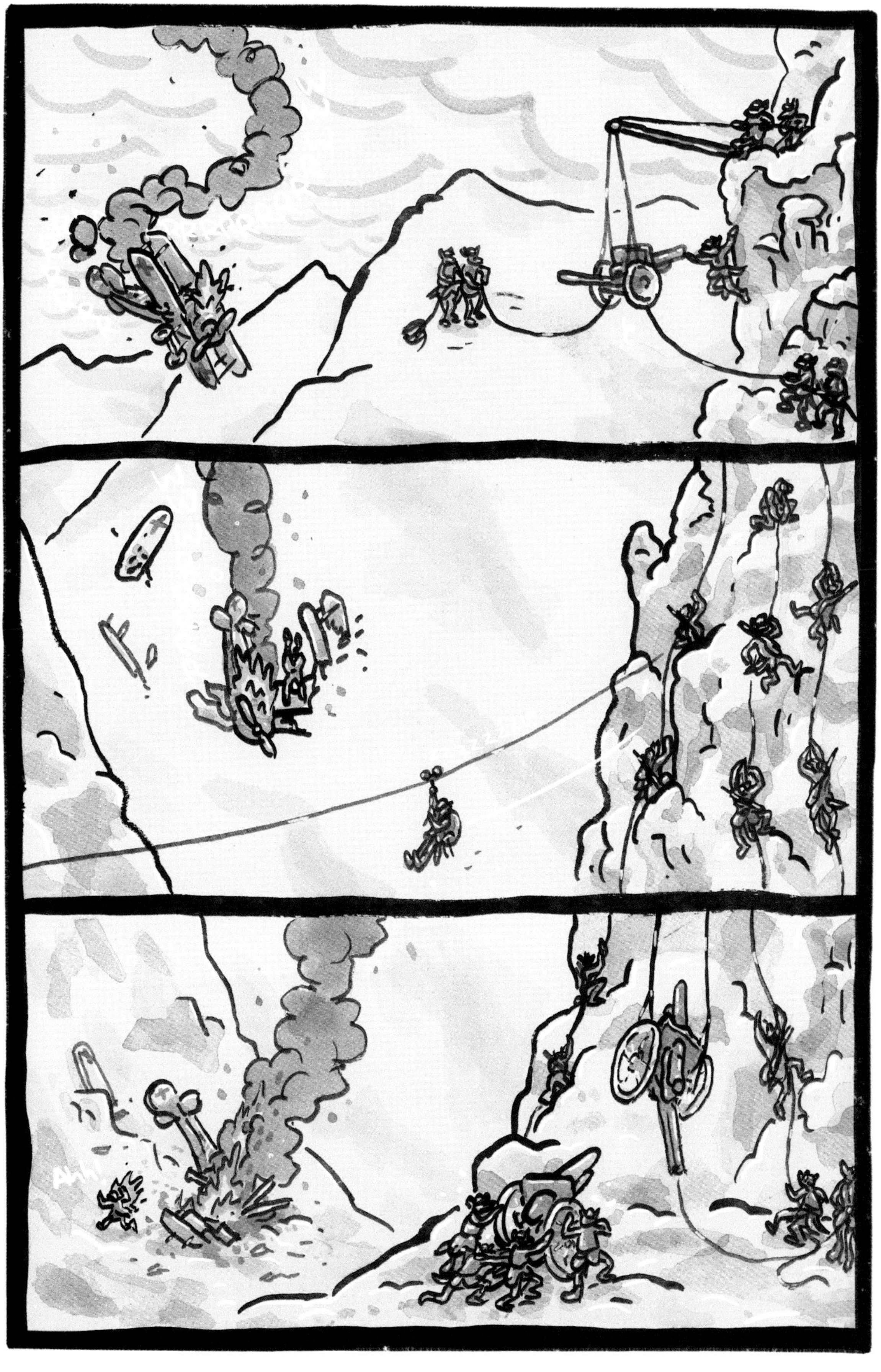
Ahh!

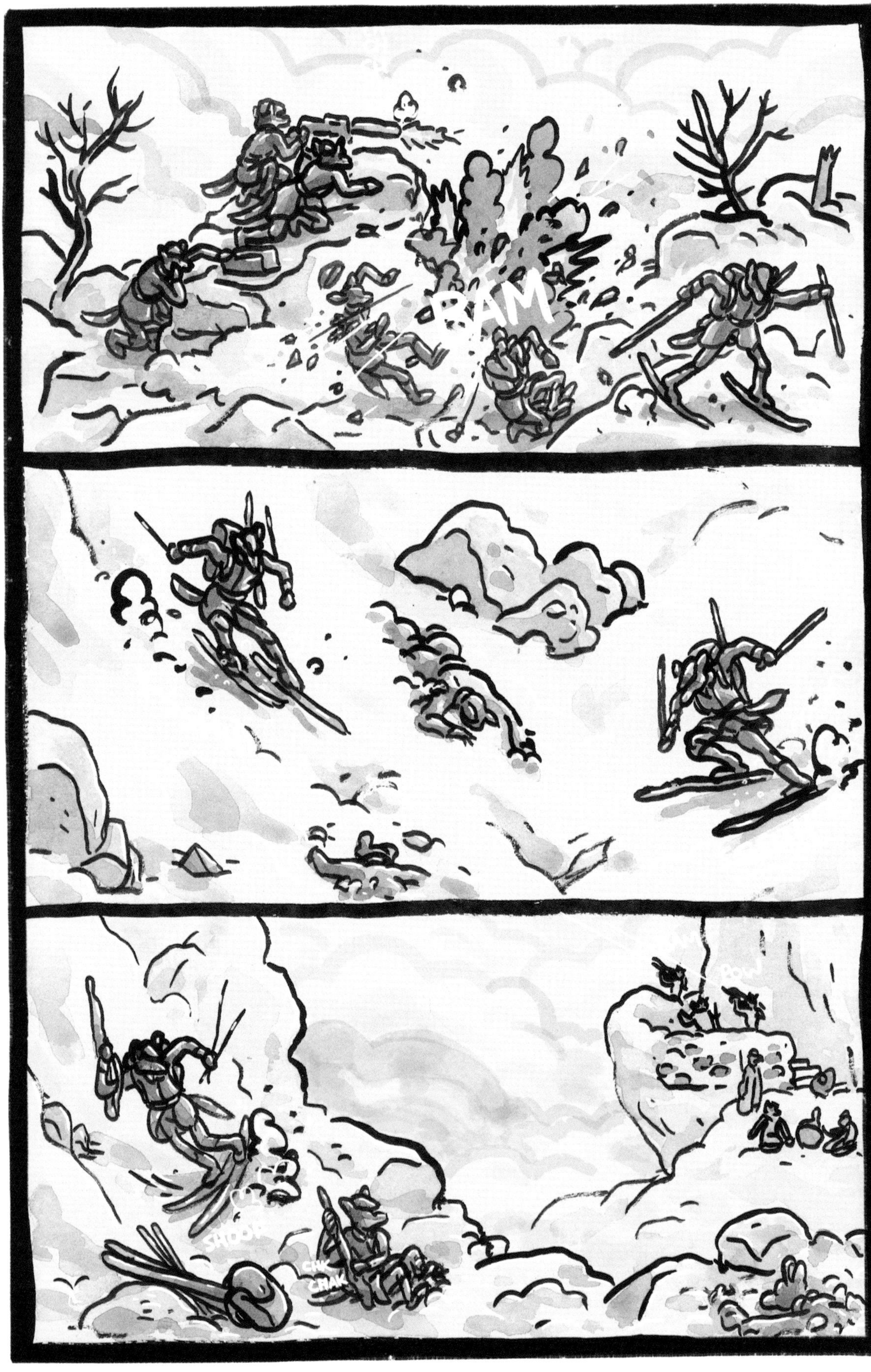
BAM
SHOOP
CHK
CHAK

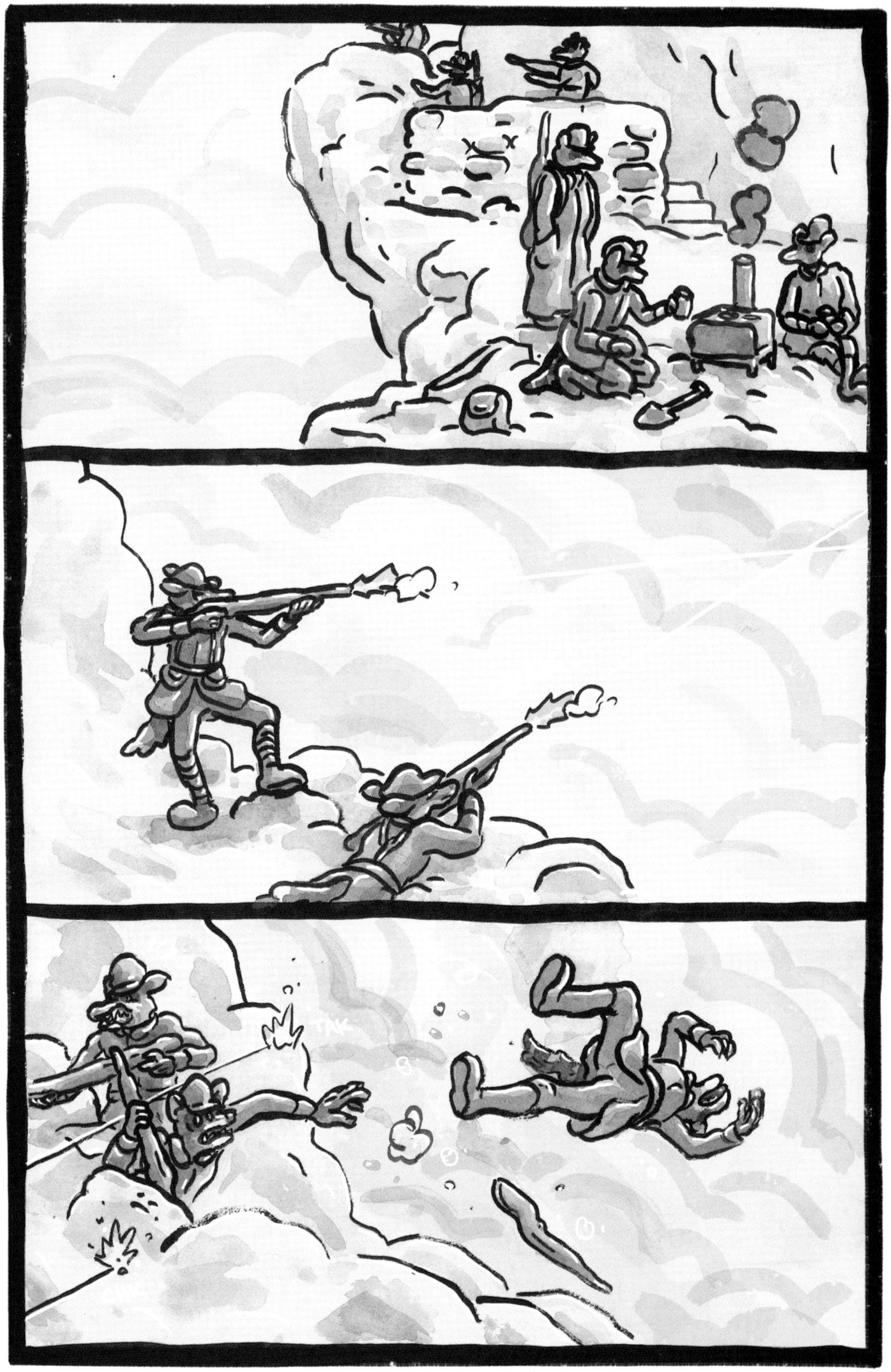
TAK

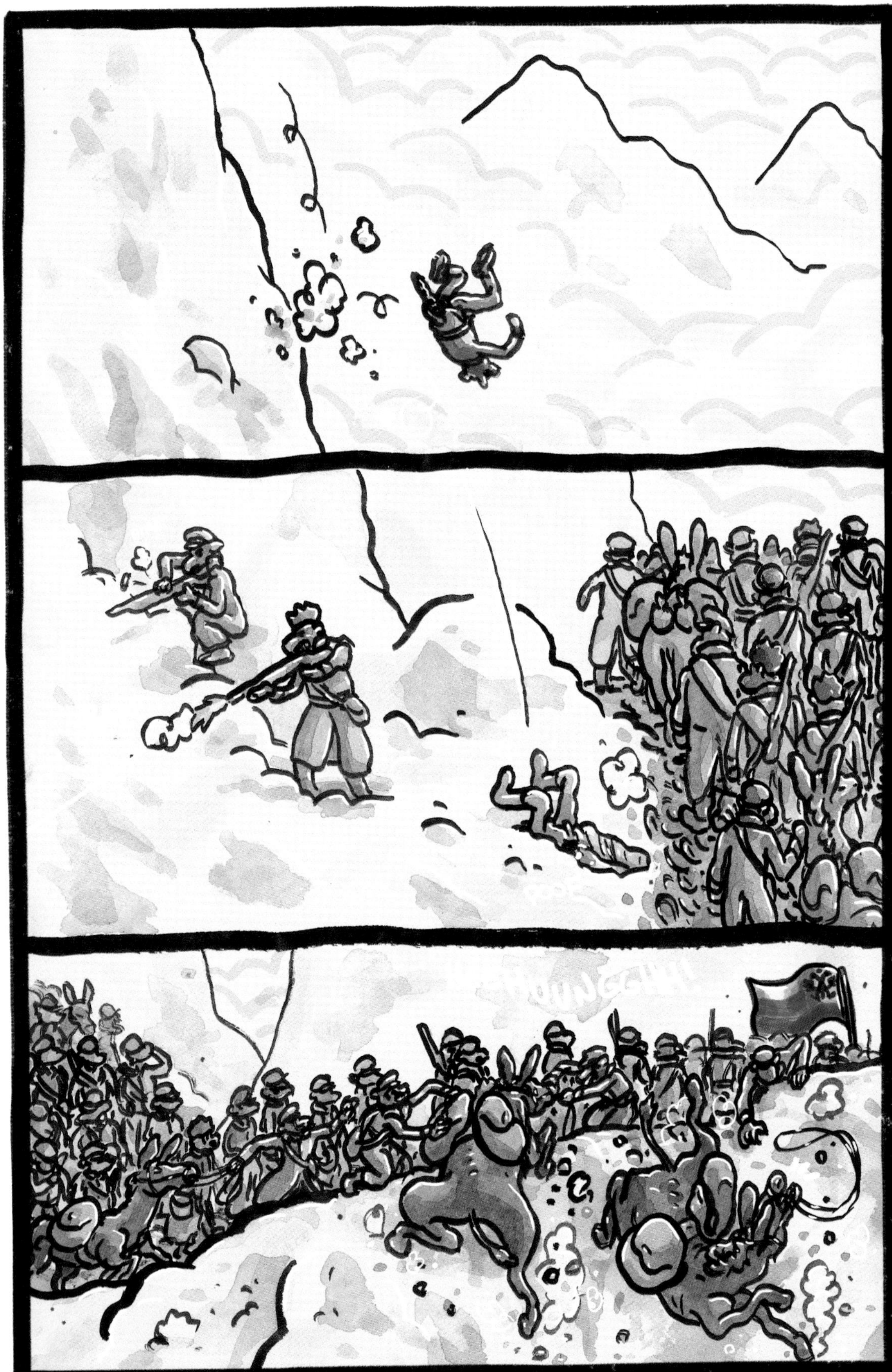

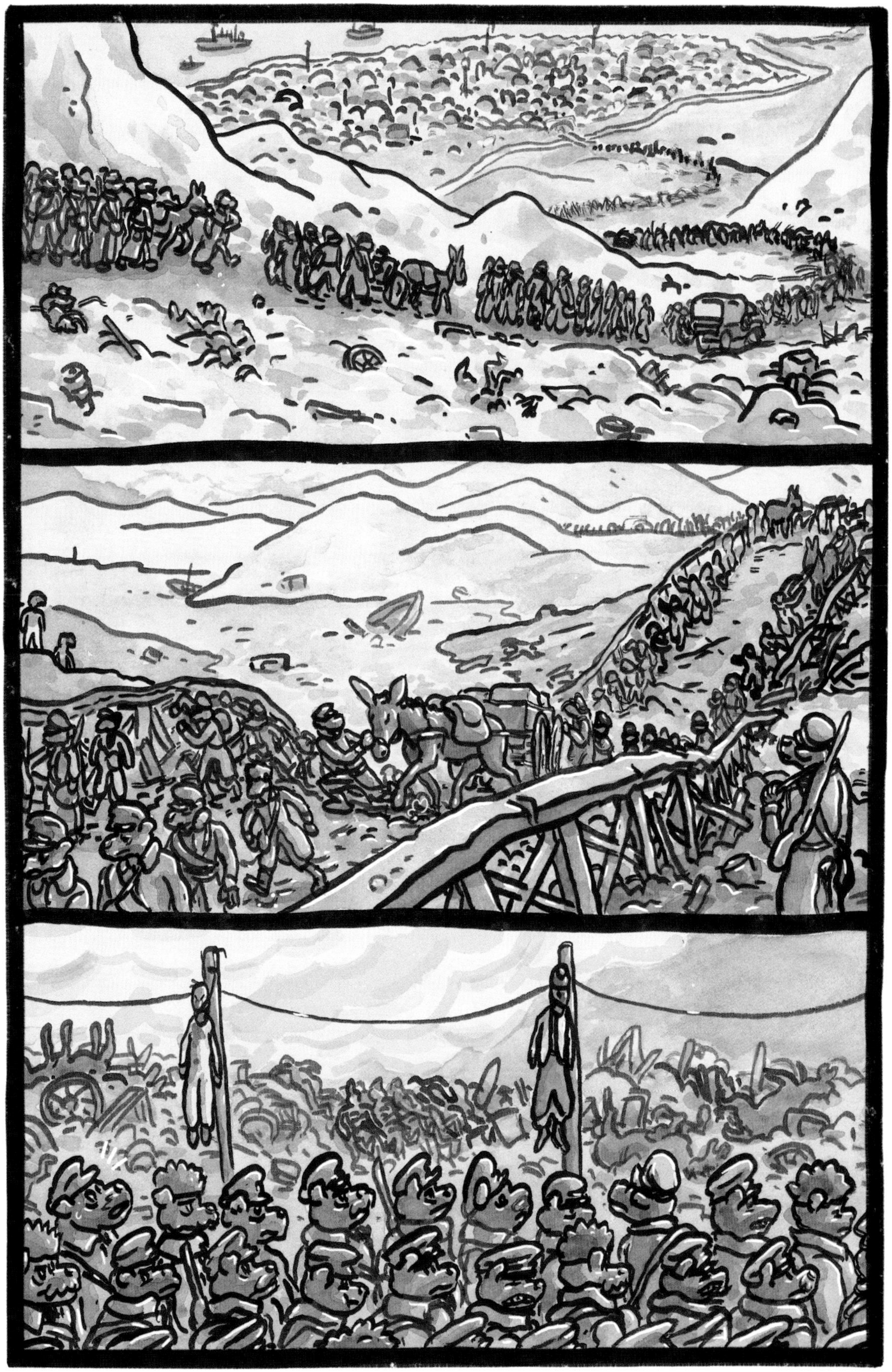

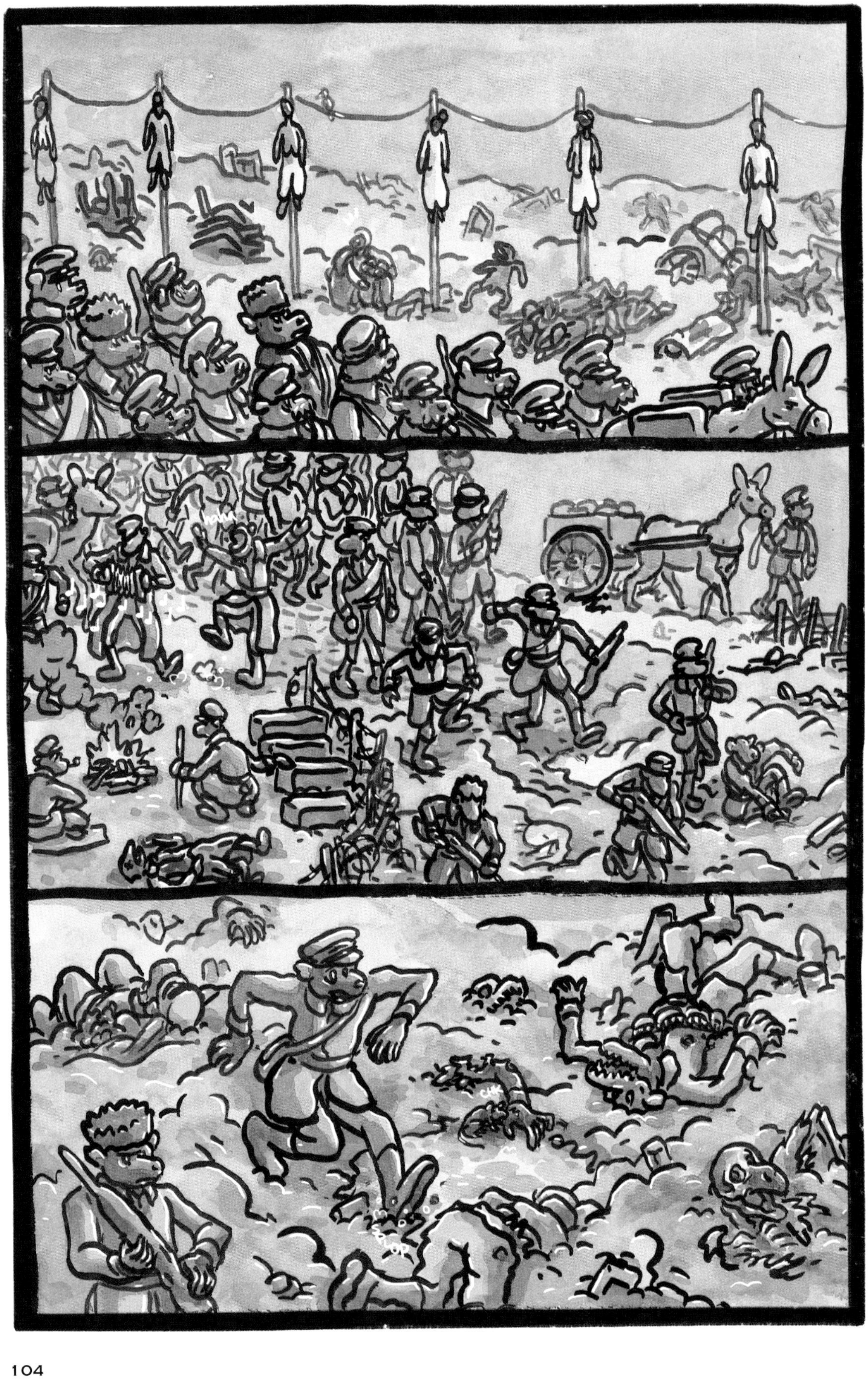
haha
CHK
SPLOP

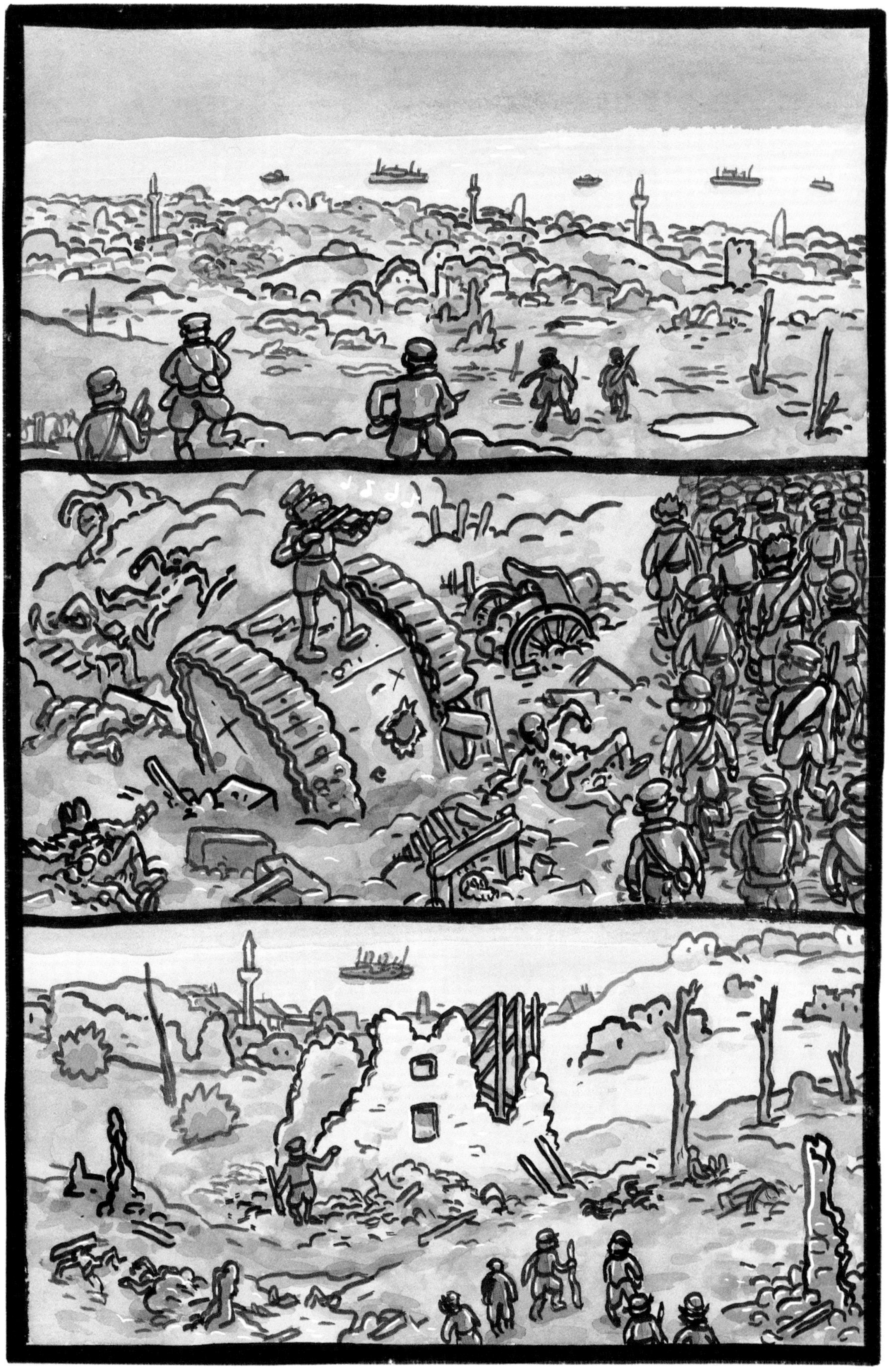

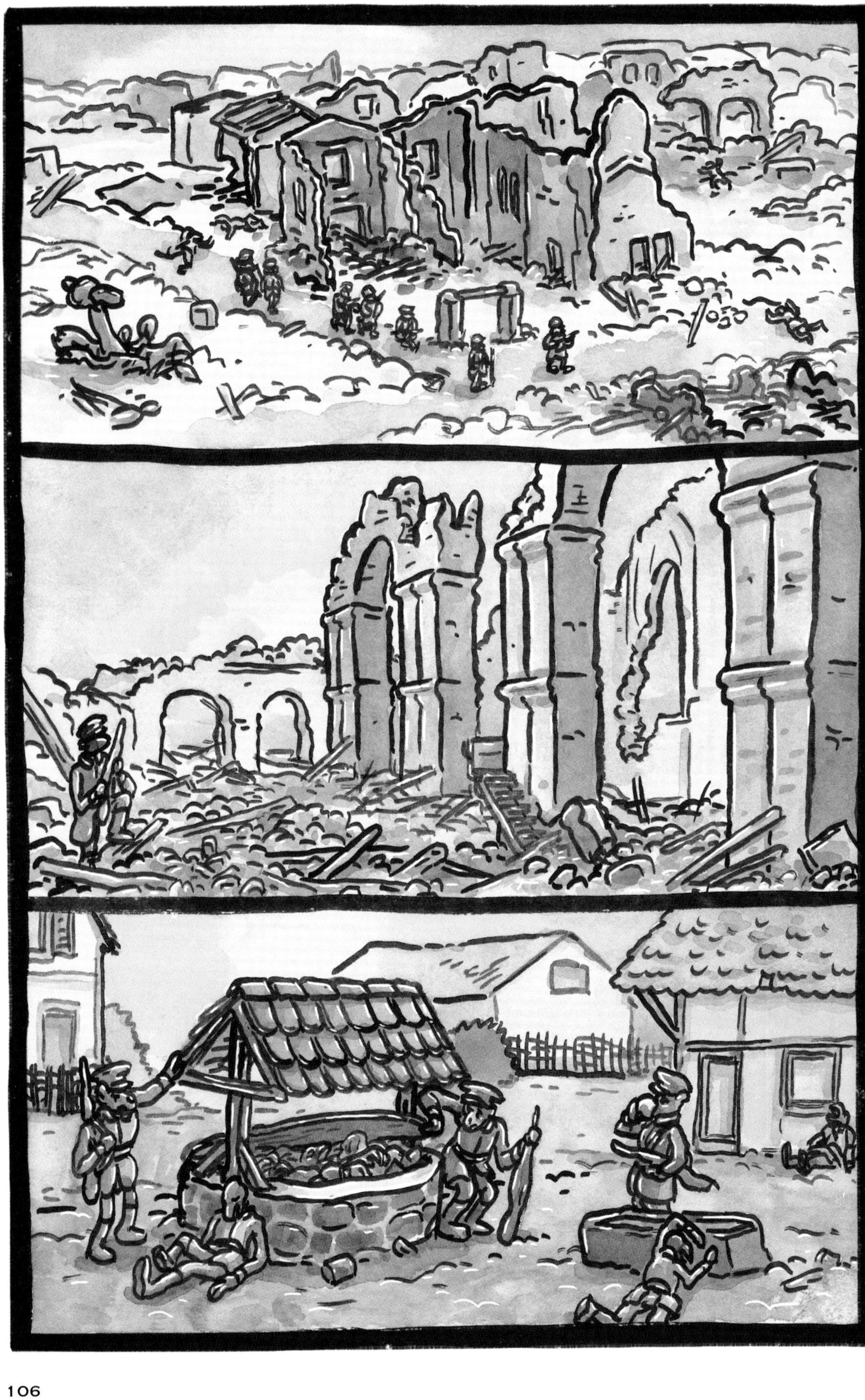

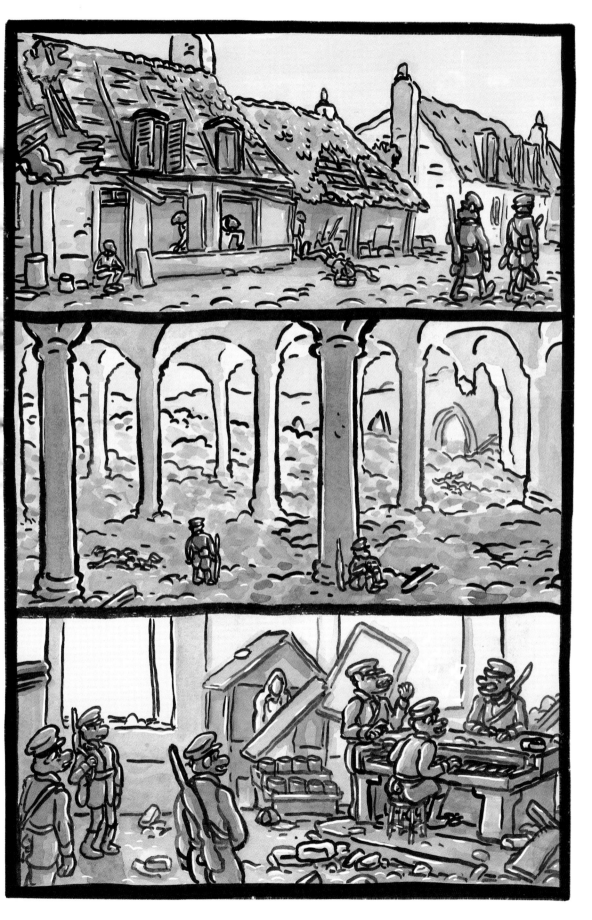

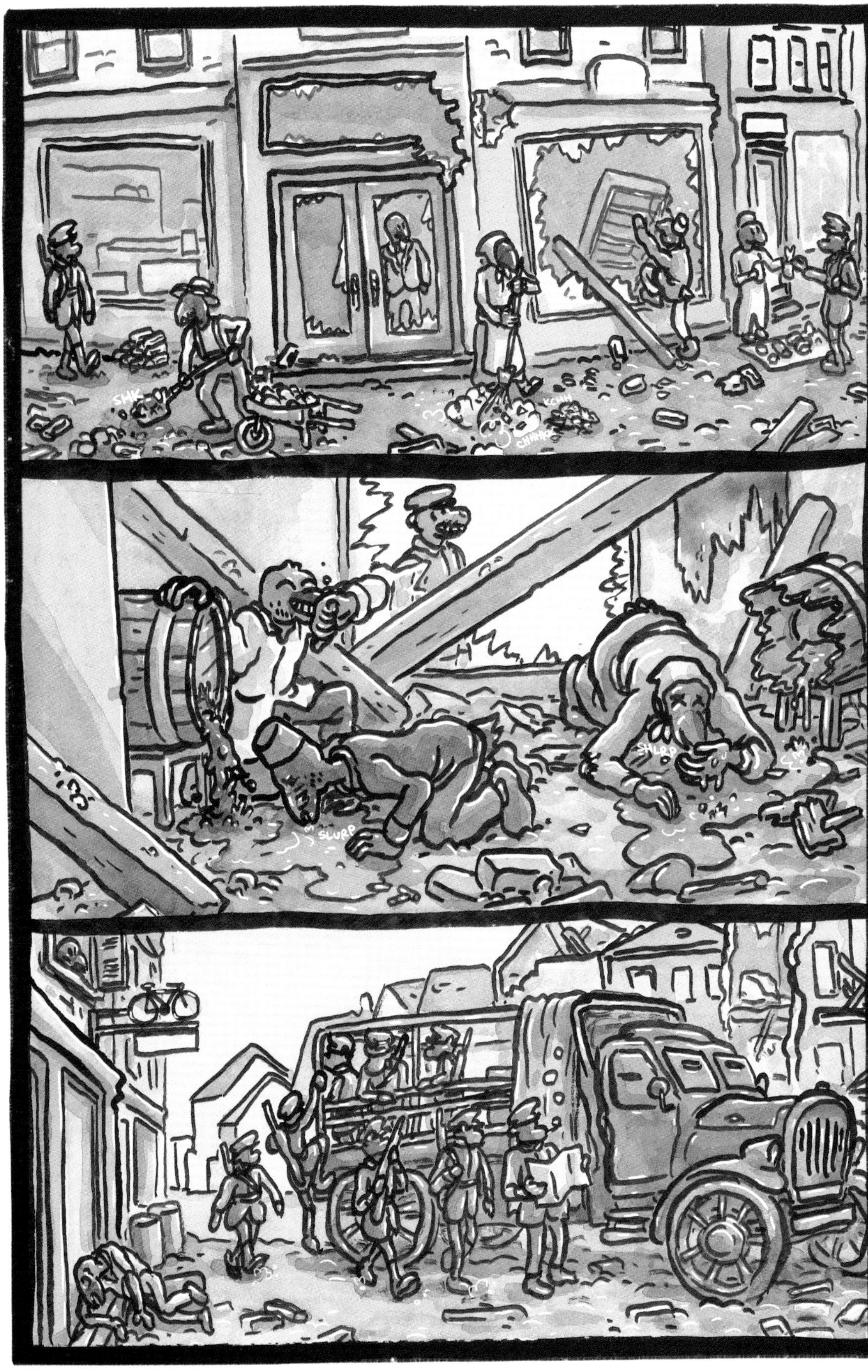
SHK
KCHH
CHHHKK
SHLRP
SLURP

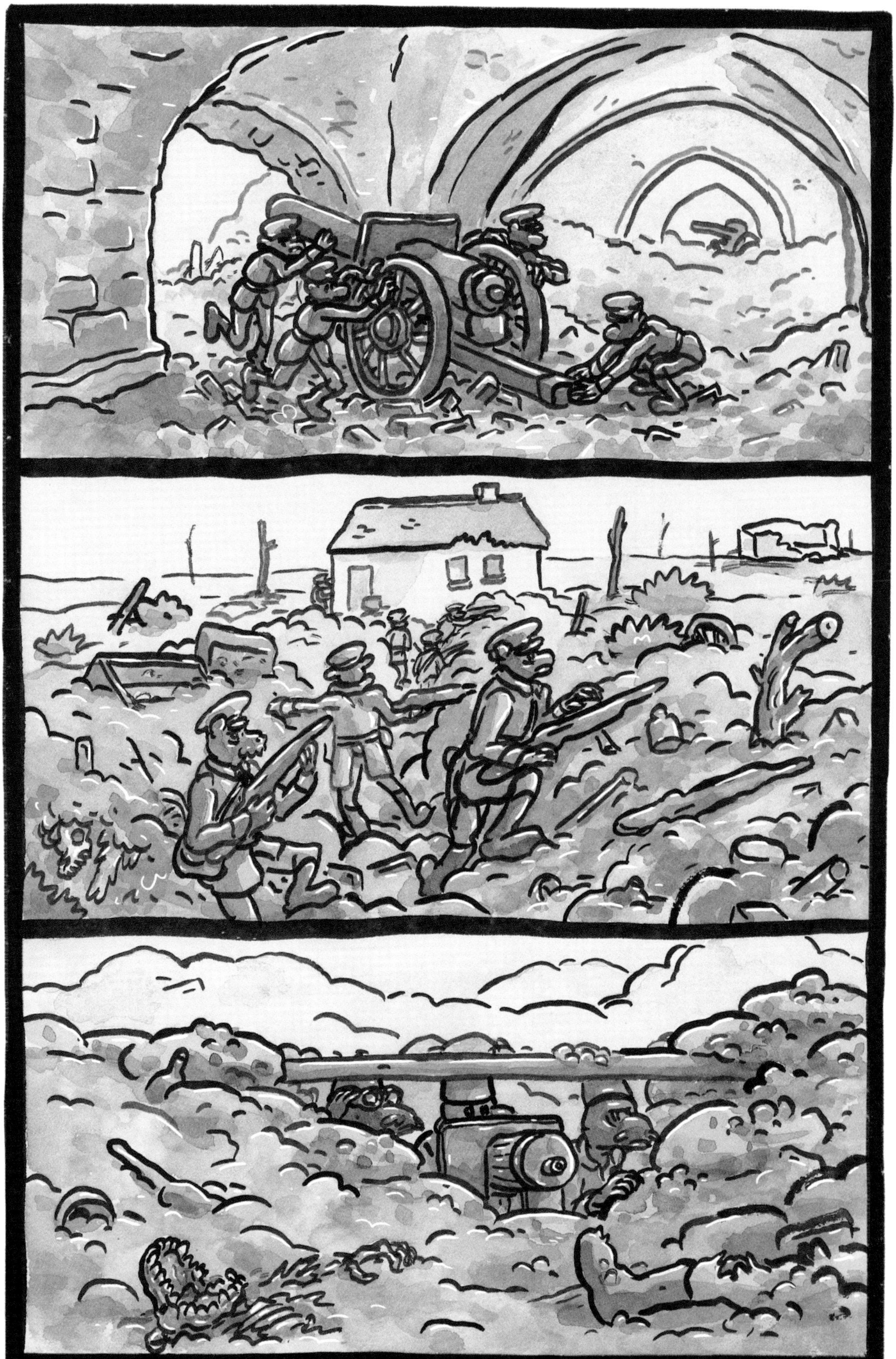

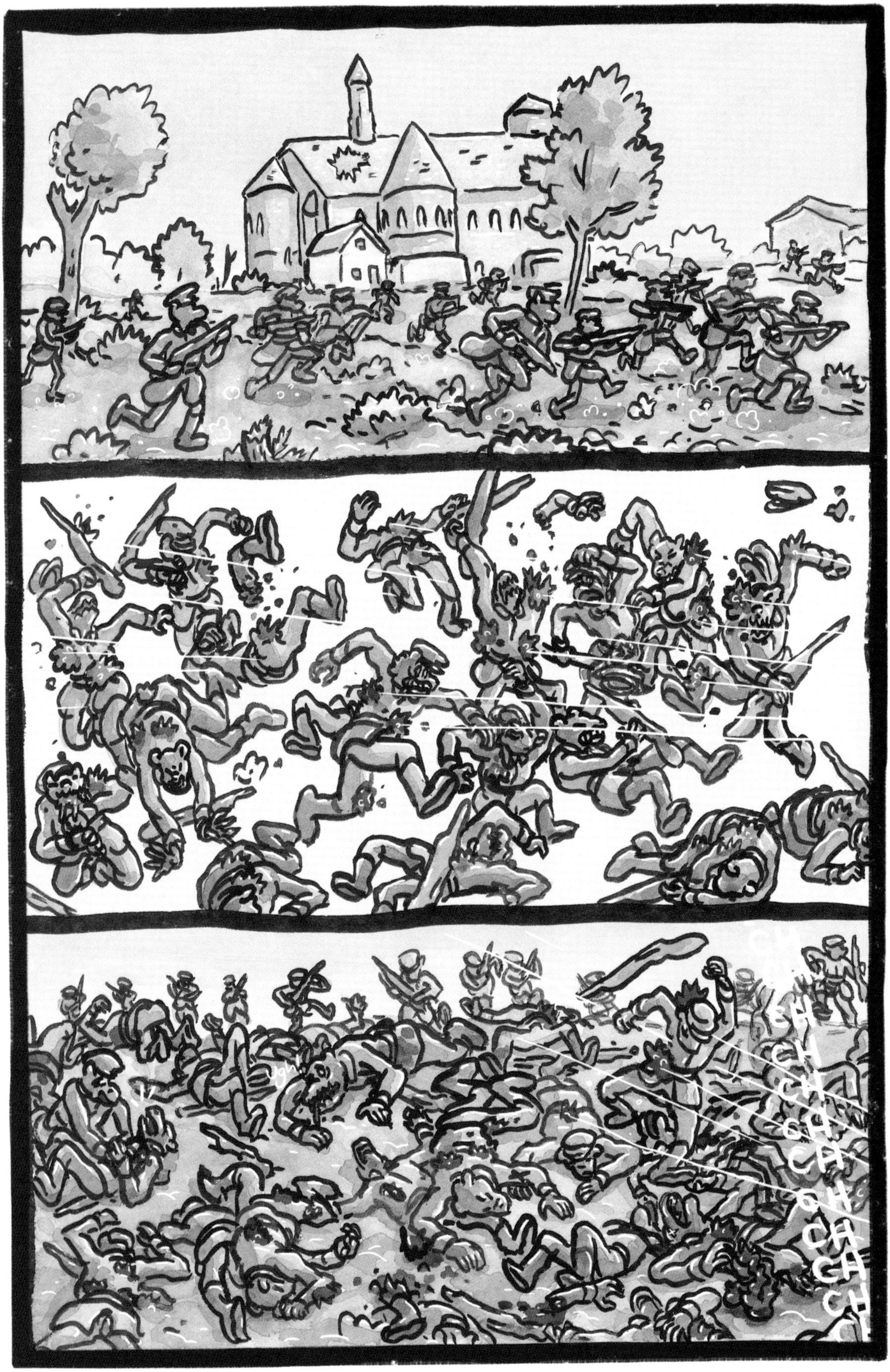
ugh!
CH CH CH CH CH CH CH CH CH CH

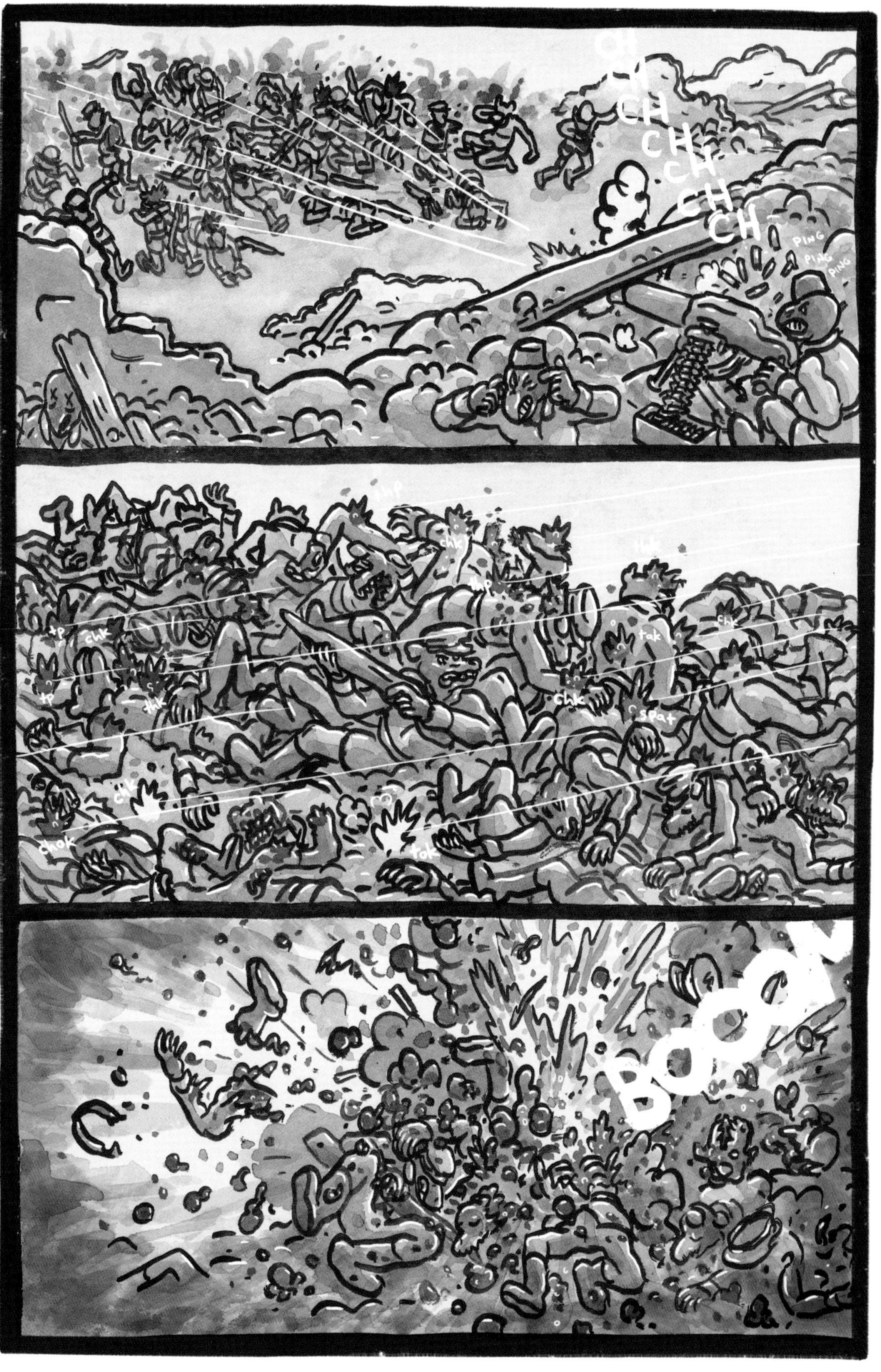
CH CH CH CH CH CH CH
PING PING PING
thp
chk
thk
thp
tp
chk
chk
tak
tp
thk
chk
spat
chk
chok
tok
BOOO

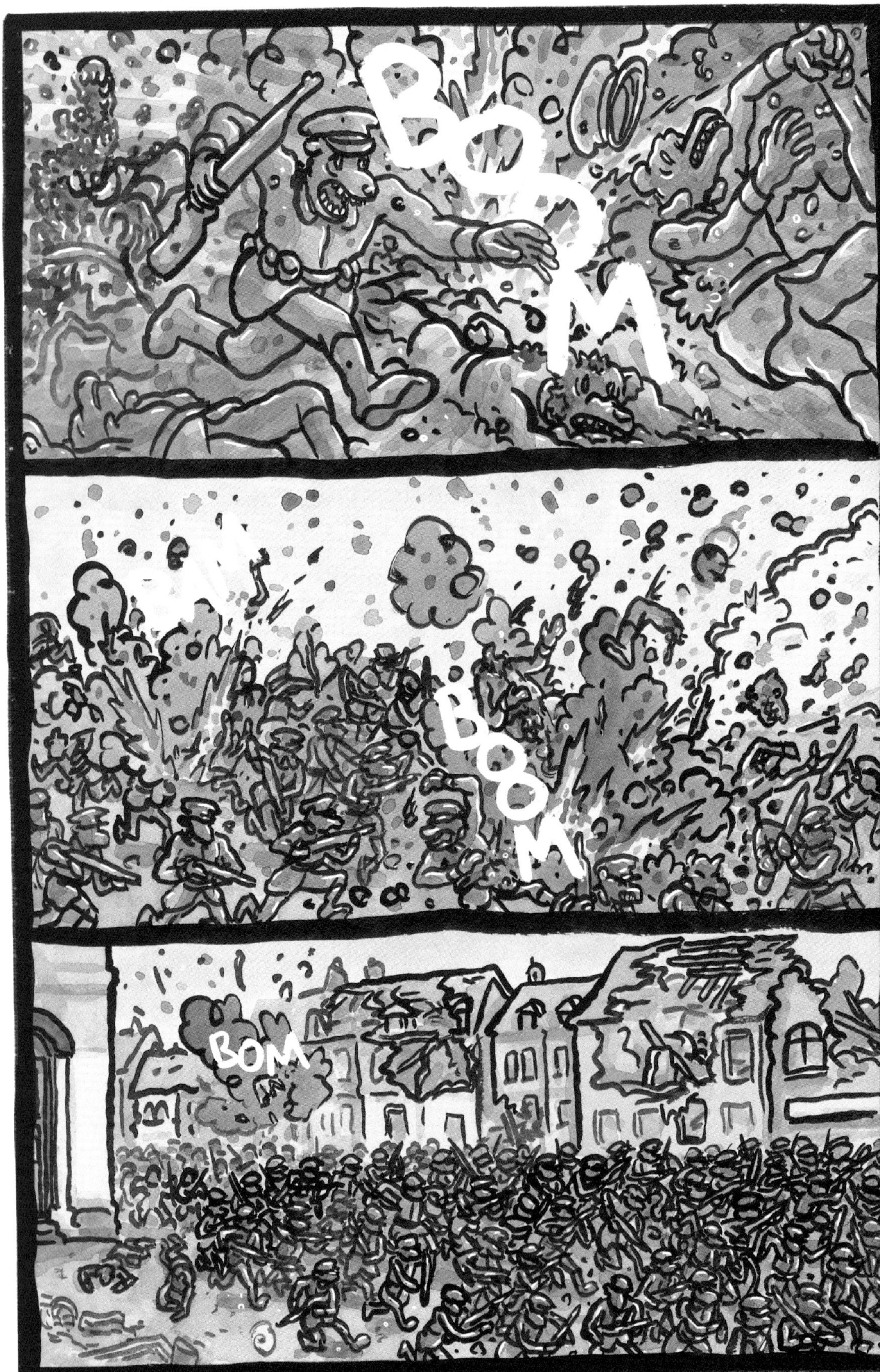
BOOM
BOOM
BOM

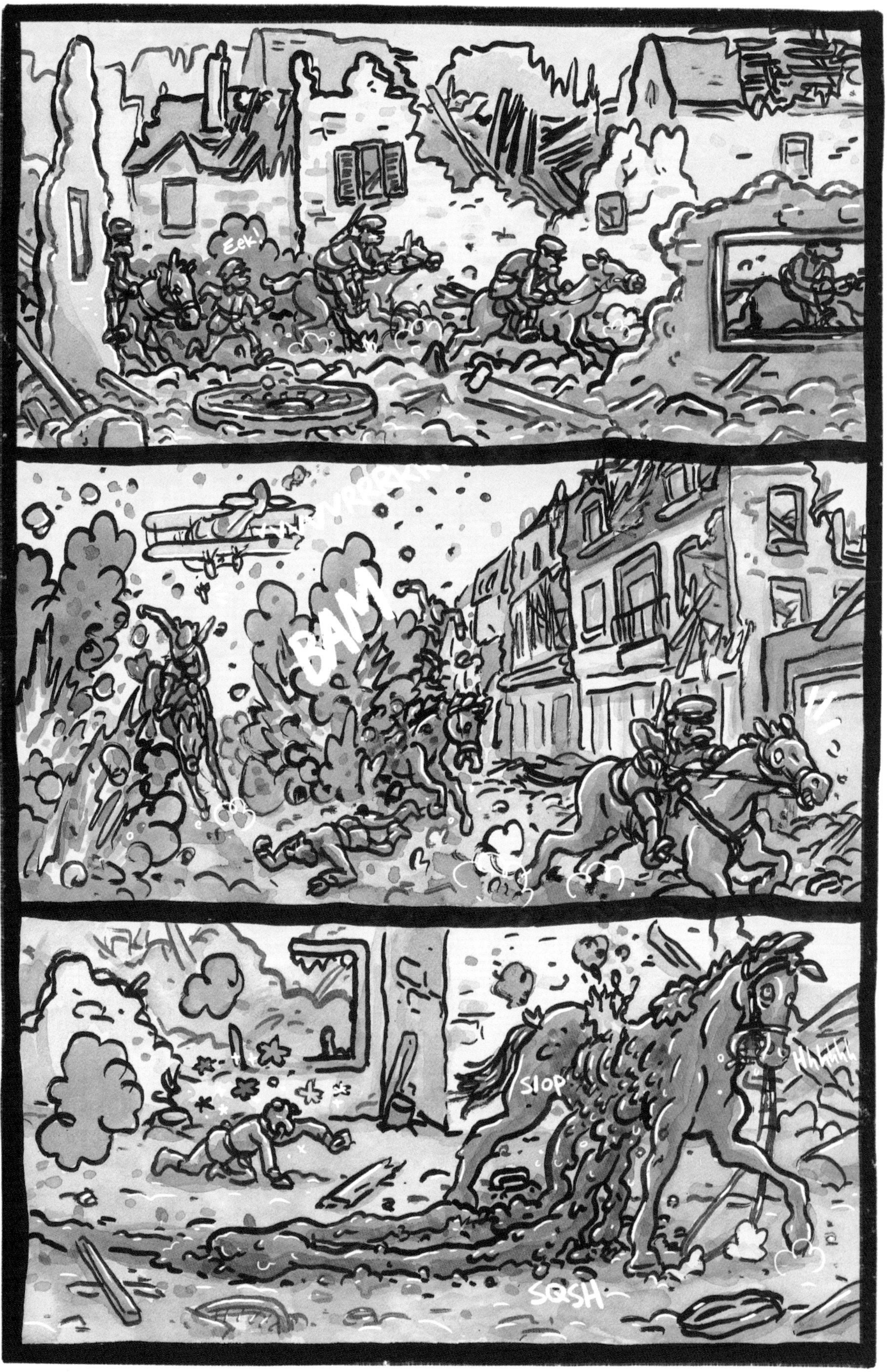
Eek!
BAM
SLOP
SQSH

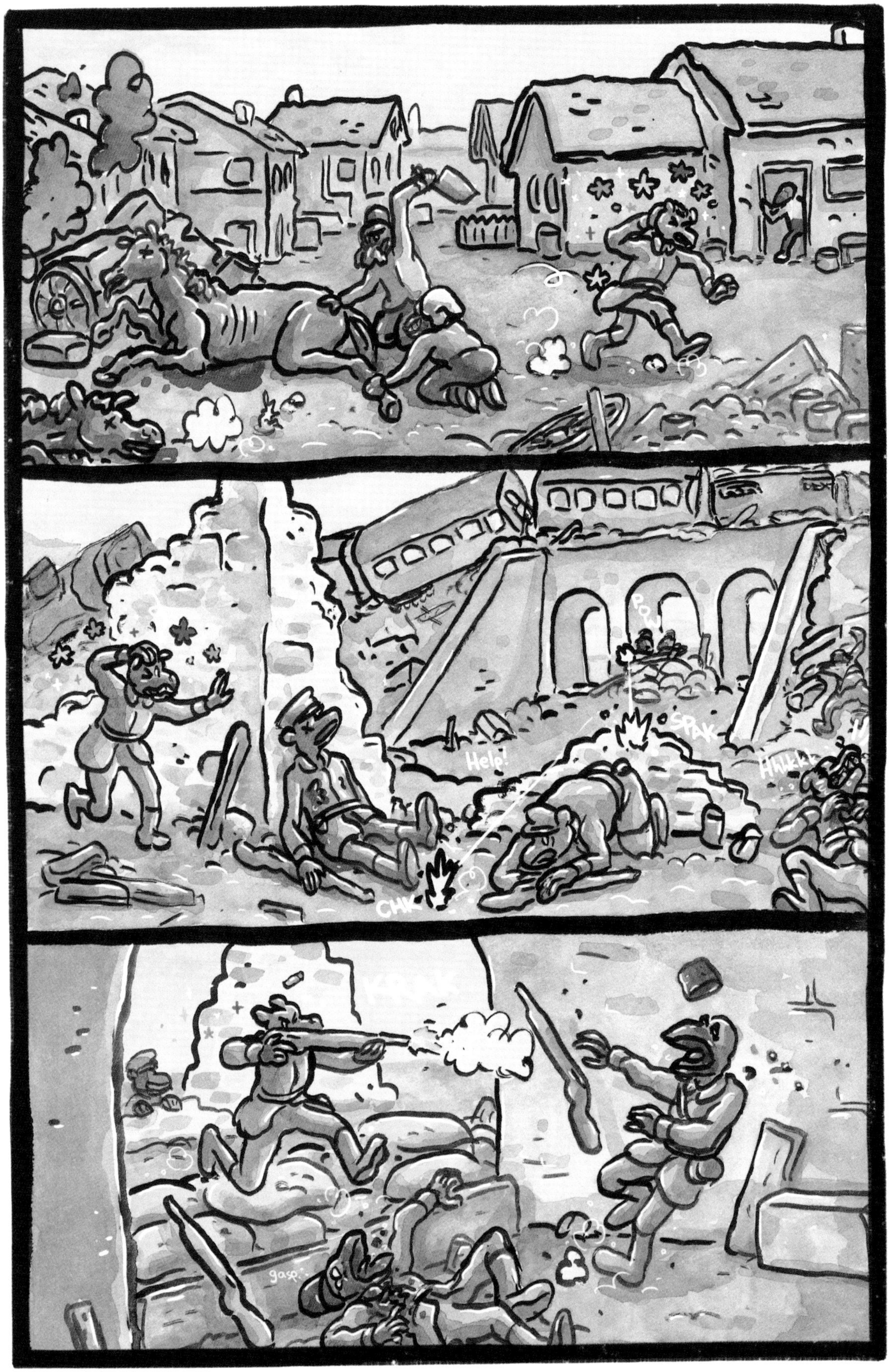
POW
SPAK
Help!
Hhkkk
CHK
KRAK
gasp

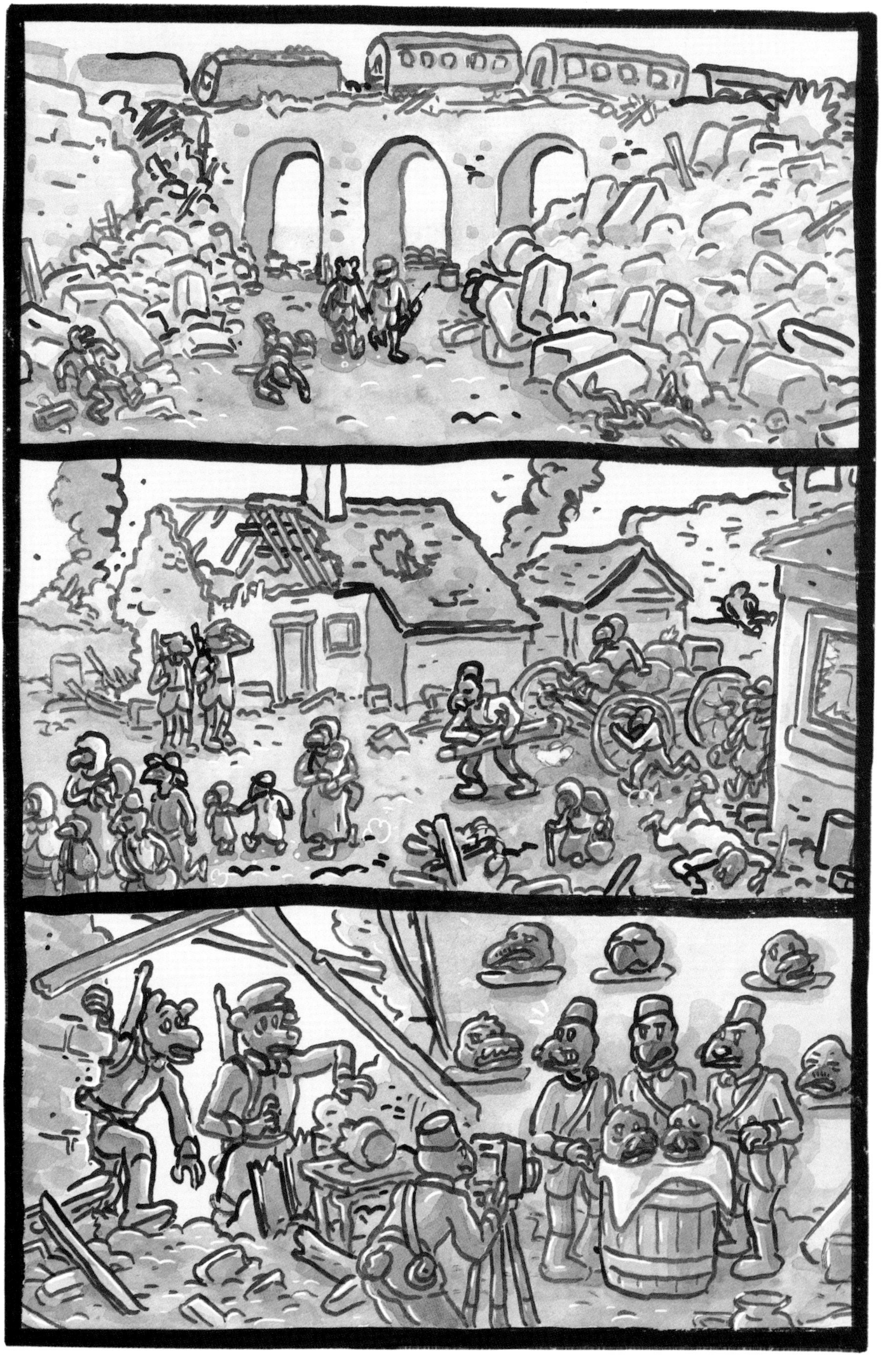

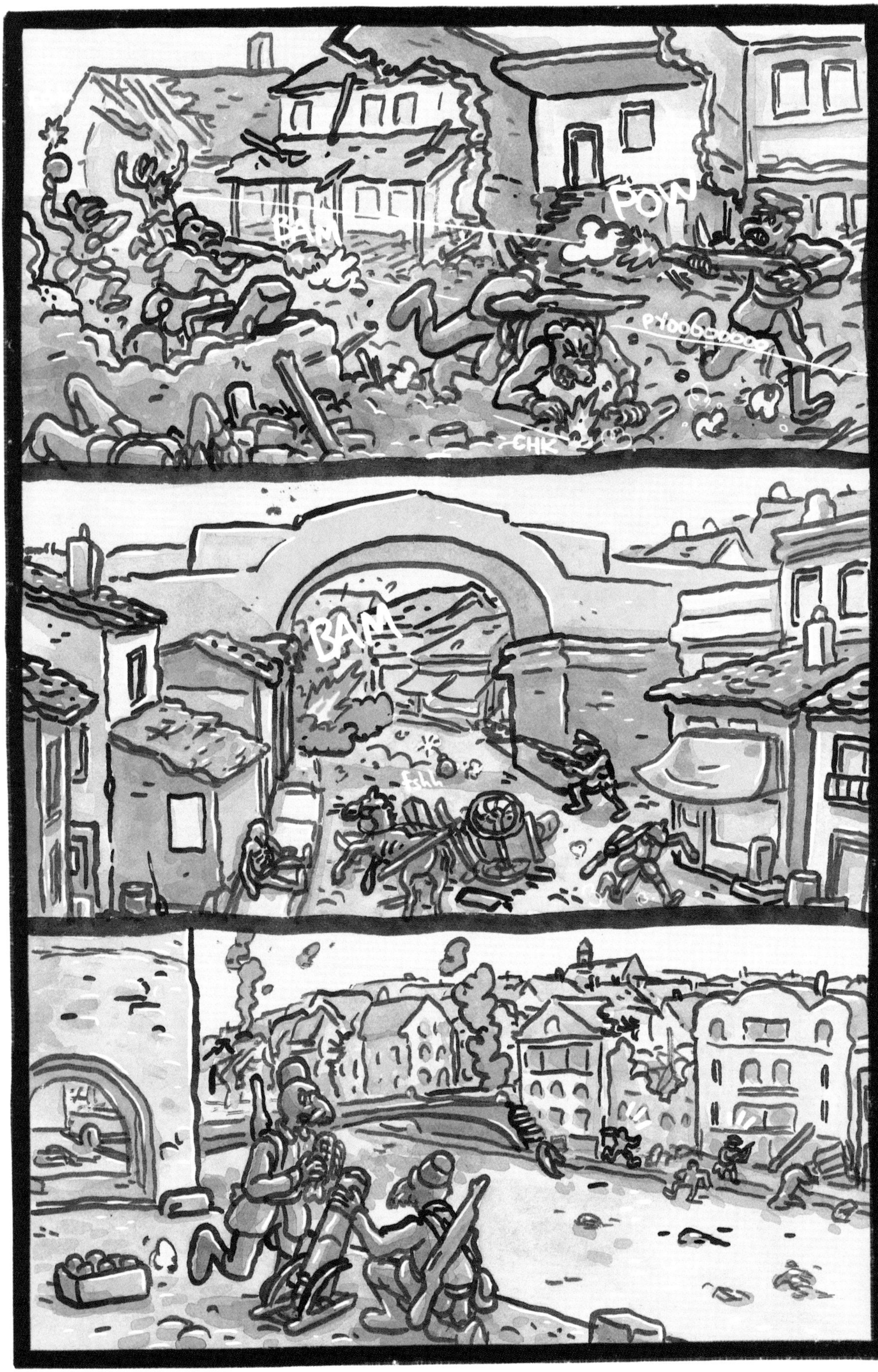
BAM
POW
PYOOOOOOOO
CHK
BAM

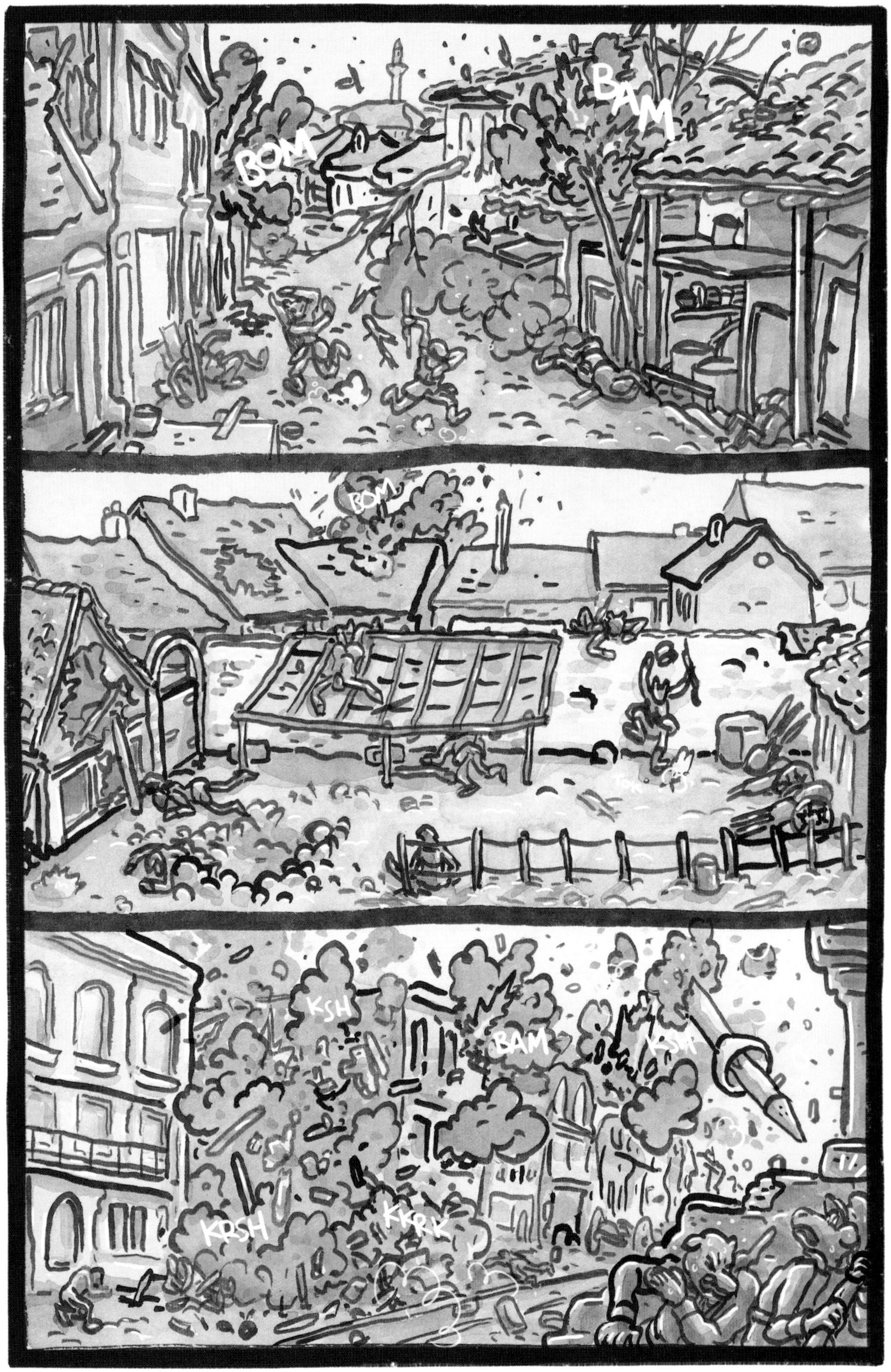
BOM
BAM
BOM
KSH
BAM
KSH
KRSH
KKRK

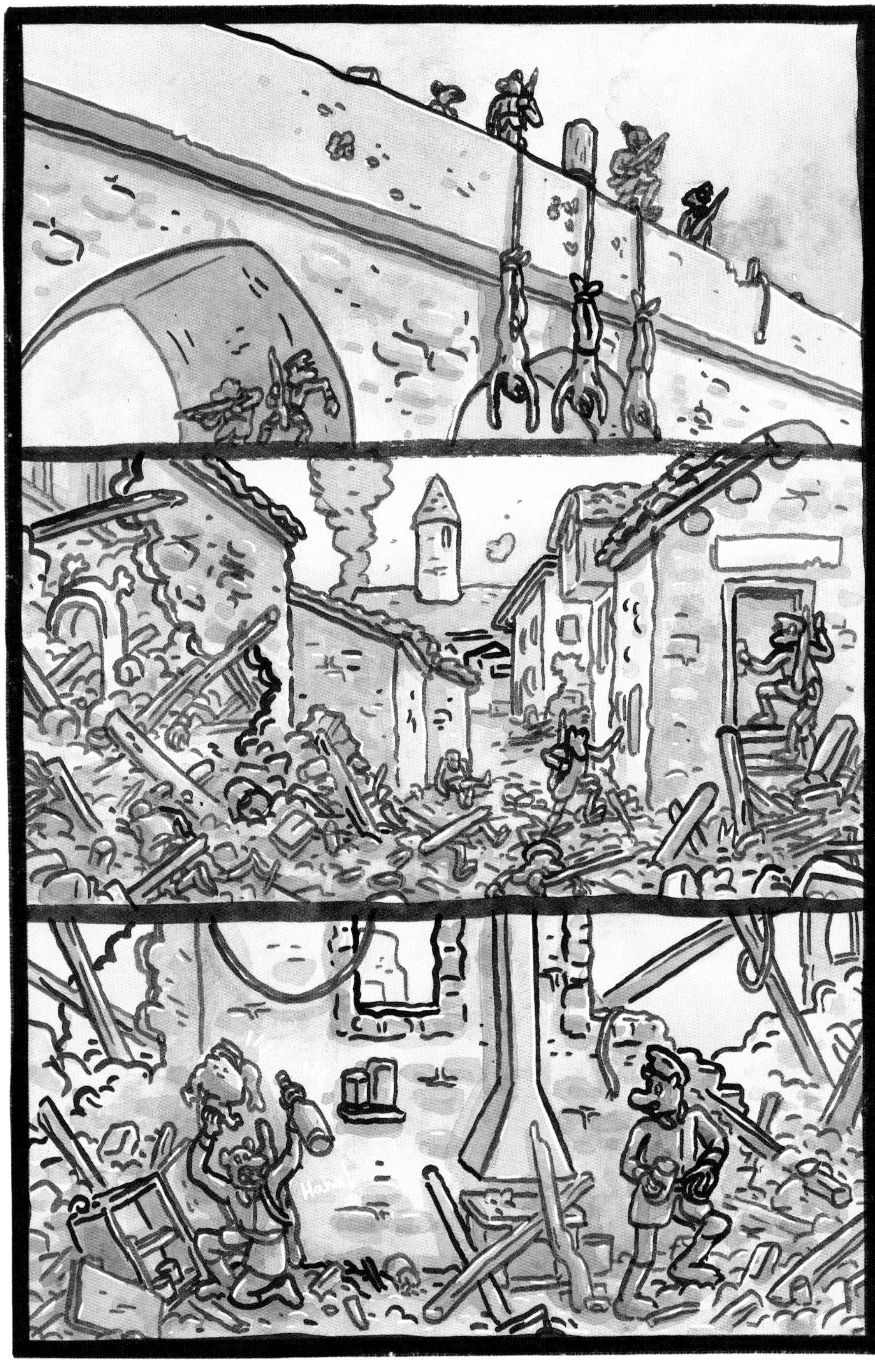

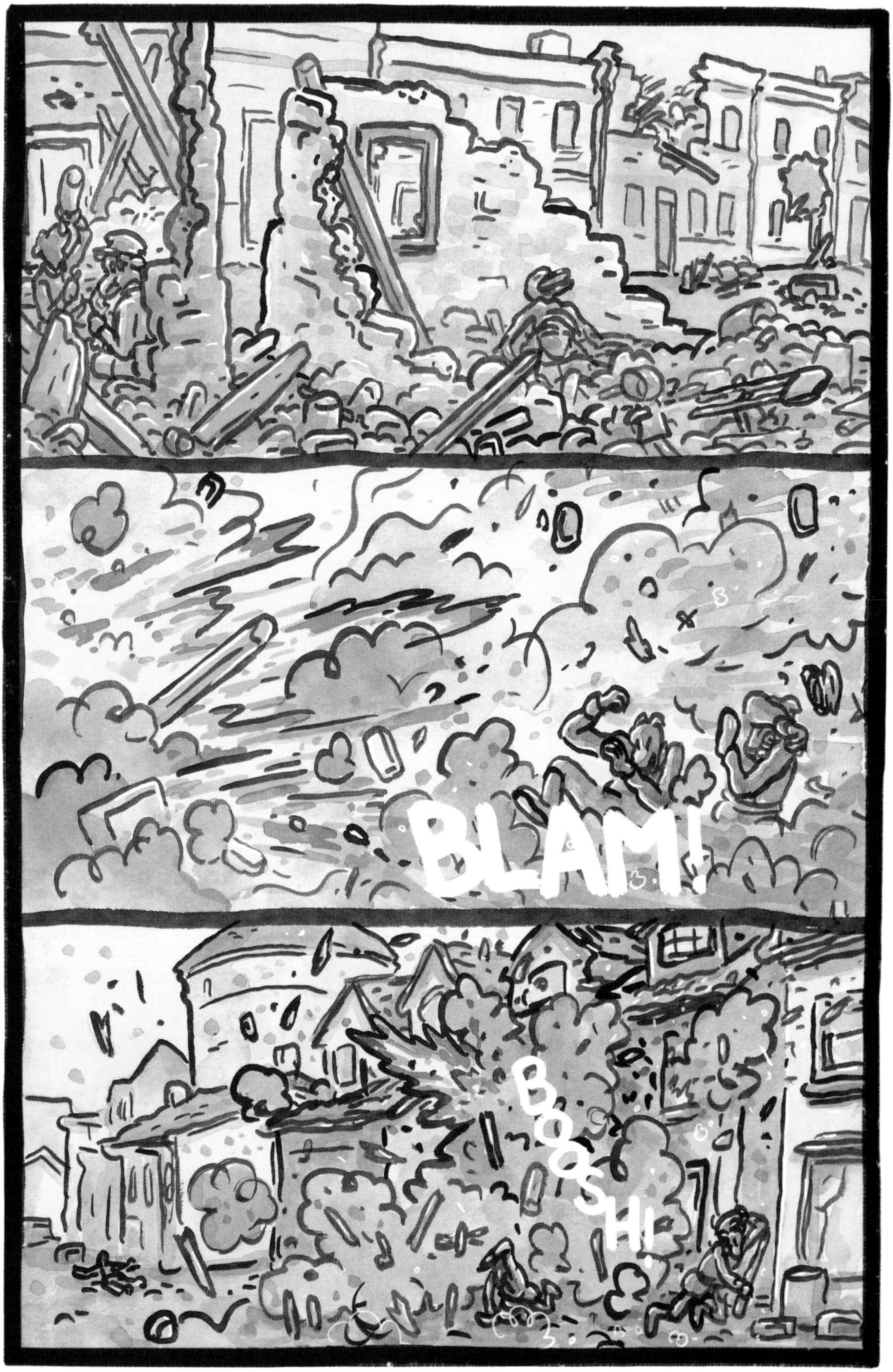
BLAM!
BOOSH!

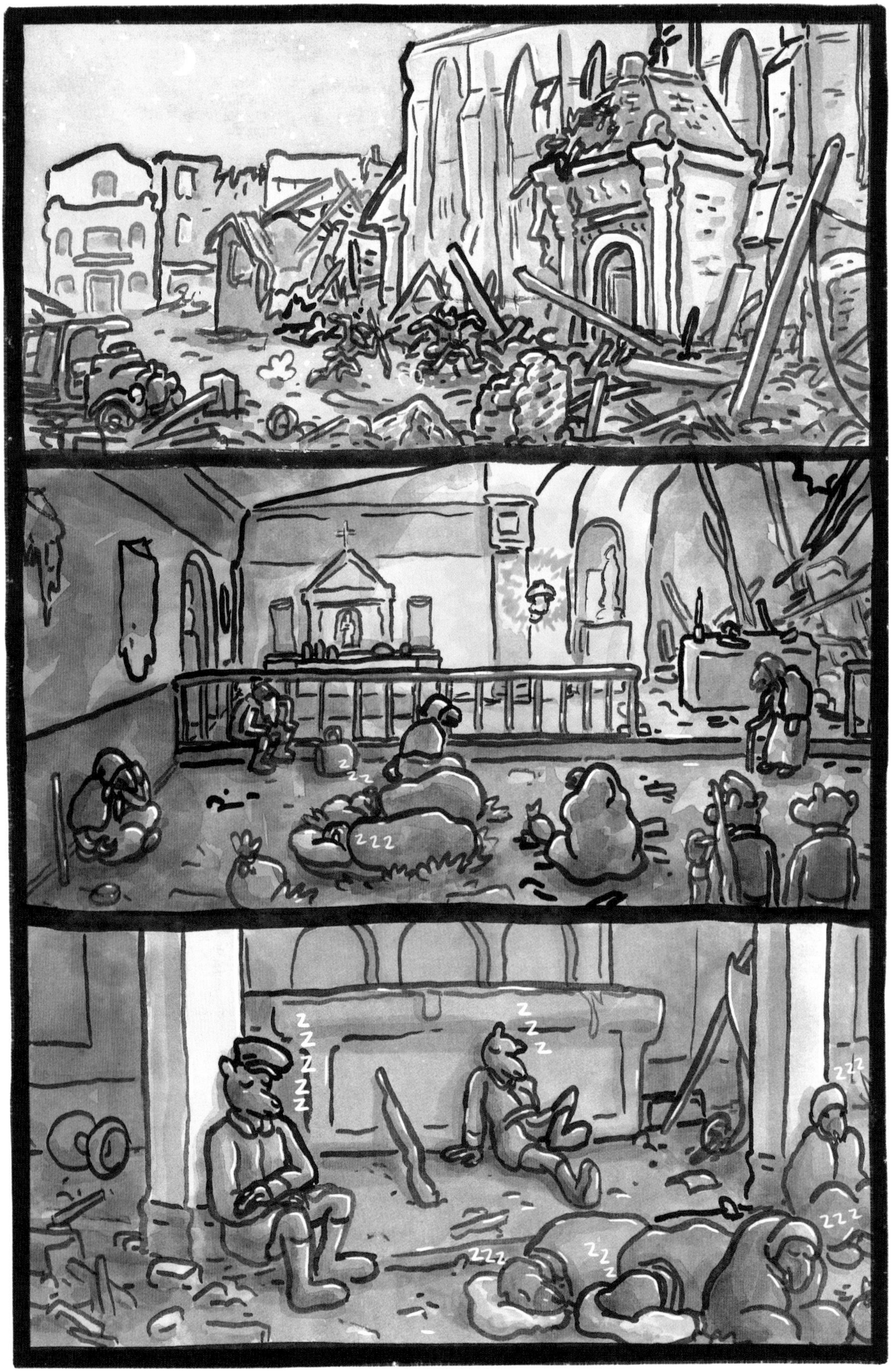
zzz
zzz
ZZZZZ
ZZZ
zzz
zzz
zzz
zzz

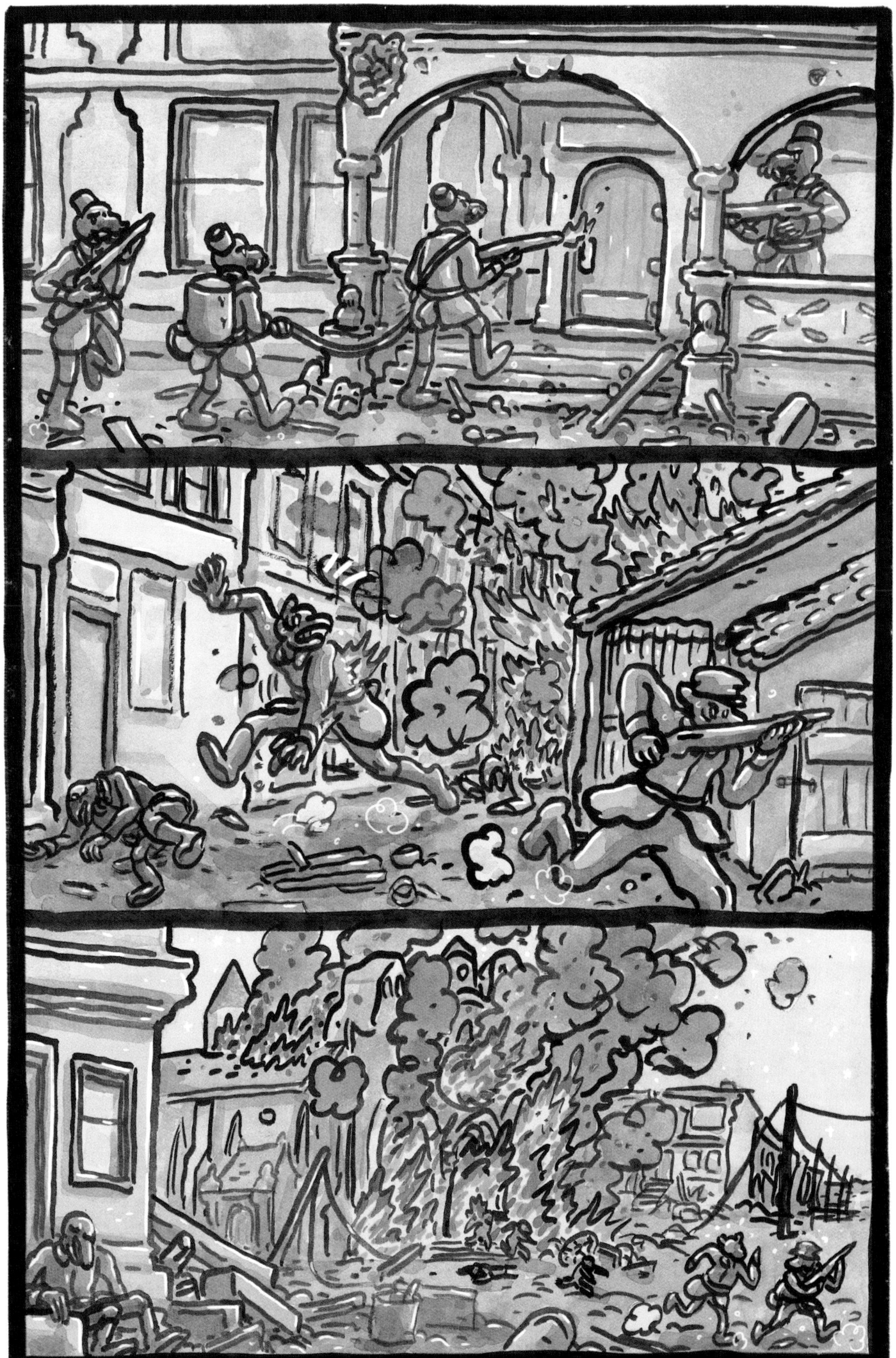

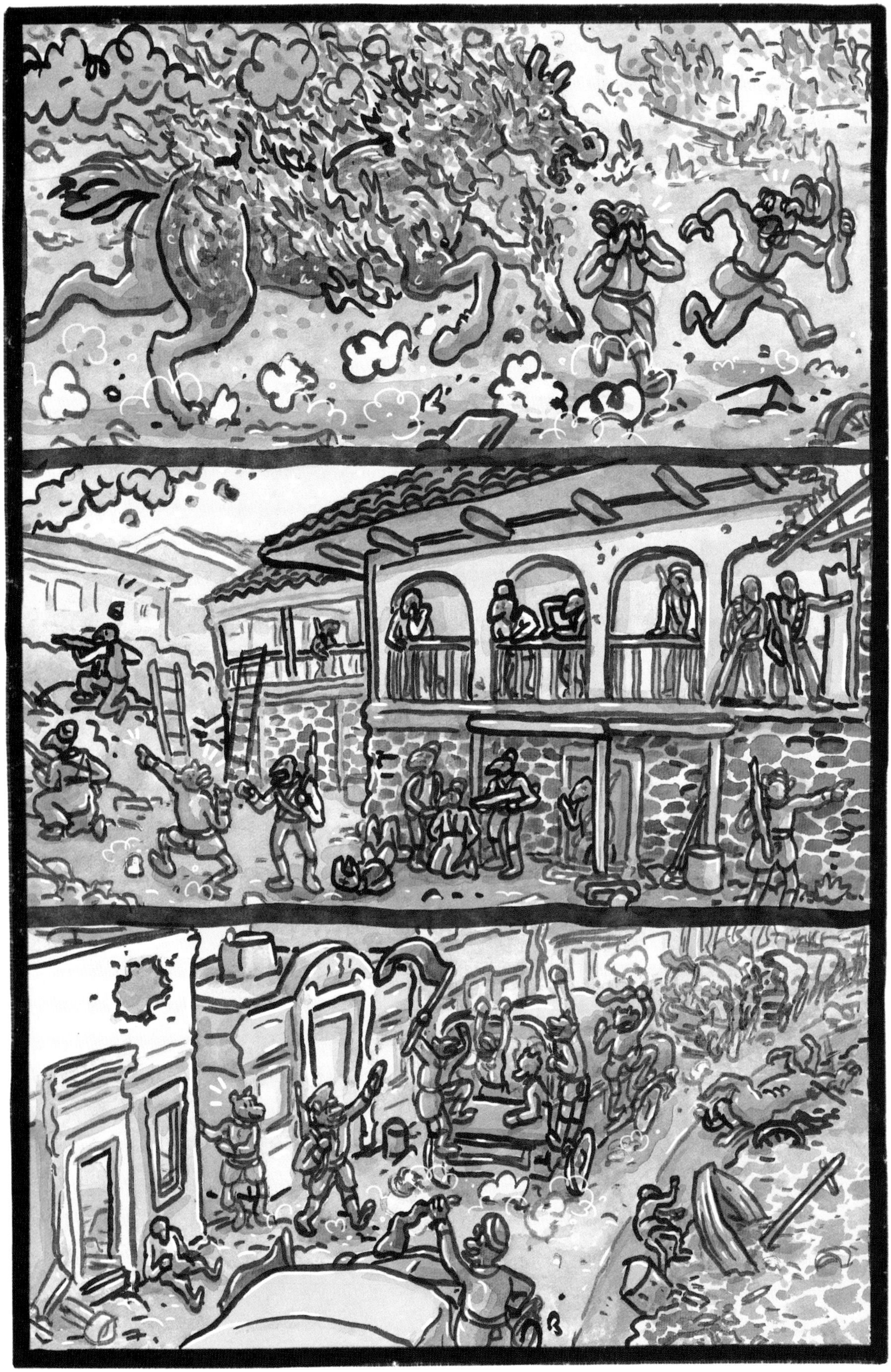

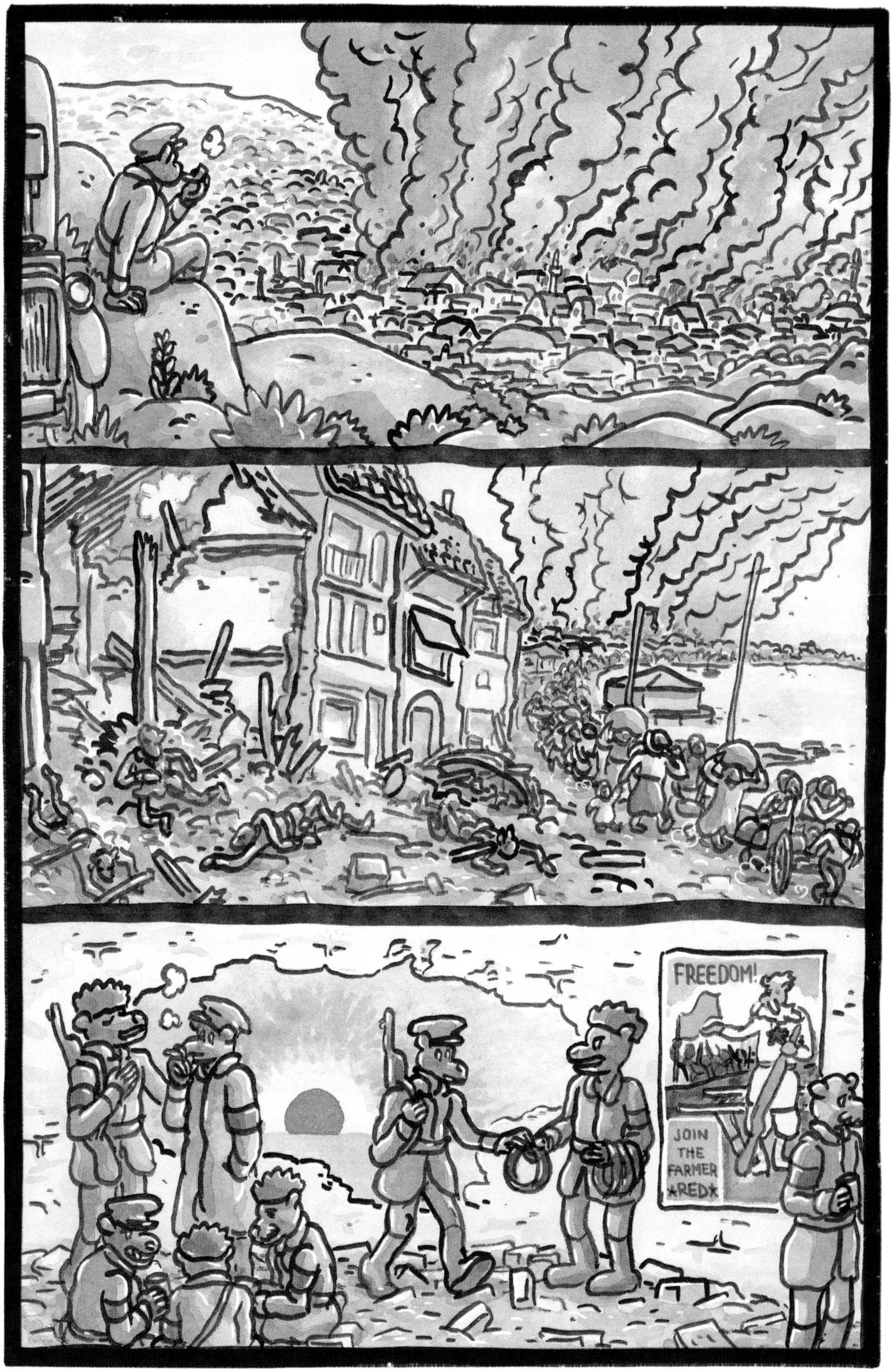
FREEDOM!
JOIN THE FARMER
★RED★

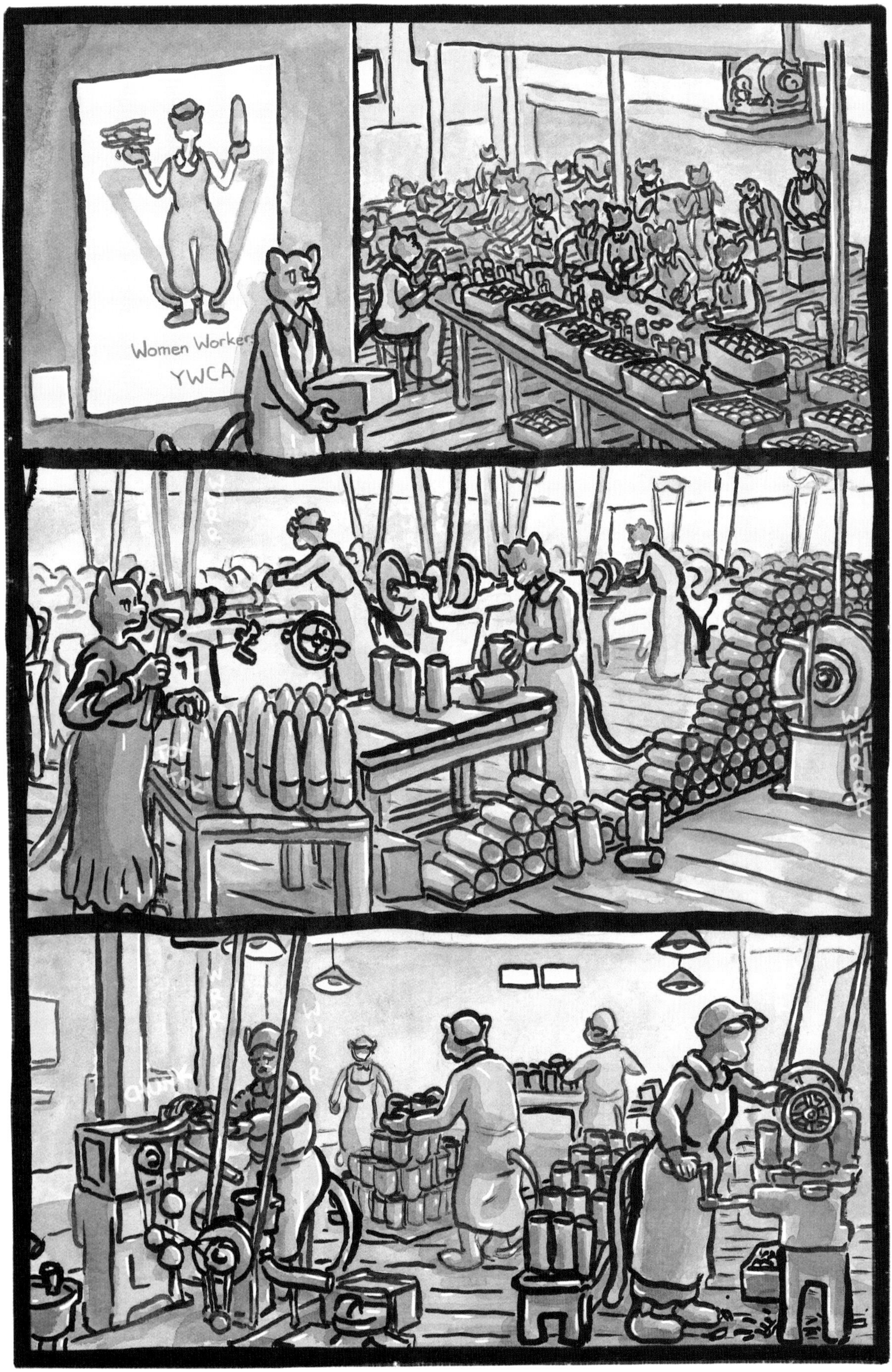
Women Workers
YWCA
TOK
TOK
WRRR
WRRR
chunk

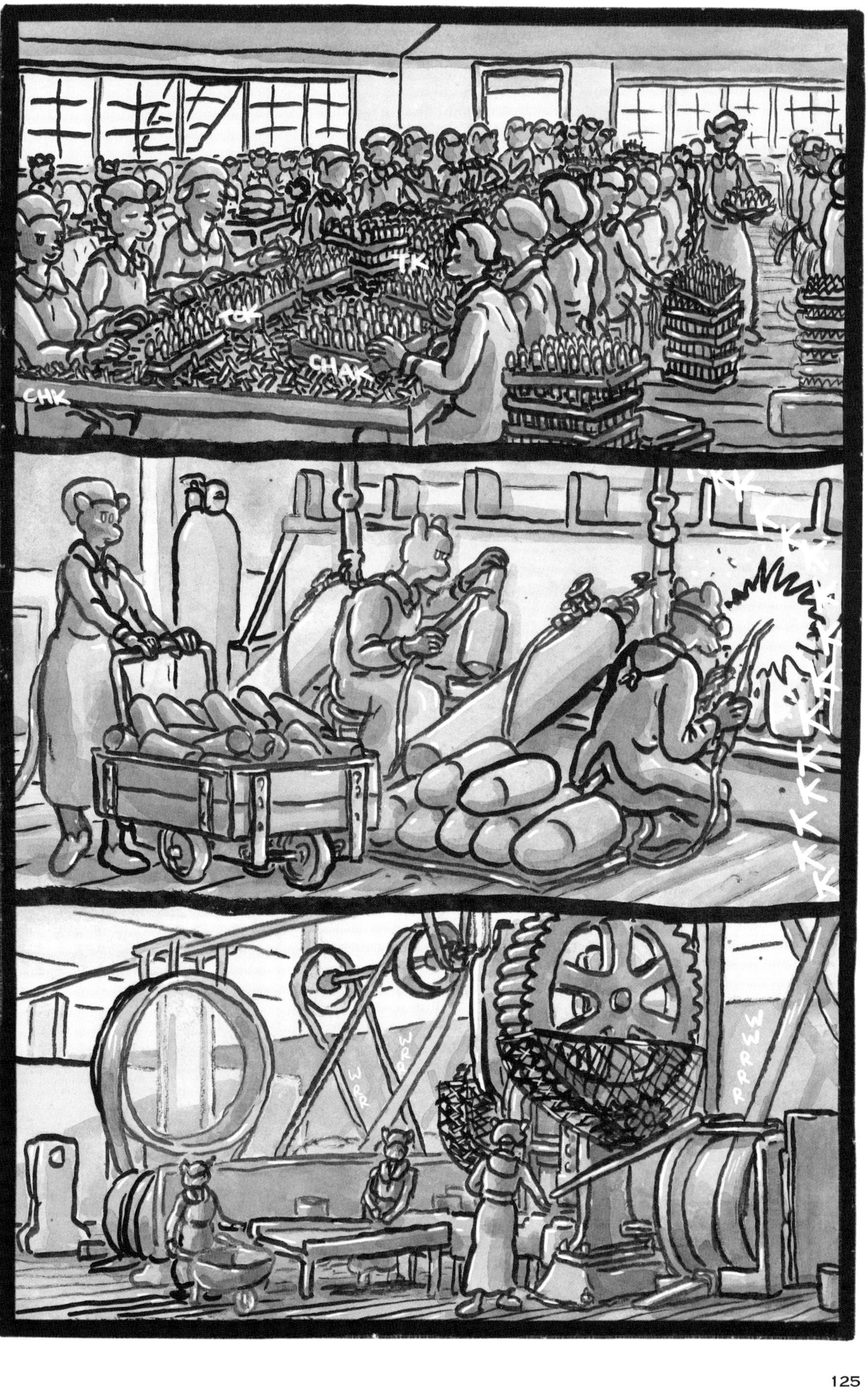
CHK
TK
CHAK
WRR
WRR
WWRRRR

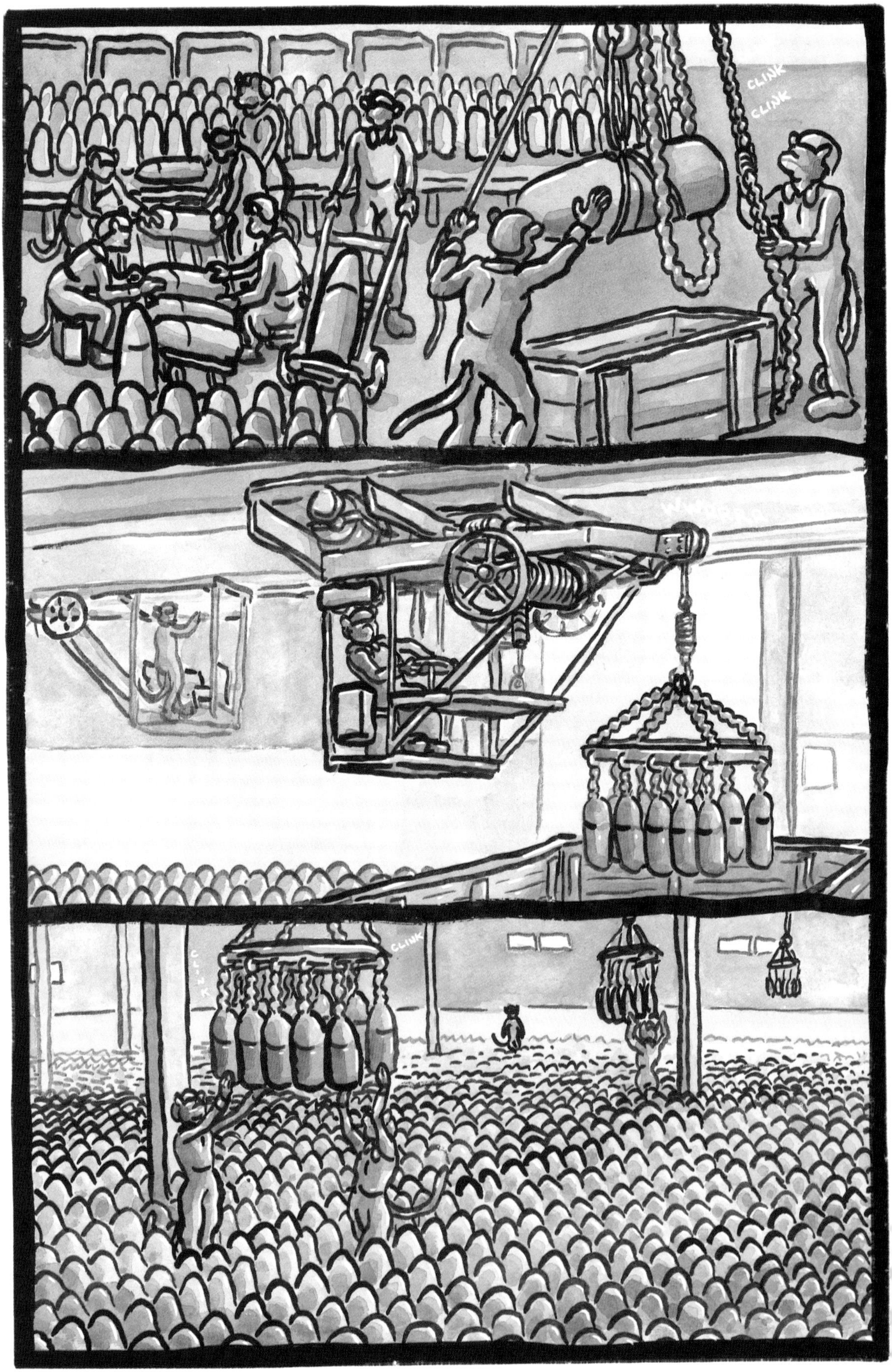
CLINK
CLINK
CLINK
CLINK

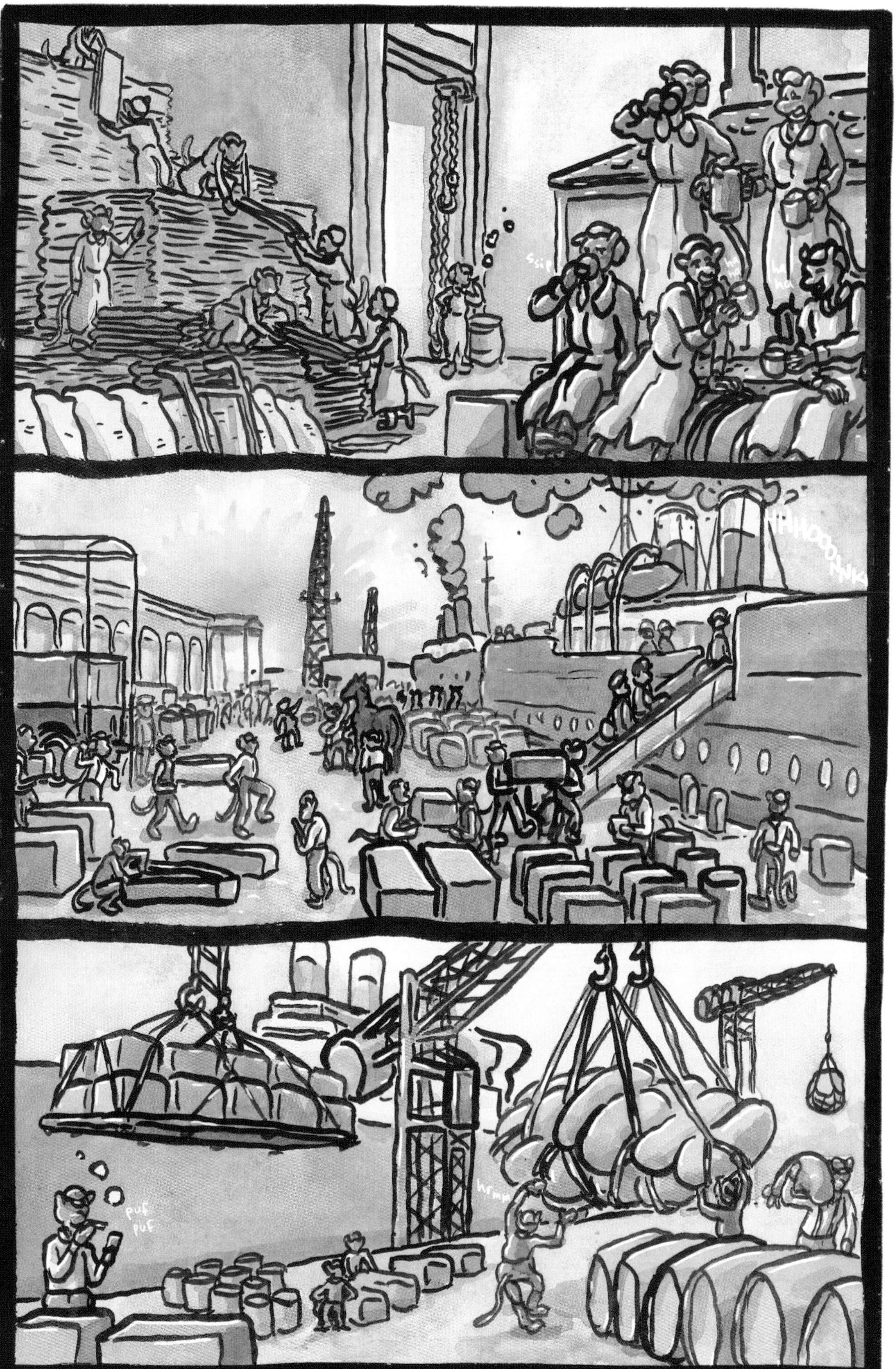
ssip
ha ha
ha ha
HHHOOOONNK
hrmph
puf puf

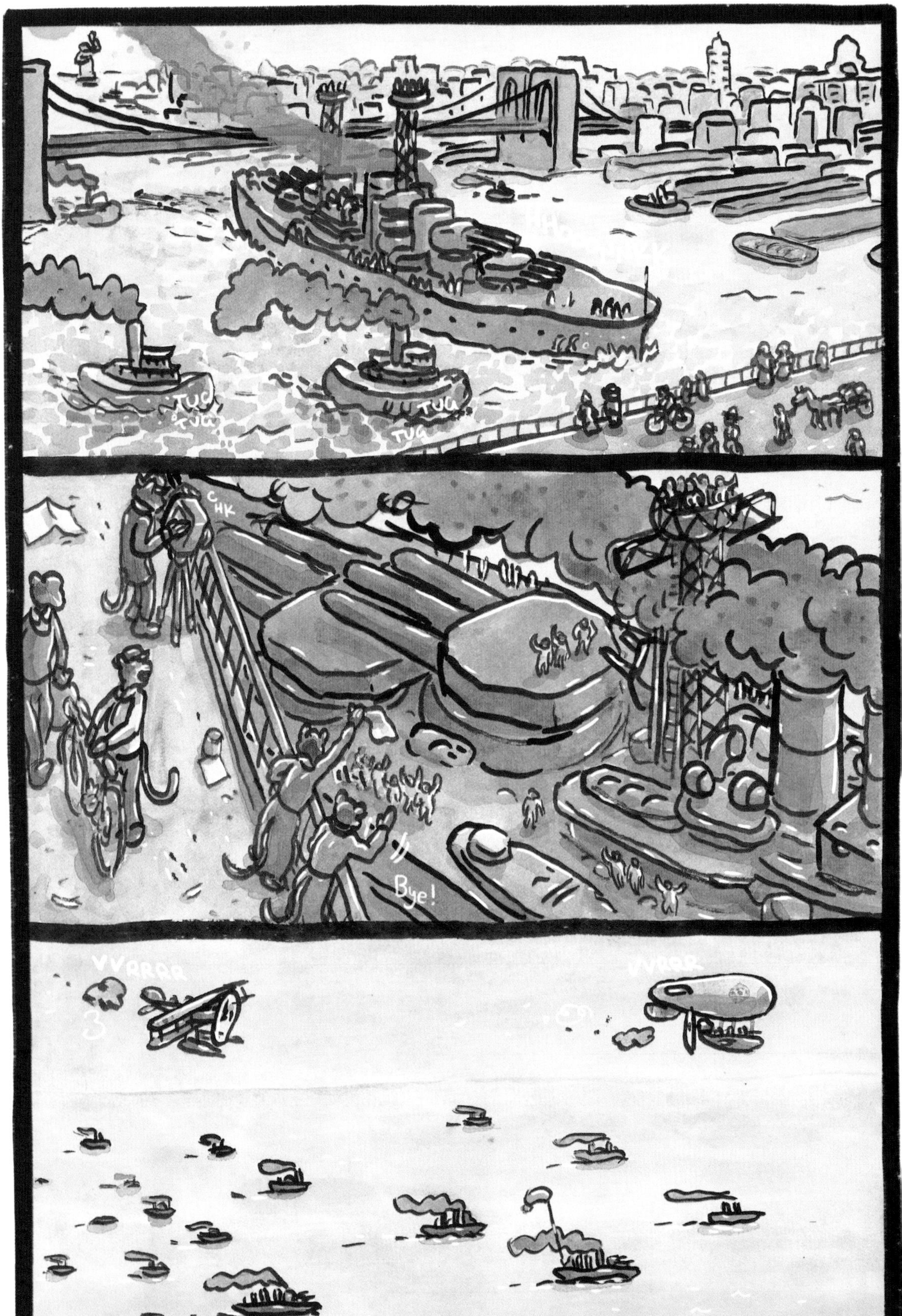
TUG
TUG
TUG
TUG
CHK
Bye!
VVRRRR
VVRRR

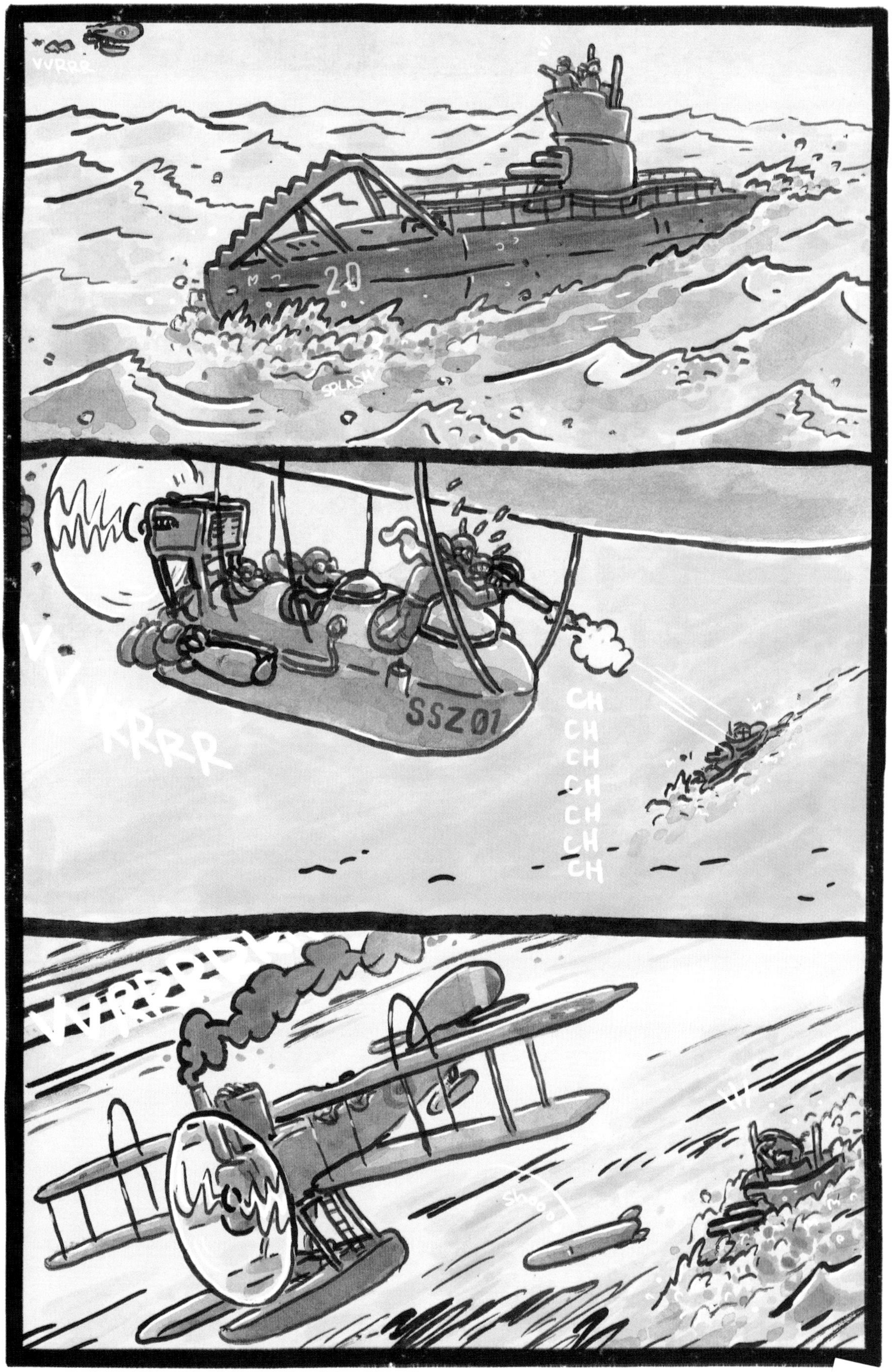

VVRRR
SPLASH
VVRRRR
SSZ01
CH
CH
CH
CH
CH
CH
CH
VVRRRR

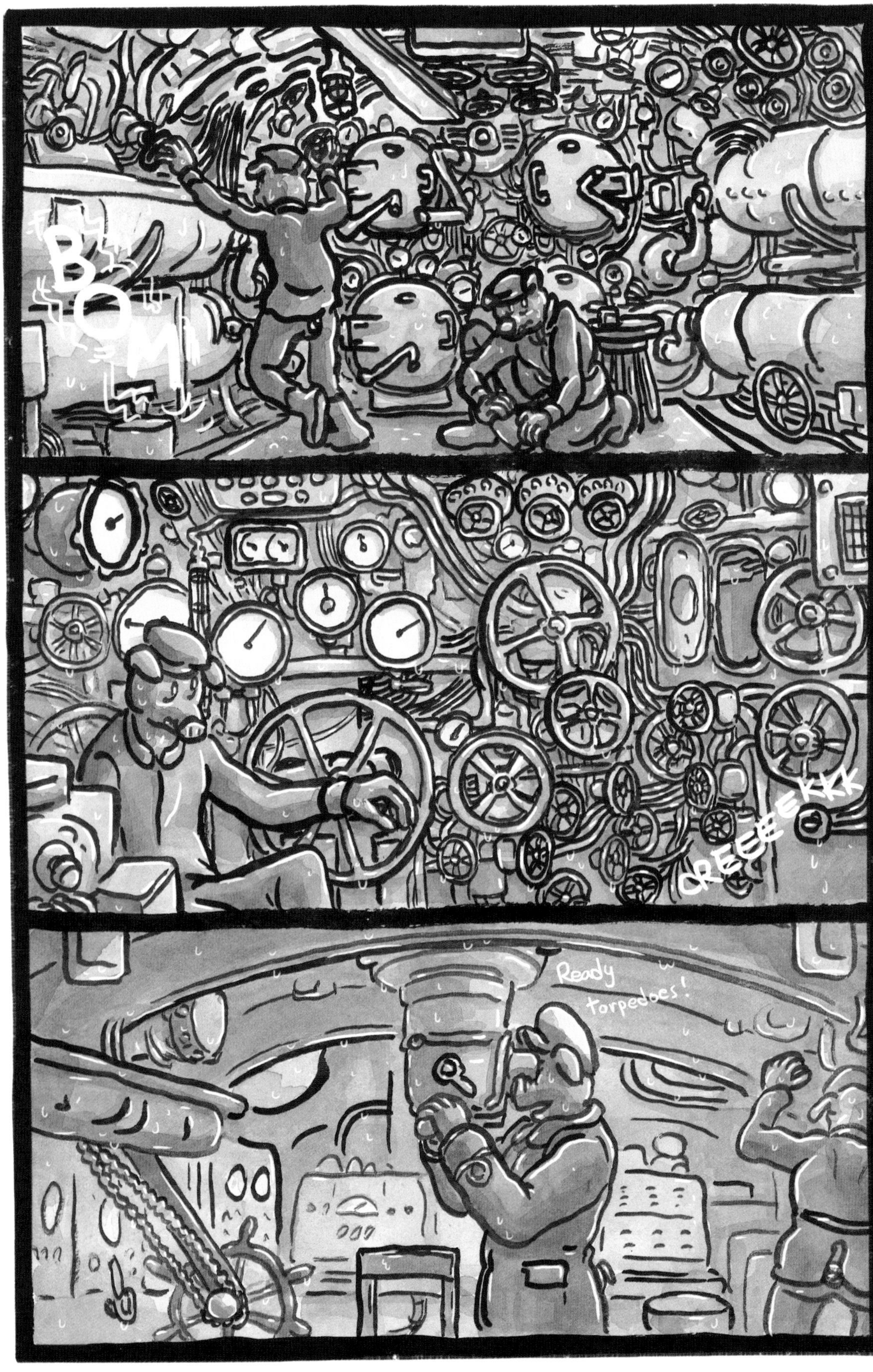
BOOM
CREEEEEKKK
Ready torpedoes!

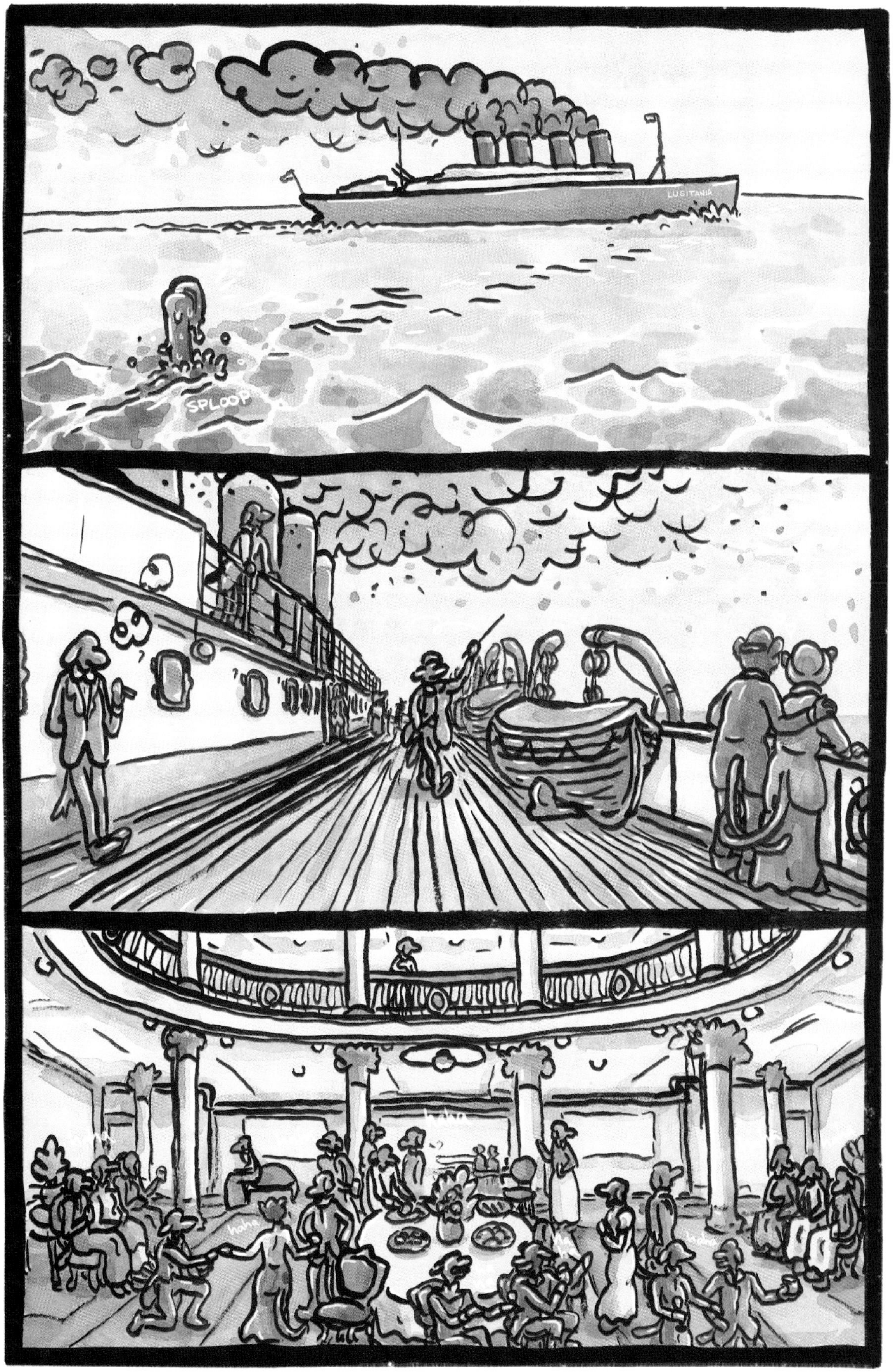
LUSITANIA
SPLOOP
haha
haha
haha

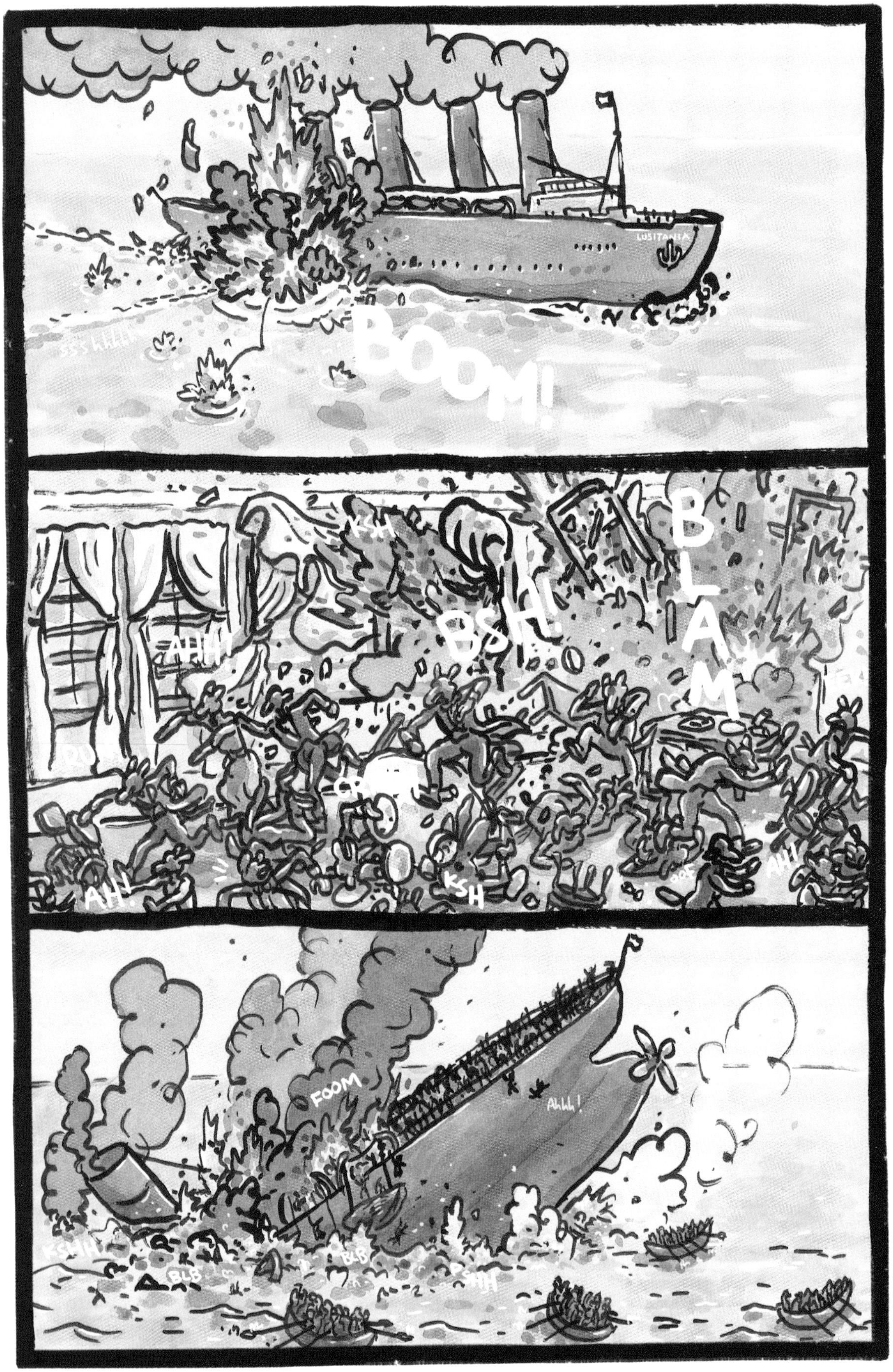

LUSITANIA
BOOM!
KSH
BSH!
BLAM
AHH!
AH!
KSH
AH!
FOOM
Ahhh!
KSHH
BLB
BLB
PSHH

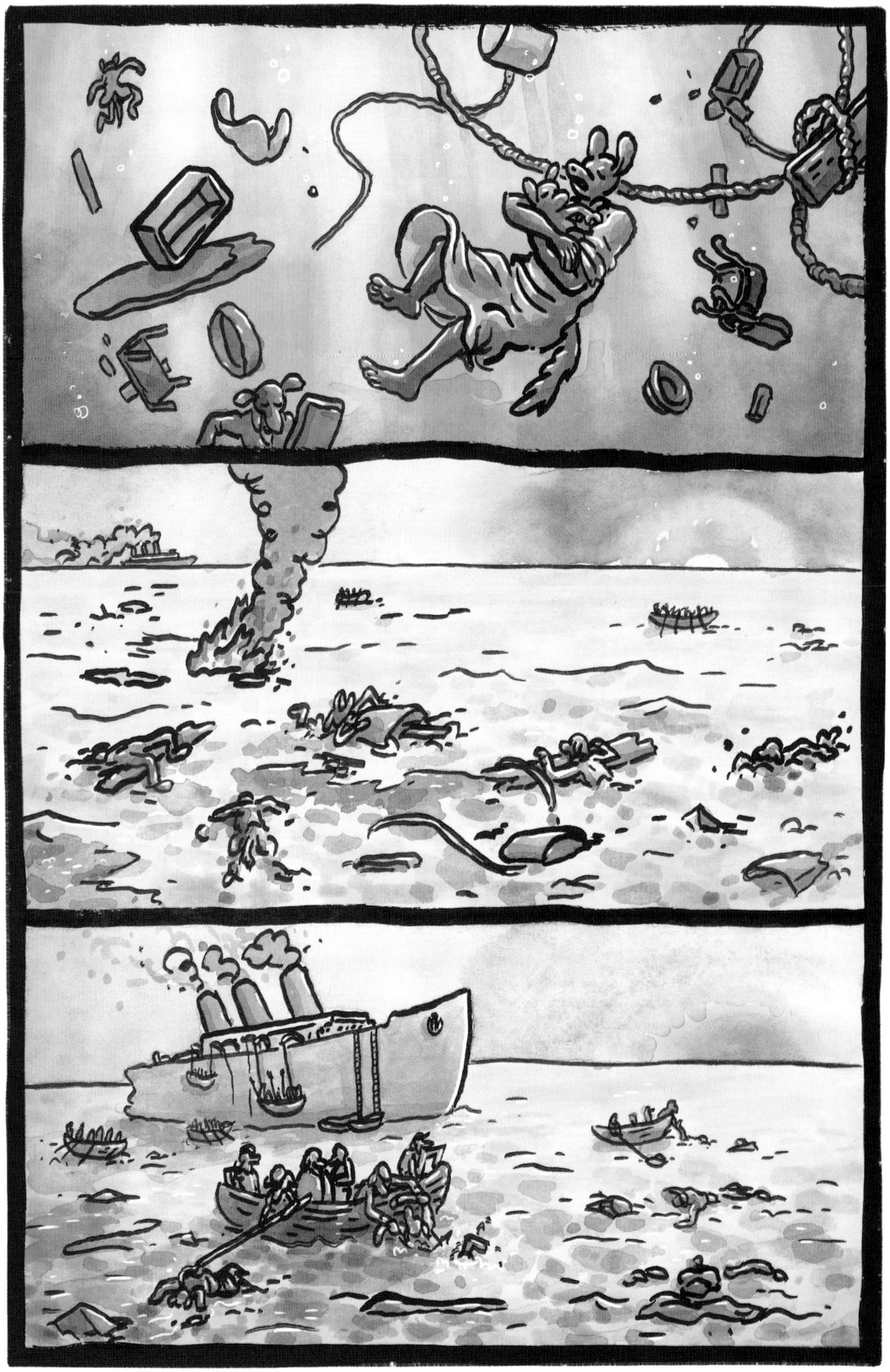

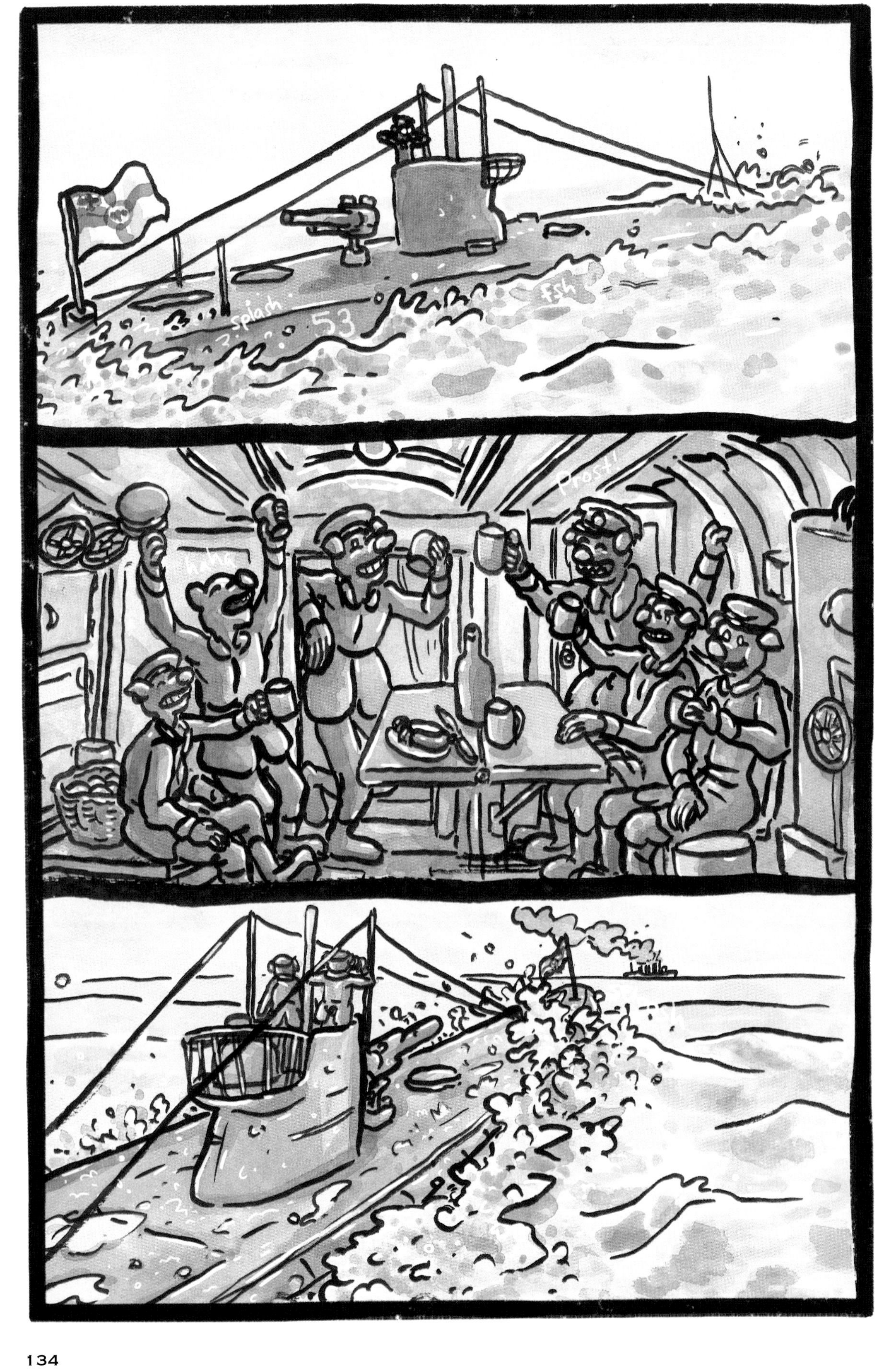
splash
53
fsh
haha
Prost!

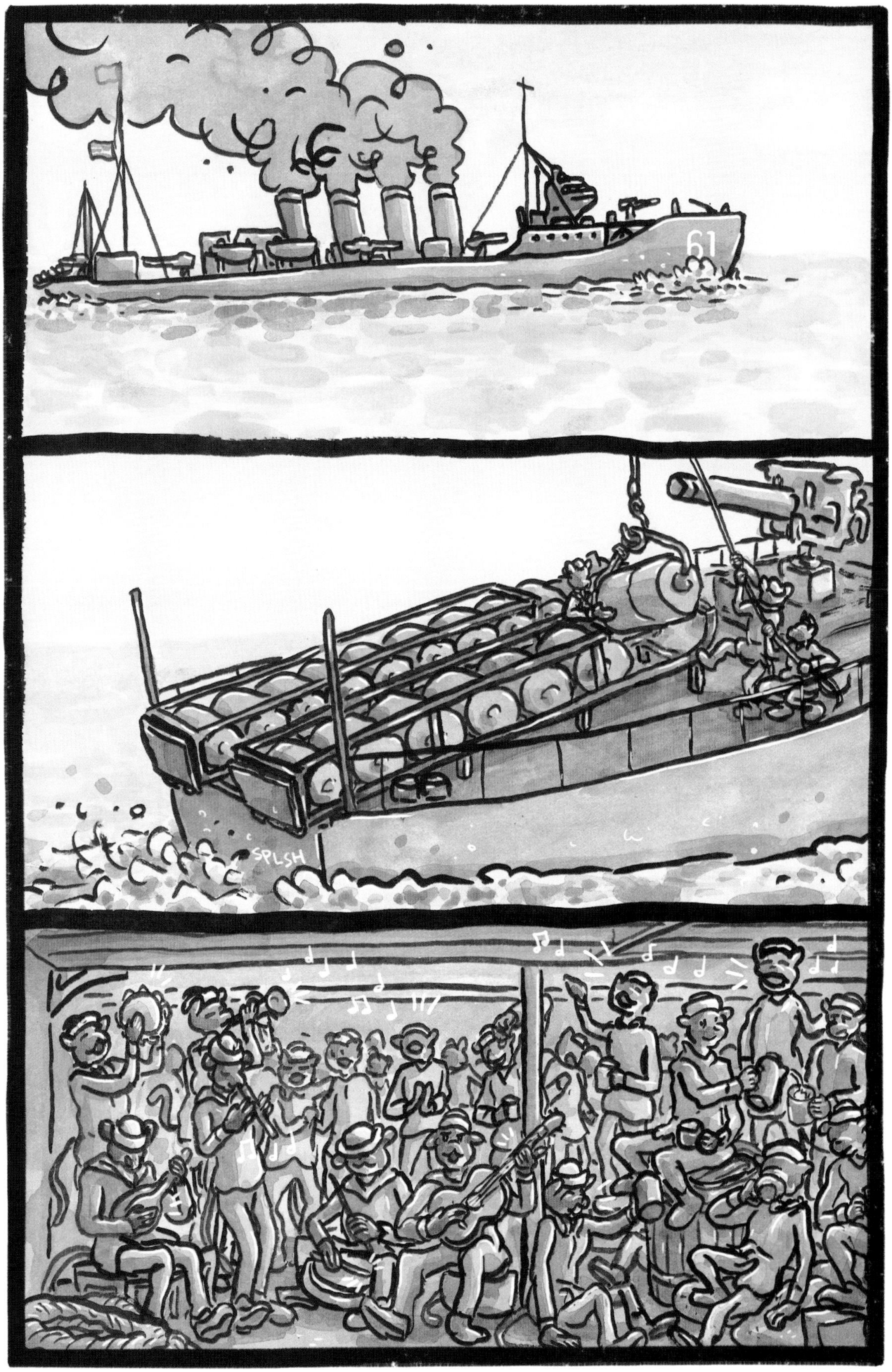
SPLSH

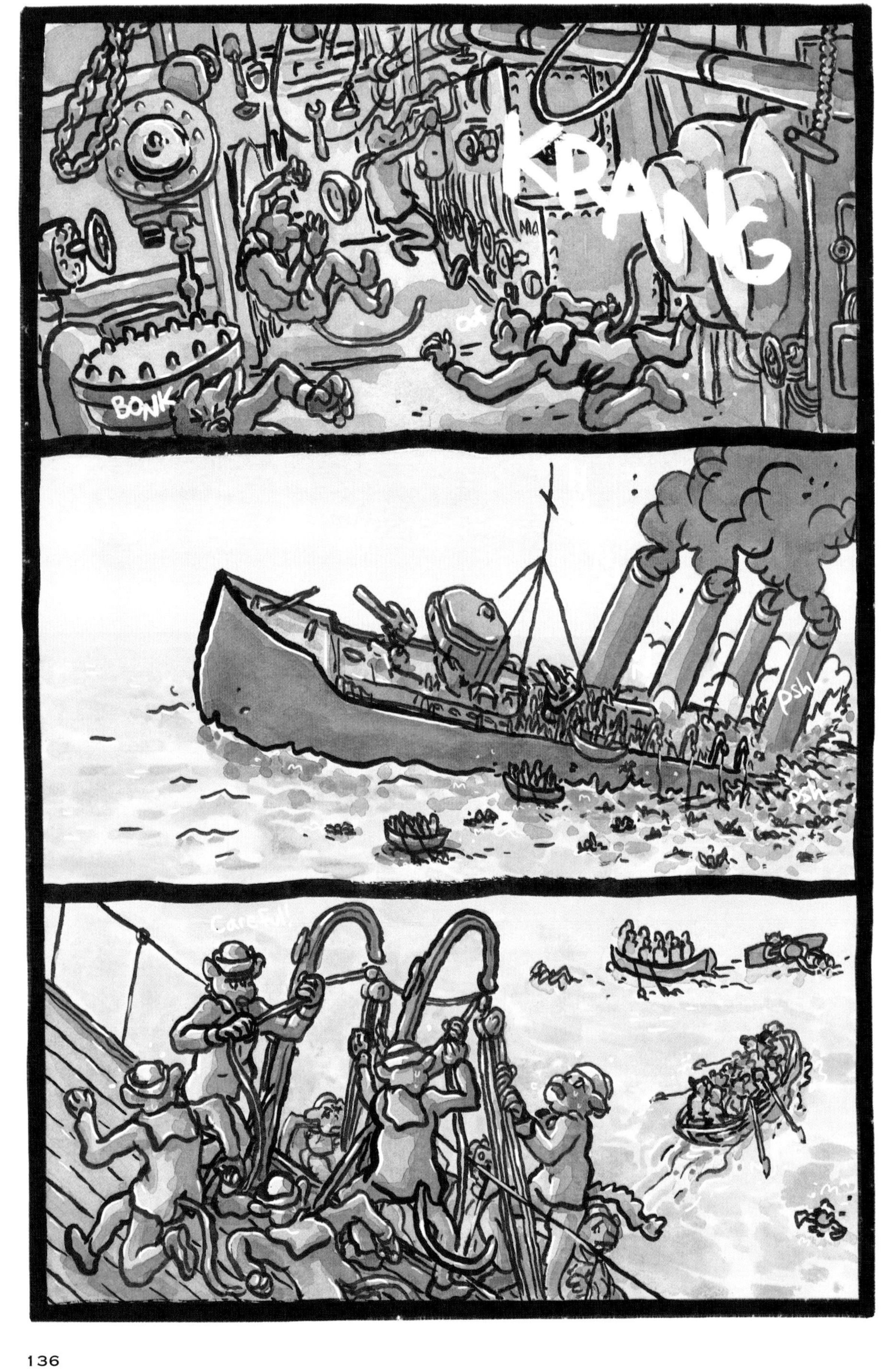
KRANG
oof
BONK
pshh
pshh
Careful!

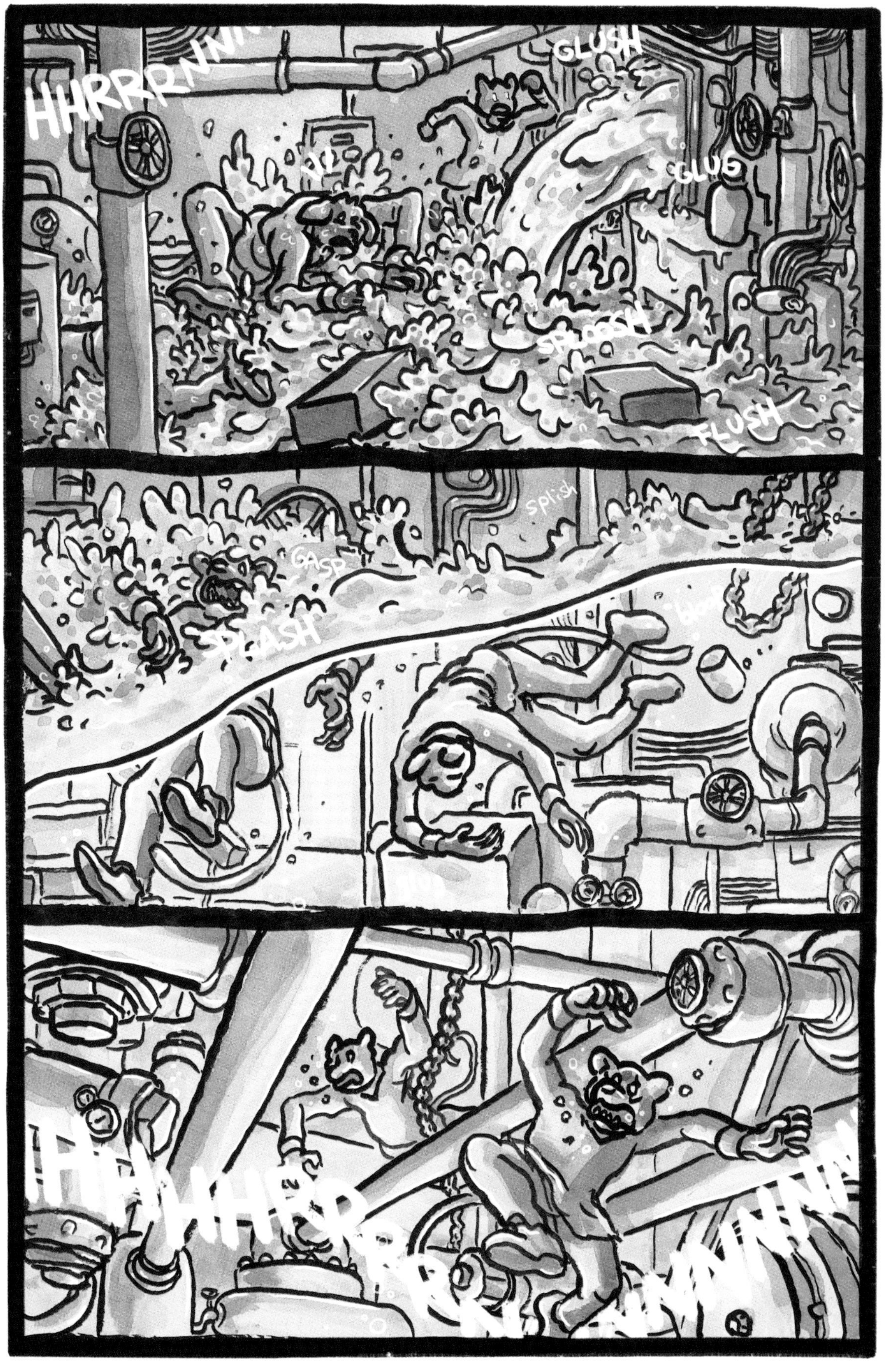
HHRRRNNN
GLUSH
GLUG
SPLOOSH
FLUSH
splish
GASP
SPLASH
bloop
HHHHRRRRNNNNNN

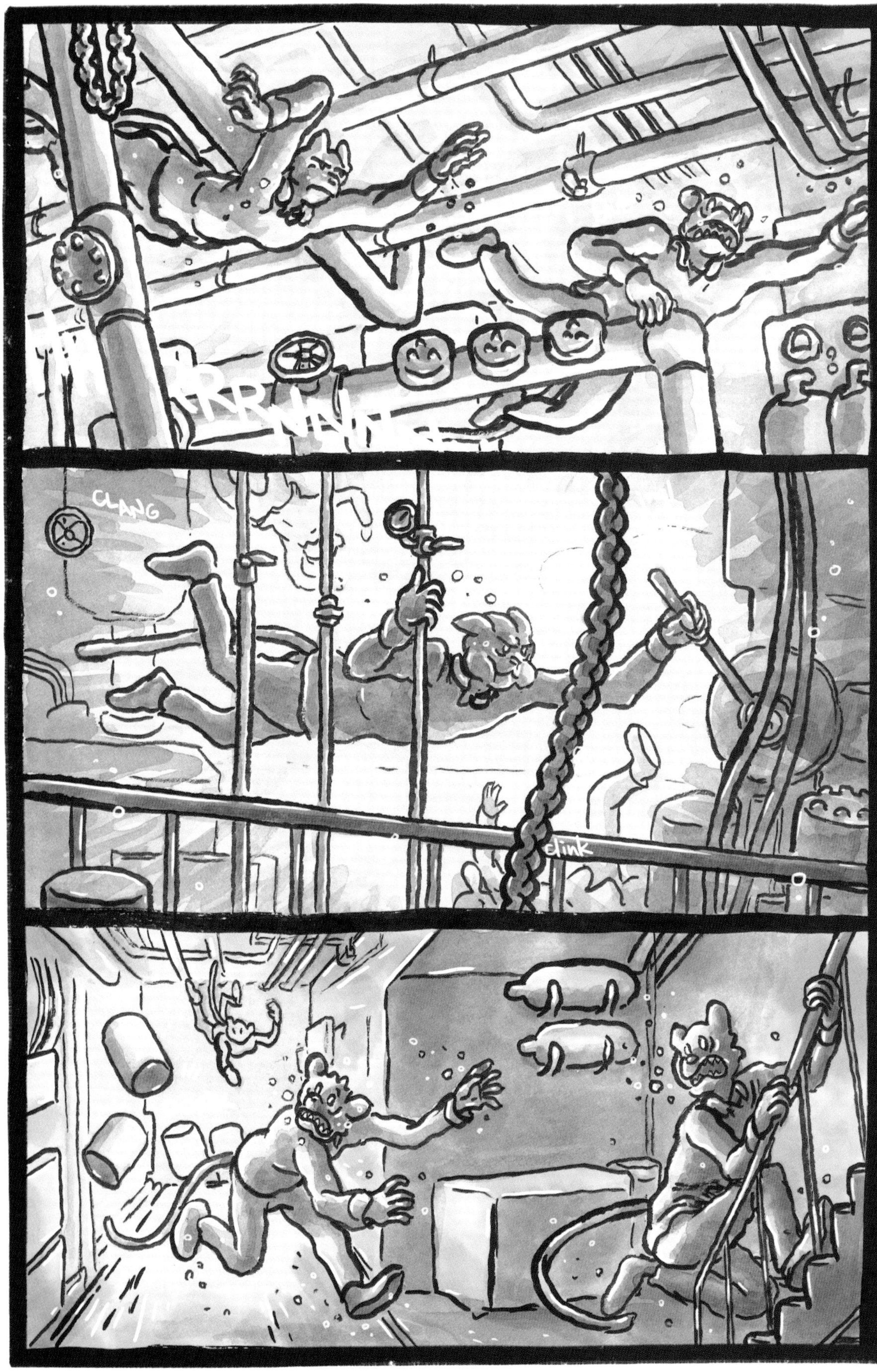
CLANG
clink

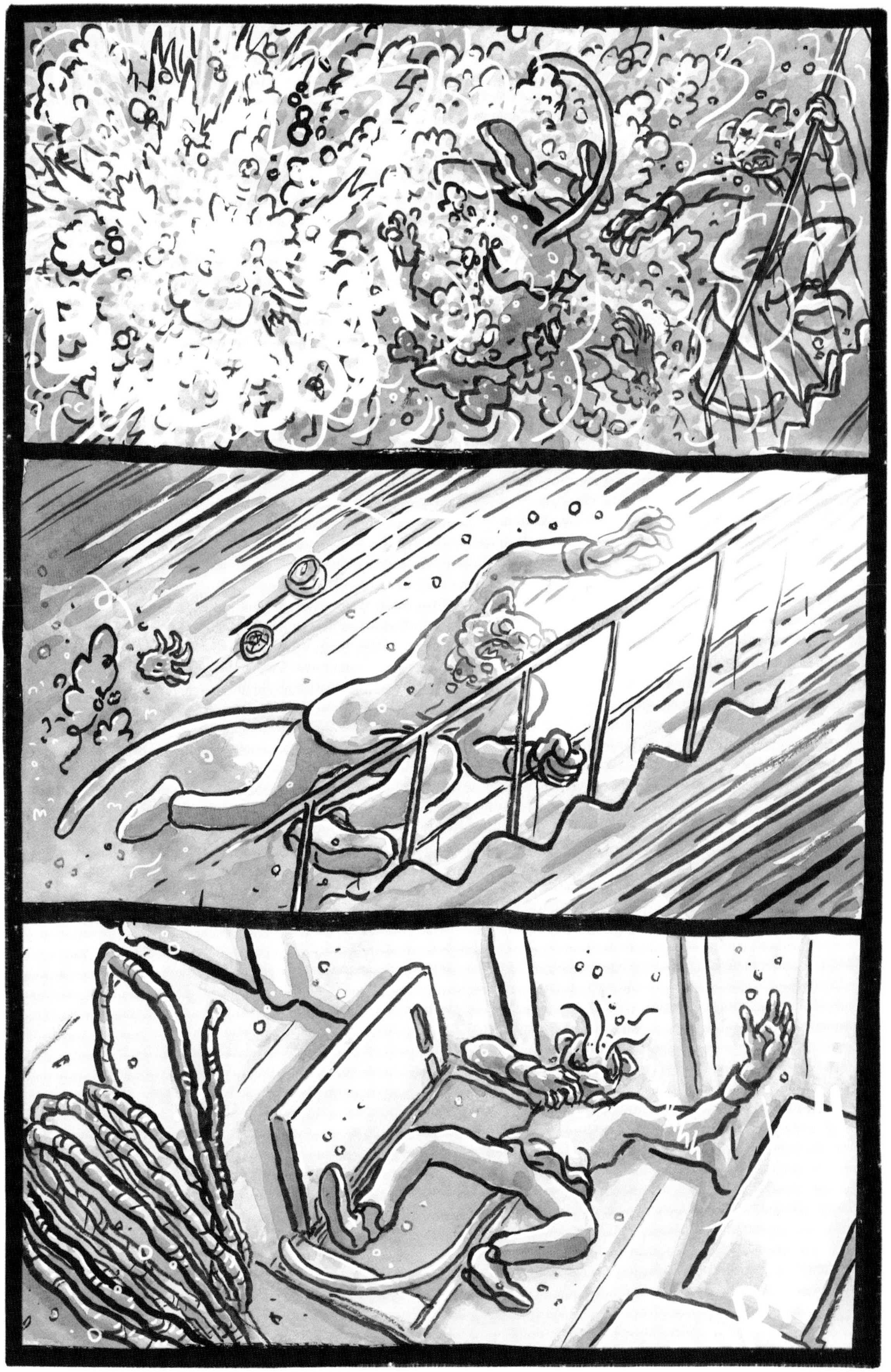

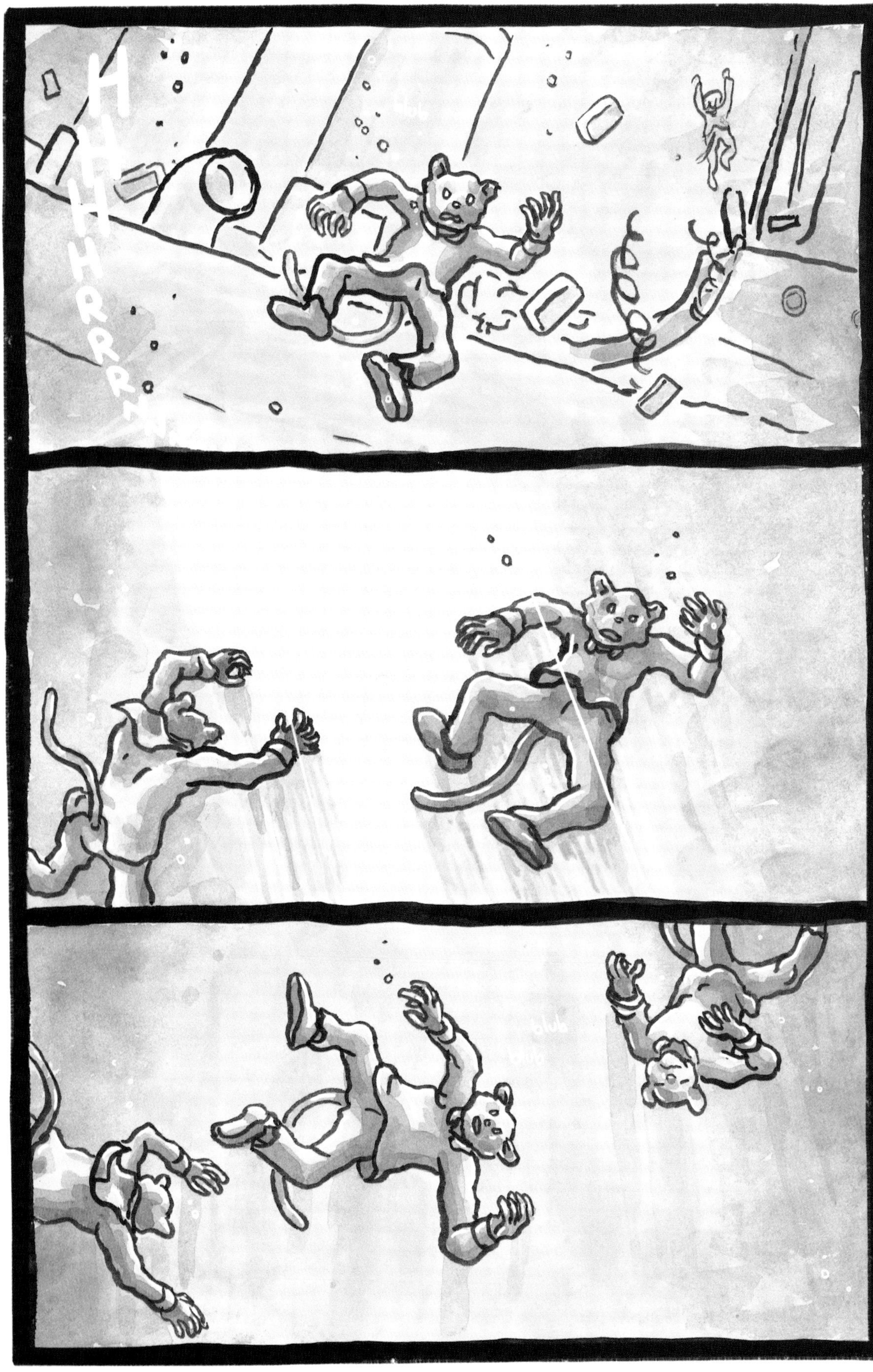
HHHHRRRR
blub

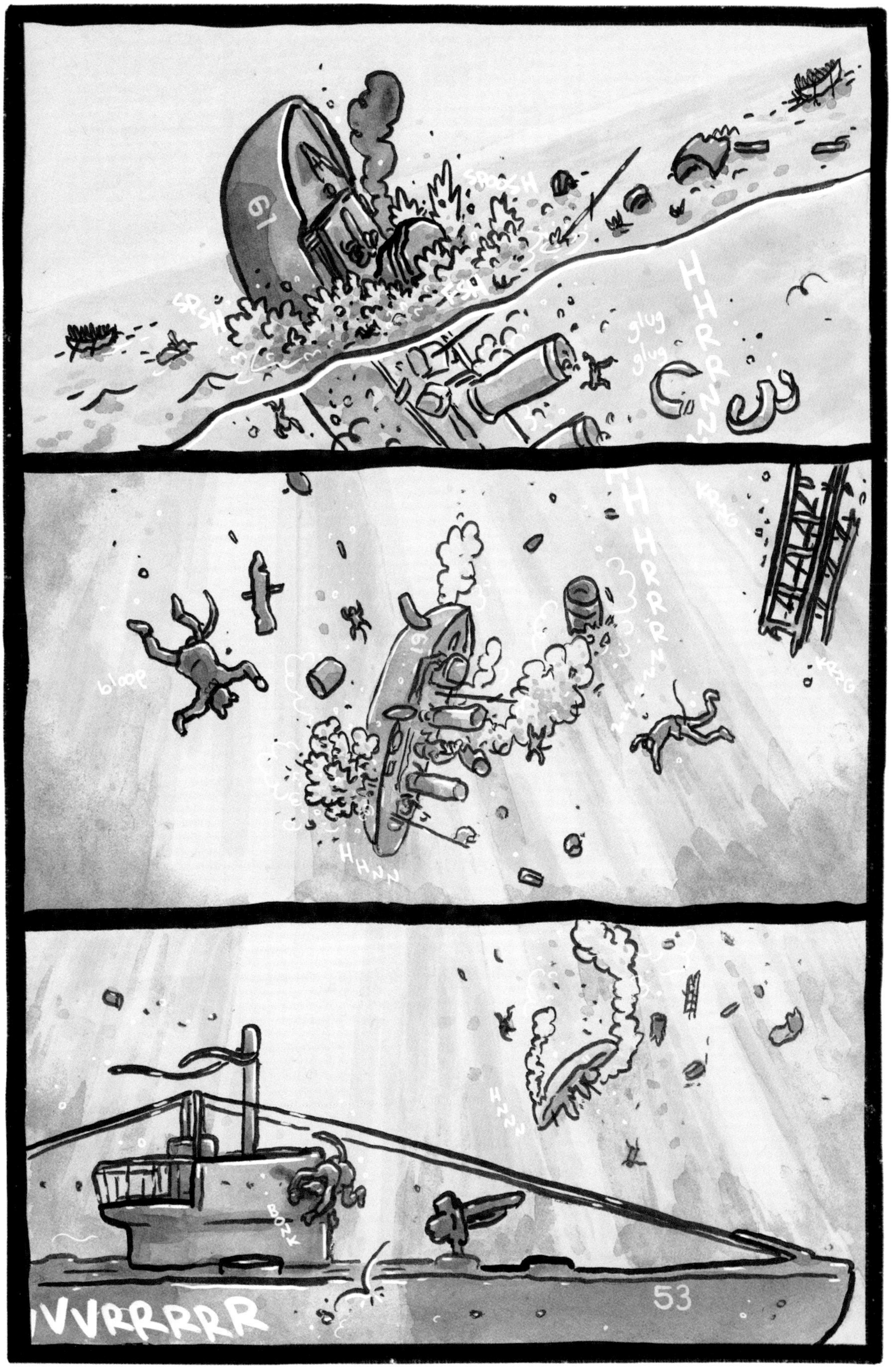
SPOOSH
SPLSH
FSH
glug
glug
HHRRNN
HHRRRNN
bloop
KRRG
KRRG
HHNN
HHNN
BONK
VVRRRRR

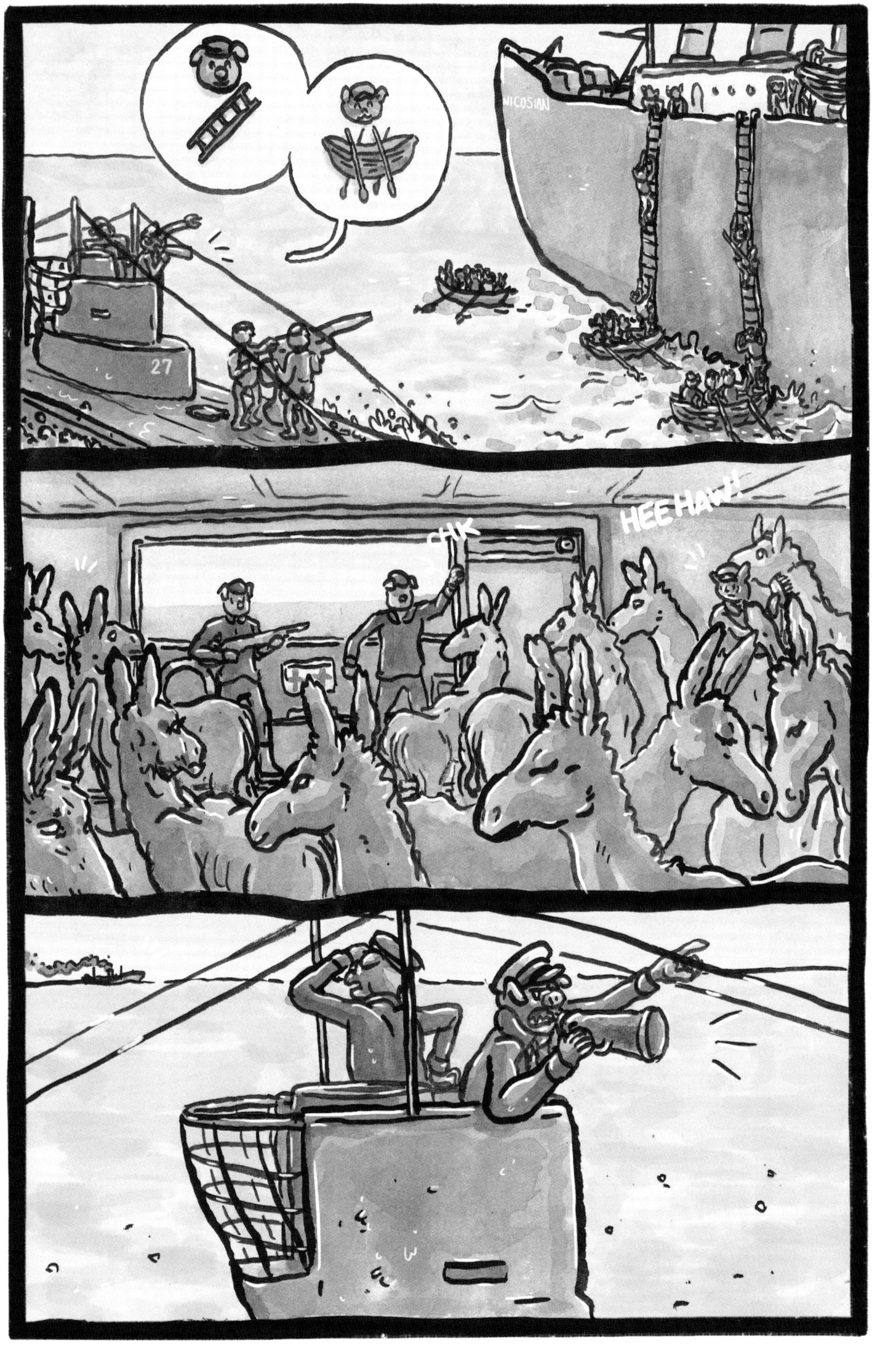
NICOSIAN
27
CHK
HEE HAW!

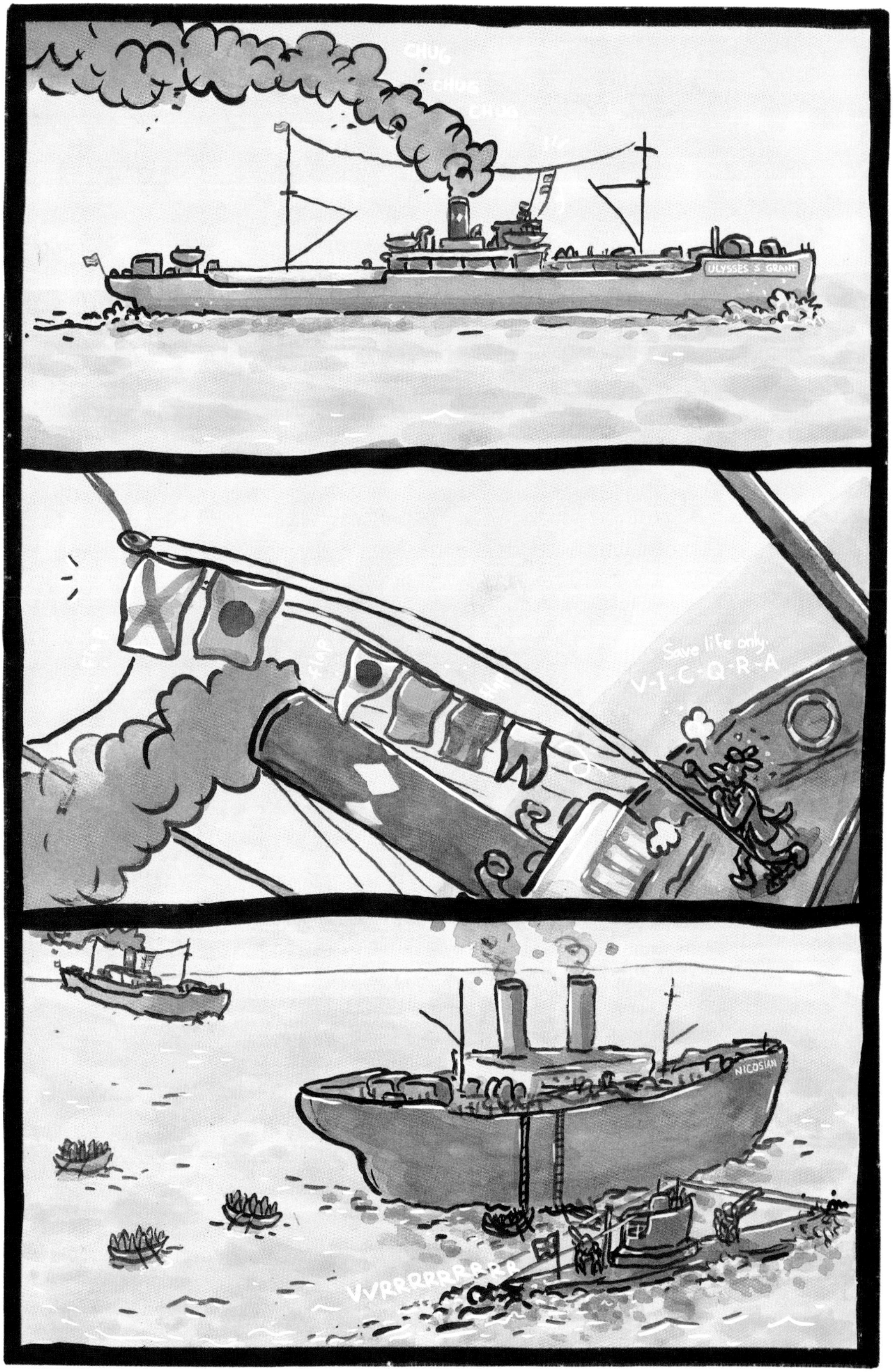
CHUG
CHUG
CHUG
ULYSSES S GRANT
flap
flap
Save life only.
V-I-C-Q-R-A
NICOSIAN
VVRRRRRRRRA

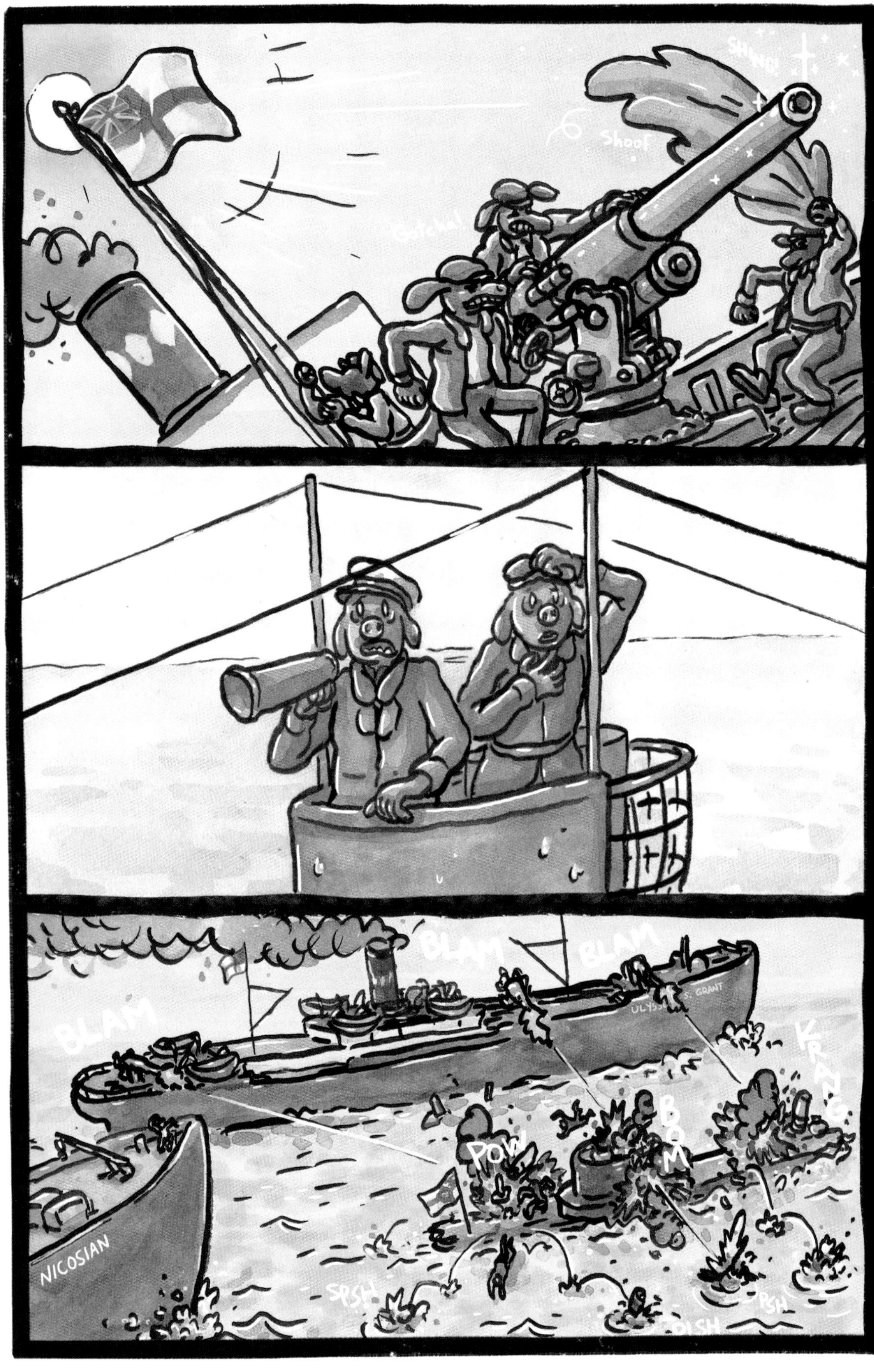
SHING!
Shoof
Gotcha!
BLAM
BLAM
BLAM
KRANG
BOM
POW
NICOSIAN
SPSH
PSH

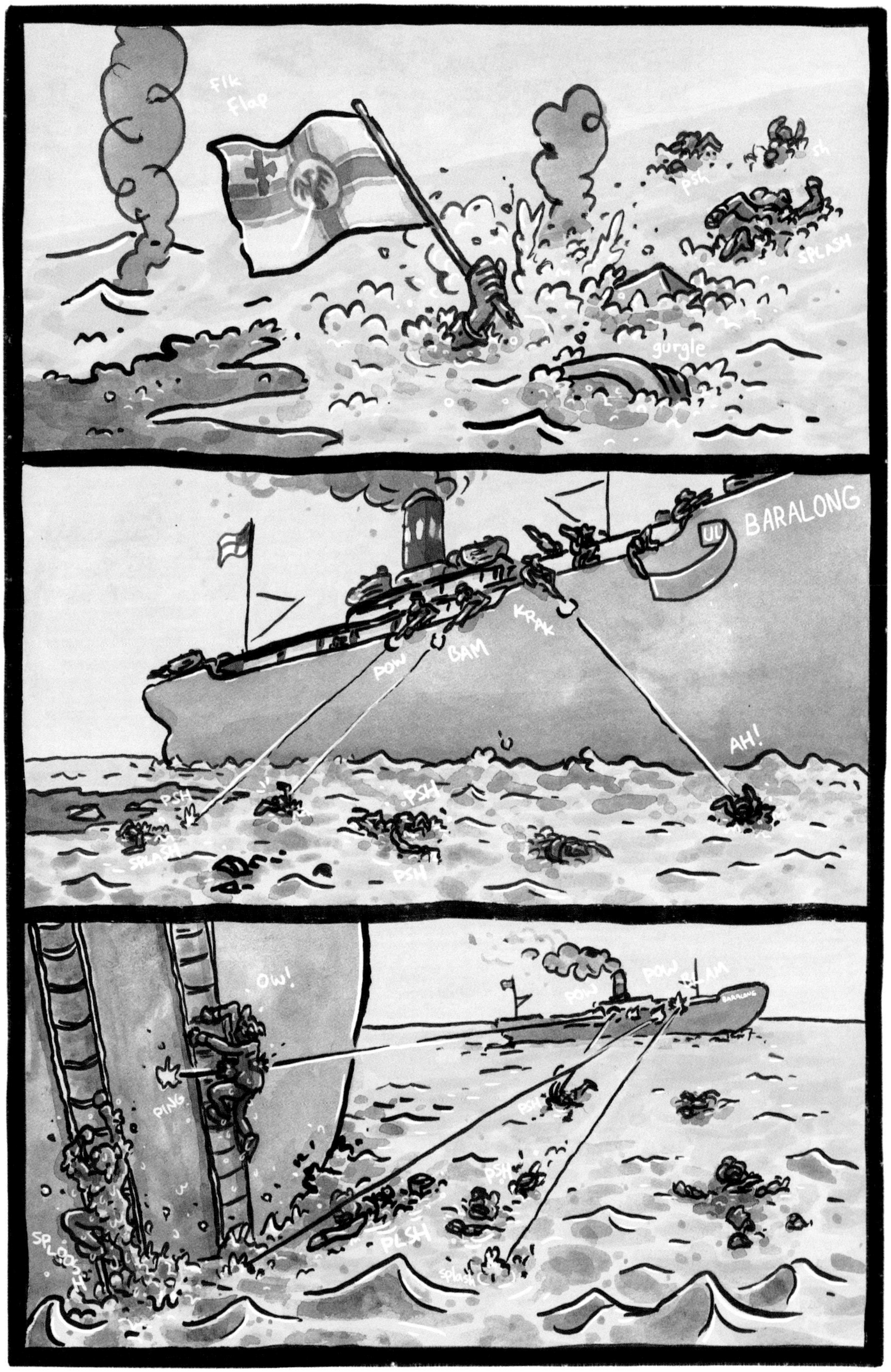

Flk
Flap
psh
sh
SPLASH
gurgle
BARALONG
KRAK
POW
BAM
AH!
PSH
PSH
SPLASH
PSH
OW!
PING
POW
POW
BLAM
BARALONG
PSH
PSH
PLSH
SPLOOSH
splash

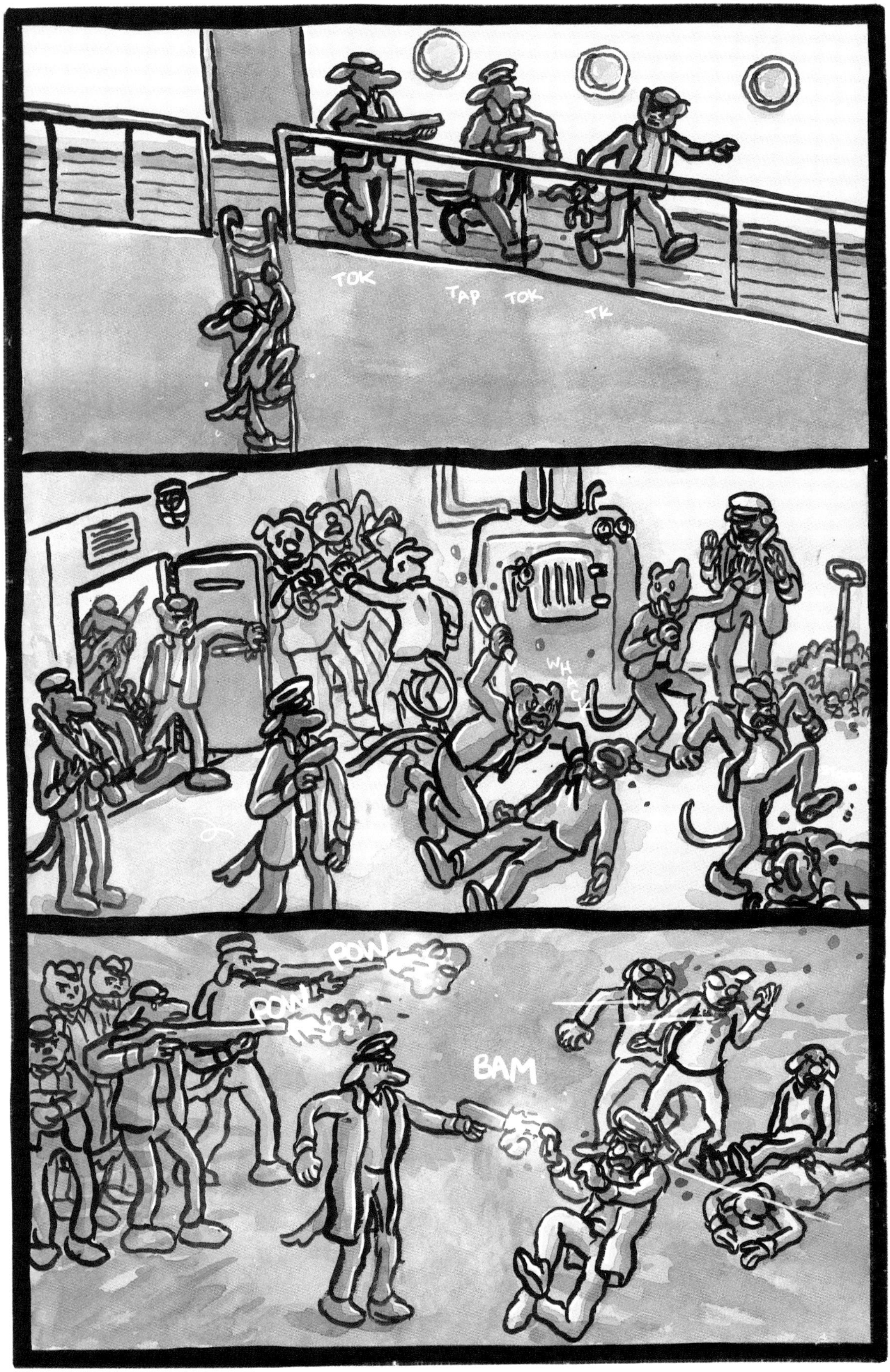
TOK
TAP
TOK
TK
WHACK
POW
POW
BAM

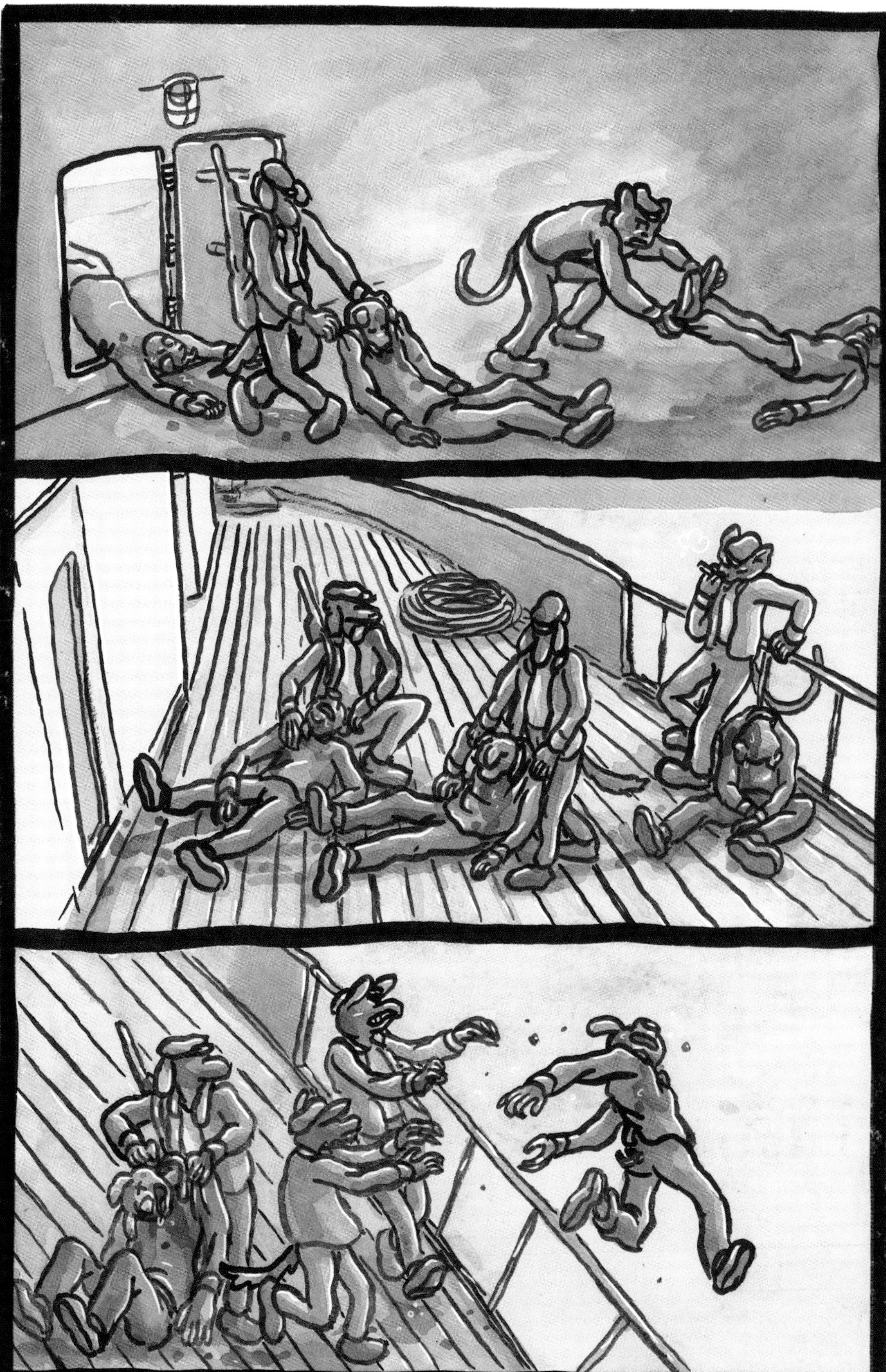

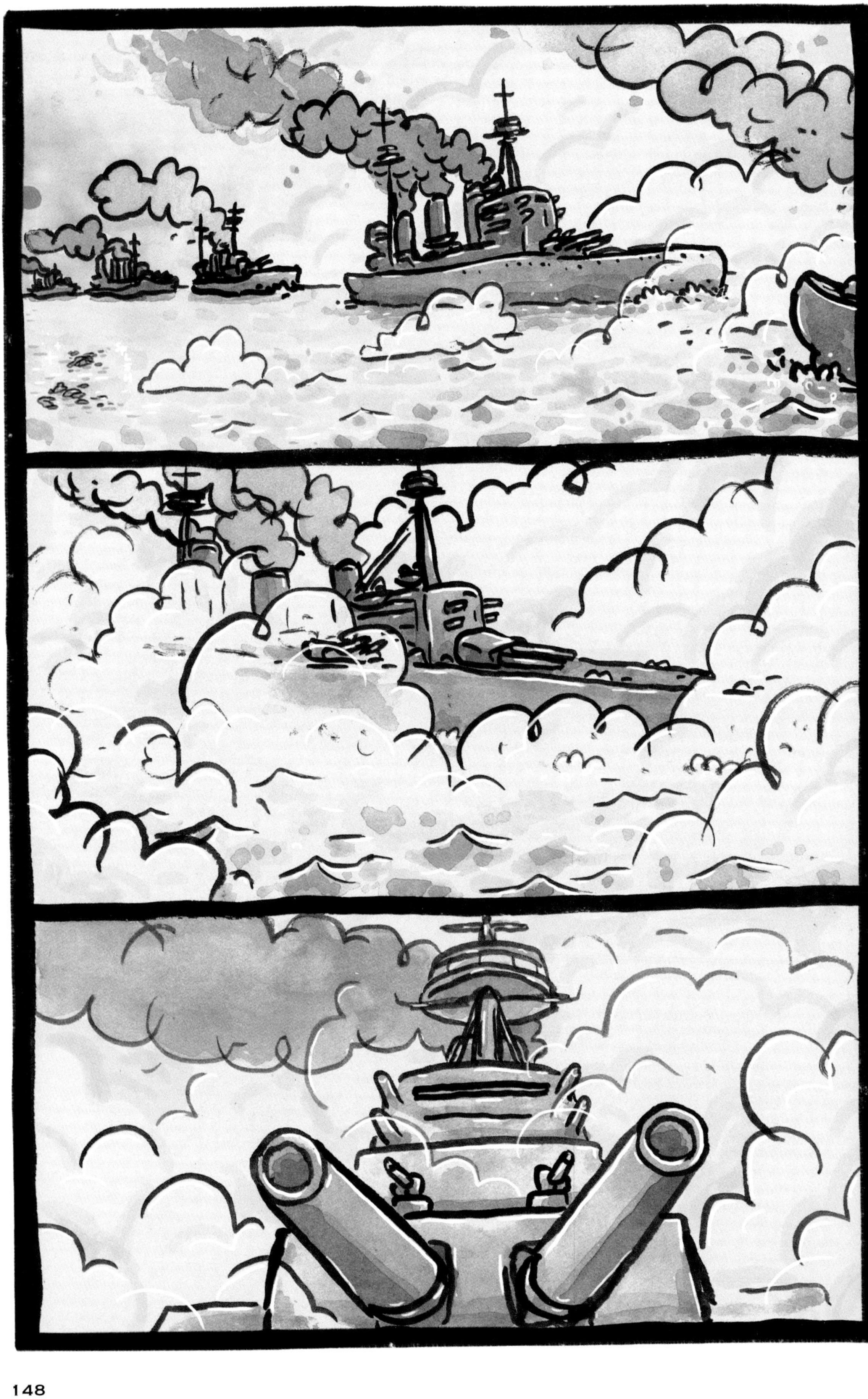

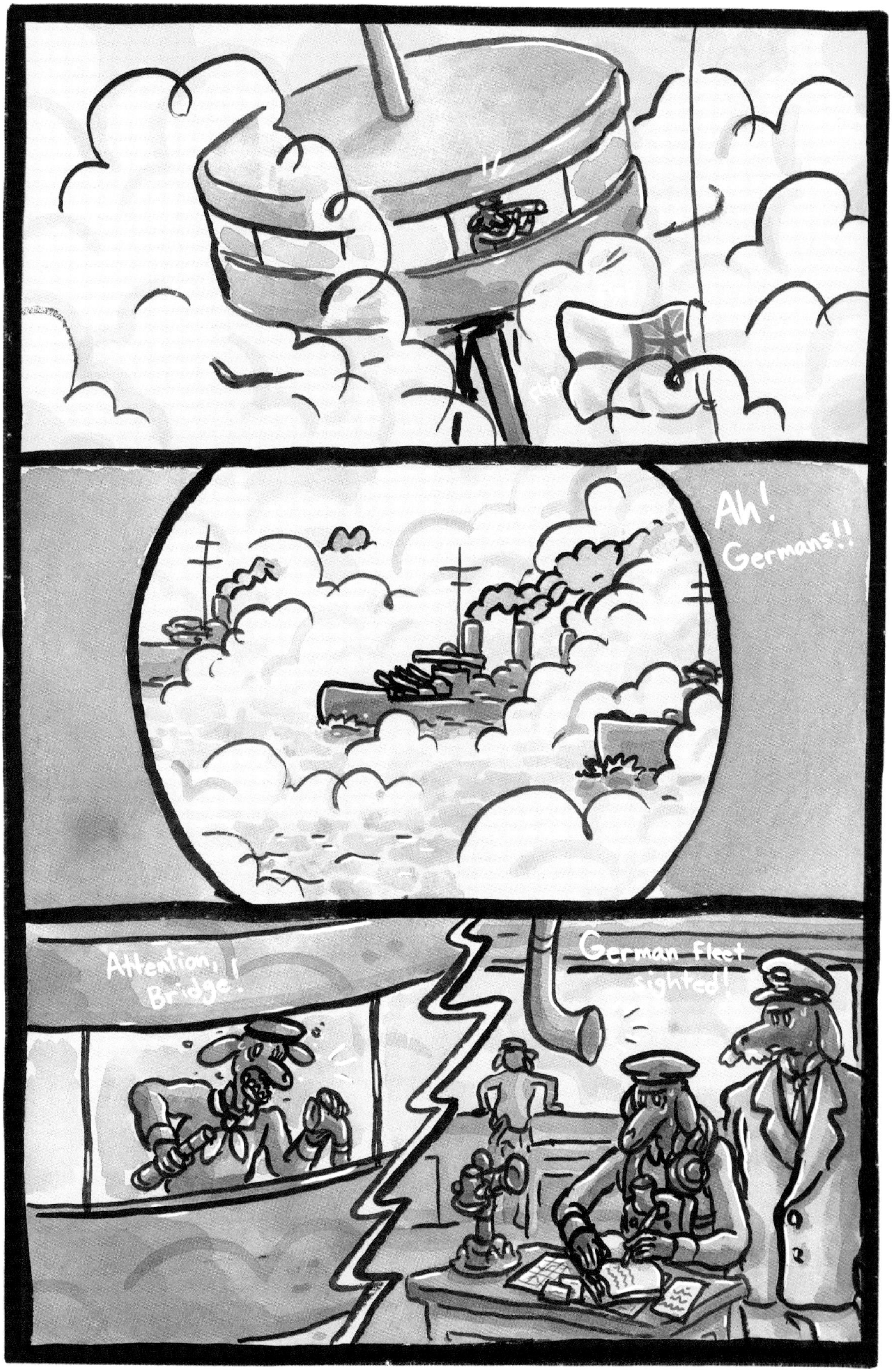

flap
Ah! Germans!!
Attention, Bridge!
German fleet sighted!

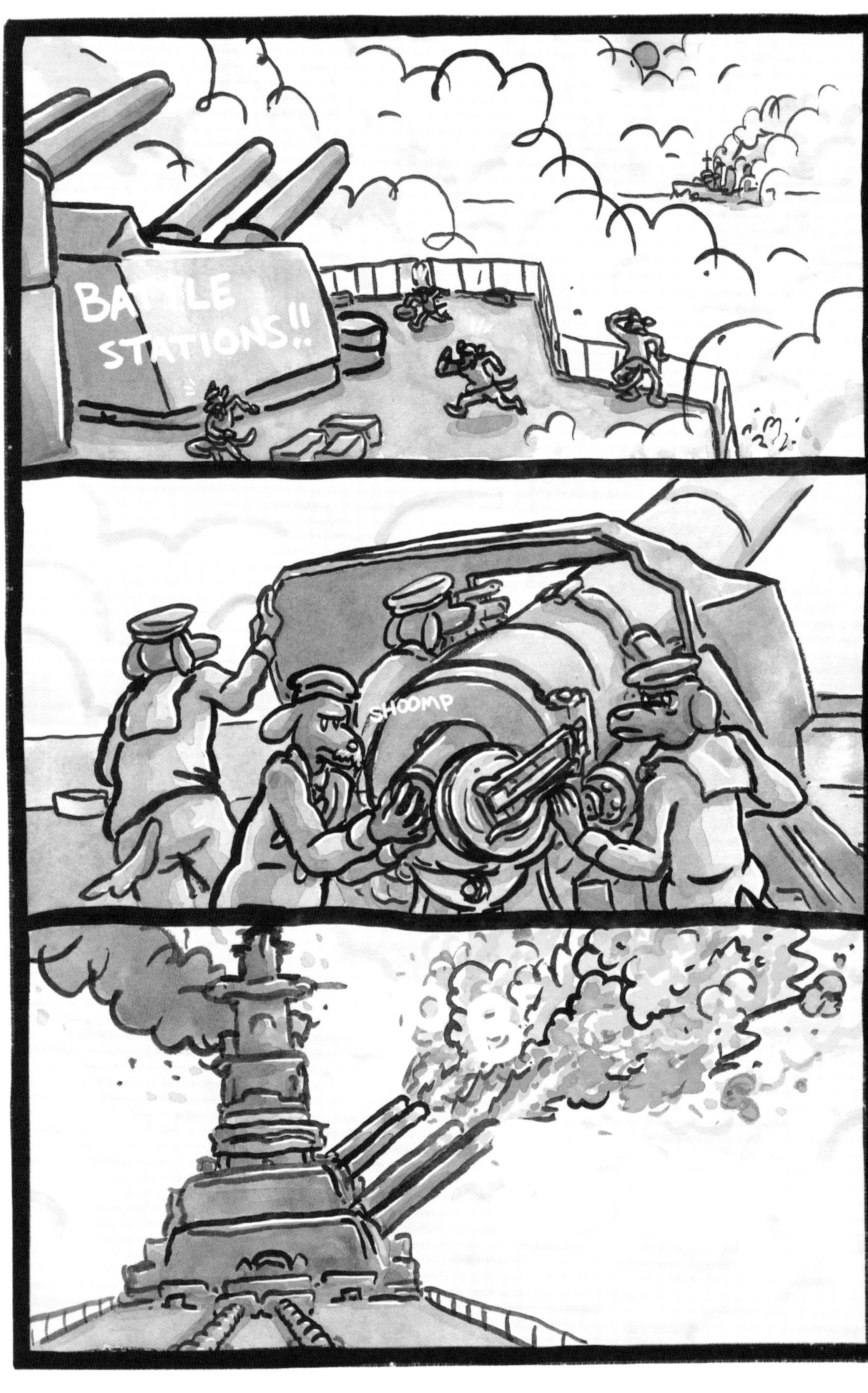
BATTLE STATIONS!!
SHOOMP

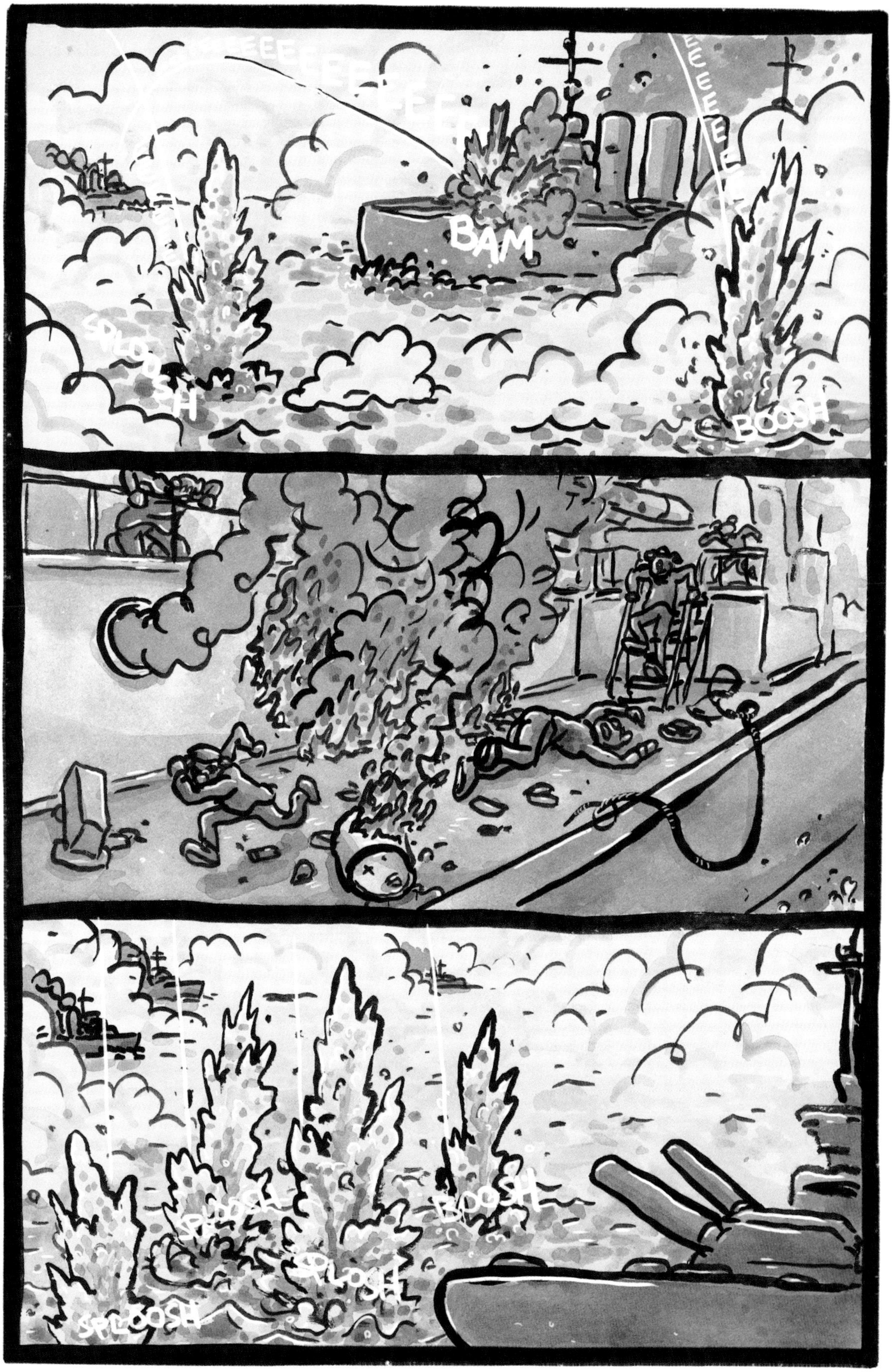
BAM
SPLOOSH
BOOSH
SPLOSH
BOOSH
SPLOSH
SPLOOSH

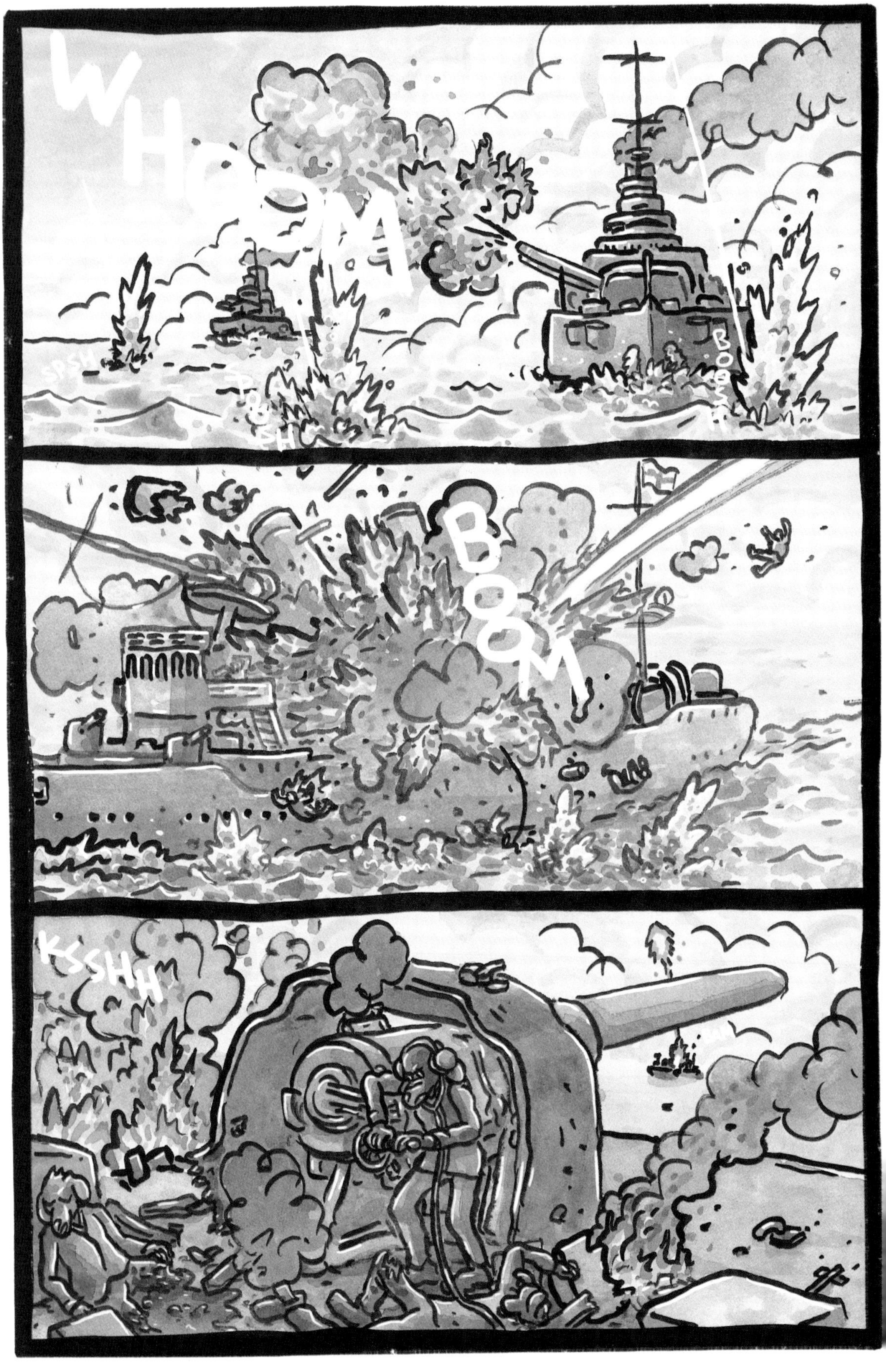
WHOOM
SPSH
POOSH
BOOSH
BOOM
KSSHH

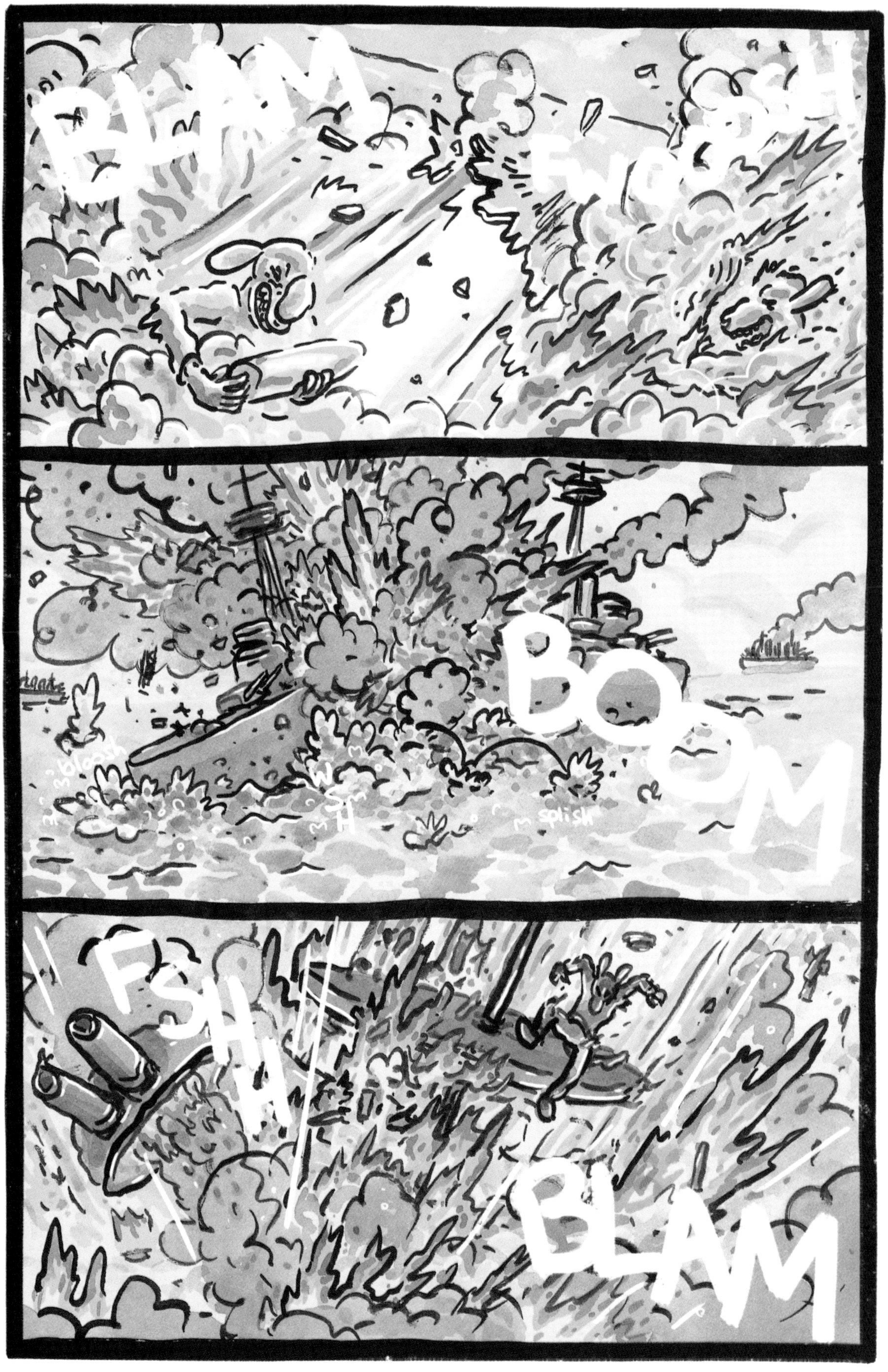
BLAM
FWOOSH
BOOM
bloosh
WSH
splish
FSHH
BLAM

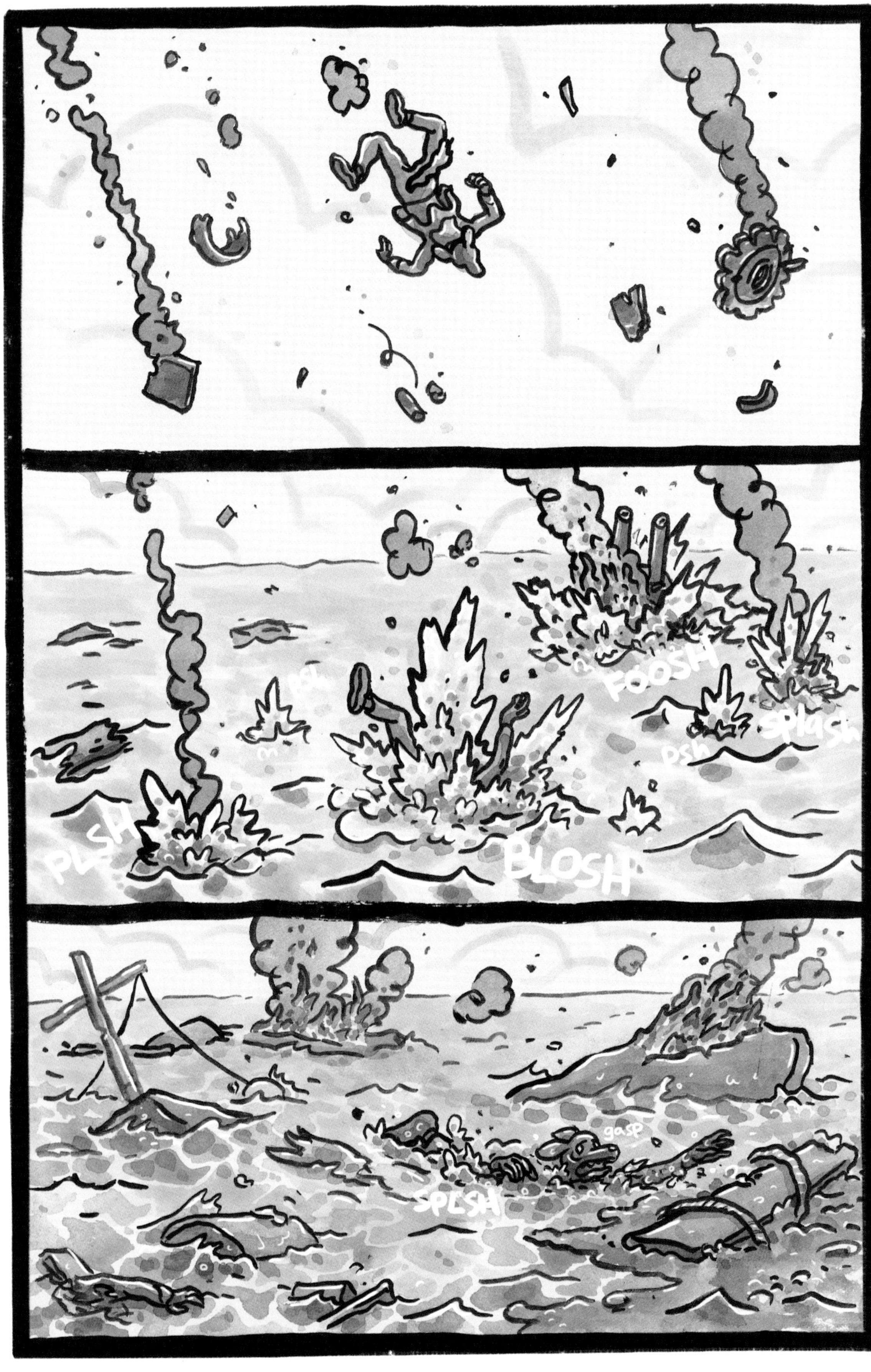
FOOSH
PLSH
BLOSH
SPLASH
PSH
gasp
SPLSH

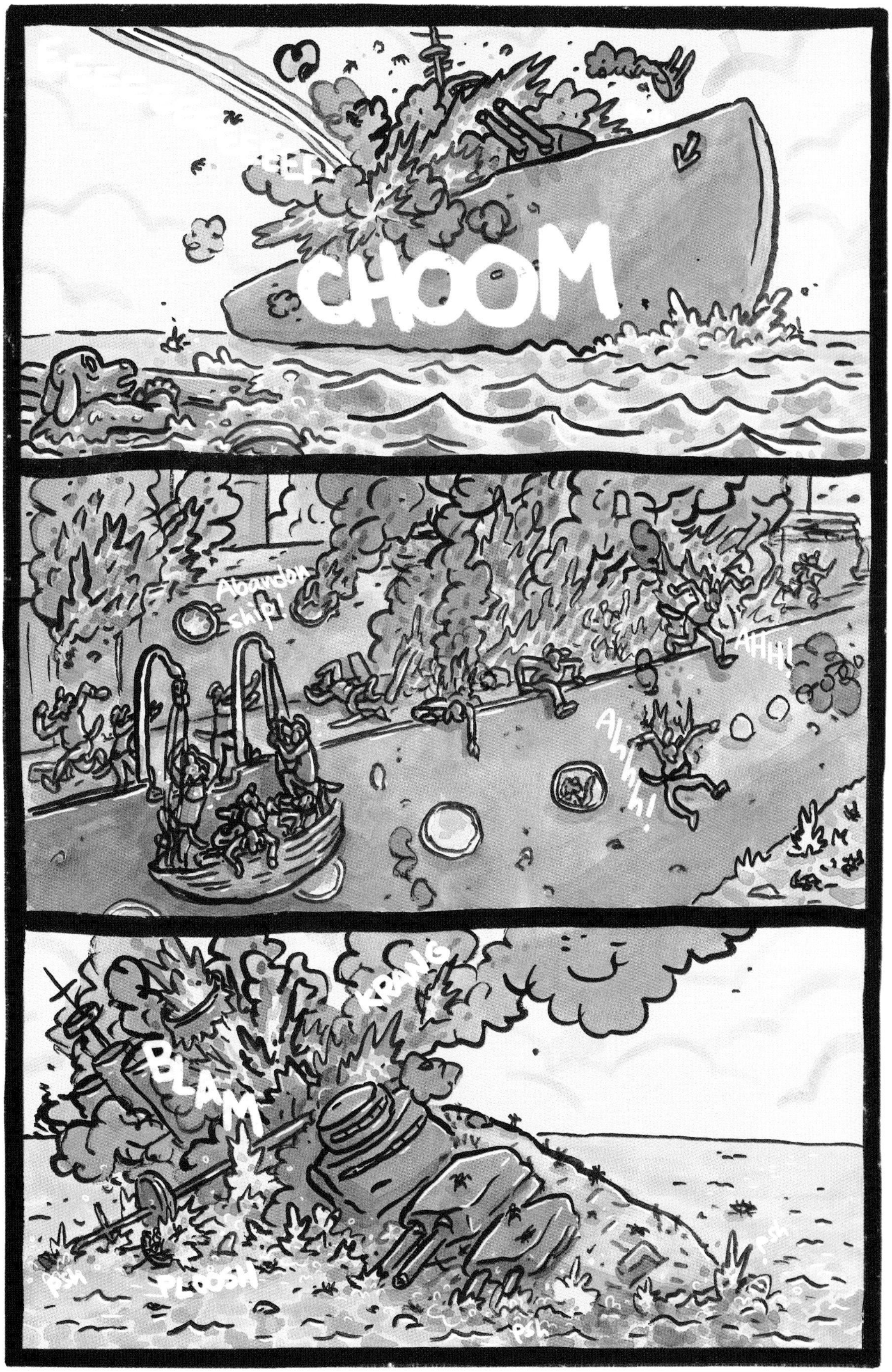
CHOOM
Abandon ship!
AHH!
Ahhhh!
KRANG
BLAM
psh
PLOOSH
psh
psh

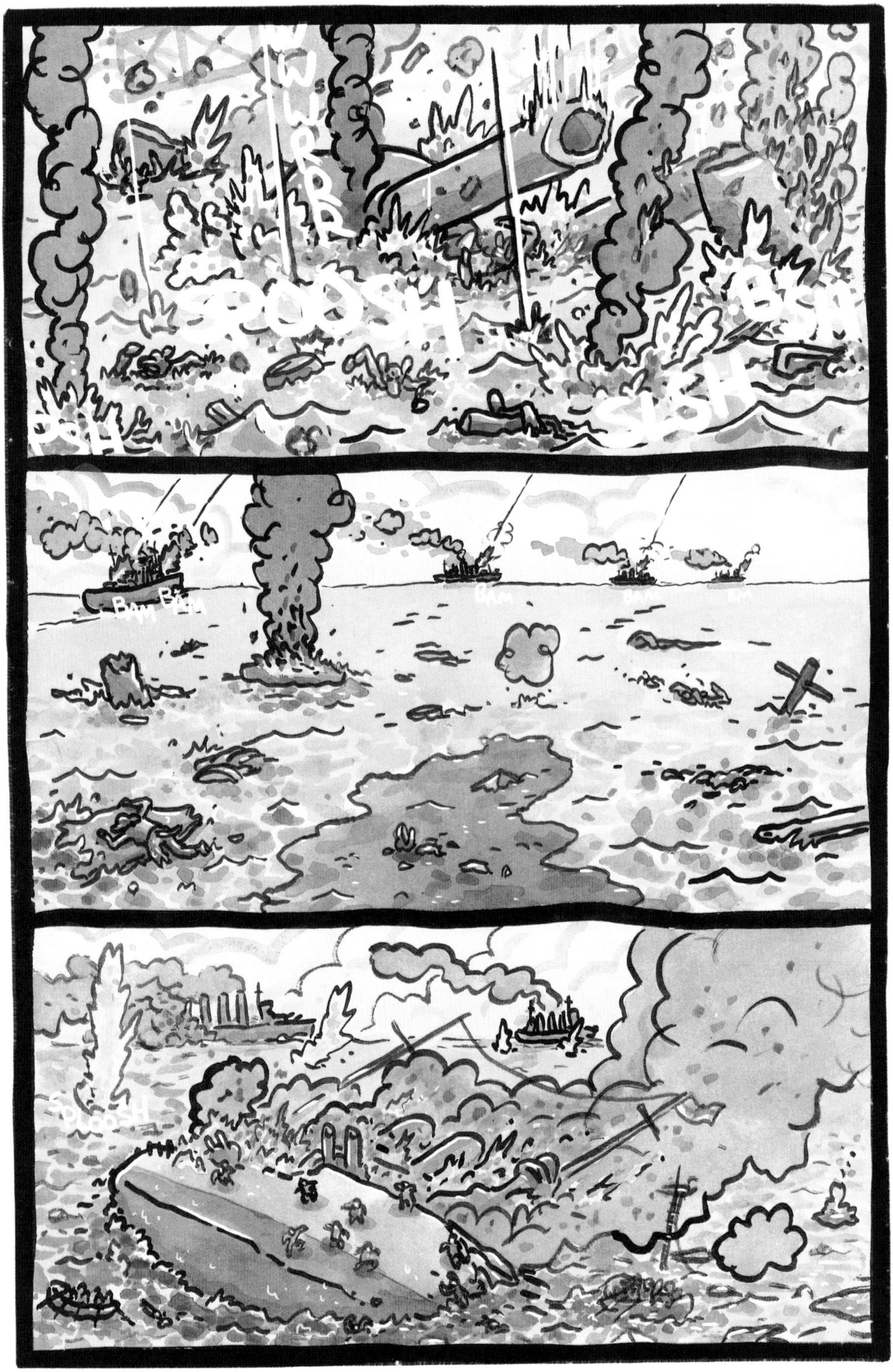
WWRRR
SPOOSH
BSH
PSH
BAM
BAM
BAM
BAM
BM
SPLOOSH

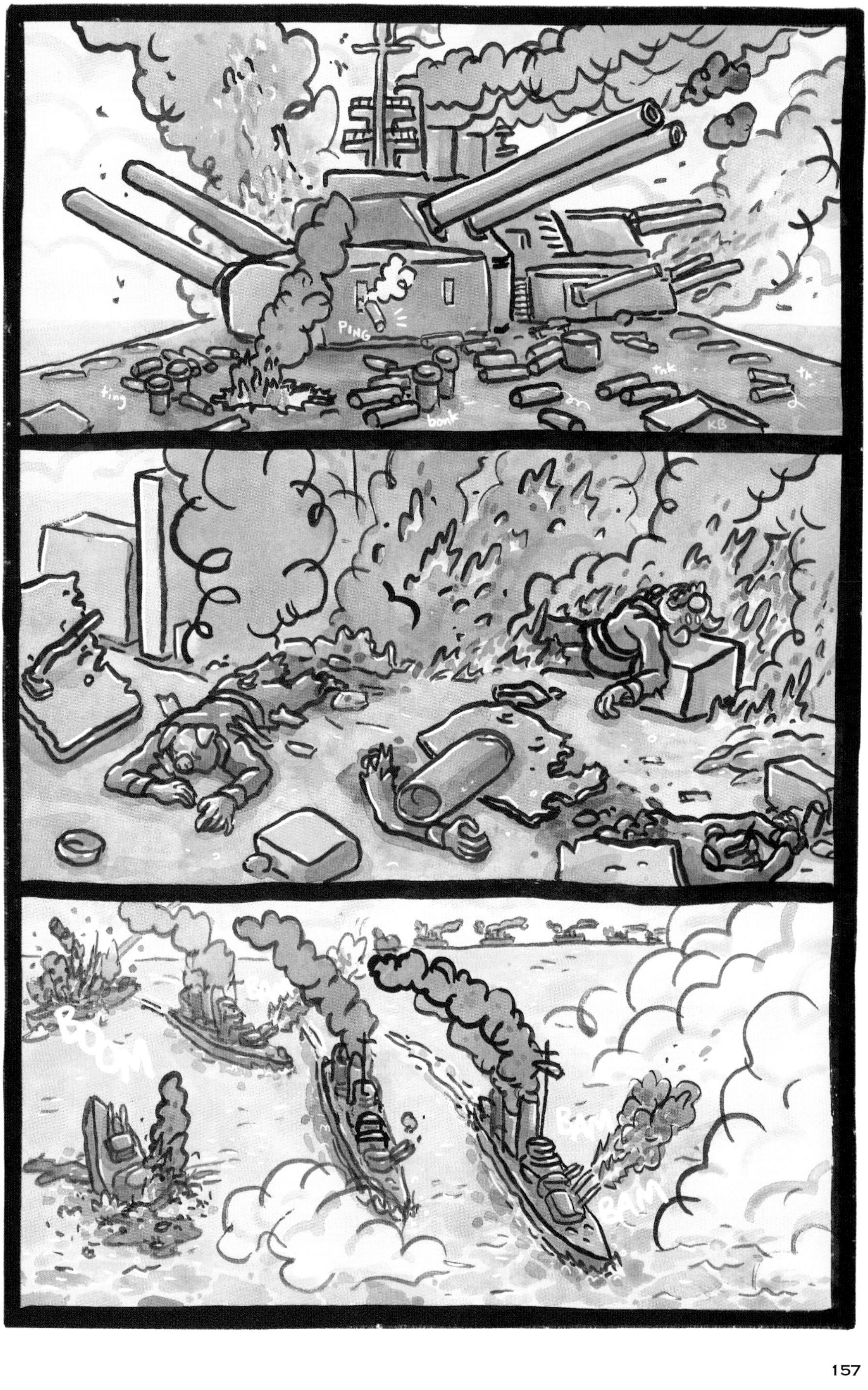
PING
ting
bonk
tnk
tk
KB
BAM
BOOM
BAM
BAM

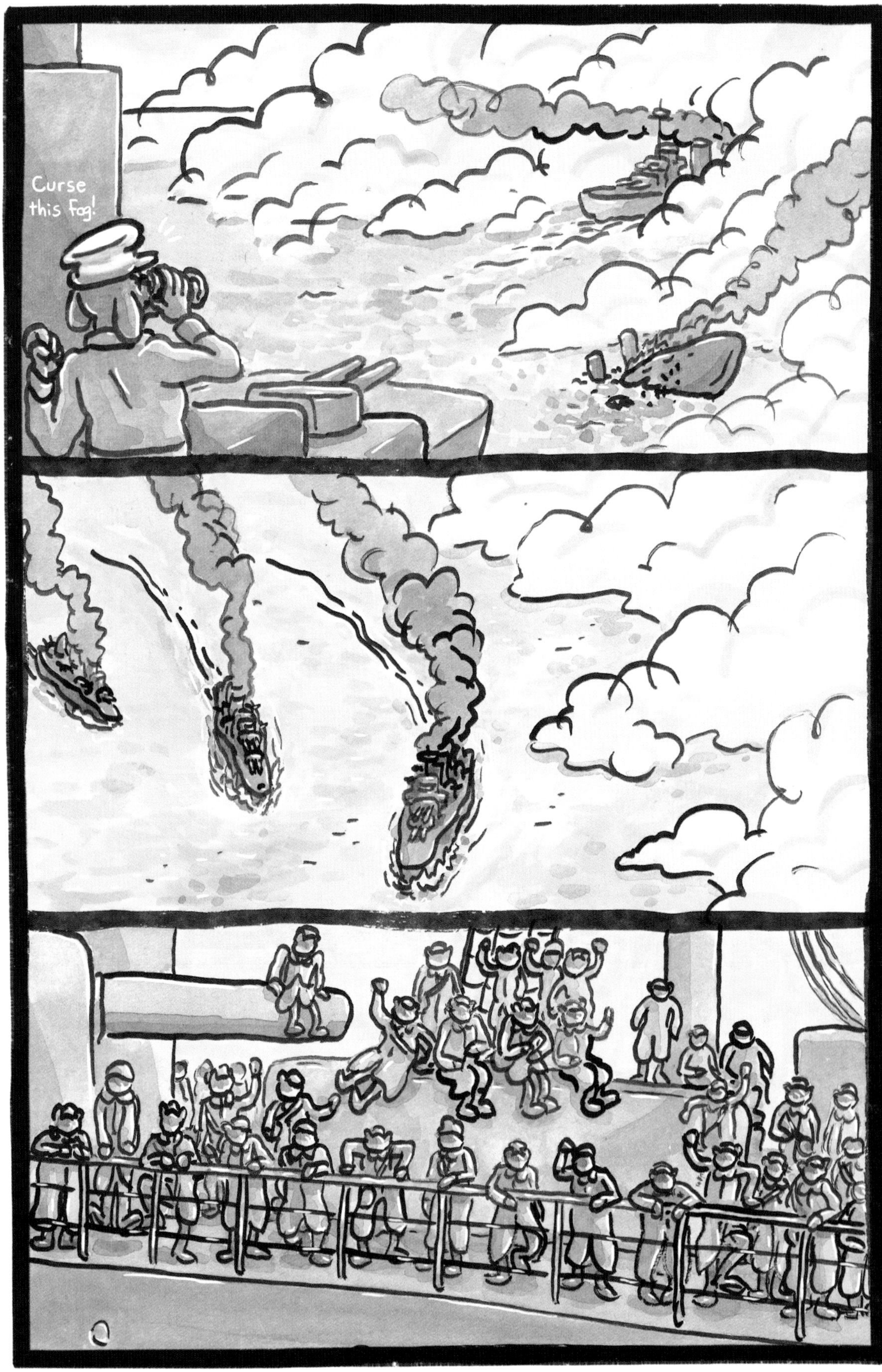
Curse this Fog!

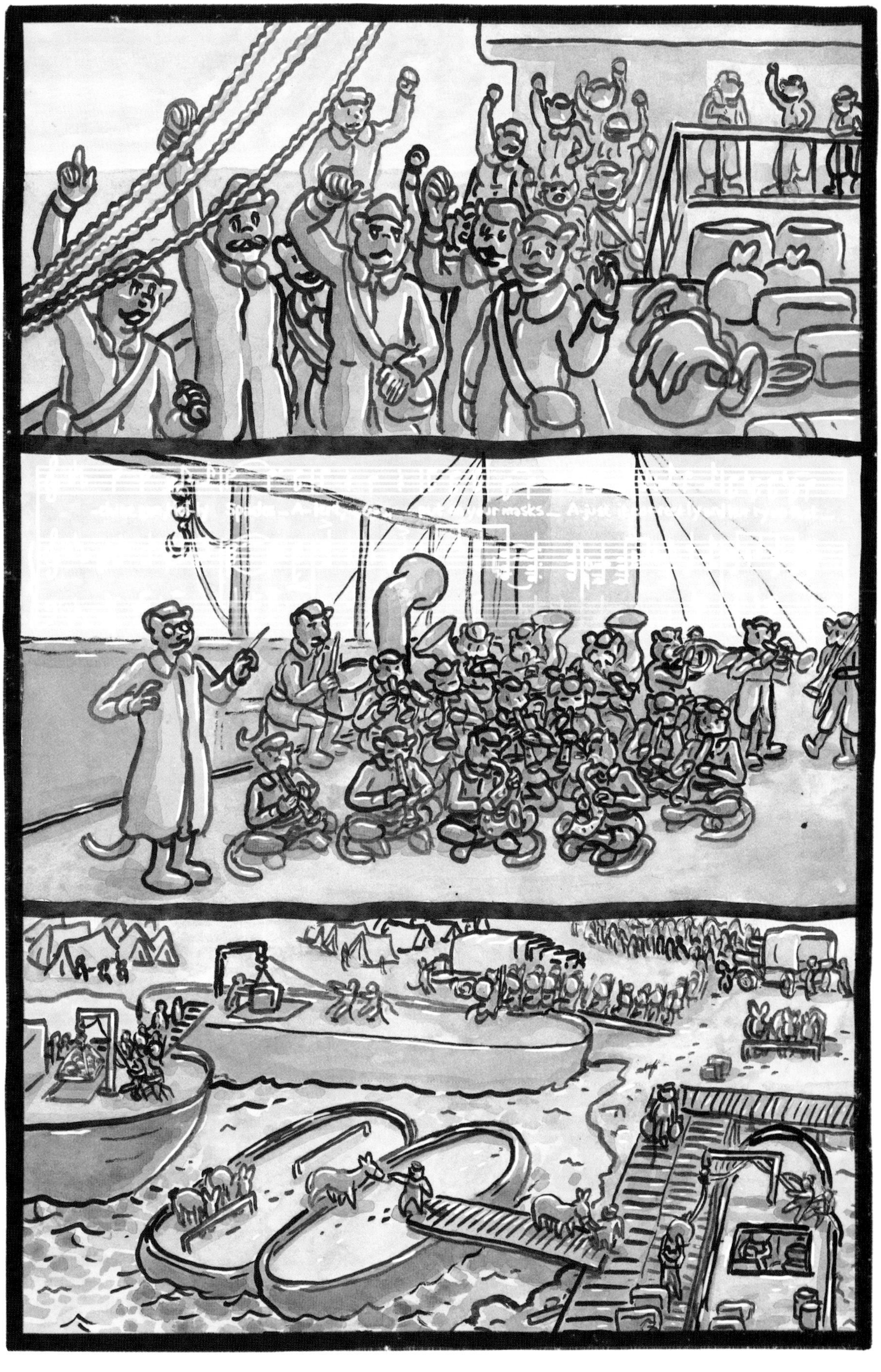
your masks_

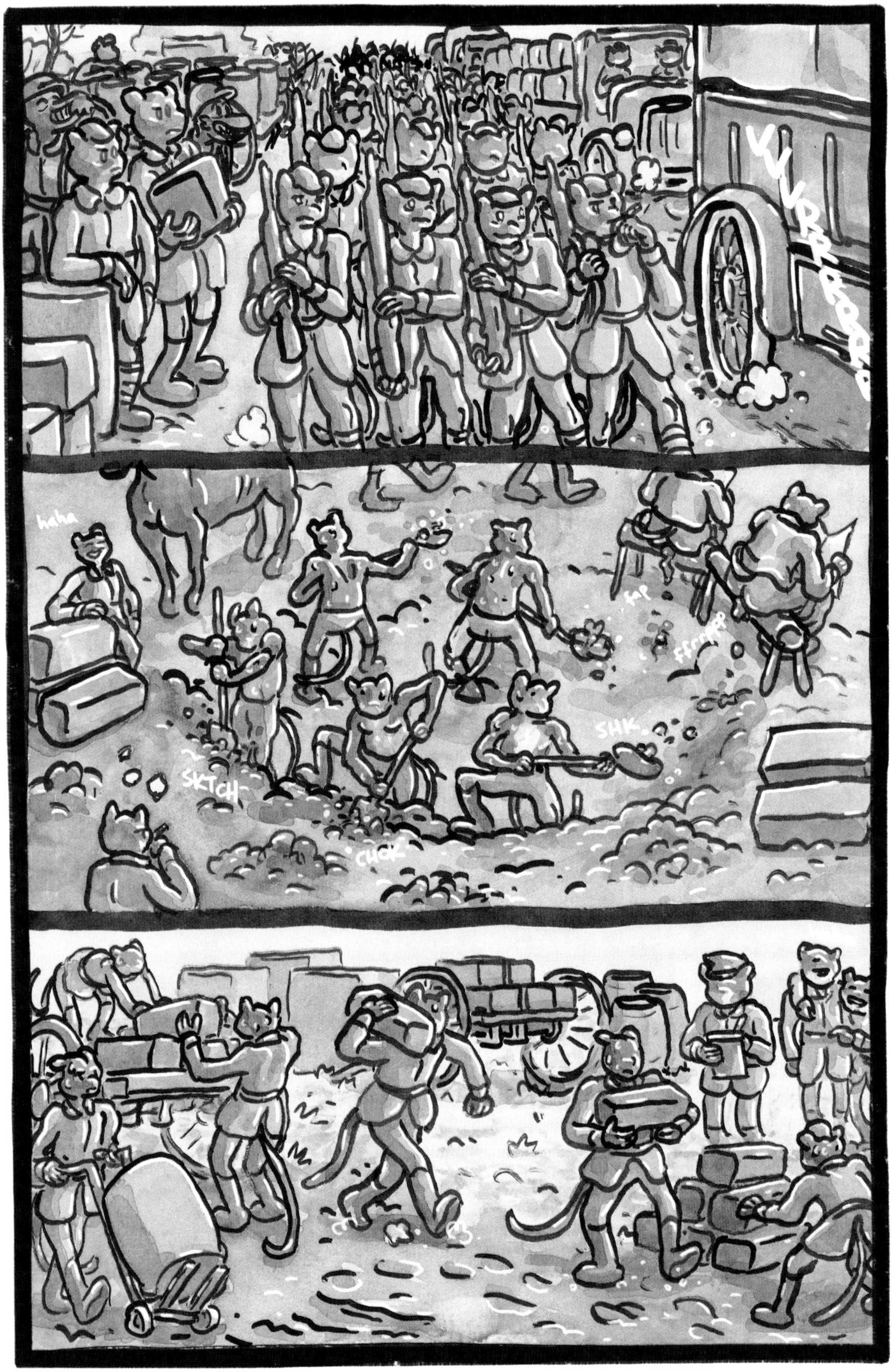
haha
fap
SHK
SKTCH
CHOK

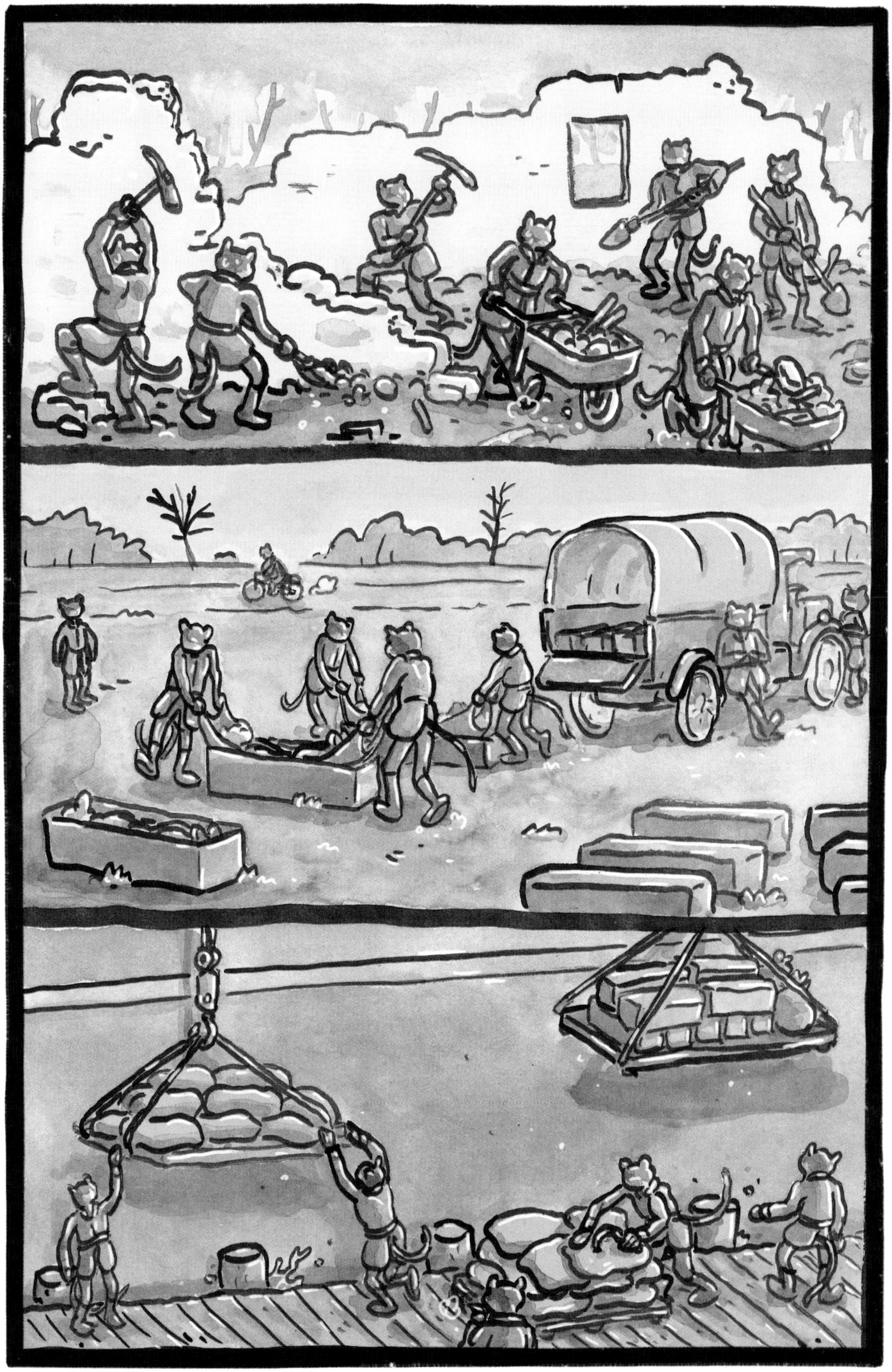

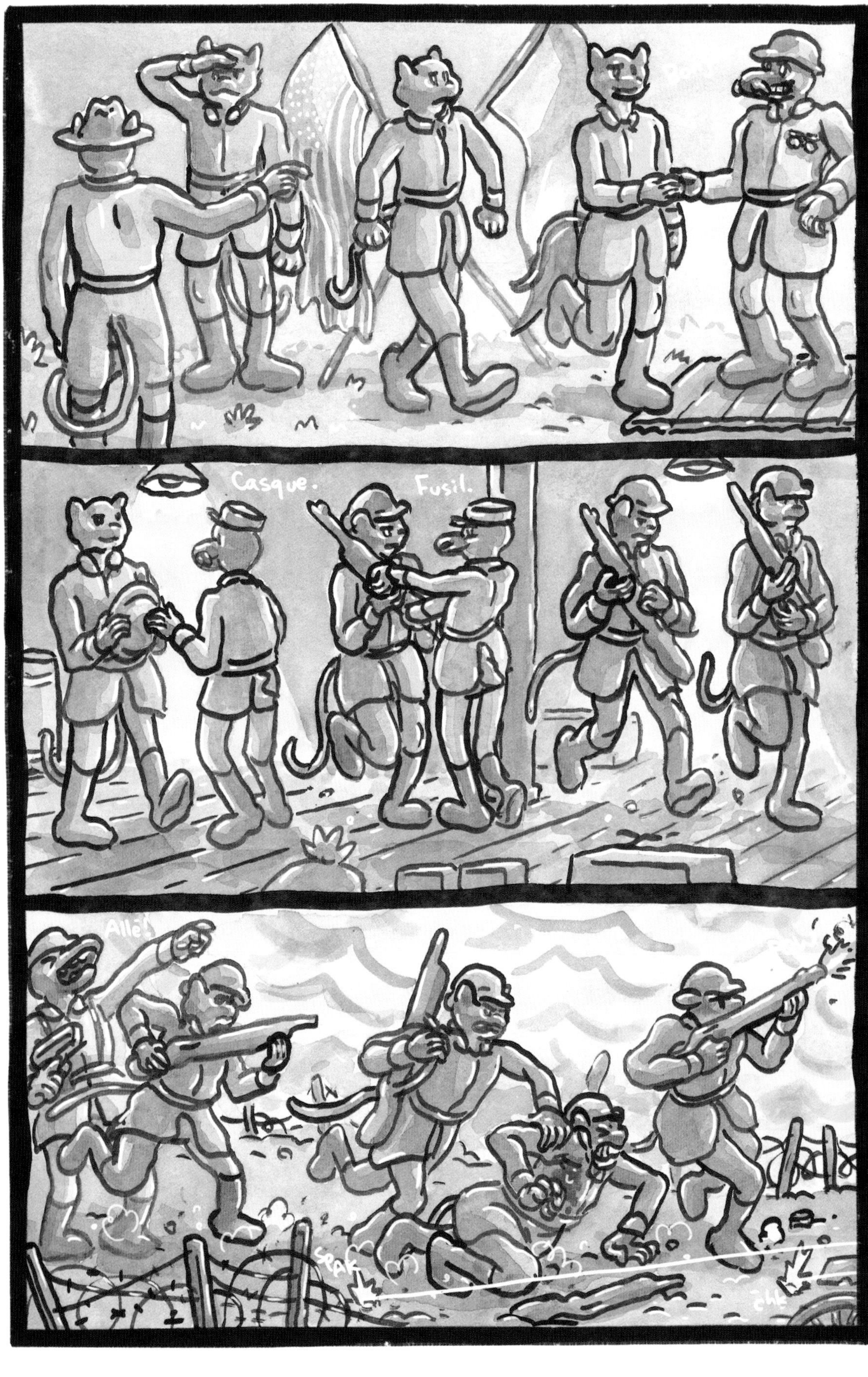
Casque.
Fusil.
Allé!
SPAK
chk

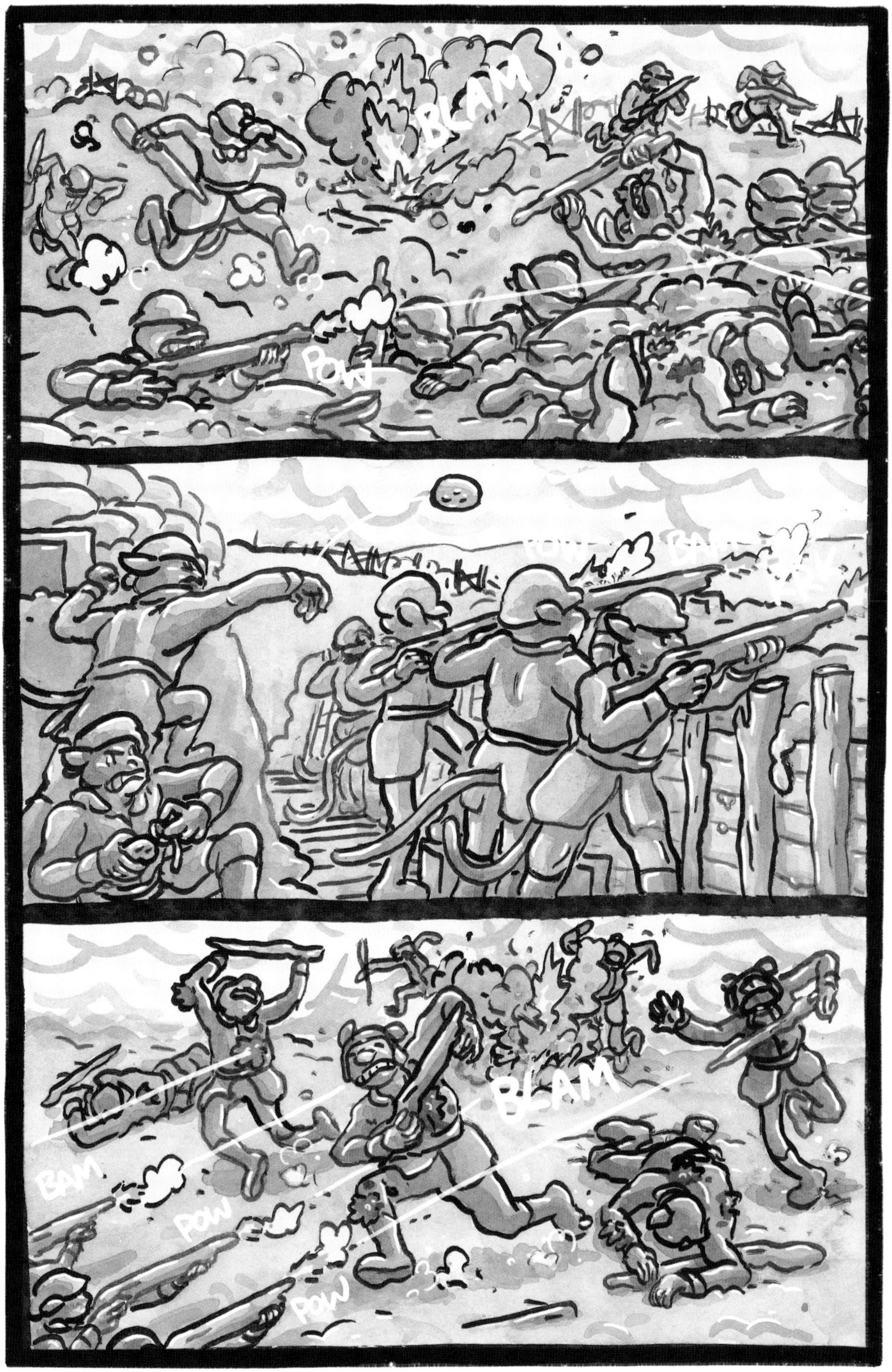
BLAM
POW
POW
BAM
BLAM
BAM
POW
POW

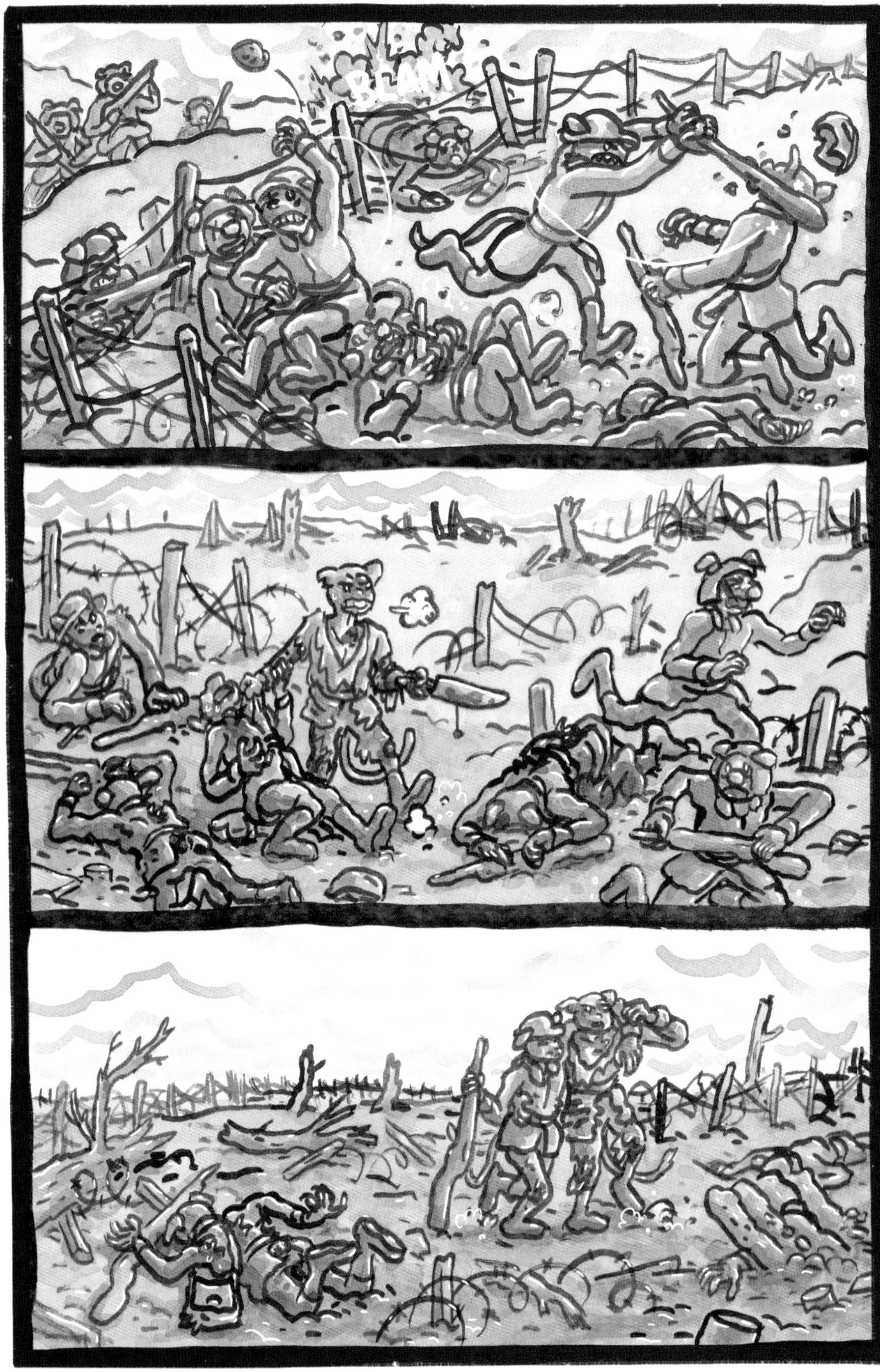
BLAM

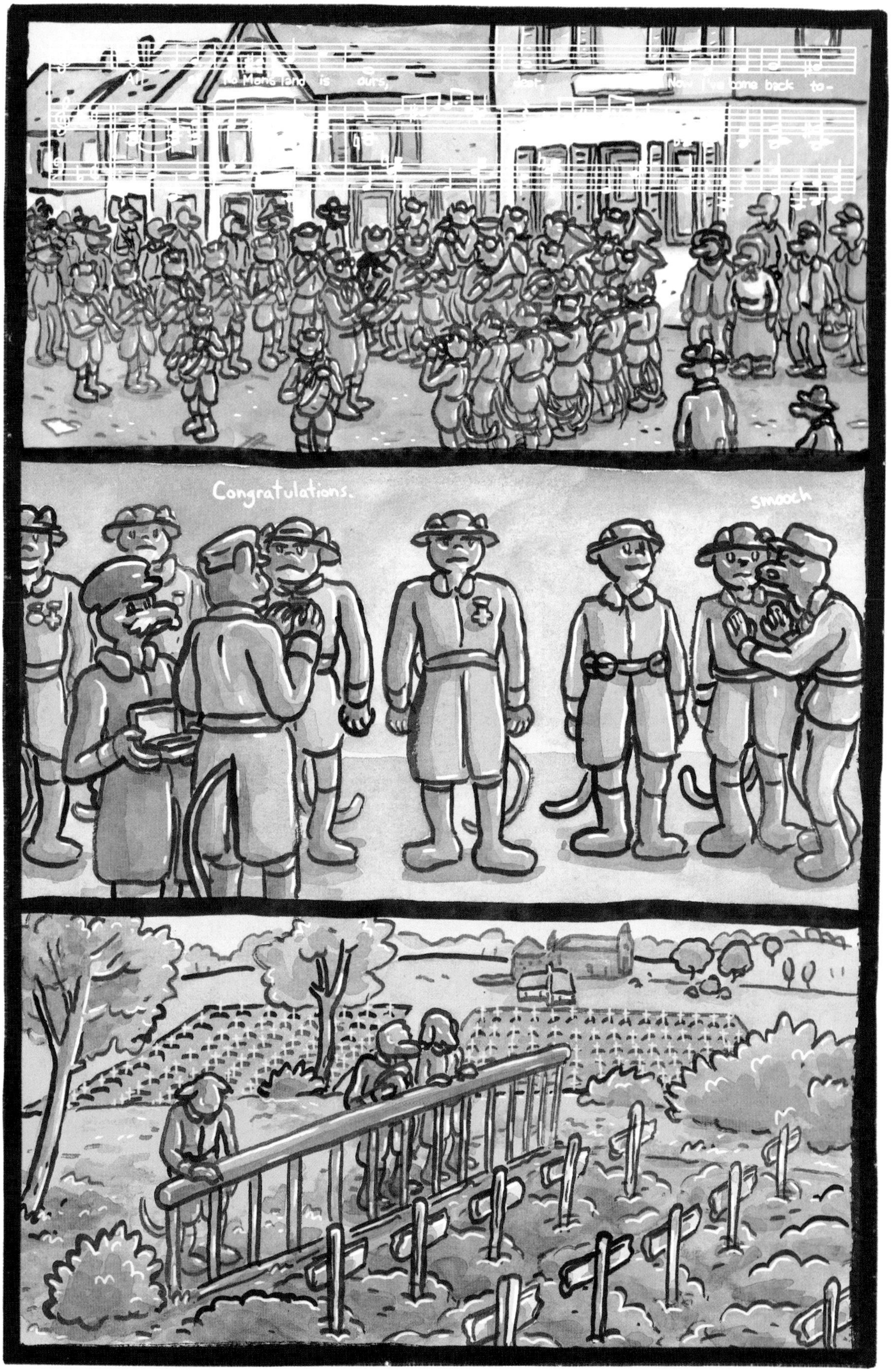
All of No Man's land is ours, dear, Now I've come back to-
Congratulations.
smooch

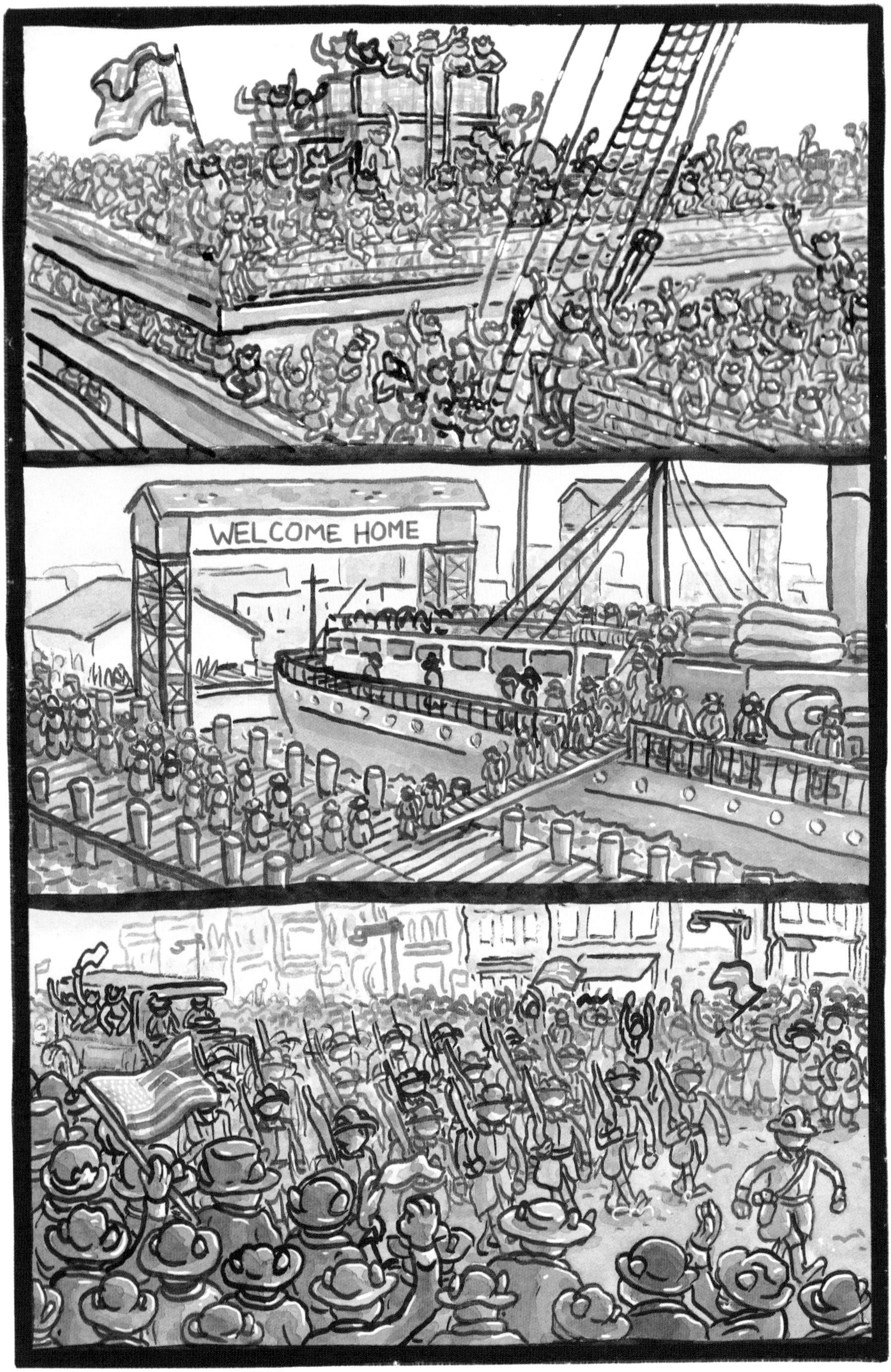
WELCOME HOME

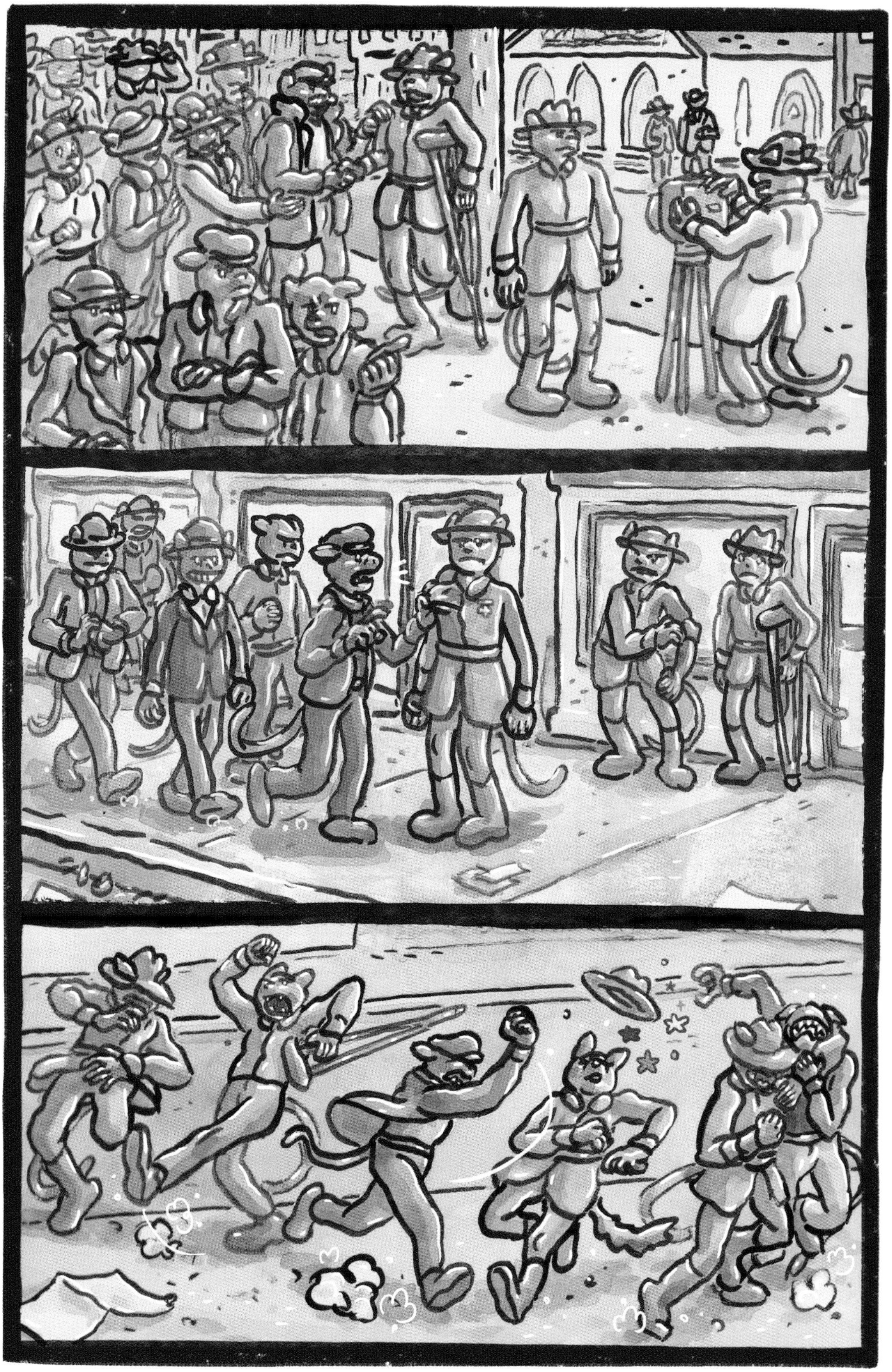

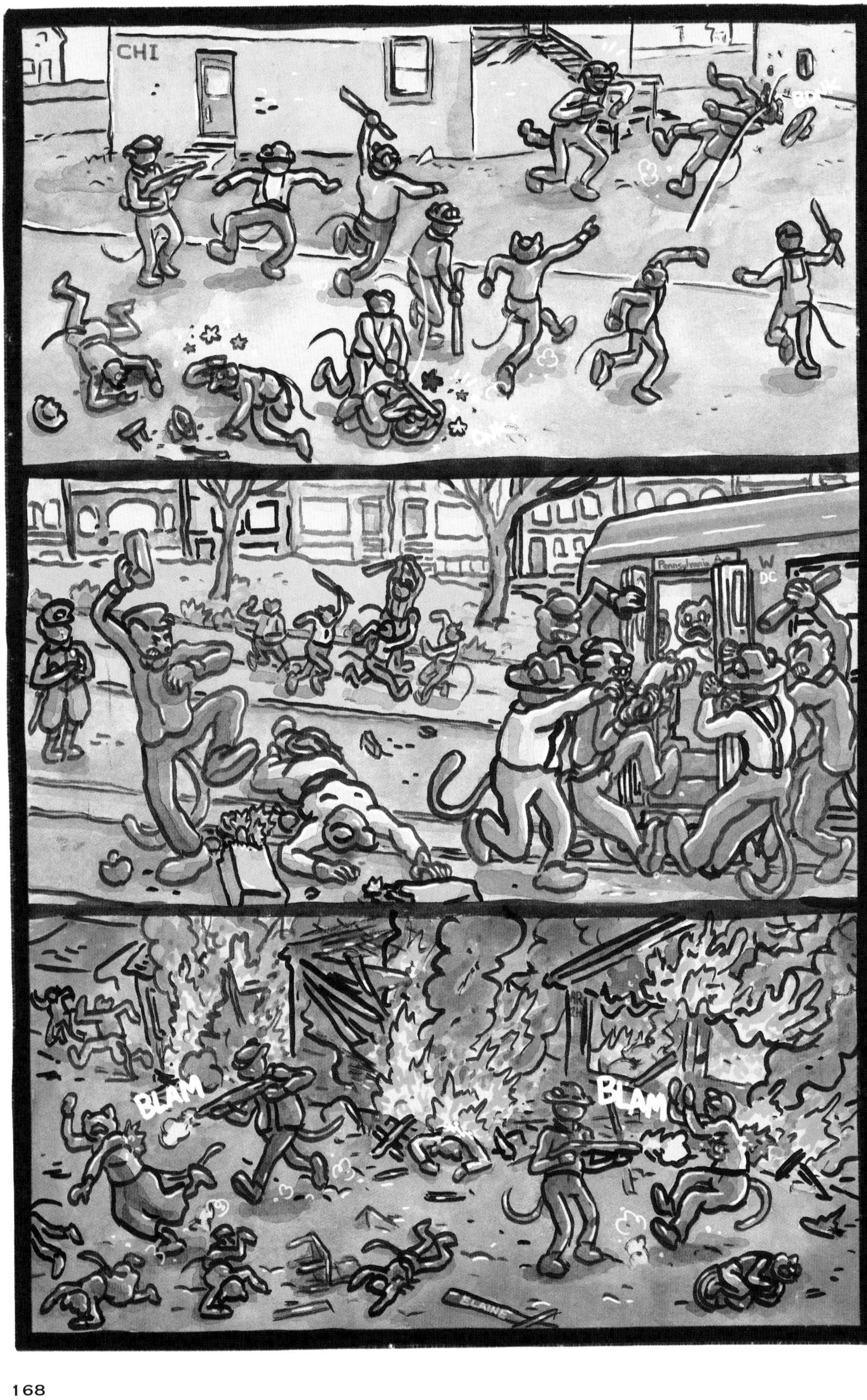

CHI
Pennsylvania
W
DC
BLAM
BLAM
ELAINE

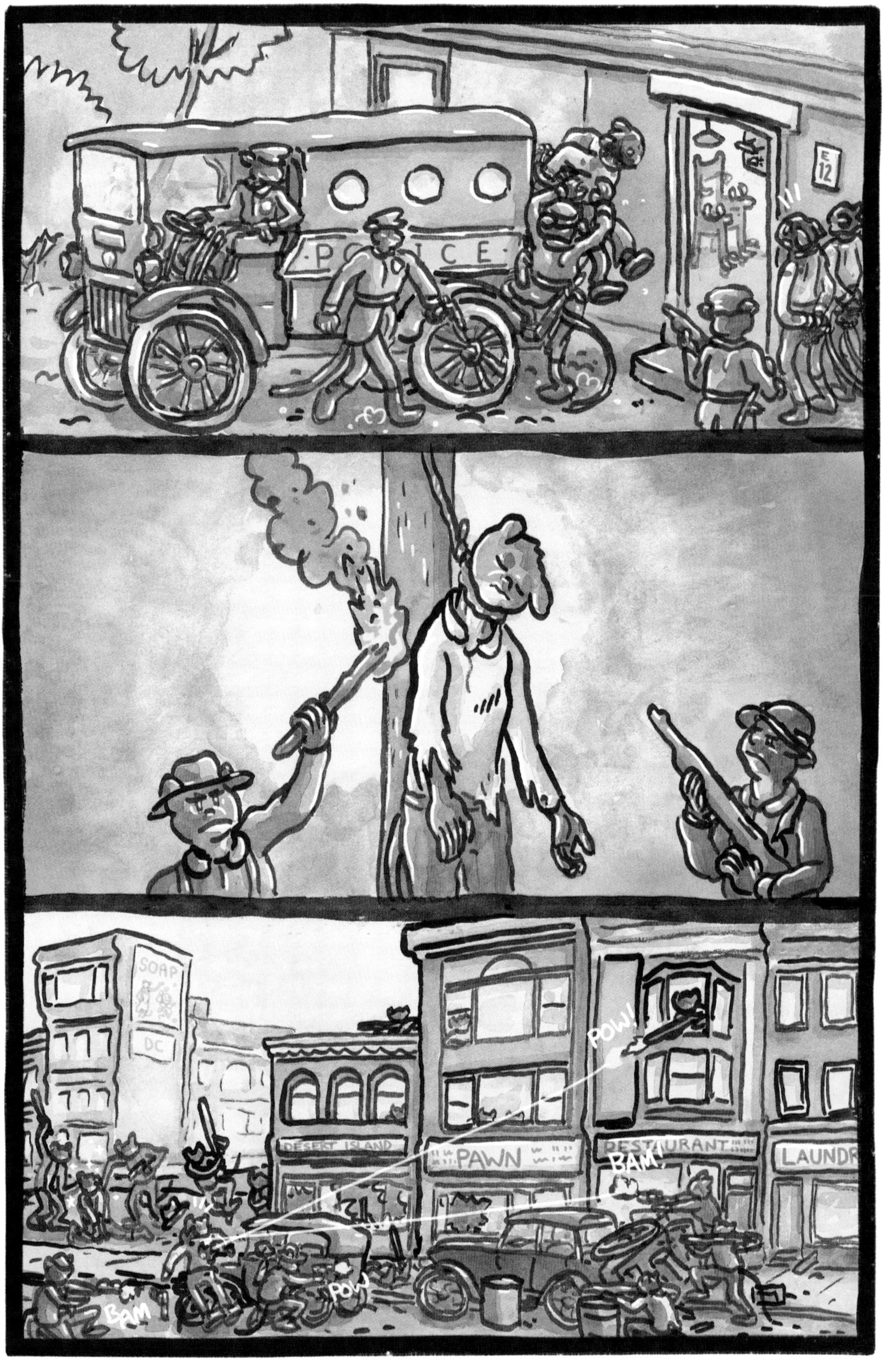
POLICE
E 12
SOAP
DC
POW!
DESERT ISLAND
PAWN
RESTAURANT
BAM!
LAUNDR
BAM
POW

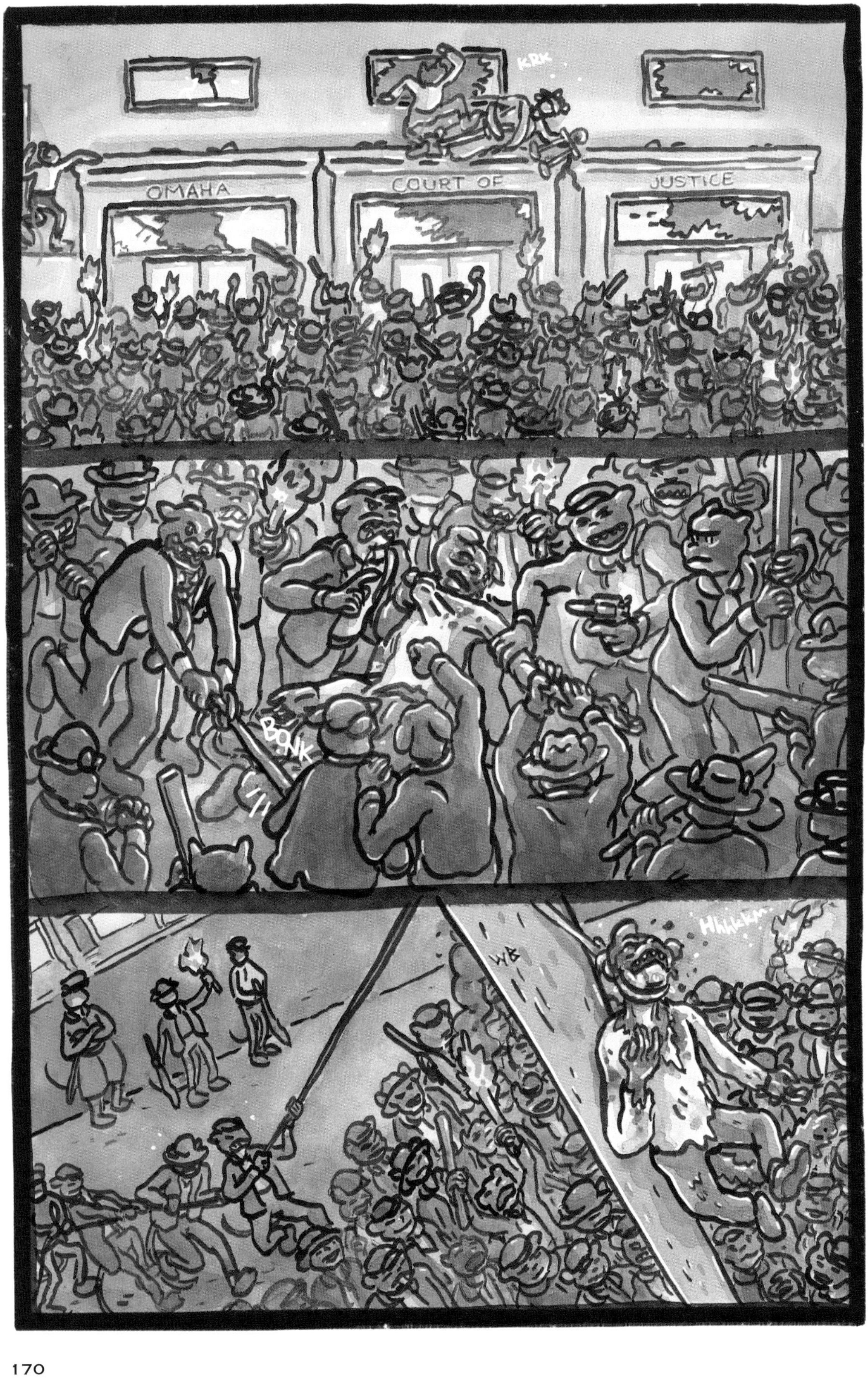
KRK
OMAHA
COURT OF
JUSTICE
BONK
WB
Hhhkkm

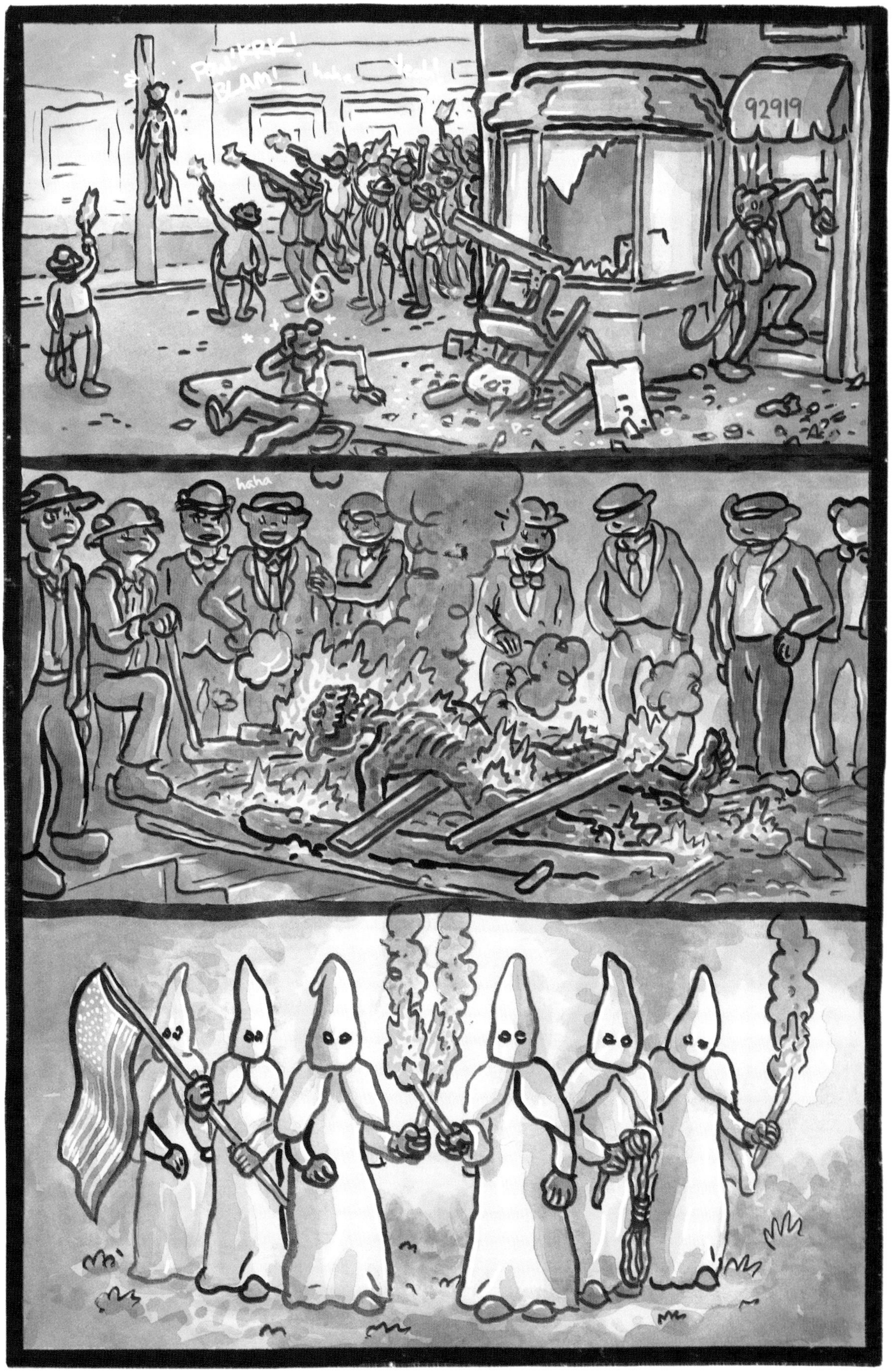
BLAM!
92919
haha

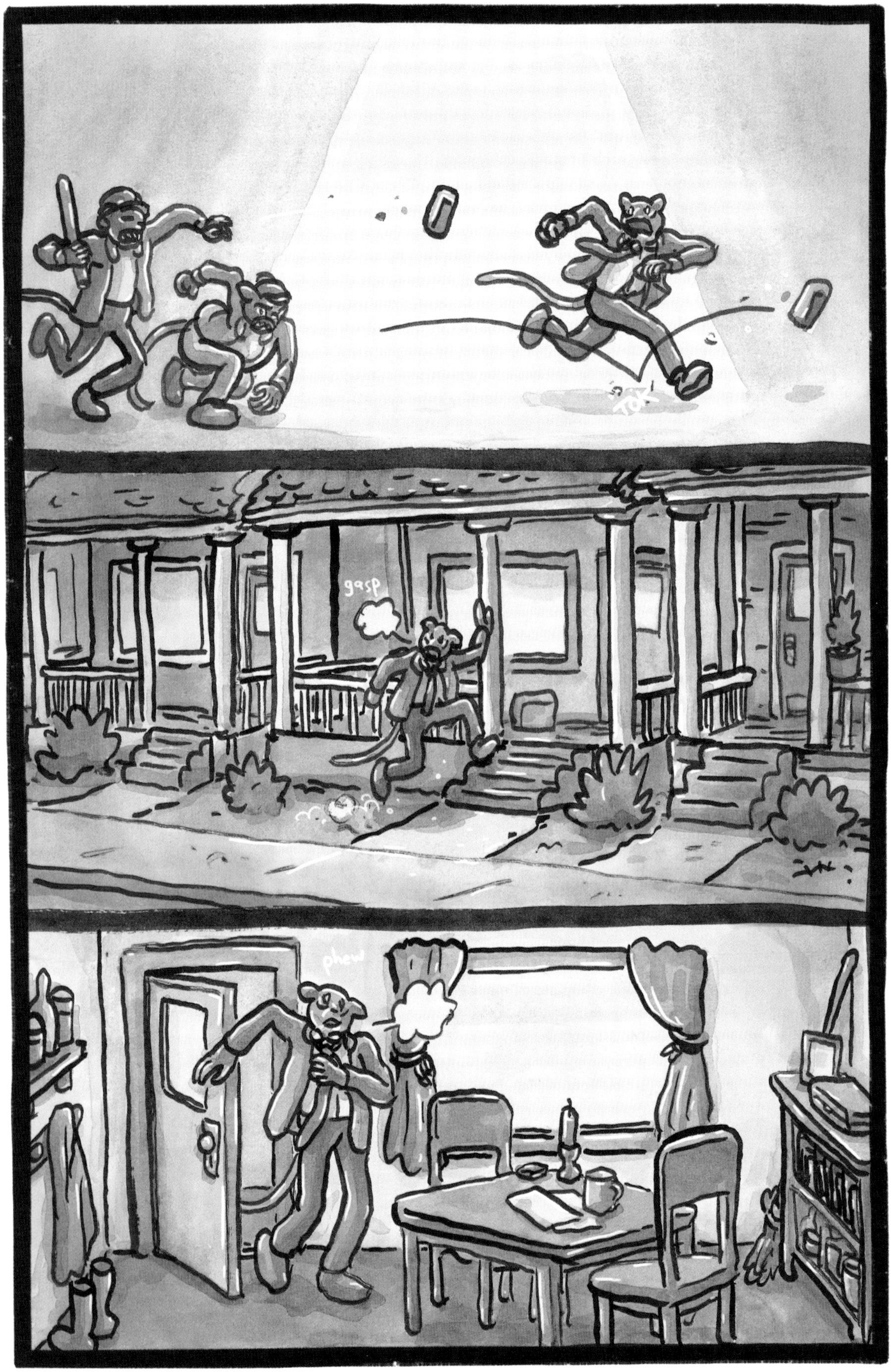
TOK
gasp
phew

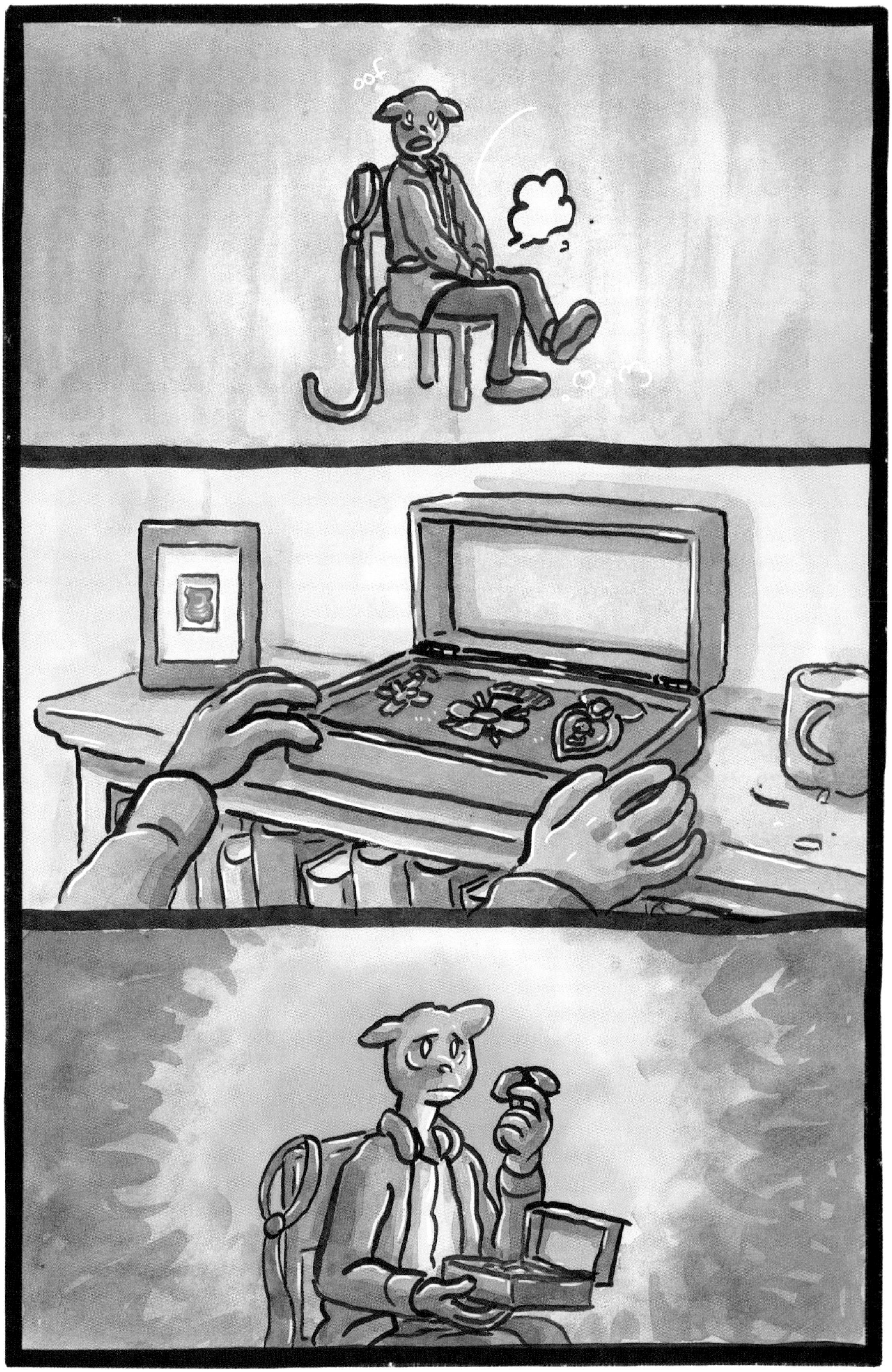
oof

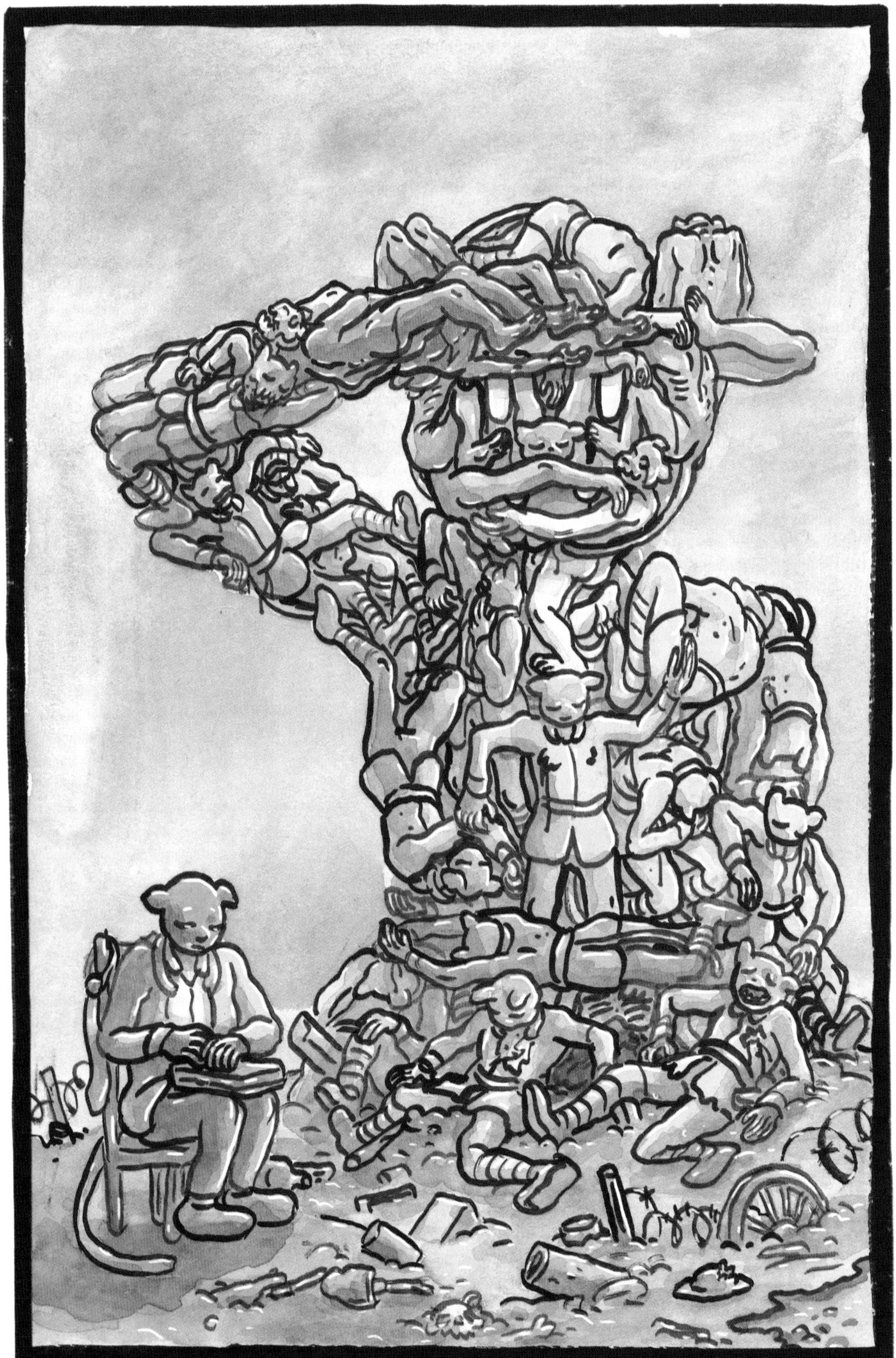

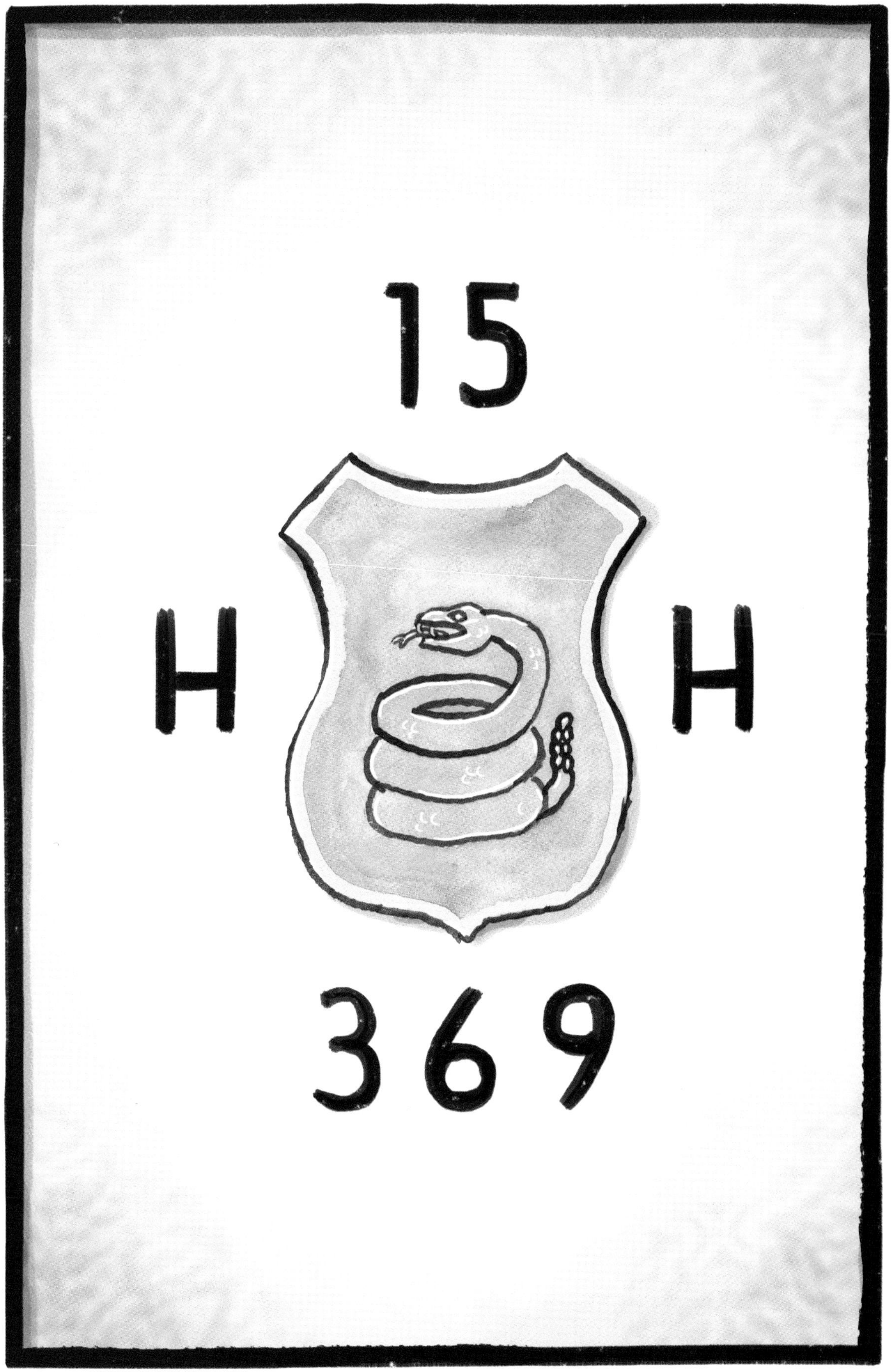
15
H
H
369

CONTINUE THE STORY

For more about WW1 and these influential figures,

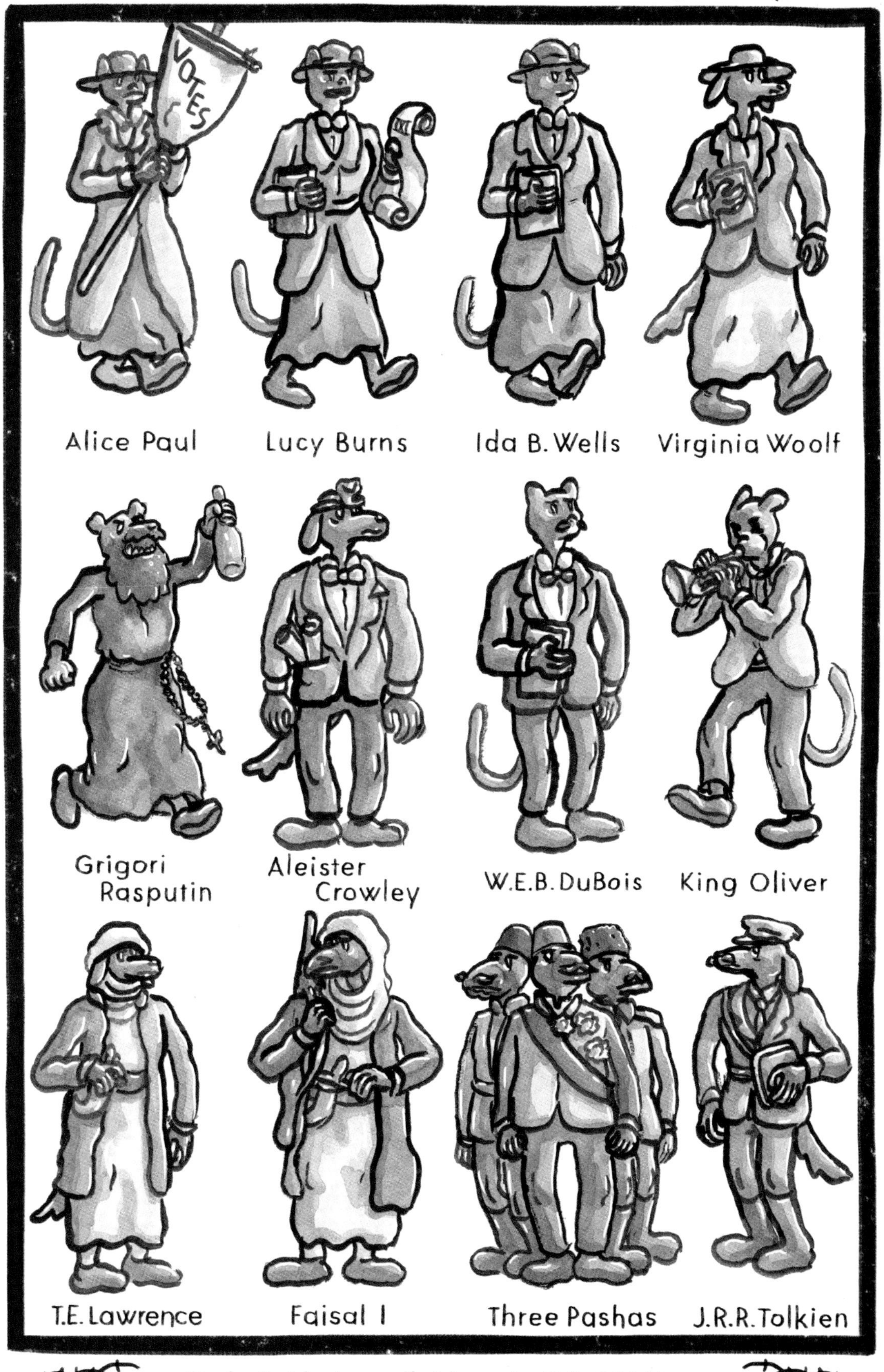

VOTES
Alice Paul
Lucy Burns
Ida B. Wells
Virginia Woolf
Grigori Rasputin
Aleister Crowley
W.E.B. DuBois
King Oliver
T.E. Lawrence
Faisal I
Three Pashas
J.R.R. Tolkien

a Study Guide is available at IANDENSFORD.com

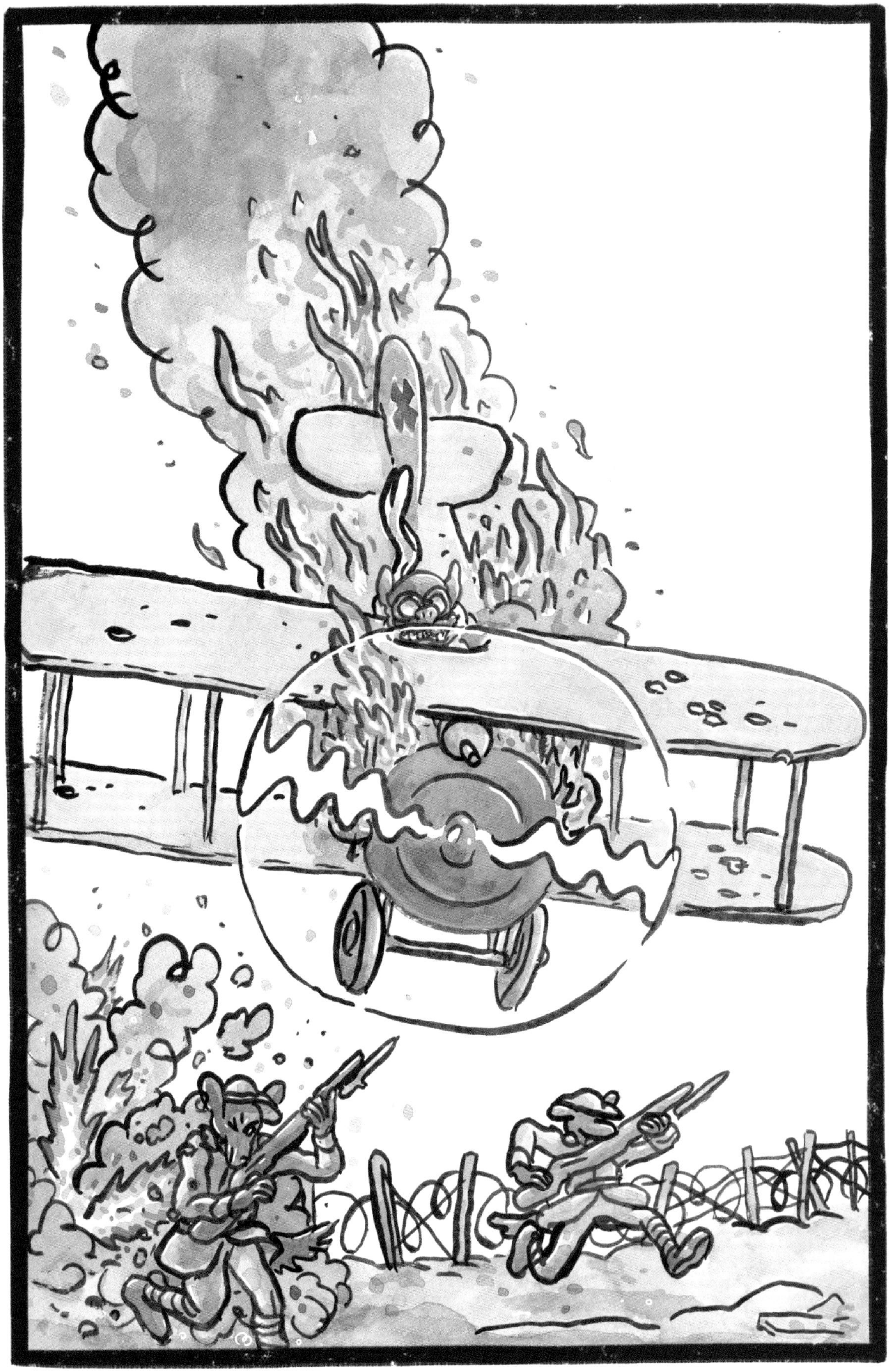

Firstly, I want to thank my wife, Tae, for her constant love and support. I would also like to thank Gary and USNI for the amazing opportunity, Alec and Chris for their feedback, Pete for his part, plus Guy and Greg for the studio time. Extra special recognition to Frank and Sally from the Comics Workbook site, where <u>Trench Dogs</u> was first conceived, and their wonderful Rowhouse Residency Program in Pittsburgh, PA.

- Ian Densford

BIBLIOGRAPHY

<u>Poilu</u>	by Louis Barthas
<u>The Harlem Hellfighters</u>	by Max Brooks
<u>Hardcore History Podcast</u>	by Dan Carlin
<u>The Beauty and the Sorrow</u>	by Peter Englund
<u>The Great War</u>	by Peter Hart
<u>Storm of Steel</u>	by Ernst Jünger
<u>Smoke and Mirrors</u>	by Deborah Lake
<u>A More Unbending Battle</u>	by Peter Nelson
<u>The Great War</u>	by Joe Sacco
<u>Goddamn This War</u>	by Jacques Tardi
Imperial War Museum	Misc. Interviews

ABOUT THE CREATOR

Author and illustrator **Ian Densford** is a working artist who lives in New York State with his wife, Tae, and their son, Anderson. When not animating on the computer or drawing in his sketchbook, you can find him frolicking in the nearby forest and rocky hillsides.